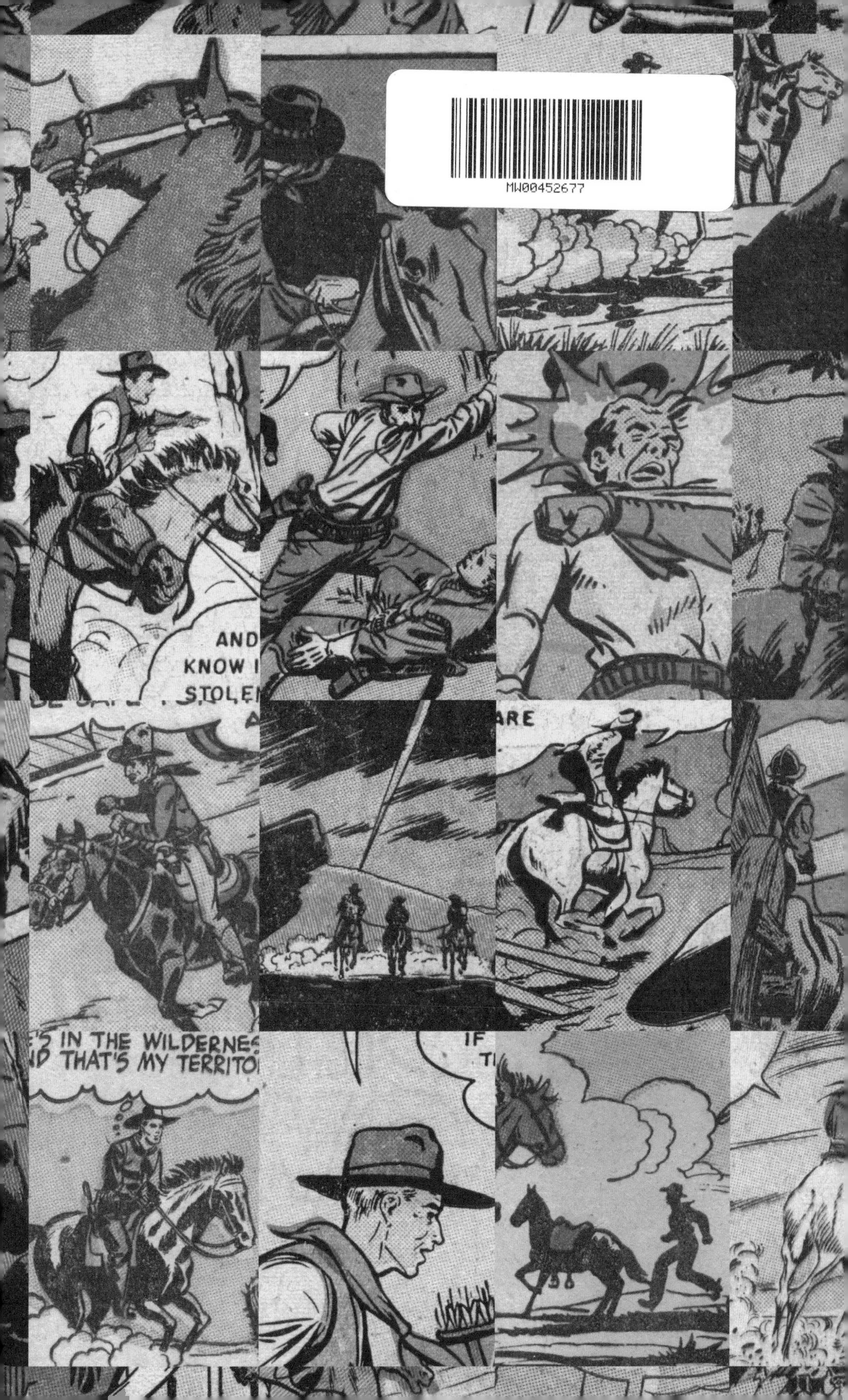
AND
KNOW I
STOLE
ARE
'S IN THE WILDERNES
ND THAT'S MY TERRITO
IF
TI

OLD
YOUR
AND

LOCUSTS! THAT OUR

---BECAUSE JOHN DAVY **ALWAYS** GETS WHAT HE WANTS !

HOLD IT, EVE

Golden Age Western Comics

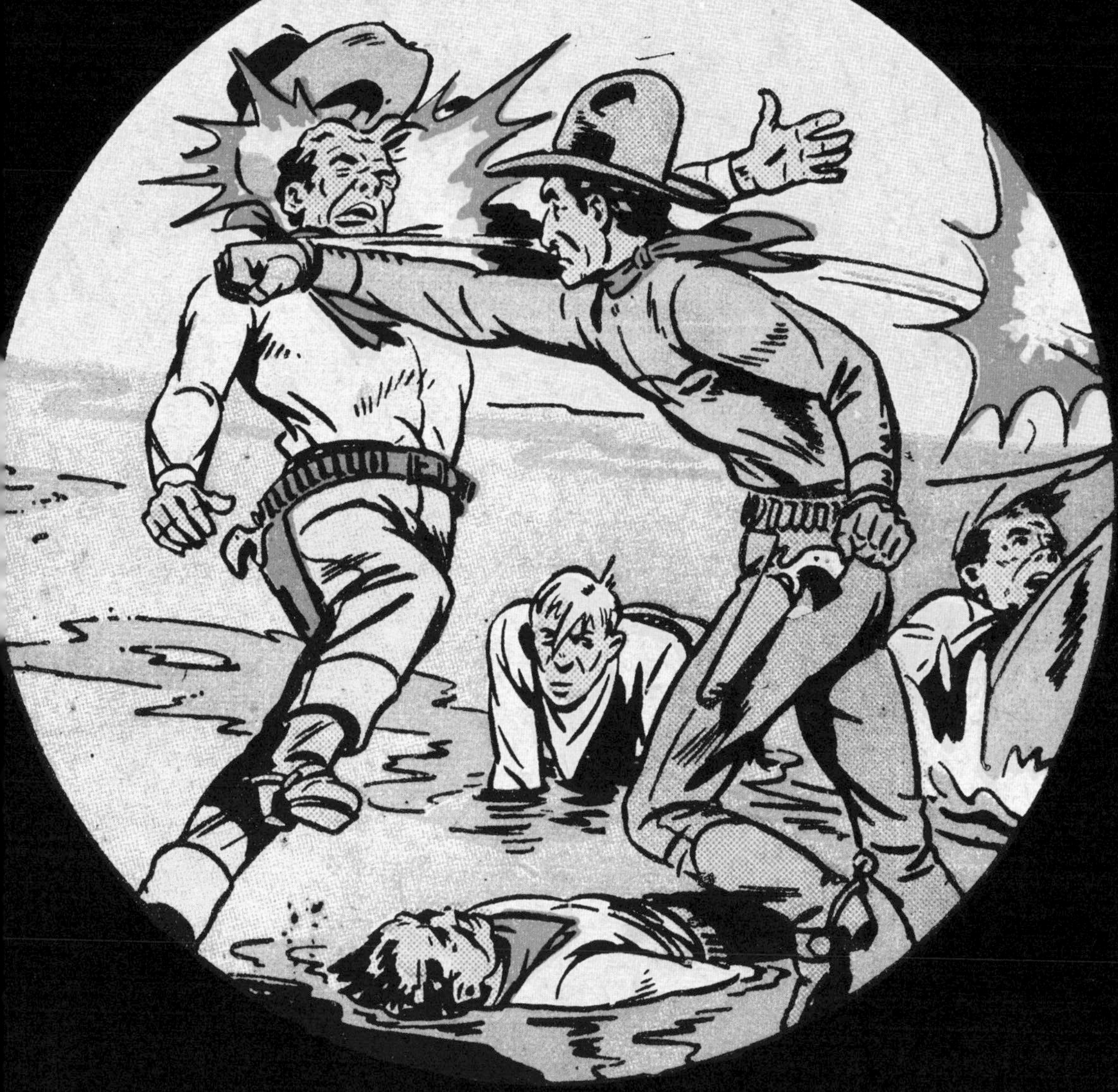

Edited by Steven Brower
Foreword by Christopher Irving

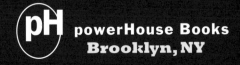

powerHouse Books
Brooklyn, NY

Golden Age Western Comics

Editor / Designer: Steven Brower
Production: Janna Brower

Published in the United States by powerHouse
Books, a division of powerHouse Cultural
Entertainment, Inc.
37 Main Street, Brooklyn, NY 11201-1021
telephone 212.604.9074, fax 212.366.5247
e-mail: westerncomics@powerhousebooks.com
website: www.powerhousebooks.com

First edition, 2012

Library of Congress Control Number: 2011945347

Hardcover ISBN 978-1-57687-594-0

Printing and binding through Asia Pacific Offset

A complete catalog of powerHouse Books and
Limited Editions is available upon request; please call,
write, or visit our website.

10 9 8 7 6 5 4 3 2 1

Printed and bound in China

TABLE OF CONTENTS

FOREWORD

Christopher Irving

When the Western was at its peak, from about the 1930s–50s, the period of the Old West had only been over for around 50 years, and the craze has since been over for about that length of time. While the current generation of kids embraces the giant robots made popular in the years following the Western's peak, the cowboy is largely forgotten in this politically correct time. Toy guns are generally taboo, and "Cowboys and Indians" just doesn't fly on today's playground.

But once, when being American was a way of life, the cowboy was king, and this collection celebrates that era in an array of spectacular and offbeat comics.

By the late-'40s and through the mid-'50s, as superheroes became less exciting and relevant, the cowboy stepped in with his spurred boots to keep the comics industry afloat. The shrinking comics industry didn't have enough room for both genres, and the cowboy was the quicker draw, beating the long underwear crowd out. The last standby, All-American Comics' *All-Star Comics* (which featured the first major superhero team in the Justice Society of America), gave way to *All-Star Western*.

After reading this assemblage of stories, put together by Steven Brower, you'll see why they were all the rage, whether for story quality or sheer kitsch factor. There were more publishers in the Golden Age of comics than badmen in a saloon, and they produced Westerns of all flavors and levels.

Several of the stories herein were published by Charlton Comics, once one of the largest publishers of comics in the United States. Founded in Seymour, Connecticut by a former Italian bricklayer and a disbarred attorney he'd met in prison, Charlton held the distinction of housing everything from editorial to distribution under one roof. The downside to Charlton is that they paid the worst rates in the business; as a result, most of their comics were hastily drawn by freelancers anxious to produce enough pages to make a living wage.

There were, however, some real diamonds in the rough, the brightest being Charlton artist, and eventual editor, Dick Giordano. A trio of Giordano's stories is presented here, showing the craftsmanship and pride he put into even the lowest paying work. He later went on to edit at DC Comics, eventually becoming the Managing Editor (his modest title for Editor-in-Chief) and then Vice President/Executive Editor in the mid-'80s. Giordano suffered from hearing loss for most of his adult life and, by the time of his death in 2010, was practically deaf.

Although not credited, chances are the Charlton Westerns were written by Joe Gill, a dyed-in-the-wool Irishman and self-professed "hack" writer. Entering the comics industry with best pal Mickey Spillane (of *Mike Hammer* fame) in the early '40s, Joe became the head writer at Charlton and stayed there until they closed shop in '86. There, he wrote every genre of story from romance to superhero to crime to Western. I was lucky enough to know Gill a few years before he died in 2007; he was a helluva character, always equipped with a wisecrack and sound writing advice.

Charlton was also a last resort for struggling artists in the '50s, which made it possible for them to occasionally score artists like Mike Sekowsky, future *Justice League of America* artist, who contributes the Masked Raider story here. His use of solid blacks and geometric shapes gives his work a kinetic nature that pops off the page. Charlton later boasted a post-*Spider-Man* Steve Ditko in their ranks, as he returned to his first major home in comics in the mid-'60s to draw *The Question* and *Blue Beetle*.

Although they only have one entry here, Magazine Enterprises produced many of the best and most offbeat Western comics ever made. It wasn't just because of their assemblage of talented, top-level cartoonists; much was undoubtedly owed to the Editor-in-Chief and top man at ME, Vin Sullivan, who was the first to discover Jerry Siegel and Joe Shuster's *Superman* in the submissions slush pile, and inadvertently helped launch the entire superhero genre. With their flag Western title *Best of the West*, ME Westerns featured stars who were crossed between superhero and cowboy, wearing masks and costumes while also living with alter egos. Their top characters were the first Ghost Rider, who wore a spooky luminescent costume and used magic to spook the baddies; Redmask, the superhero identity of cowboy star Tim Holt; and the masked cowgirl Black Phantom.

Our ME entry here is from *Dan'l Boone*, featuring the legendary frontiersman, with art by Joe Certa. While he was never considered a huge name, Certa dutifully worked in comics from the '40s through the '70s, drawing *Martian Manhunter* for DC Comics, the syndicated *Straight Arrow* strip, and also working at Gold Key comics on TV adaptations, including the *Dark Shadows* comic. While his work has a certain stiffness to it, it is far from lacking in charm. Certa was one of many talented journeymen who was like a character actor, always delivering a solid job yet never considered a star.

Not even a character actor, even though he assisted Will Eisner on *The Spirit*, Manny Stallman's art is so stiff and off-putting that it instantly delves into kitsch territory. His work on the truly bizarre "Little Eagle" story presented here is a great example of a platypus of a character. Another (and even greater) Eisner connection in this book is Jerry Iger, who drew the "Annie Oakley" story for Charlton and is the person most

responsible for giving the legendary Eisner his start in comics. When Eisner met Iger in the late-'30s, the latter was editor of a comics magazine called *Wow, What a Magazine!*, and gave Will his first work. After the mag folded, the two went into business together packaging comics as Universal Phoenix, with Eisner doing all of the art and Iger pounding the pavement to find wannabe comics publishers to sell their stories to.

It's a mighty good thing that the cowboy was around to help keep comics aloft throughout the early '50s. It didn't hurt that the Western was experiencing a wave of popularity through Western characters like The Lone Ranger, Cisco Kid, Zorro, and Hopalong Cassidy, and stars such as Roy Rogers, the King of the Cowboys. Even depictions of his sidekick, Gabby Hayes, had a long-running presence in comics: a former Shakespearean actor, Hayes removed his dentures and played a laughable prospector type, a Little Tramp for the Old West, and we also have him here. Their time was running out, however, as new genres were getting ready to overtake them in Cold War America.

Kids were giving up their six-shooter cap pistols for toy ray guns, or growing up and embracing the new adult Western in the form of the long-running *Gunsmoke* TV and radio programs. Many of them just moved on to rock 'n' roll when exploring the prairies of adolescence. The superhero came back with a vengeance in 1956, as the Flash was revamped for a new generation of National Comics readers, bringing the rest of his superhero buddies back to life in a superhero revival. Pretty soon, the cowboy was replaced with new versions of dusted-off old superheroes at National, and revolutionary angst-ridden ones at Marvel Comics.

But for now, let's pretend there are no power rings or radioactive spider bites, and we'll grab a spot at the saloon bar or around a campfire in the middle of the desert, and parlay with these old-school, print cowboys (and girls). Yeehaw!

WESTERN COMICS

Steven Brower

No sooner had the era ended than it was romanticized in the arts. Automobiles had barely replaced horse driven wagons when a plethora of cowboy films entertained the masses alongside melodramas and comedies. The earliest silent Westerns appeared as soon as the technology to create them was available. There was the less-than-one-minute-long *Cripple Creek Bar-Room Scene* (literally the prototypical barroom scene), and *Poker at Dawson City*, set during the Alaska gold rush underway at the time, both produced in 1899. In 1903, the first commercial film, *The Great Train Robbery*, written and directed by Edwin S. Porter, gave birth to the genre. D.W. Griffith experimented with the form in the *Twisted Trail* (1910), with Mary Pickford; *The Last Drop of Water* (1911); and *Fighting Blood* (1911).

The first feature-length Western was the six-reel *Arizona* (1913), directed by Augustus E. Thomas. Cecil B. DeMille's first motion picture was *The Squaw Man* (1914). Soon real-life cowboys and legendary Western figures appeared in films, such as Buffalo Bill Cody in *The Adventures of Buffalo Bill* (1914).

This burgeoning genre soon introduced the first Hollywood cowboy star, William S. Hart, who appeared in over three-dozen films from 1914 until 1925. Next up was Gilbert M. "Broncho Billy" Anderson, starting with *Broncho Billy and the Baby* (1915), and ending with *The Son-of-a-Gun* (1919). But by far the best-known and lasting star was Tom Mix. Beginning in 1916 he often produced and directed his own films and bridged the gap between the silent era and "speakies." Sound film ushered in the "singing cowboy," spawning stars such as Gene Autry, Tex Ritter, and Roy Rogers, a member of the singing group the Sons of the Pioneers. Another successful singing cowboy was William "Hopalong Cassidy" Boyd, who appeared in almost 70 films between 1935 and 1952 and went on to a starring role in a long-running TV series, as did Rogers.

More serious Western fare hit the screen as well, starring non-cowboy actors, such as director John Ford's classic *Stagecoach* (1939) starring John Wayne. Others followed: *Northwest Passage* (1940) with Spencer Tracy; and *Dodge City* (1939), and *Virginia City* (1940), starring English actor Errol Flynn as a cowboy. He then portrayed General Custer in director Raoul Walsh's romanticized biography *They Died with Their Boots On* (1941). Of note as well were director/producer Howard Hawks' collaborations with John Wayne on four films, *Red River* (1948), *Rio Bravo* (1959), *El Dorado* (1966), and *Rio Lobo* (1970). Perhaps the genre reached its zenith with Fred Zinnemann's *High Noon* in 1952, starring Gary Cooper in the ultimate shoot out.

Over on radio the genre flourished as well with a wealth of Western shows airing: *The American Trail, Death Valley Days, Frontier Town, Gene Autry's Melody Ranch, Gunsmoke, Hopalong Cassidy, The Roy Rogers Show, Tales of the Texas Rangers, The Cisco Kid*, and *Tom Mix Ralston Straight Shooters*, to name a few. And with the advent of the new technology of television Western programs flourished, including: *The Adventures of Jim Bowie, The Cisco Kid, The Adventures of Kit Carson, The Lone Ranger, The Roy Rogers Show, The Adventures of Wild Bill Hickok, Hopalong Cassidy, Annie Oakley, Death Valley Days, Zorro, Gunsmoke, Bonanza, The Rifleman, Bat Masterson, Have Gun — Will Travel*, and *Wagon Train*, among many others.

Considering their success on film and radio, and later on TV, one would think that Westerns appearing in newspaper comic strips would be natural, but the converse is true. There was *Texas Slim* by Ferd Johnson (later of Frank Willard's *Moon Mullins* fame), which began in 1925, and was revived in 1940 under the new title, *Texas Slim and Dirty Dalton*. And *Broncho Bill* by Harry O'Neill debuted in 1928 as *Young Buffalo Bill* and continued until 1950. But those were the exceptions. It wasn't until the mid-1930s that the genre began to take hold. Zane Grey's *King of the Royal Mounted*, illustrated by Allen Dean, and *Bronc Peeler* both debuted in 1935. *Red Ryder*, created by writer Stephen Slesinger and artist Fred Harman, began in 1938. *Big Chief Wahoo* (which began as *The Great Gusto*) by Elmer Woggon, and *The Lone Ranger*, adapted from the radio show by Fran Stricker and Charles Flanders, soon premiered as well. Also making their debut in the '30s were Garrett Price's *White Boy*, Ed Leffingwell's *Little Joe*, and Vic Forsythe's *Way out West*.

In February 1937, more than a year before Superman's debut in *Action Comics* #1, the first Western comic book premiered, published by the Comics Magazine Company, titled *Western Picture Stories*, featuring art by the legendary Will Eisner. However, this series lasted only four issues. The same month another Western comic book, *Star Ranger* #1, was published by Chesler/Centaur Publications and ran for 12 issues. It later became *Cowboy Comics* and then the title was changed again to *Star Ranger Funnies*, which lasted until October 1939. In April of the same year Dell published *Western Action Thrillers*, but it lasted only one issue. The first Western photo comic cover featured Roy Rogers, *Dell's Four Color Comics* #38 in April 1944. The same year *Cisco Kid Comics*, a one-shot comic book by Baily Publishing appeared.

But it wasn't until 1948 that Western comic books came into their own. After the war, interest in superheroes diminished as real heroes returned home, and publishers were scrambling for new material. Soon, matinee Western stars had comic series based on them: Gene Autry, Monte Hale, Gabby Hayes, Tim Holt, Lash LaRue, Tom Mix, Tex Ritter, Roy Rogers, John Wayne, et al, all had their own titles. Historical and mythological figures were also well represented: Annie Oakley, Buffalo Bill, the Cisco Kid, Daniel Boone, Davy Crockett, Jesse James, Kit Carson, the Lone Ranger, Wild Bill Hickcock. In addition, new Western characters and titles were created, such as: *Bullseye* and *Boy's Ranch* by Simon and Kirby; Mort Weisinger and Mort Meskin's *Vigilante* at DC; *The Hawk* at Ziff-Davis; and the *Two-Gun Kid*, *Kid Colt Outlaw*, and *Rawhide Kid* over at Atlas.

Within the stories of this anthology the usual Western tropes appear—the sharpshooter, the kid, the gunslinger, the city slicker, the posse, the pony express, the jailbreak, the stagecoach holdup, barrooms aplenty—but there are many surprises in store as well. And while the portrayal of Native Americans belies the mindset of the time in which these comics were created, there's actually quite a variety of how their story is told. There are "good" Indians (usually those who assist the white man), peaceful tribes, and warring factions. Treaties are in threat of being broken and peace is laid claim to.

Another subgenre of the Western comic was a combination of two disparate ones that became popular after the war: Romance and Cowboys. I would be remiss not to include one here, the familiar tale of the "sassy" gal in need of taming. Still, although several of these stories contain familiar clichés, these tales are imbued with charm and surprises. Often these stories display excellent art and dynamic page design as well.

Created mostly by men working in crowded New York offices, or cramped apartments throughout the city, the tales of the range, barroom brawls, shoot outs, wagon trains, campfires, bank robberies, are all collected here for us to enjoy once again, preserved before they fade into the sunset.

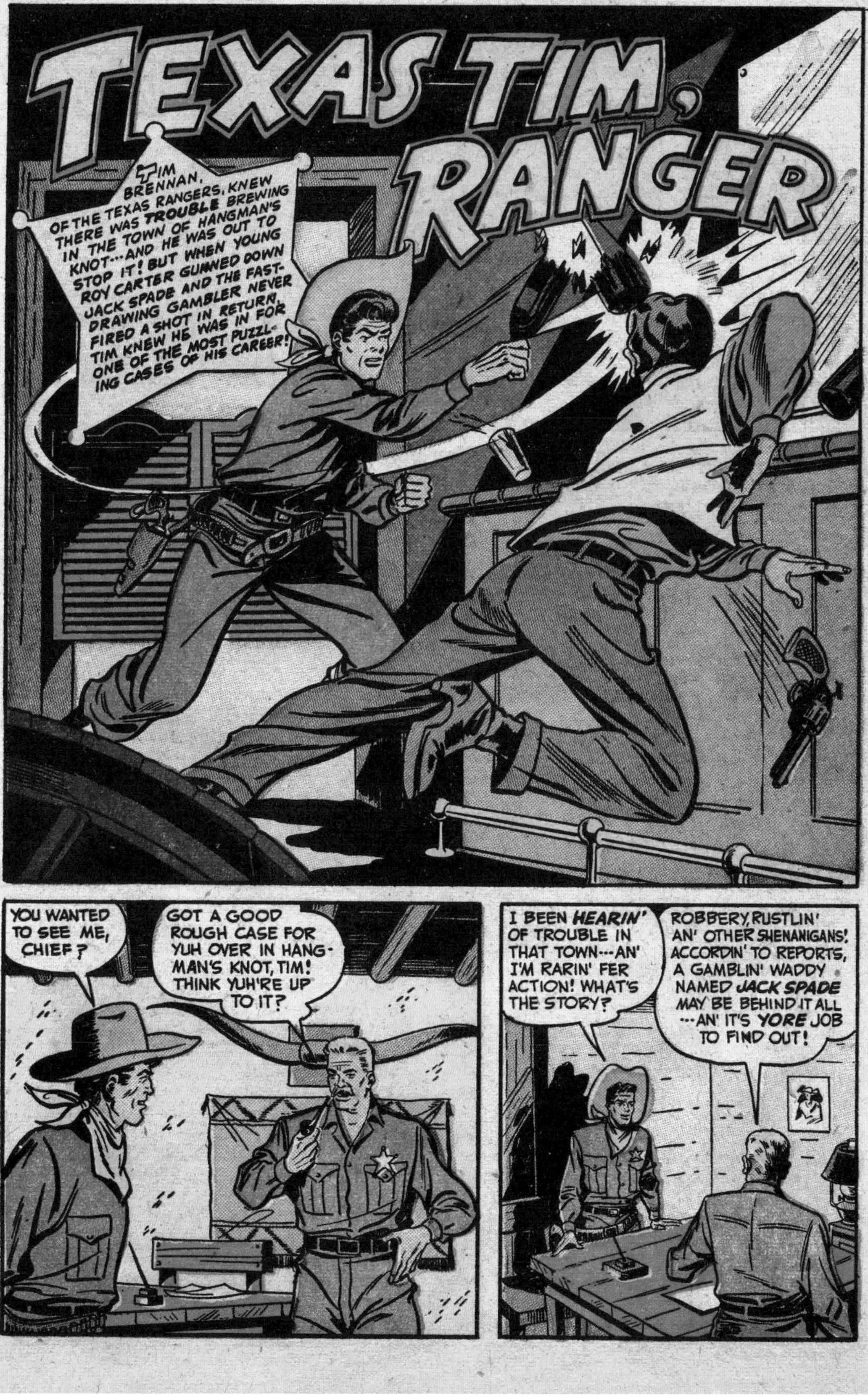
TEXAS TIM, RANGER
TIM BRENNAN, OF THE TEXAS RANGERS, KNEW THERE WAS TROUBLE BREWING IN THE TOWN OF HANGMAN'S KNOT---AND HE WAS OUT TO STOP IT! BUT WHEN YOUNG ROY CARTER GUNNED DOWN JACK SPADE AND THE FAST-DRAWING GAMBLER NEVER FIRED A SHOT IN RETURN, TIM KNEW HE WAS IN FOR ONE OF THE MOST PUZZLING CASES OF HIS CAREER!
YOU WANTED TO SEE ME, CHIEF?
GOT A GOOD ROUGH CASE FOR YUH OVER IN HANGMAN'S KNOT, TIM! THINK YUH'RE UP TO IT?
I BEEN HEARIN' OF TROUBLE IN THAT TOWN---AN' I'M RARIN' FER ACTION! WHAT'S THE STORY?
ROBBERY, RUSTLIN' AN' OTHER SHENANIGANS! ACCORDIN' TO REPORTS, A GAMBLIN' WADDY NAMED JACK SPADE MAY BE BEHIND IT ALL ---AN' IT'S YORE JOB TO FIND OUT!

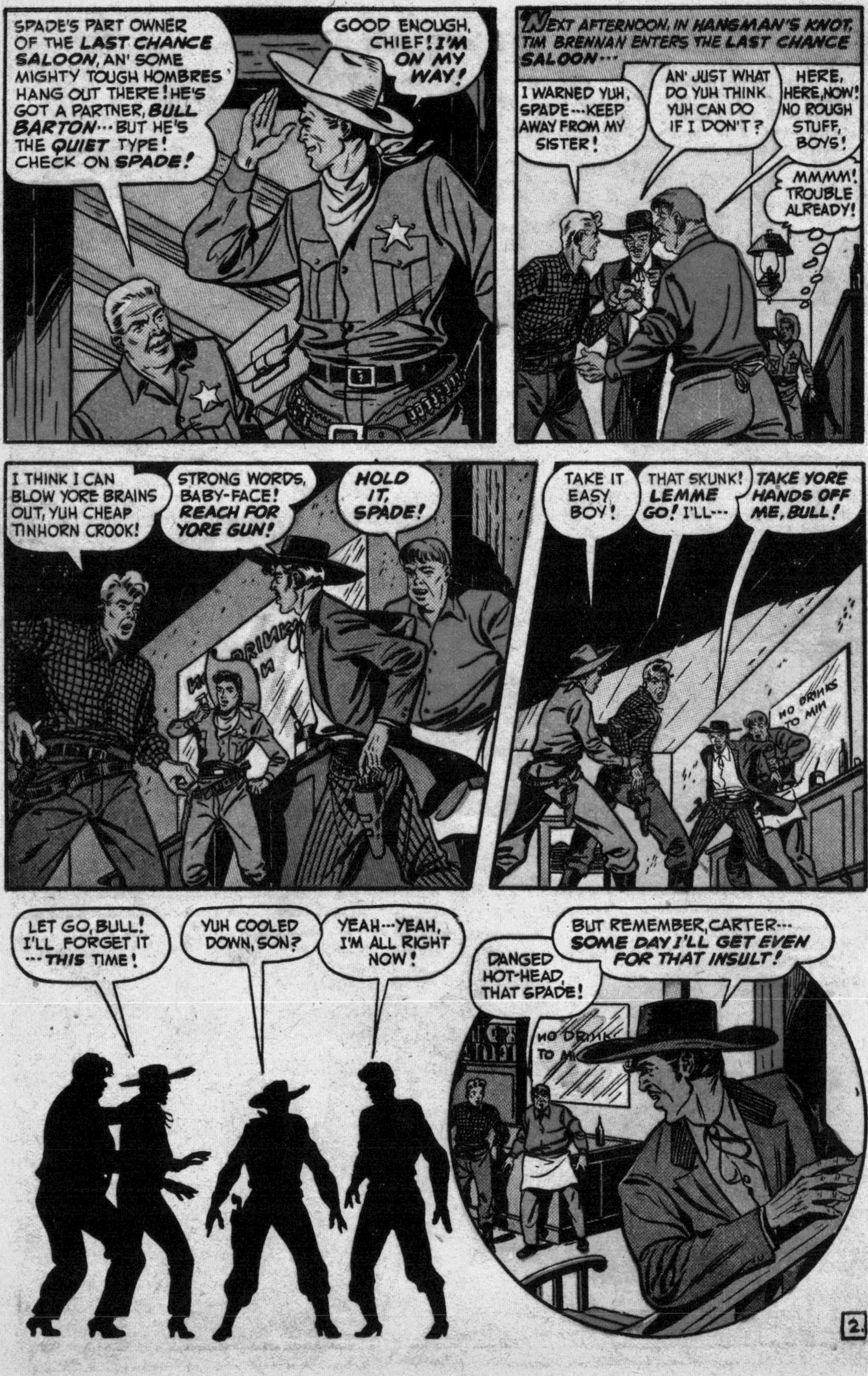
SPADE'S PART OWNER OF THE LAST CHANCE SALOON, AN' SOME MIGHTY TOUGH HOMBRES HANG OUT THERE! HE'S GOT A PARTNER, BULL BARTON... BUT HE'S THE QUIET TYPE! CHECK ON SPADE!
GOOD ENOUGH, CHIEF! I'M ON MY WAY!
NEXT AFTERNOON, IN HANGMAN'S KNOT, TIM BRENNAN ENTERS THE LAST CHANCE SALOON...
I WARNED YUH, SPADE...KEEP AWAY FROM MY SISTER!
AN' JUST WHAT DO YUH THINK YUH CAN DO IF I DON'T?
HERE, HERE, NOW! NO ROUGH STUFF, BOYS!
MMMM! TROUBLE ALREADY!
I THINK I CAN BLOW YORE BRAINS OUT, YUH CHEAP TINHORN CROOK!
STRONG WORDS, BABY-FACE! REACH FOR YORE GUN!
HOLD IT, SPADE!
TAKE IT EASY, BOY!
THAT SKUNK! LEMME GO! I'LL---
TAKE YORE HANDS OFF ME, BULL!
NO DRINKS TO HIM
LET GO, BULL! I'LL FORGET IT ---THIS TIME!
YUH COOLED DOWN, SON?
YEAH---YEAH, I'M ALL RIGHT NOW!
DANGED HOT-HEAD, THAT SPADE!
BUT REMEMBER, CARTER--- SOME DAY I'LL GET EVEN FOR THAT INSULT!
2.

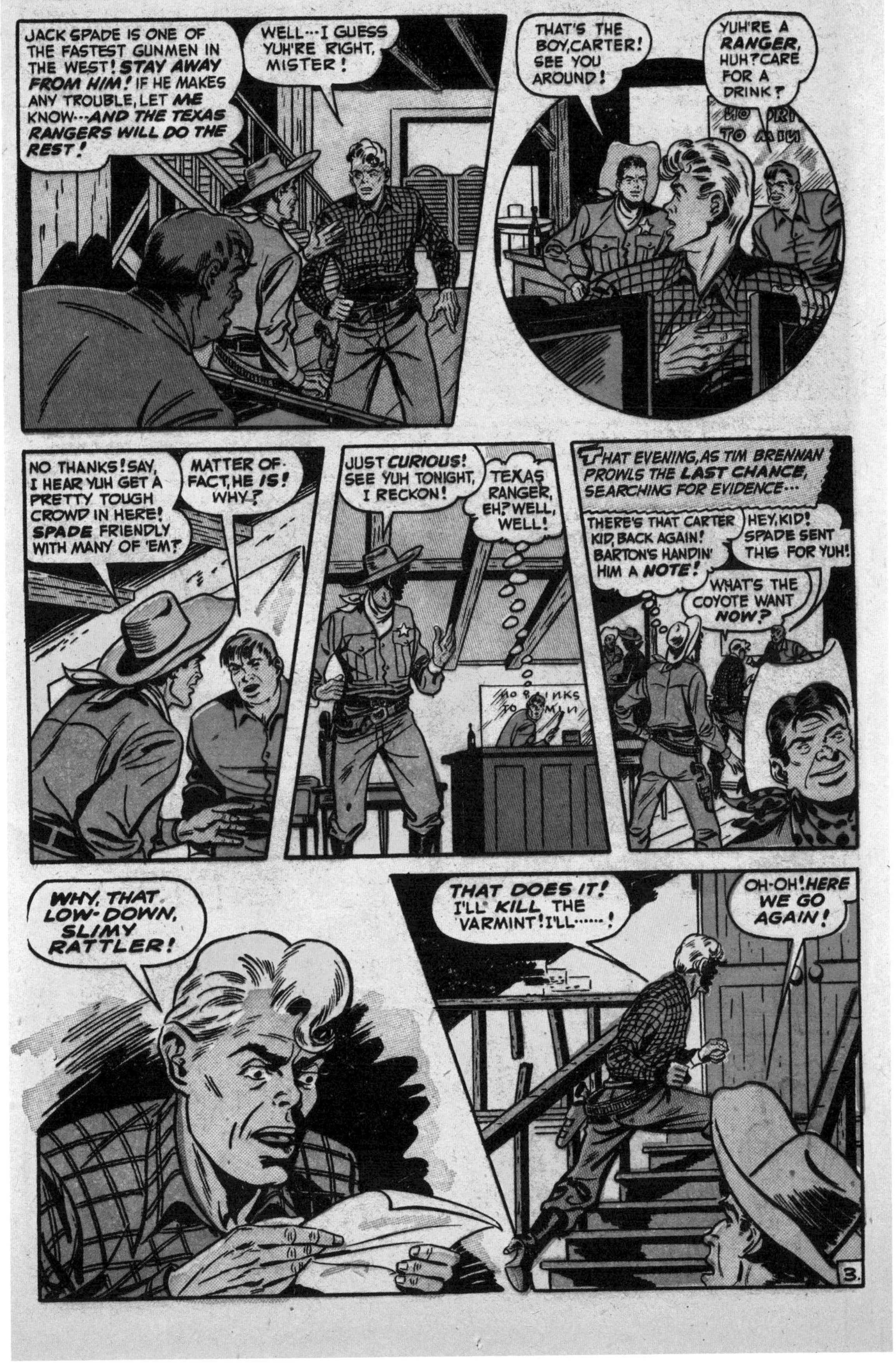

JACK SPADE IS ONE OF THE FASTEST GUNMEN IN THE WEST! STAY AWAY FROM HIM! IF HE MAKES ANY TROUBLE, LET ME KNOW---AND THE TEXAS RANGERS WILL DO THE REST!
WELL---I GUESS YUH'RE RIGHT, MISTER!
THAT'S THE BOY, CARTER! SEE YOU AROUND!
YUH'RE A RANGER, HUH? CARE FOR A DRINK?
NO THANKS! SAY, I HEAR YUH GET A PRETTY TOUGH CROWD IN HERE! SPADE FRIENDLY WITH MANY OF 'EM?
MATTER OF FACT, HE IS! WHY?
JUST CURIOUS! SEE YUH TONIGHT, I RECKON!
TEXAS RANGER, EH? WELL, WELL!
THAT EVENING, AS TIM BRENNAN PROWLS THE LAST CHANCE, SEARCHING FOR EVIDENCE---
THERE'S THAT CARTER KID, BACK AGAIN! BARTON'S HANDIN' HIM A NOTE!
HEY, KID! SPADE SENT THIS FOR YUH!
WHAT'S THE COYOTE WANT NOW?
WHY, THAT LOW-DOWN, SLIMY RATTLER!
THAT DOES IT! I'LL KILL THE VARMINT! I'LL......!
OH-OH! HERE WE GO AGAIN!
3.

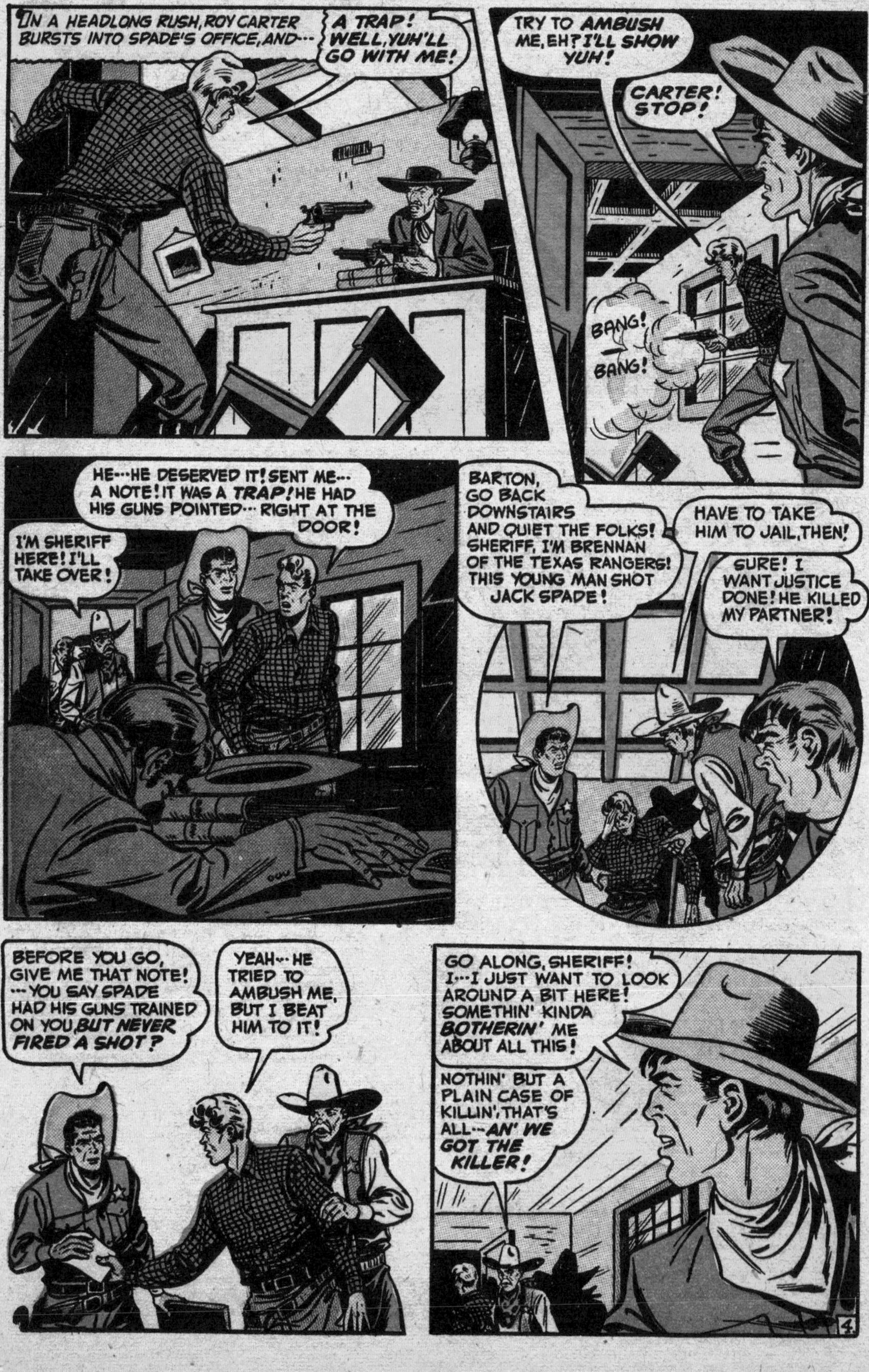
IN A HEADLONG RUSH, ROY CARTER BURSTS INTO SPADE'S OFFICE, AND---
A TRAP! WELL, YUH'LL GO WITH ME!
TRY TO AMBUSH ME, EH? I'LL SHOW YUH!
CARTER! STOP!
BANG! — BANG!
HE---HE DESERVED IT! SENT ME--- A NOTE! IT WAS A TRAP! HE HAD HIS GUNS POINTED--- RIGHT AT THE DOOR!
I'M SHERIFF HERE! I'LL TAKE OVER!
BARTON, GO BACK DOWNSTAIRS AND QUIET THE FOLKS! SHERIFF, I'M BRENNAN OF THE TEXAS RANGERS! THIS YOUNG MAN SHOT JACK SPADE!
HAVE TO TAKE HIM TO JAIL, THEN!
SURE! I WANT JUSTICE DONE! HE KILLED MY PARTNER!
BEFORE YOU GO, GIVE ME THAT NOTE! ---YOU SAY SPADE HAD HIS GUNS TRAINED ON YOU, BUT NEVER FIRED A SHOT?
YEAH--HE TRIED TO AMBUSH ME, BUT I BEAT HIM TO IT!
GO ALONG, SHERIFF! I---I JUST WANT TO LOOK AROUND A BIT HERE! SOMETHIN' KINDA BOTHERIN' ME ABOUT ALL THIS!
NOTHIN' BUT A PLAIN CASE OF KILLIN', THAT'S ALL--AN' WE GOT THE KILLER!
4

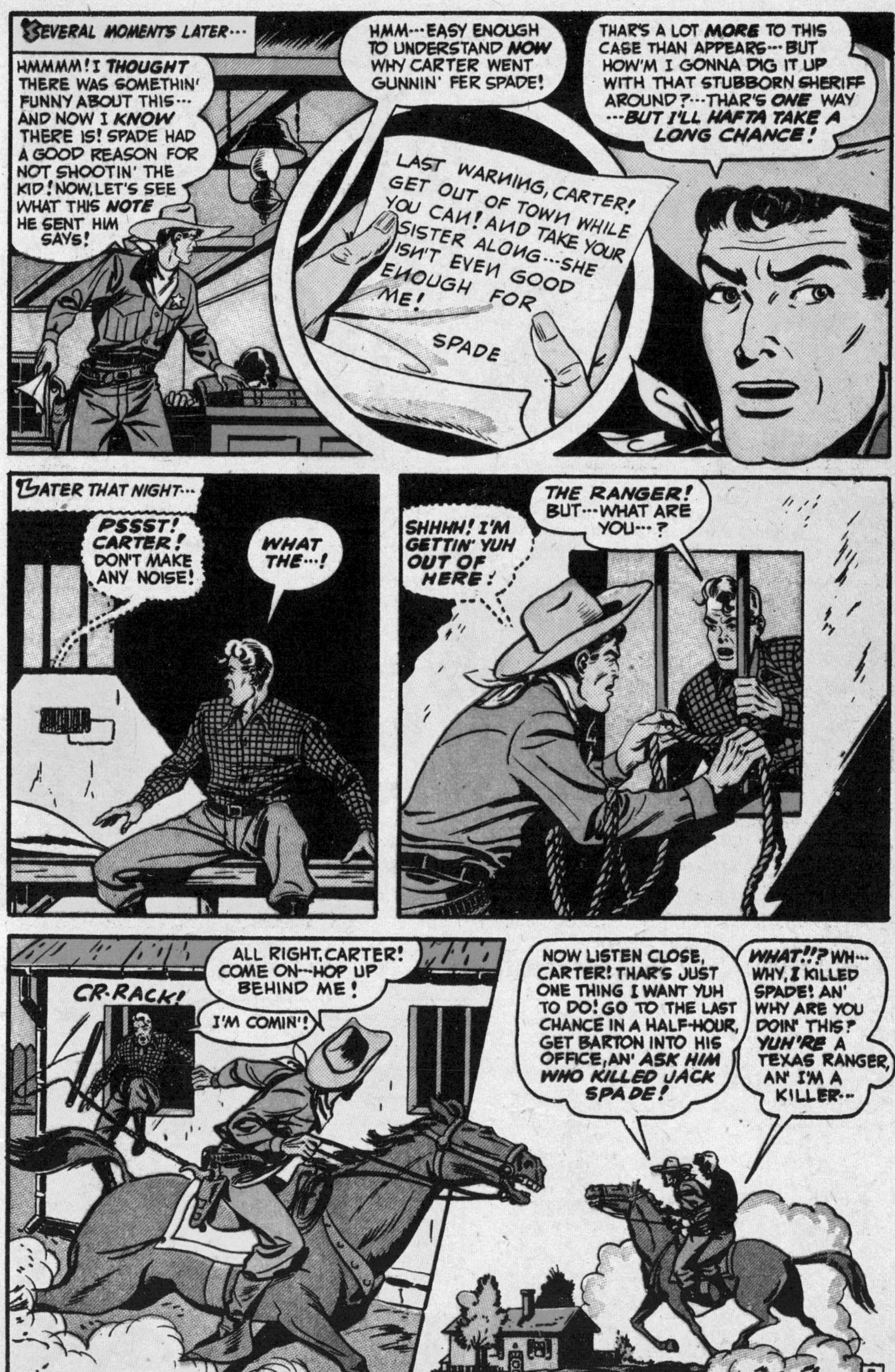
SEVERAL MOMENTS LATER···
HMMMM! I THOUGHT THERE WAS SOMETHIN' FUNNY ABOUT THIS··· AND NOW I KNOW THERE IS! SPADE HAD A GOOD REASON FOR NOT SHOOTIN' THE KID! NOW, LET'S SEE WHAT THIS NOTE HE SENT HIM SAYS!
HMM··· EASY ENOUGH TO UNDERSTAND NOW WHY CARTER WENT GUNNIN' FER SPADE!
LAST WARNING, CARTER! GET OUT OF TOWN WHILE YOU CAN! AND TAKE YOUR SISTER ALONG···SHE ISN'T EVEN GOOD ENOUGH FOR ME!
SPADE
THAR'S A LOT MORE TO THIS CASE THAN APPEARS··· BUT HOW'M I GONNA DIG IT UP WITH THAT STUBBORN SHERIFF AROUND?··· THAR'S ONE WAY ···BUT I'LL HAFTA TAKE A LONG CHANCE!
LATER THAT NIGHT···
PSSST! CARTER! DON'T MAKE ANY NOISE!
WHAT THE···!
SHHHH! I'M GETTIN' YUH OUT OF HERE!
THE RANGER! BUT···WHAT ARE YOU···?
CR-RACK!
ALL RIGHT, CARTER! COME ON···HOP UP BEHIND ME!
I'M COMIN'!
NOW LISTEN CLOSE, CARTER! THAR'S JUST ONE THING I WANT YUH TO DO! GO TO THE LAST CHANCE IN A HALF-HOUR, GET BARTON INTO HIS OFFICE, AN' ASK HIM WHO KILLED JACK SPADE!
WHAT!!? WH··· WHY, I KILLED SPADE! AN' WHY ARE YOU DOIN' THIS? YUH'RE A TEXAS RANGER, AN' I'M A KILLER··
5.

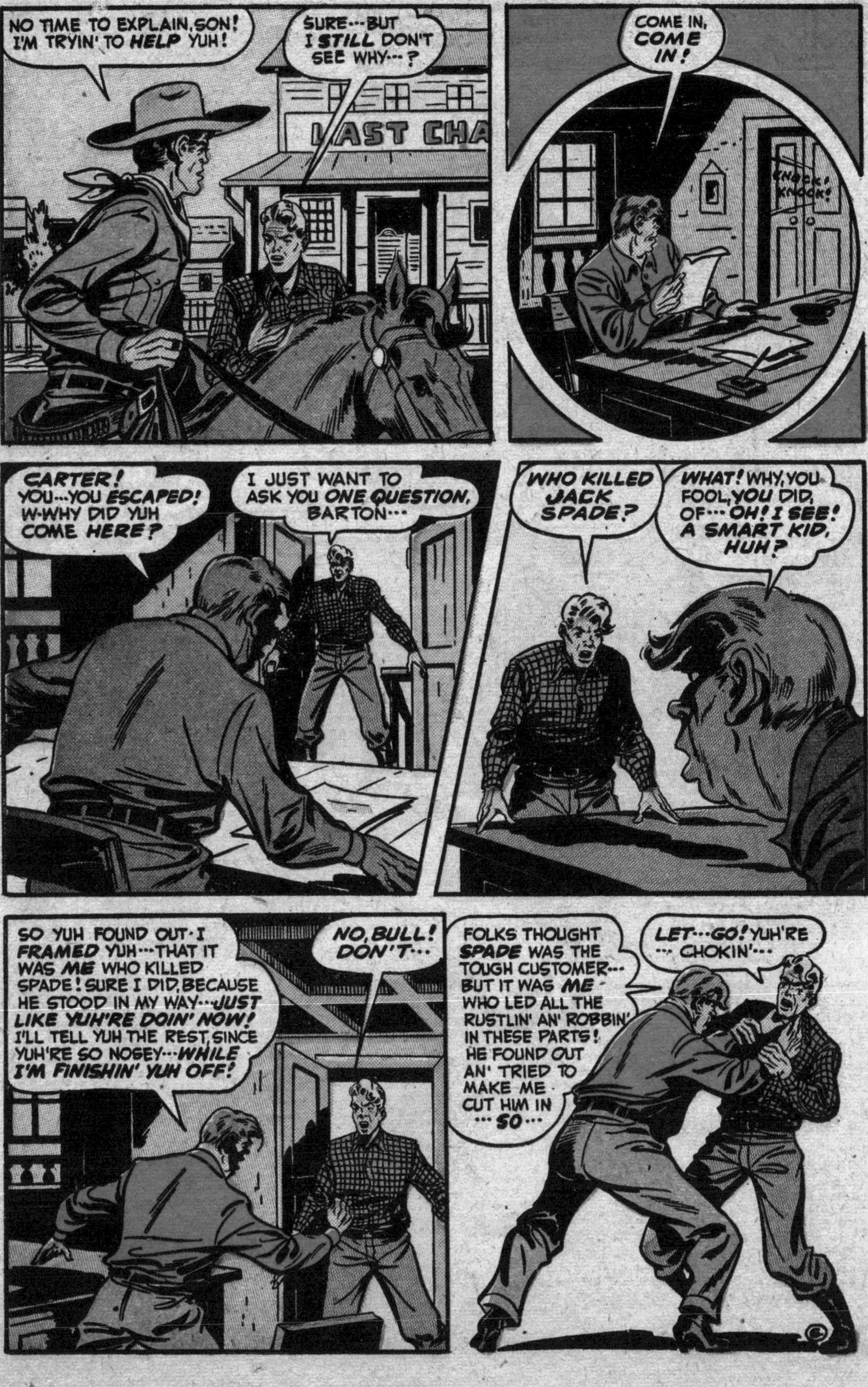
NO TIME TO EXPLAIN, SON! I'M TRYIN' TO HELP YUH!
SURE---BUT I STILL DON'T SEE WHY---?
LAST CHA
COME IN, COME IN!
KNOCK! KNOCK!
CARTER! YOU---YOU ESCAPED! W-WHY DID YUH COME HERE?
I JUST WANT TO ASK YOU ONE QUESTION, BARTON---
WHO KILLED JACK SPADE?
WHAT! WHY, YOU FOOL, YOU DID, OF--- OH! I SEE! A SMART KID, HUH?
SO YUH FOUND OUT I FRAMED YUH---THAT IT WAS ME WHO KILLED SPADE! SURE I DID, BECAUSE HE STOOD IN MY WAY---JUST LIKE YUH'RE DOIN' NOW! I'LL TELL YUH THE REST, SINCE YUH'RE SO NOSEY---WHILE I'M FINISHIN' YUH OFF!
NO, BULL! DON'T---
FOLKS THOUGHT SPADE WAS THE TOUGH CUSTOMER--- BUT IT WAS ME WHO LED ALL THE RUSTLIN' AN' ROBBIN' IN THESE PARTS! HE FOUND OUT AN' TRIED TO MAKE ME CUT HIM IN ---SO---
LET---GO! YUH'RE ---CHOKIN'---

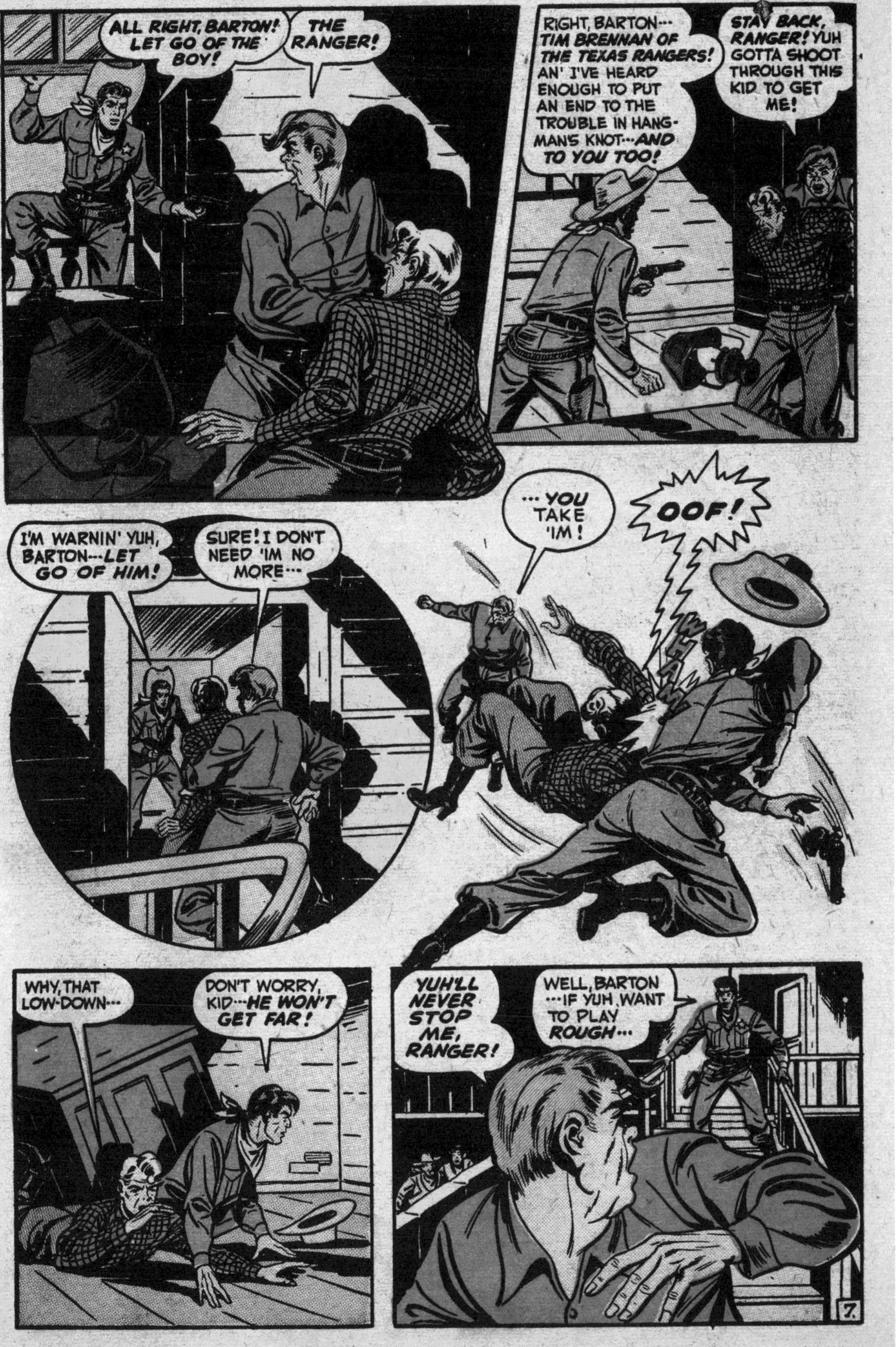
ALL RIGHT, BARTON! LET GO OF THE BOY!
THE RANGER!
RIGHT, BARTON... TIM BRENNAN OF THE TEXAS RANGERS! AN' I'VE HEARD ENOUGH TO PUT AN END TO THE TROUBLE IN HANG-MAN'S KNOT... AND TO YOU TOO!
STAY BACK, RANGER! YUH GOTTA SHOOT THROUGH THIS KID TO GET ME!
I'M WARNIN' YUH, BARTON... LET GO OF HIM!
SURE! I DON'T NEED 'IM NO MORE...
...YOU TAKE 'IM!
OOF!
WHAM
WHY, THAT LOW-DOWN...
DON'T WORRY, KID... HE WON'T GET FAR!
YUH'LL NEVER STOP ME, RANGER!
WELL, BARTON ...IF YUH WANT TO PLAY ROUGH...
7.

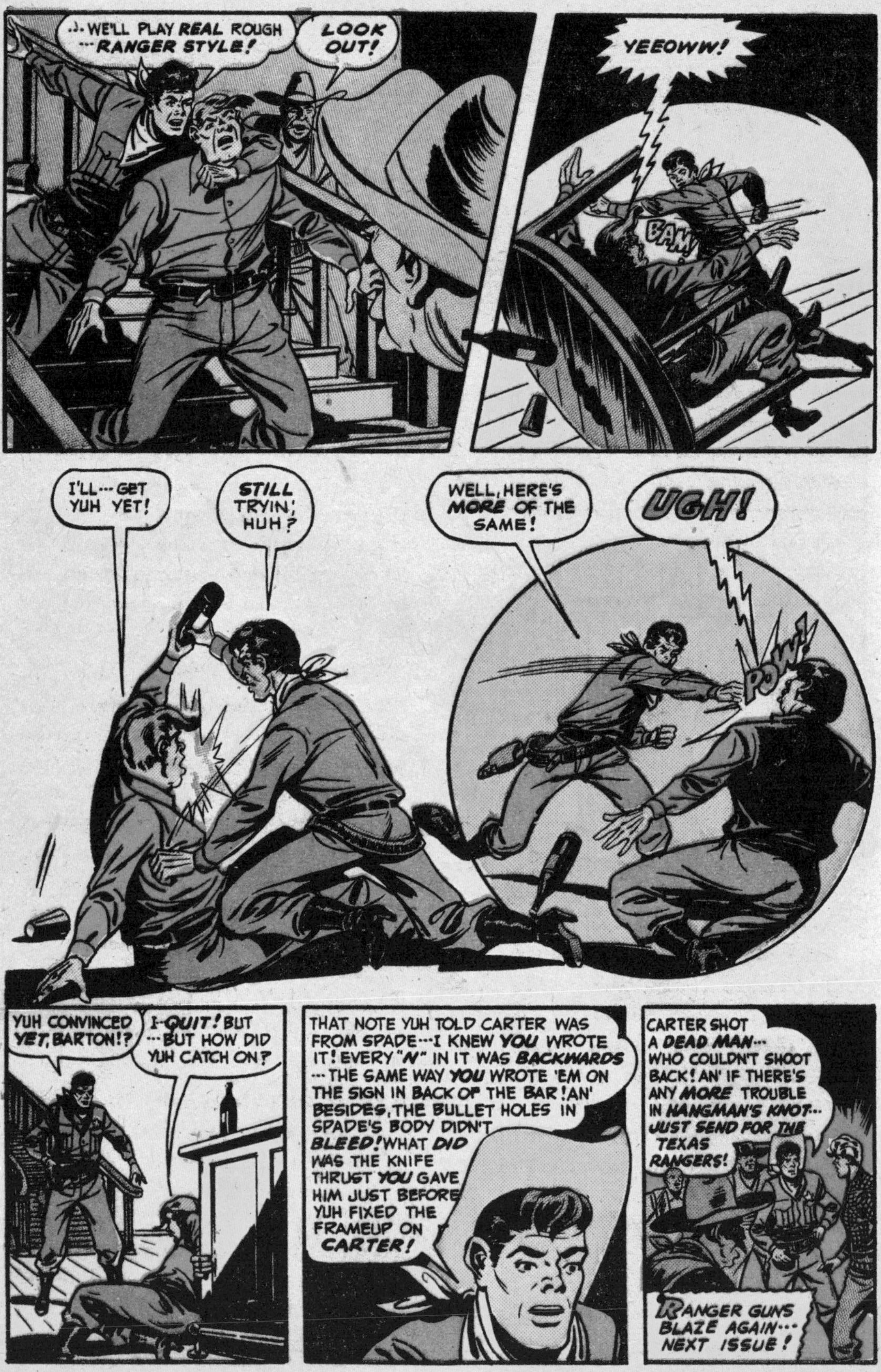

..WE'LL PLAY REAL ROUGH ---RANGER STYLE!
LOOK OUT!
YEEOWW!
BAM
I'LL--- GET YUH YET!
STILL TRYIN', HUH?
WELL, HERE'S MORE OF THE SAME!
UGH!
POW
YUH CONVINCED YET, BARTON!?
I--QUIT! BUT ---BUT HOW DID YUH CATCH ON?
THAT NOTE YUH TOLD CARTER WAS FROM SPADE---I KNEW YOU WROTE IT! EVERY "N" IN IT WAS BACKWARDS ---THE SAME WAY YOU WROTE 'EM ON THE SIGN IN BACK OF THE BAR! AN' BESIDES, THE BULLET HOLES IN SPADE'S BODY DIDN'T BLEED! WHAT DID WAS THE KNIFE THRUST YOU GAVE HIM JUST BEFORE YUH FIXED THE FRAMEUP ON CARTER!
CARTER SHOT A DEAD MAN--- WHO COULDN'T SHOOT BACK! AN' IF THERE'S ANY MORE TROUBLE IN HANGMAN'S KNOT... JUST SEND FOR THE TEXAS RANGERS!
RANGER GUNS BLAZE AGAIN--- NEXT ISSUE!

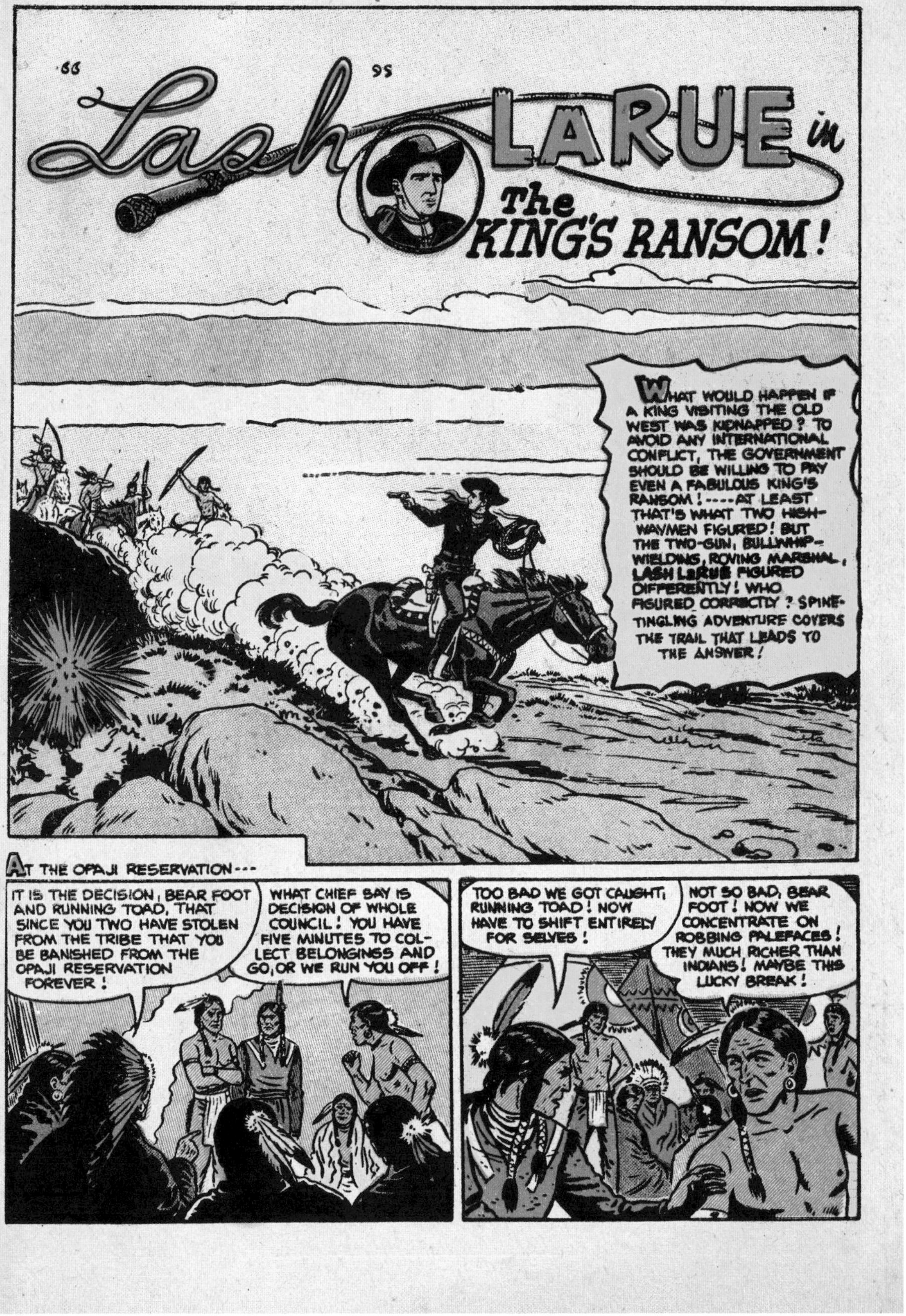
"Lash" LARUE in
The KING'S RANSOM!
WHAT WOULD HAPPEN IF A KING VISITING THE OLD WEST WAS KIDNAPPED? TO AVOID ANY INTERNATIONAL CONFLICT, THE GOVERNMENT SHOULD BE WILLING TO PAY EVEN A FABULOUS KING'S RANSOM!----AT LEAST THAT'S WHAT TWO HIGH-WAYMEN FIGURED! BUT THE TWO-GUN, BULLWHIP-WIELDING, ROVING MARSHAL, LASH LaRUE FIGURED DIFFERENTLY! WHO FIGURED CORRECTLY? SPINE-TINGLING ADVENTURE COVERS THE TRAIL THAT LEADS TO THE ANSWER!
AT THE OPAJI RESERVATION---
IT IS THE DECISION, BEAR FOOT AND RUNNING TOAD, THAT SINCE YOU TWO HAVE STOLEN FROM THE TRIBE THAT YOU BE BANISHED FROM THE OPAJI RESERVATION FOREVER!
WHAT CHIEF SAY IS DECISION OF WHOLE COUNCIL! YOU HAVE FIVE MINUTES TO COL-LECT BELONGINGS AND GO, OR WE RUN YOU OFF!
TOO BAD WE GOT CAUGHT, RUNNING TOAD! NOW HAVE TO SHIFT ENTIRELY FOR SELVES!
NOT SO BAD, BEAR FOOT! NOW WE CONCENTRATE ON ROBBING PALEFACES! THEY MUCH RICHER THAN INDIANS! MAYBE THIS LUCKY BREAK!

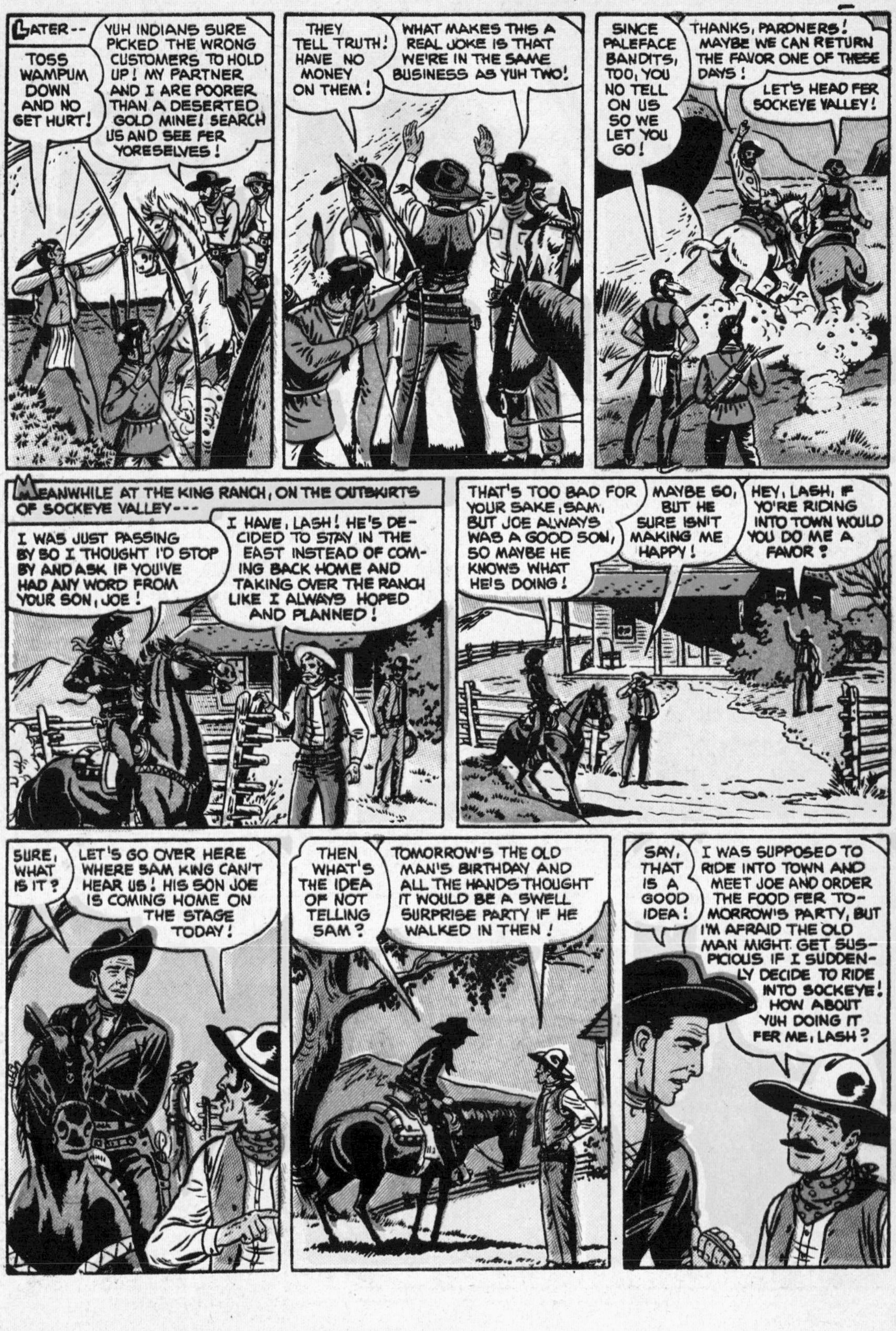
LATER--
TOSS WAMPUM DOWN AND NO GET HURT!
YUH INDIANS SURE PICKED THE WRONG CUSTOMERS TO HOLD UP! MY PARTNER AND I ARE POORER THAN A DESERTED GOLD MINE! SEARCH US AND SEE FER YORESELVES!
THEY TELL TRUTH! HAVE NO MONEY ON THEM!
WHAT MAKES THIS A REAL JOKE IS THAT WE'RE IN THE SAME BUSINESS AS YUH TWO!
SINCE PALEFACE BANDITS, TOO, YOU NO TELL ON US SO WE LET YOU GO!
THANKS, PARDNERS! MAYBE WE CAN RETURN THE FAVOR ONE OF THESE DAYS!
LET'S HEAD FER SOCKEYE VALLEY!
MEANWHILE AT THE KING RANCH, ON THE OUTSKIRTS OF SOCKEYE VALLEY---
I WAS JUST PASSING BY SO I THOUGHT I'D STOP BY AND ASK IF YOU'VE HAD ANY WORD FROM YOUR SON, JOE!
I HAVE, LASH! HE'S DECIDED TO STAY IN THE EAST INSTEAD OF COMING BACK HOME AND TAKING OVER THE RANCH LIKE I ALWAYS HOPED AND PLANNED!
THAT'S TOO BAD FOR YOUR SAKE, SAM, BUT JOE ALWAYS WAS A GOOD SON, SO MAYBE HE KNOWS WHAT HE'S DOING!
MAYBE SO, BUT HE SURE ISN'T MAKING ME HAPPY!
HEY, LASH, IF YO'RE RIDING INTO TOWN WOULD YOU DO ME A FAVOR?
SURE, WHAT IS IT?
LET'S GO OVER HERE WHERE SAM KING CAN'T HEAR US! HIS SON JOE IS COMING HOME ON THE STAGE TODAY!
THEN WHAT'S THE IDEA OF NOT TELLING SAM?
TOMORROW'S THE OLD MAN'S BIRTHDAY AND ALL THE HANDS THOUGHT IT WOULD BE A SWELL SURPRISE PARTY IF HE WALKED IN THEN!
SAY, THAT IS A GOOD IDEA!
I WAS SUPPOSED TO RIDE INTO TOWN AND MEET JOE AND ORDER THE FOOD FER TOMORROW'S PARTY, BUT I'M AFRAID THE OLD MAN MIGHT GET SUSPICIOUS IF I SUDDENLY DECIDE TO RIDE INTO SOCKEYE! HOW ABOUT YUH DOING IT FER ME, LASH?

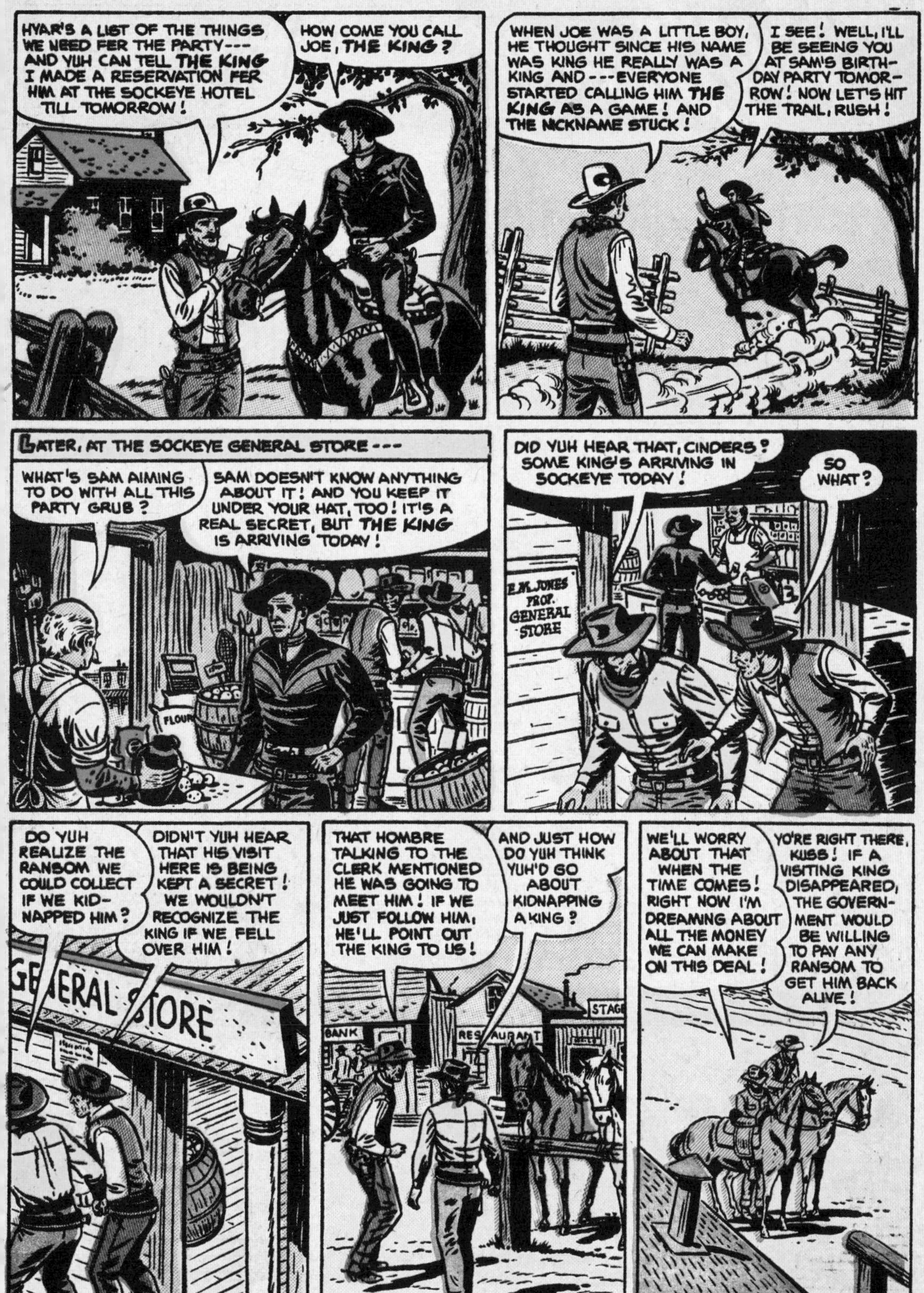
HYAR'S A LIST OF THE THINGS WE NEED FER THE PARTY--- AND YUH CAN TELL THE KING I MADE A RESERVATION FER HIM AT THE SOCKEYE HOTEL TILL TOMORROW!
HOW COME YOU CALL JOE, THE KING?
WHEN JOE WAS A LITTLE BOY, HE THOUGHT SINCE HIS NAME WAS KING HE REALLY WAS A KING AND---EVERYONE STARTED CALLING HIM THE KING AS A GAME! AND THE NICKNAME STUCK!
I SEE! WELL, I'LL BE SEEING YOU AT SAM'S BIRTHDAY PARTY TOMORROW! NOW LET'S HIT THE TRAIL, RUSH!
LATER, AT THE SOCKEYE GENERAL STORE---
WHAT'S SAM AIMING TO DO WITH ALL THIS PARTY GRUB?
SAM DOESN'T KNOW ANYTHING ABOUT IT! AND YOU KEEP IT UNDER YOUR HAT, TOO! IT'S A REAL SECRET, BUT THE KING IS ARRIVING TODAY!
FLOUR
DID YUH HEAR THAT, CINDERS? SOME KING'S ARRIVING IN SOCKEYE TODAY!
SO WHAT?
E.M. JONES PROP. GENERAL STORE
DO YUH REALIZE THE RANSOM WE COULD COLLECT IF WE KIDNAPPED HIM?
DIDN'T YUH HEAR THAT HIS VISIT HERE IS BEING KEPT A SECRET! WE WOULDN'T RECOGNIZE THE KING IF WE FELL OVER HIM!
GENERAL STORE
THAT HOMBRE TALKING TO THE CLERK MENTIONED HE WAS GOING TO MEET HIM! IF WE JUST FOLLOW HIM, HE'LL POINT OUT THE KING TO US!
AND JUST HOW DO YUH THINK YUH'D GO ABOUT KIDNAPPING A KING?
BANK
RESTAURANT
STAGE
WE'LL WORRY ABOUT THAT WHEN THE TIME COMES! RIGHT NOW I'M DREAMING ABOUT ALL THE MONEY WE CAN MAKE ON THIS DEAL!
YO'RE RIGHT THERE, KISS! IF A VISITING KING DISAPPEARED, THE GOVERNMENT WOULD BE WILLING TO PAY ANY RANSOM TO GET HIM BACK ALIVE!

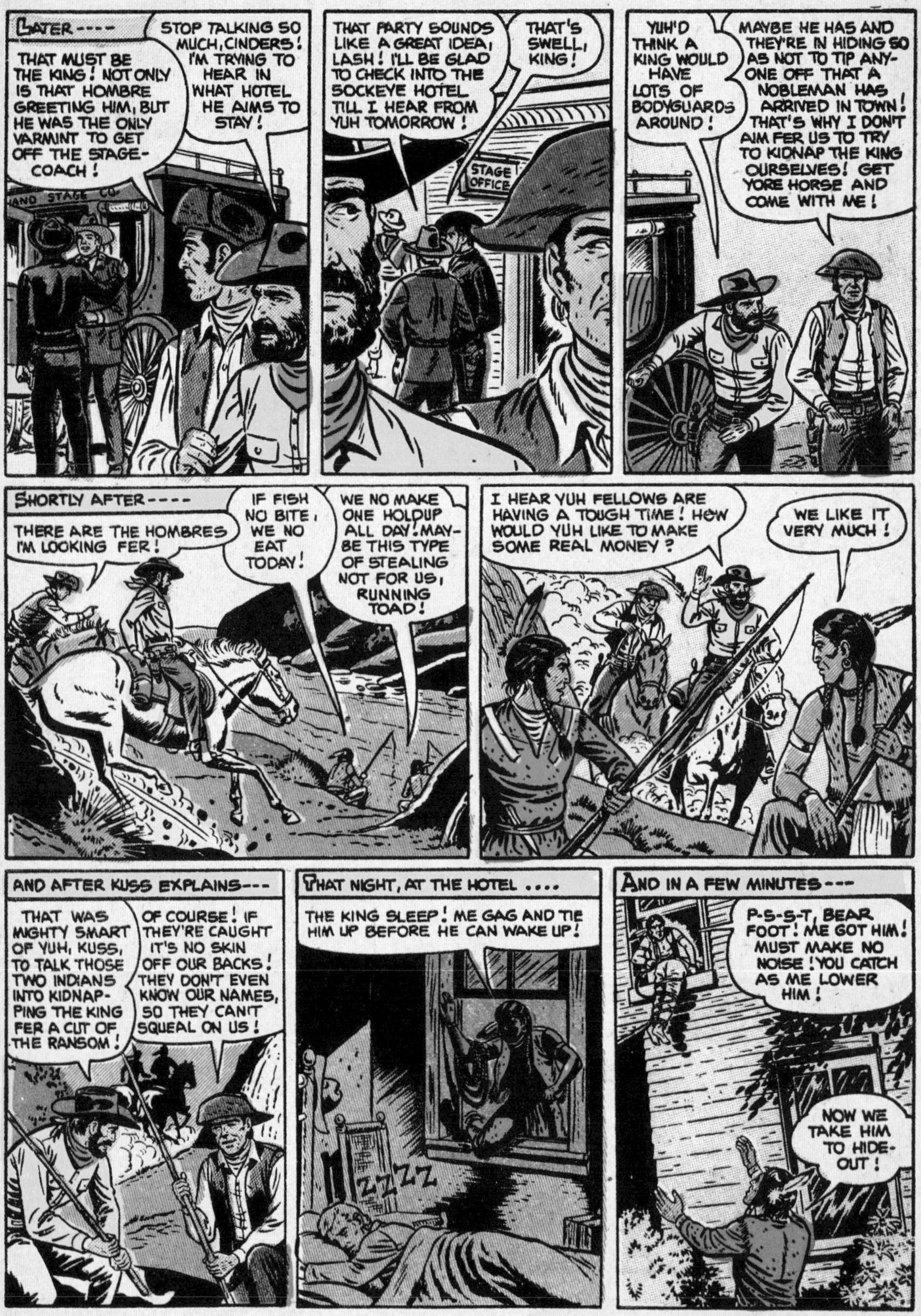
LATER ----
THAT MUST BE THE KING! NOT ONLY IS THAT HOMBRE GREETING HIM, BUT HE WAS THE ONLY VARMINT TO GET OFF THE STAGE-COACH!
STOP TALKING SO MUCH, CINDERS! I'M TRYING TO HEAR IN WHAT HOTEL HE AIMS TO STAY!
THAT PARTY SOUNDS LIKE A GREAT IDEA, LASH! I'LL BE GLAD TO CHECK INTO THE SOCKEYE HOTEL TILL I HEAR FROM YUH TOMORROW!
THAT'S SWELL, KING!
STAGE OFFICE
YUH'D THINK A KING WOULD HAVE LOTS OF BODYGUARDS AROUND!
MAYBE HE HAS AND THEY'RE IN HIDING SO AS NOT TO TIP ANY-ONE OFF THAT A NOBLEMAN HAS ARRIVED IN TOWN! THAT'S WHY I DON'T AIM FER US TO TRY TO KIDNAP THE KING OURSELVES! GET YORE HORSE AND COME WITH ME!
SHORTLY AFTER ----
THERE ARE THE HOMBRES I'M LOOKING FER!
IF FISH NO BITE, WE NO EAT TODAY!
WE NO MAKE ONE HOLDUP ALL DAY! MAY-BE THIS TYPE OF STEALING NOT FOR US, RUNNING TOAD!
I HEAR YUH FELLOWS ARE HAVING A TOUGH TIME! HOW WOULD YUH LIKE TO MAKE SOME REAL MONEY?
WE LIKE IT VERY MUCH!
AND AFTER KUSS EXPLAINS---
THAT WAS MIGHTY SMART OF YUH, KUSS, TO TALK THOSE TWO INDIANS INTO KIDNAP-PING THE KING FER A CUT OF THE RANSOM!
OF COURSE! IF THEY'RE CAUGHT IT'S NO SKIN OFF OUR BACKS! THEY DON'T EVEN KNOW OUR NAMES, SO THEY CAN'T SQUEAL ON US!
THAT NIGHT, AT THE HOTEL ....
THE KING SLEEP! ME GAG AND TIE HIM UP BEFORE HE CAN WAKE UP!
ZZZZ
AND IN A FEW MINUTES ---
P-S-S-T, BEAR FOOT! ME GOT HIM! MUST MAKE NO NOISE! YOU CATCH AS ME LOWER HIM!
NOW WE TAKE HIM TO HIDE-OUT!

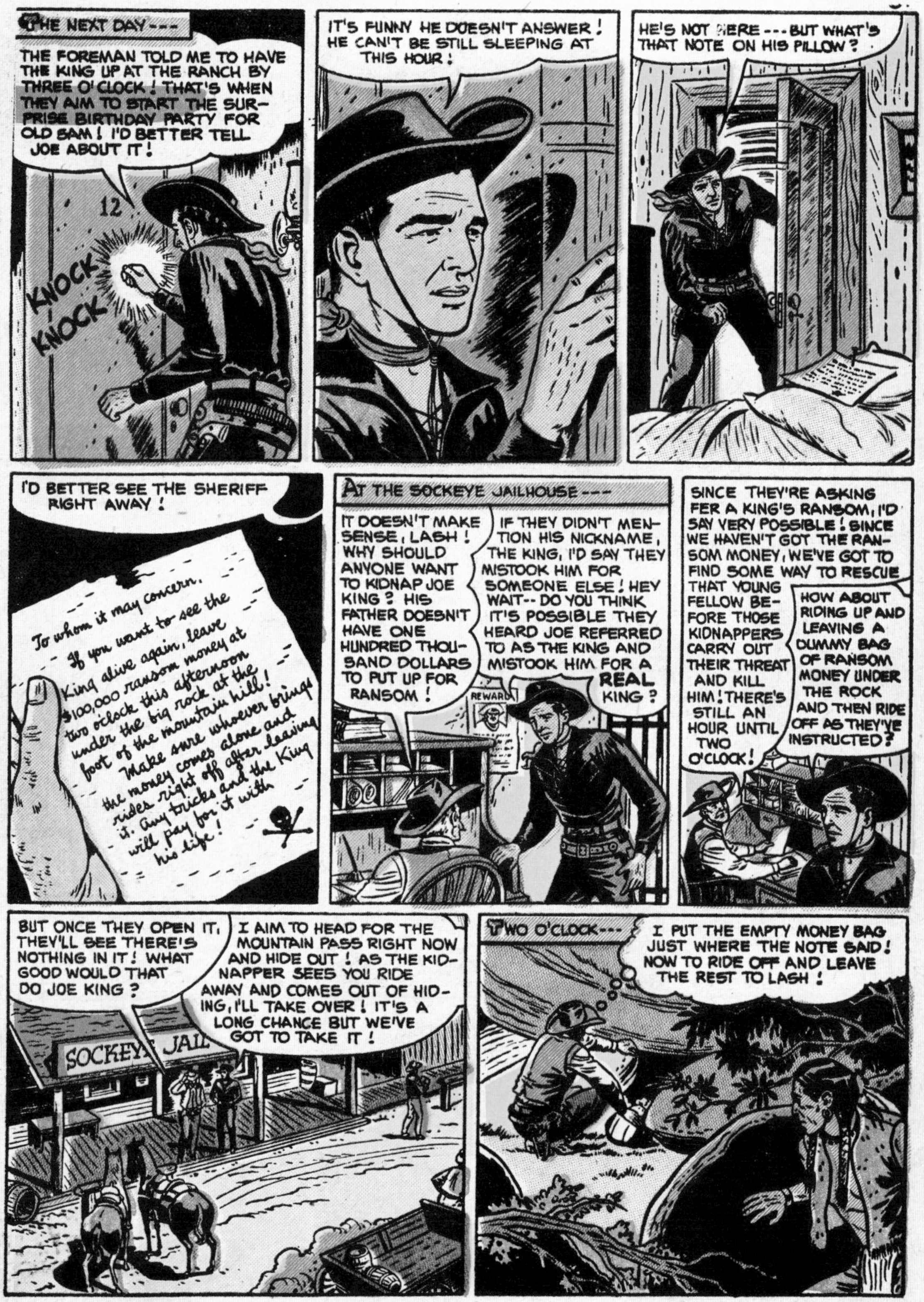
THE NEXT DAY---
THE FOREMAN TOLD ME TO HAVE THE KING UP AT THE RANCH BY THREE O'CLOCK! THAT'S WHEN THEY AIM TO START THE SURPRISE BIRTHDAY PARTY FOR OLD SAM! I'D BETTER TELL JOE ABOUT IT!
12
KNOCK KNOCK
IT'S FUNNY HE DOESN'T ANSWER! HE CAN'T BE STILL SLEEPING AT THIS HOUR!
HE'S NOT HERE---BUT WHAT'S THAT NOTE ON HIS PILLOW?
I'D BETTER SEE THE SHERIFF RIGHT AWAY!
To whom it may concern.
If you want to see the King alive again, leave $100,000 ransom money at two o'clock this afternoon under the big rock at the foot of the mountain hill!
Make sure whoever brings the money comes alone and rides right off after leaving it. Any tricks and the King will pay for it with his life!
AT THE SOCKEYE JAILHOUSE---
IT DOESN'T MAKE SENSE, LASH! WHY SHOULD ANYONE WANT TO KIDNAP JOE KING? HIS FATHER DOESN'T HAVE ONE HUNDRED THOUSAND DOLLARS TO PUT UP FOR RANSOM!
IF THEY DIDN'T MENTION HIS NICKNAME, THE KING, I'D SAY THEY MISTOOK HIM FOR SOMEONE ELSE! HEY WAIT-- DO YOU THINK IT'S POSSIBLE THEY HEARD JOE REFERRED TO AS THE KING AND MISTOOK HIM FOR A REAL KING?
REWARD
SINCE THEY'RE ASKING FER A KING'S RANSOM, I'D SAY VERY POSSIBLE! SINCE WE HAVEN'T GOT THE RANSOM MONEY, WE'VE GOT TO FIND SOME WAY TO RESCUE THAT YOUNG FELLOW BEFORE THOSE KIDNAPPERS CARRY OUT THEIR THREAT AND KILL HIM! THERE'S STILL AN HOUR UNTIL TWO O'CLOCK!
HOW ABOUT RIDING UP AND LEAVING A DUMMY BAG OF RANSOM MONEY UNDER THE ROCK AND THEN RIDE OFF AS THEY'VE INSTRUCTED?
BUT ONCE THEY OPEN IT, THEY'LL SEE THERE'S NOTHING IN IT! WHAT GOOD WOULD THAT DO JOE KING?
I AIM TO HEAD FOR THE MOUNTAIN PASS RIGHT NOW AND HIDE OUT! AS THE KIDNAPPER SEES YOU RIDE AWAY AND COMES OUT OF HIDING, I'LL TAKE OVER! IT'S A LONG CHANCE BUT WE'VE GOT TO TAKE IT!
SOCKEYE JAIL
TWO O'CLOCK---
I PUT THE EMPTY MONEY BAG JUST WHERE THE NOTE SAID! NOW TO RIDE OFF AND LEAVE THE REST TO LASH!

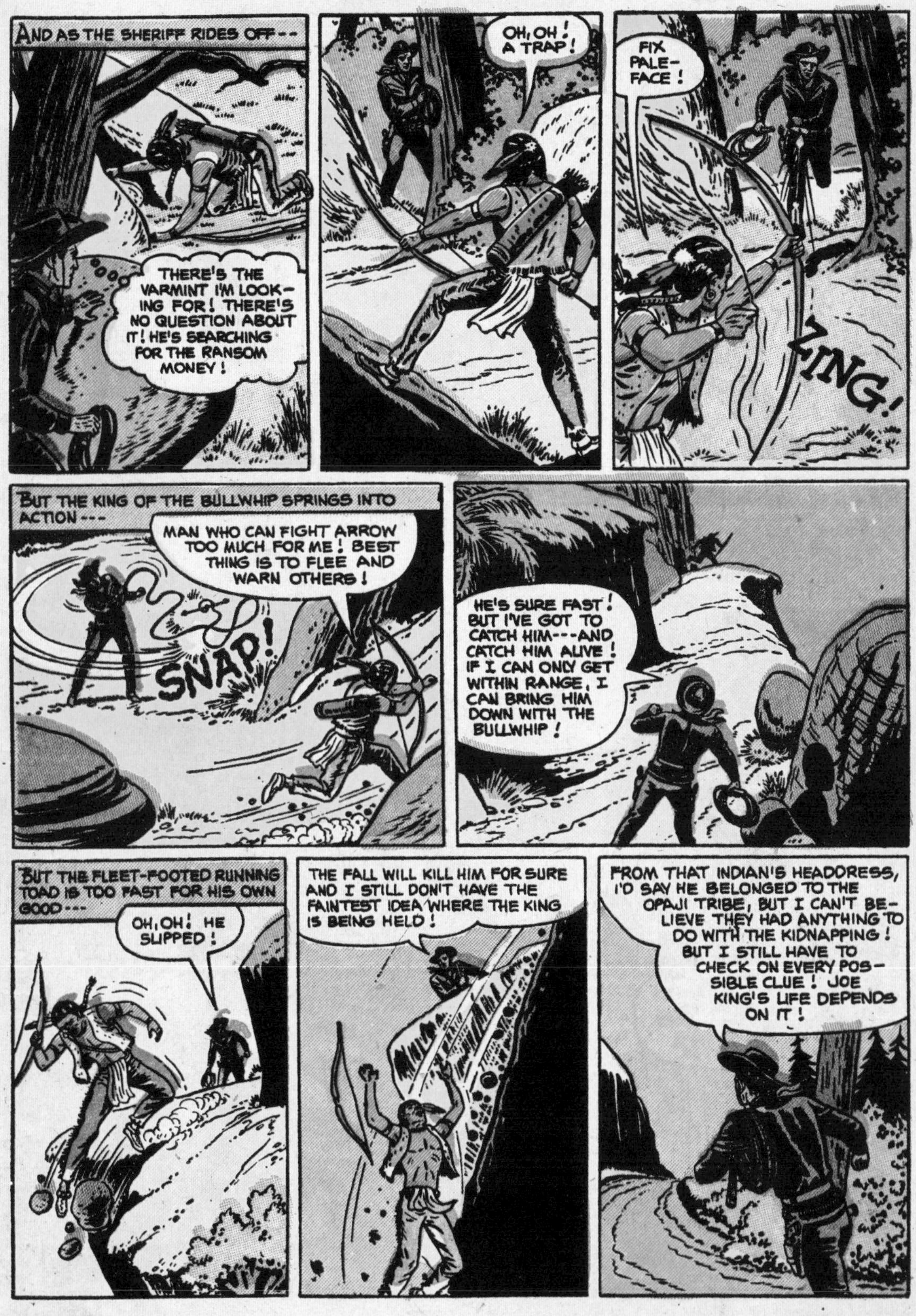

AND AS THE SHERIFF RIDES OFF --
THERE'S THE VARMINT I'M LOOKING FOR! THERE'S NO QUESTION ABOUT IT! HE'S SEARCHING FOR THE RANSOM MONEY!
OH, OH! A TRAP!
FIX PALE-FACE!
ZING!
BUT THE KING OF THE BULLWHIP SPRINGS INTO ACTION ---
MAN WHO CAN FIGHT ARROW TOO MUCH FOR ME! BEST THING IS TO FLEE AND WARN OTHERS!
SNAP!
HE'S SURE FAST! BUT I'VE GOT TO CATCH HIM---AND CATCH HIM ALIVE! IF I CAN ONLY GET WITHIN RANGE, I CAN BRING HIM DOWN WITH THE BULLWHIP!
BUT THE FLEET-FOOTED RUNNING TOAD IS TOO FAST FOR HIS OWN GOOD ---
OH, OH! HE SLIPPED!
THE FALL WILL KILL HIM FOR SURE AND I STILL DON'T HAVE THE FAINTEST IDEA WHERE THE KING IS BEING HELD!
FROM THAT INDIAN'S HEADDRESS, I'D SAY HE BELONGED TO THE OPAJI TRIBE, BUT I CAN'T BELIEVE THEY HAD ANYTHING TO DO WITH THE KIDNAPPING! BUT I STILL HAVE TO CHECK ON EVERY POSSIBLE CLUE! JOE KING'S LIFE DEPENDS ON IT!

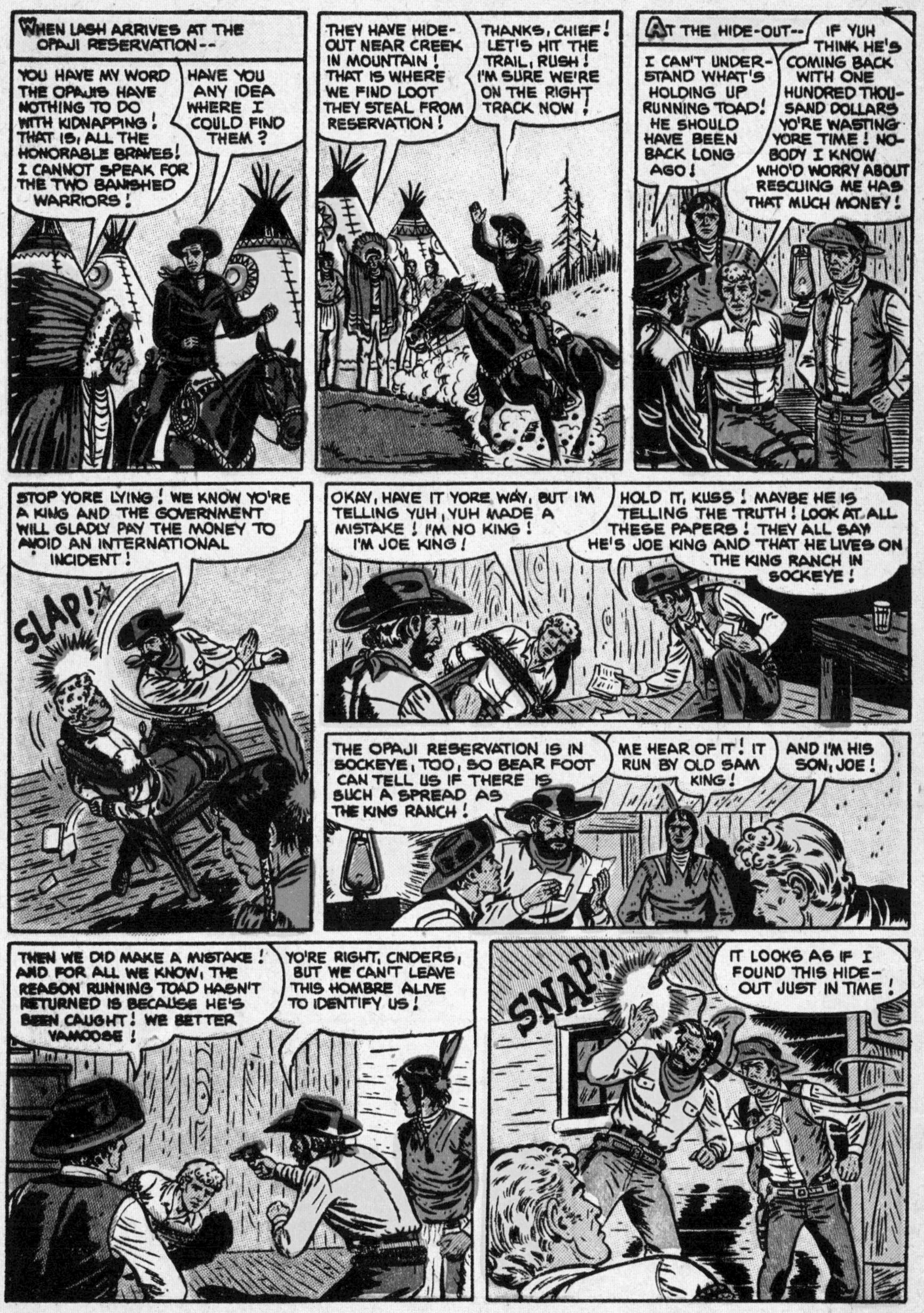
WHEN LASH ARRIVES AT THE OPAJI RESERVATION--
YOU HAVE MY WORD THE OPAJIS HAVE NOTHING TO DO WITH KIDNAPPING! THAT IS, ALL THE HONORABLE BRAVES! I CANNOT SPEAK FOR THE TWO BANISHED WARRIORS!
HAVE YOU ANY IDEA WHERE I COULD FIND THEM?
THEY HAVE HIDE-OUT NEAR CREEK IN MOUNTAIN! THAT IS WHERE WE FIND LOOT THEY STEAL FROM RESERVATION!
THANKS, CHIEF! LET'S HIT THE TRAIL, RUSH! I'M SURE WE'RE ON THE RIGHT TRACK NOW!
AT THE HIDE-OUT--
I CAN'T UNDERSTAND WHAT'S HOLDING UP RUNNING TOAD! HE SHOULD HAVE BEEN BACK LONG AGO!
IF YUH THINK HE'S COMING BACK WITH ONE HUNDRED THOUSAND DOLLARS YO'RE WASTING YORE TIME! NOBODY I KNOW WHO'D WORRY ABOUT RESCUING ME HAS THAT MUCH MONEY!
STOP YORE LYING! WE KNOW YO'RE A KING AND THE GOVERNMENT WILL GLADLY PAY THE MONEY TO AVOID AN INTERNATIONAL INCIDENT!
SLAP!
OKAY, HAVE IT YORE WAY. BUT I'M TELLING YUH, YUH MADE A MISTAKE! I'M NO KING! I'M JOE KING!
HOLD IT, KUSS! MAYBE HE IS TELLING THE TRUTH! LOOK AT ALL THESE PAPERS! THEY ALL SAY HE'S JOE KING AND THAT HE LIVES ON THE KING RANCH IN SOCKEYE!
THE OPAJI RESERVATION IS IN SOCKEYE, TOO, SO BEAR FOOT CAN TELL US IF THERE IS SUCH A SPREAD AS THE KING RANCH!
ME HEAR OF IT! IT RUN BY OLD SAM KING!
AND I'M HIS SON, JOE!
THEN WE DID MAKE A MISTAKE! AND FOR ALL WE KNOW, THE REASON RUNNING TOAD HASN'T RETURNED IS BECAUSE HE'S BEEN CAUGHT! WE BETTER VAMOOSE!
YO'RE RIGHT, CINDERS, BUT WE CAN'T LEAVE THIS HOMBRE ALIVE TO IDENTIFY US!
SNAP!
IT LOOKS AS IF I FOUND THIS HIDE-OUT JUST IN TIME!

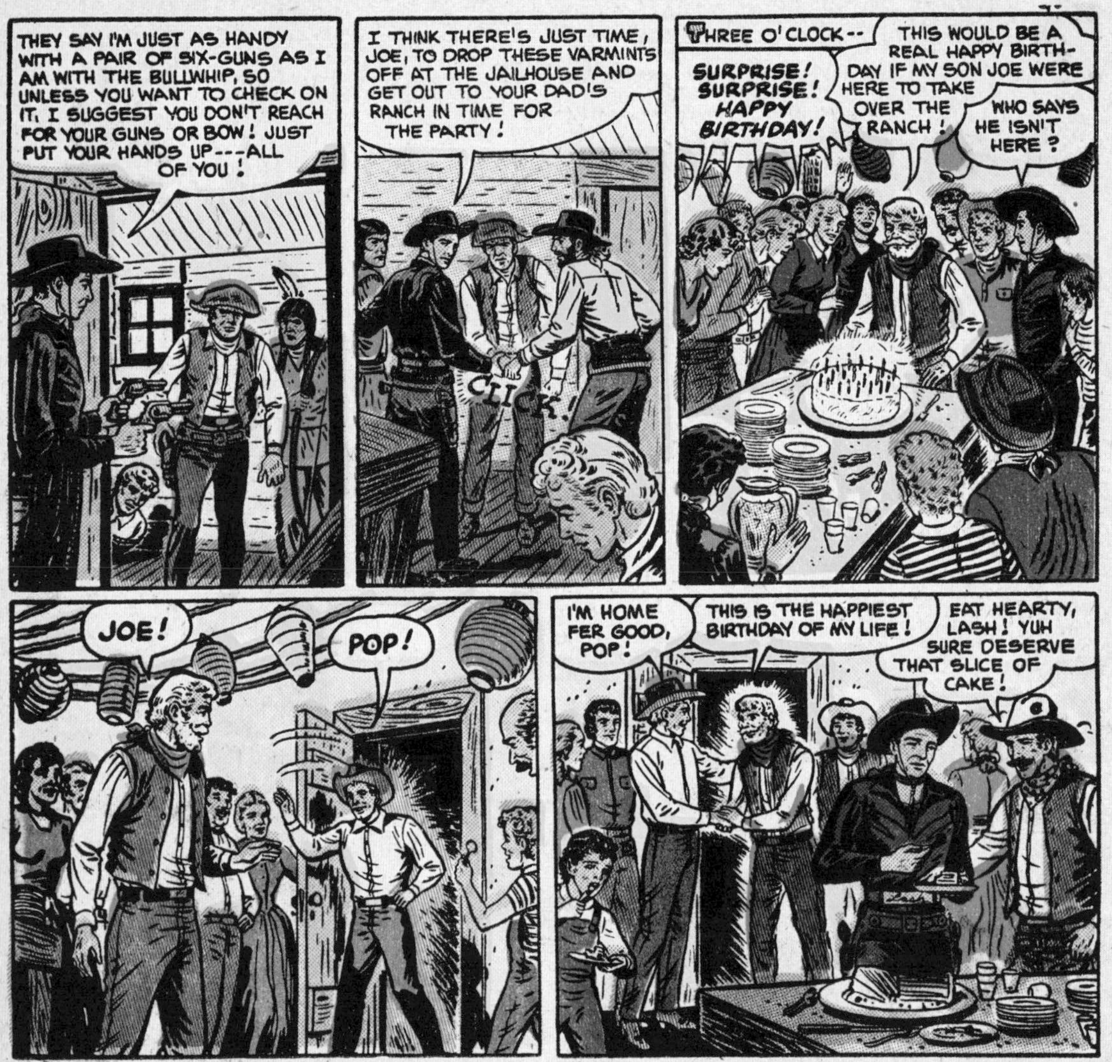
THEY SAY I'M JUST AS HANDY WITH A PAIR OF SIX-GUNS AS I AM WITH THE BULLWHIP, SO UNLESS YOU WANT TO CHECK ON IT, I SUGGEST YOU DON'T REACH FOR YOUR GUNS OR BOW! JUST PUT YOUR HANDS UP---ALL OF YOU!
I THINK THERE'S JUST TIME, JOE, TO DROP THESE VARMINTS OFF AT THE JAILHOUSE AND GET OUT TO YOUR DAD'S RANCH IN TIME FOR THE PARTY!
CLICK
THREE O' CLOCK--
SURPRISE! SURPRISE! HAPPY BIRTHDAY!
THIS WOULD BE A REAL HAPPY BIRTHDAY IF MY SON JOE WERE HERE TO TAKE OVER THE RANCH!
WHO SAYS HE ISN'T HERE?
JOE!
POP!
I'M HOME FER GOOD, POP!
THIS IS THE HAPPIEST BIRTHDAY OF MY LIFE!
EAT HEARTY, LASH! YUH SURE DESERVE THAT SLICE OF CAKE!

QUIZ

1. THERE WERE "15 MEN ON A DEAD MAN'S CHEST."

☐ True

☐ False

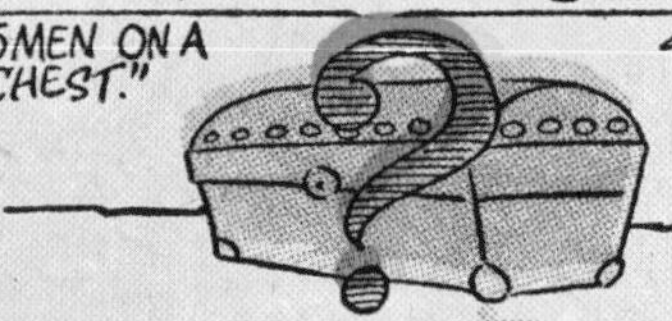

4. THE EVENING STAR IS A PLANET.

☐ True

☐ False

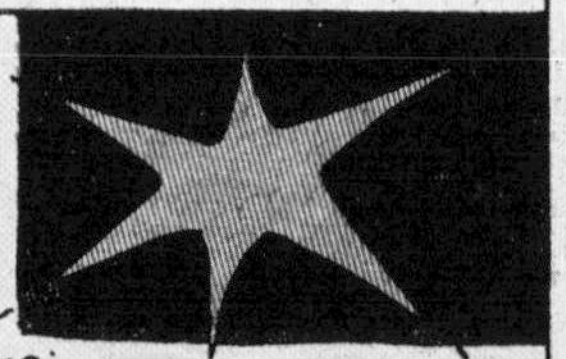

2. OF ALL THE PRESIDENTS OF THE UNITED STATES ONLY SEVEN WERE'NT LAWYERS.

☐ True ☐ False

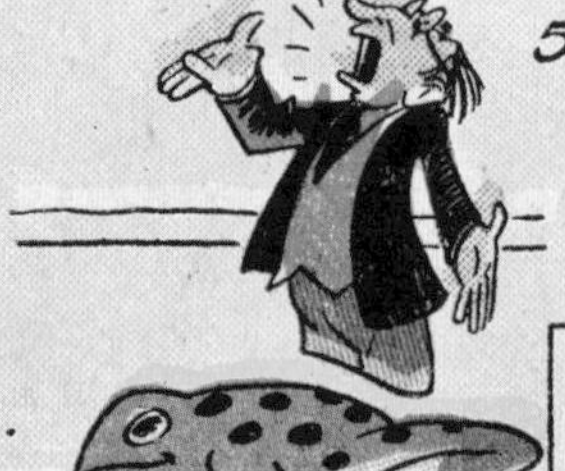

5. THE TROPIC OF CANCER IS SOUTH OF THE EQUATOR.

☐ True ☐ False

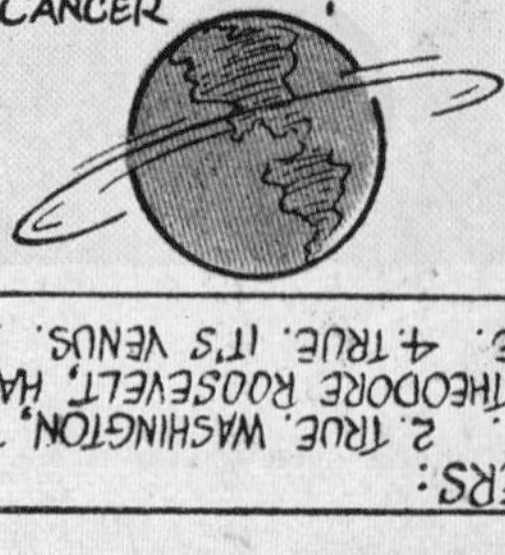

3. FROGS DRINK THROUGH THEIR SKINS.

☐ True ☐ False

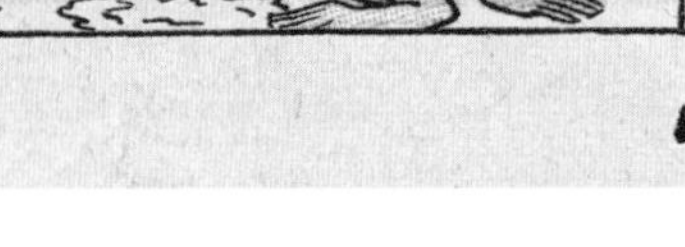

ANSWERS: 1. TRUE. 2. TRUE. WASHINGTON, TAYLOR, JOHNSON, GRANT, THEODORE ROOSEVELT, HARDING & HOOVER. 3. TRUE. 4. TRUE. IT'S VENUS. 5. FALSE. IT'S NORTH.

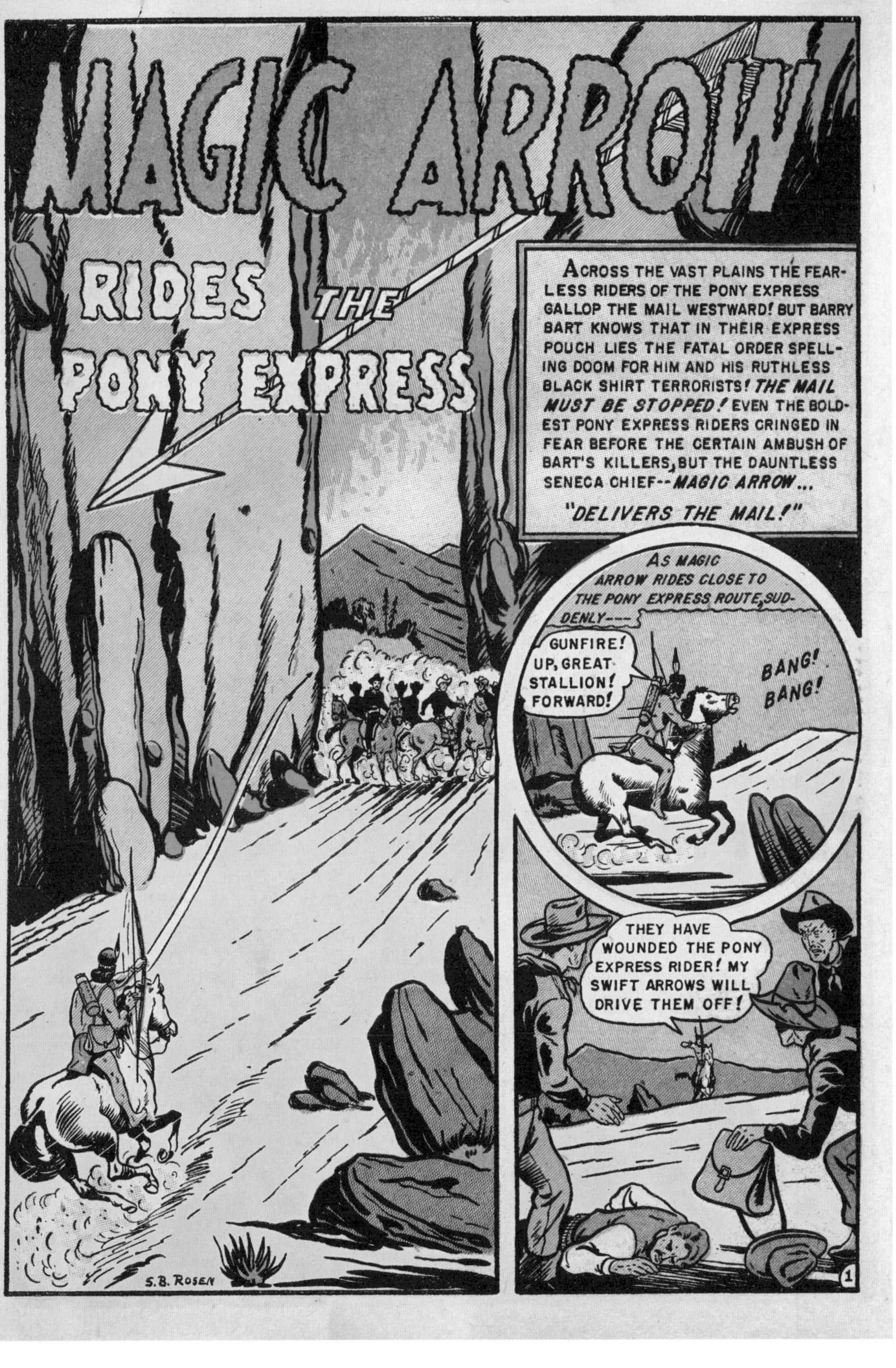

MAGIC ARROW
RIDES THE PONY EXPRESS
ACROSS THE VAST PLAINS THE FEARLESS RIDERS OF THE PONY EXPRESS GALLOP THE MAIL WESTWARD! BUT BARRY BART KNOWS THAT IN THEIR EXPRESS POUCH LIES THE FATAL ORDER SPELLING DOOM FOR HIM AND HIS RUTHLESS BLACK SHIRT TERRORISTS! THE MAIL MUST BE STOPPED! EVEN THE BOLDEST PONY EXPRESS RIDERS CRINGED IN FEAR BEFORE THE CERTAIN AMBUSH OF BART'S KILLERS, BUT THE DAUNTLESS SENECA CHIEF--MAGIC ARROW...
"DELIVERS THE MAIL!"
S.B. ROSEN
AS MAGIC ARROW RIDES CLOSE TO THE PONY EXPRESS ROUTE, SUDDENLY---
GUNFIRE! UP, GREAT STALLION! FORWARD!
BANG! BANG!
THEY HAVE WOUNDED THE PONY EXPRESS RIDER! MY SWIFT ARROWS WILL DRIVE THEM OFF!
1

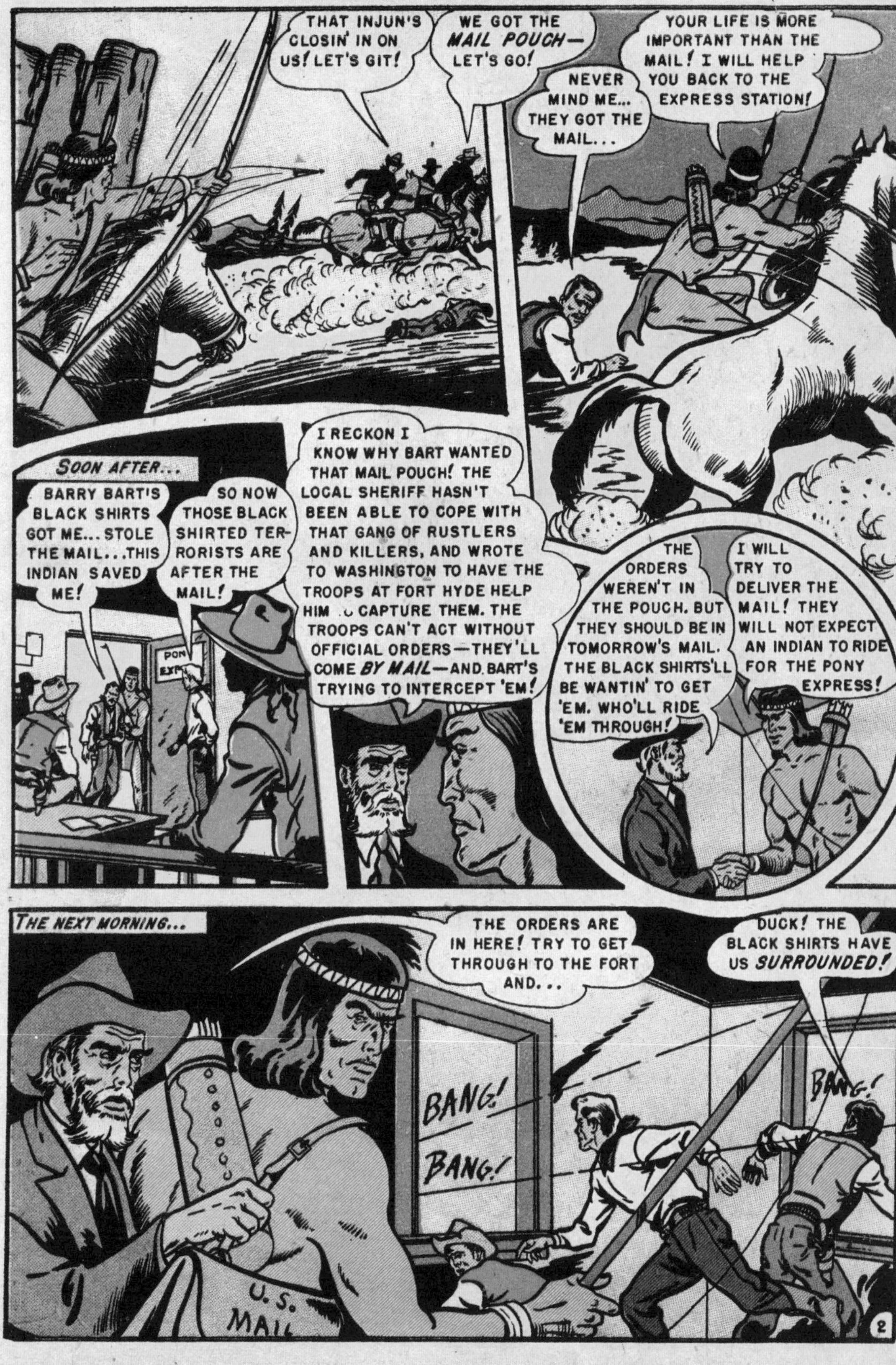

THAT INJUN'S CLOSIN' IN ON US! LET'S GIT!
WE GOT THE *MAIL POUCH*— LET'S GO!
NEVER MIND ME... THEY GOT THE MAIL...
YOUR LIFE IS MORE IMPORTANT THAN THE MAIL! I WILL HELP YOU BACK TO THE EXPRESS STATION!
SOON AFTER...
BARRY BART'S BLACK SHIRTS GOT ME... STOLE THE MAIL... THIS INDIAN SAVED ME!
SO NOW THOSE BLACK SHIRTED TERRORISTS ARE AFTER THE MAIL!
I RECKON I KNOW WHY BART WANTED THAT MAIL POUCH! THE LOCAL SHERIFF HASN'T BEEN ABLE TO COPE WITH THAT GANG OF RUSTLERS AND KILLERS, AND WROTE TO WASHINGTON TO HAVE THE TROOPS AT FORT HYDE HELP HIM TO CAPTURE THEM. THE TROOPS CAN'T ACT WITHOUT OFFICIAL ORDERS—THEY'LL COME *BY MAIL*—AND BART'S TRYING TO INTERCEPT 'EM!
THE ORDERS WEREN'T IN THE POUCH. BUT THEY SHOULD BE IN TOMORROW'S MAIL. THE BLACK SHIRTS'LL BE WANTIN' TO GET 'EM. WHO'LL RIDE 'EM THROUGH!
I WILL TRY TO DELIVER THE MAIL! THEY WILL NOT EXPECT AN INDIAN TO RIDE FOR THE PONY EXPRESS!
THE NEXT MORNING...
THE ORDERS ARE IN HERE! TRY TO GET THROUGH TO THE FORT AND...
DUCK! THE BLACK SHIRTS HAVE US *SURROUNDED*!
BANG!
BANG!
BANG!
U.S. MAIL
2

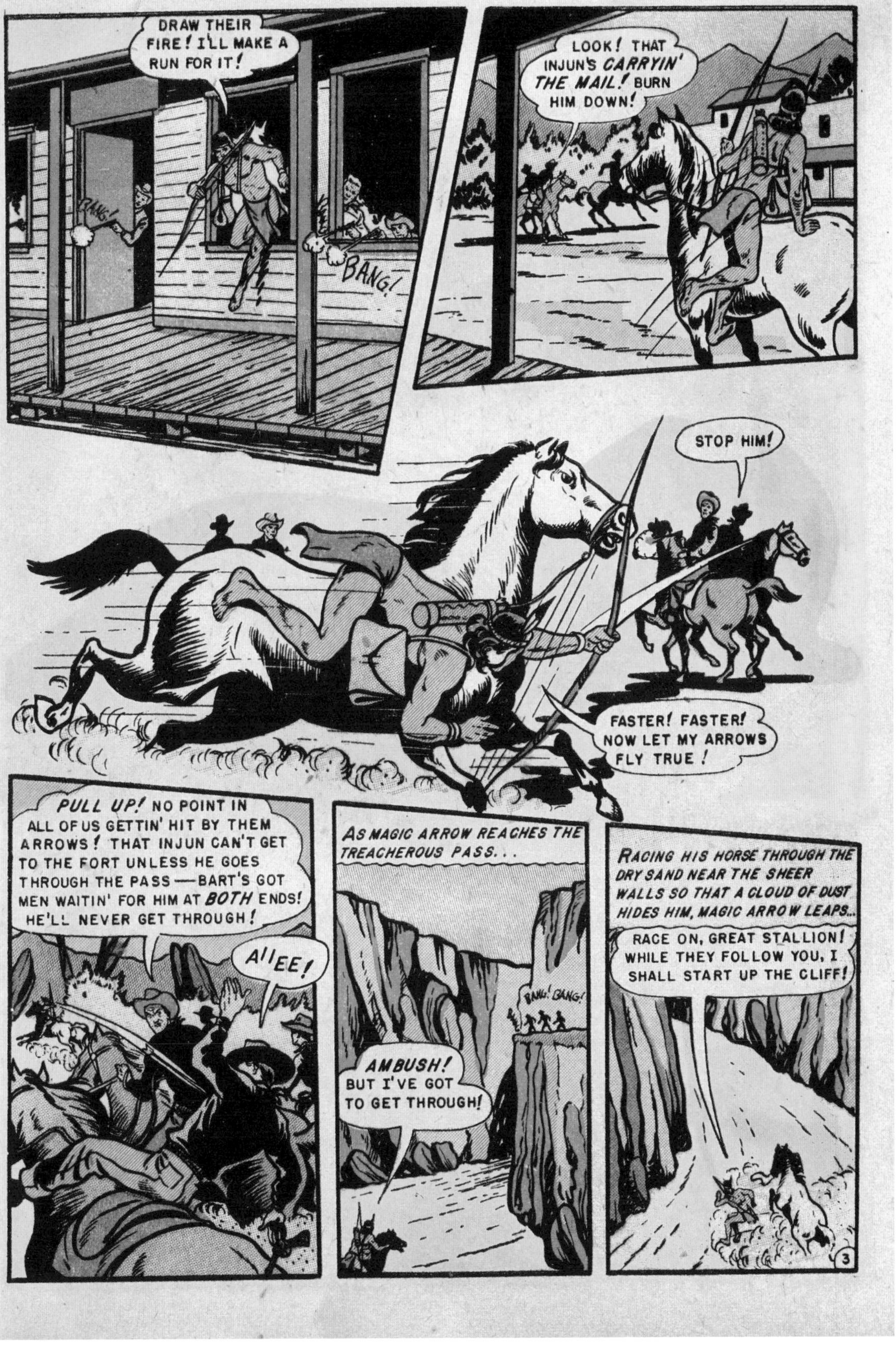
DRAW THEIR FIRE! I'LL MAKE A RUN FOR IT!
BANG!
BANG!
LOOK! THAT INJUN'S CARRYIN' THE MAIL! BURN HIM DOWN!
STOP HIM!
FASTER! FASTER! NOW LET MY ARROWS FLY TRUE!
PULL UP! NO POINT IN ALL OF US GETTIN' HIT BY THEM ARROWS! THAT INJUN CAN'T GET TO THE FORT UNLESS HE GOES THROUGH THE PASS — BART'S GOT MEN WAITIN' FOR HIM AT BOTH ENDS! HE'LL NEVER GET THROUGH!
AIIEE!
AS MAGIC ARROW REACHES THE TREACHEROUS PASS...
BANG! BANG!
AMBUSH! BUT I'VE GOT TO GET THROUGH!
RACING HIS HORSE THROUGH THE DRY SAND NEAR THE SHEER WALLS SO THAT A CLOUD OF DUST HIDES HIM, MAGIC ARROW LEAPS...
RACE ON, GREAT STALLION! WHILE THEY FOLLOW YOU, I SHALL START UP THE CLIFF!
3

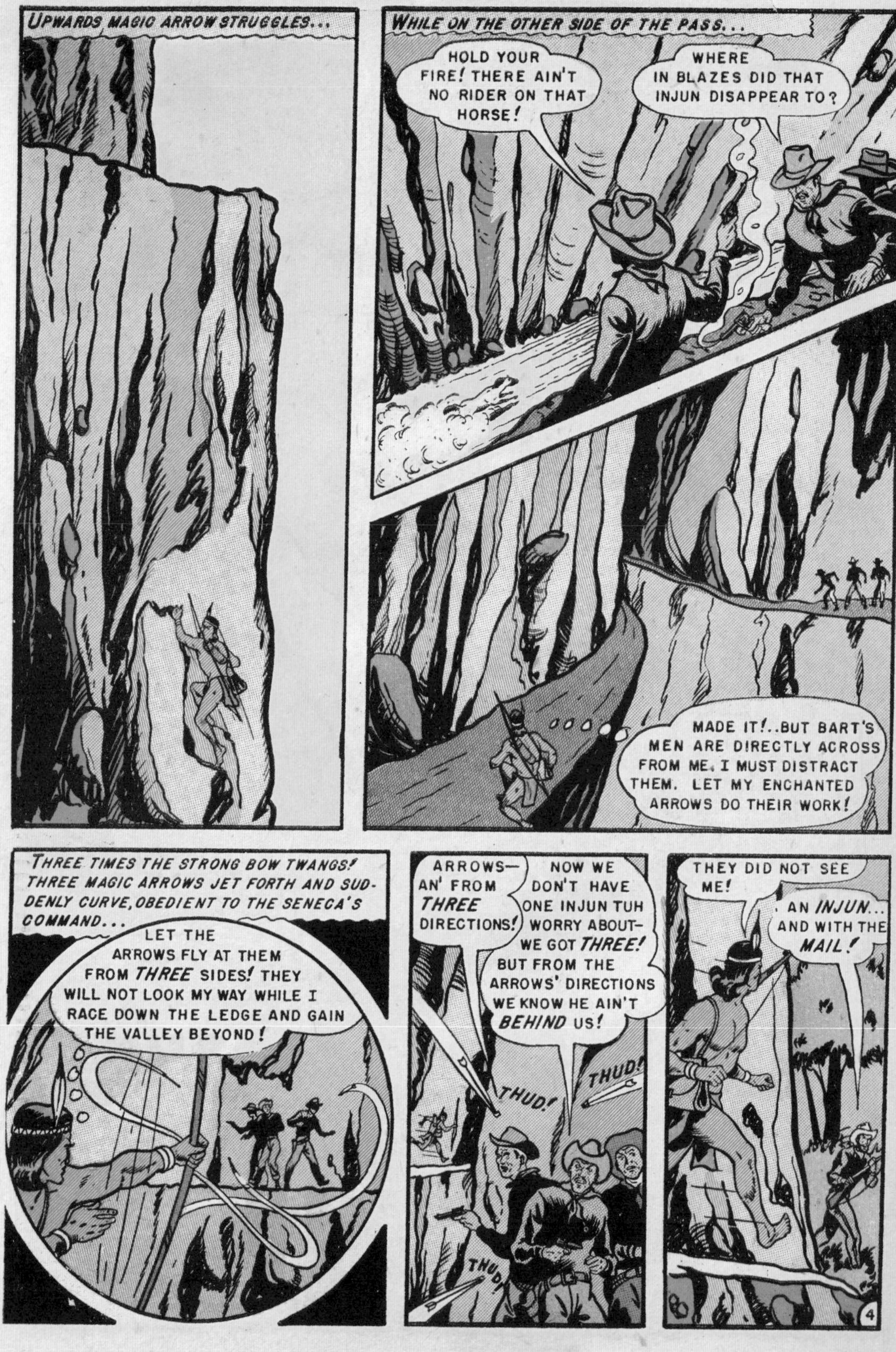

UPWARDS MAGIC ARROW STRUGGLES...
WHILE ON THE OTHER SIDE OF THE PASS...
HOLD YOUR FIRE! THERE AIN'T NO RIDER ON THAT HORSE!
WHERE IN BLAZES DID THAT INJUN DISAPPEAR TO?
MADE IT!..BUT BART'S MEN ARE DIRECTLY ACROSS FROM ME. I MUST DISTRACT THEM. LET MY ENCHANTED ARROWS DO THEIR WORK!
THREE TIMES THE STRONG BOW TWANGS! THREE MAGIC ARROWS JET FORTH AND SUDDENLY CURVE, OBEDIENT TO THE SENECA'S COMMAND...
LET THE ARROWS FLY AT THEM FROM THREE SIDES! THEY WILL NOT LOOK MY WAY WHILE I RACE DOWN THE LEDGE AND GAIN THE VALLEY BEYOND!
ARROWS— AN' FROM THREE DIRECTIONS!
NOW WE DON'T HAVE ONE INJUN TUH WORRY ABOUT— WE GOT THREE! BUT FROM THE ARROWS' DIRECTIONS WE KNOW HE AIN'T BEHIND US!
THUD!
THUD!
THUD!
THEY DID NOT SEE ME!
AN INJUN... AND WITH THE MAIL!
4

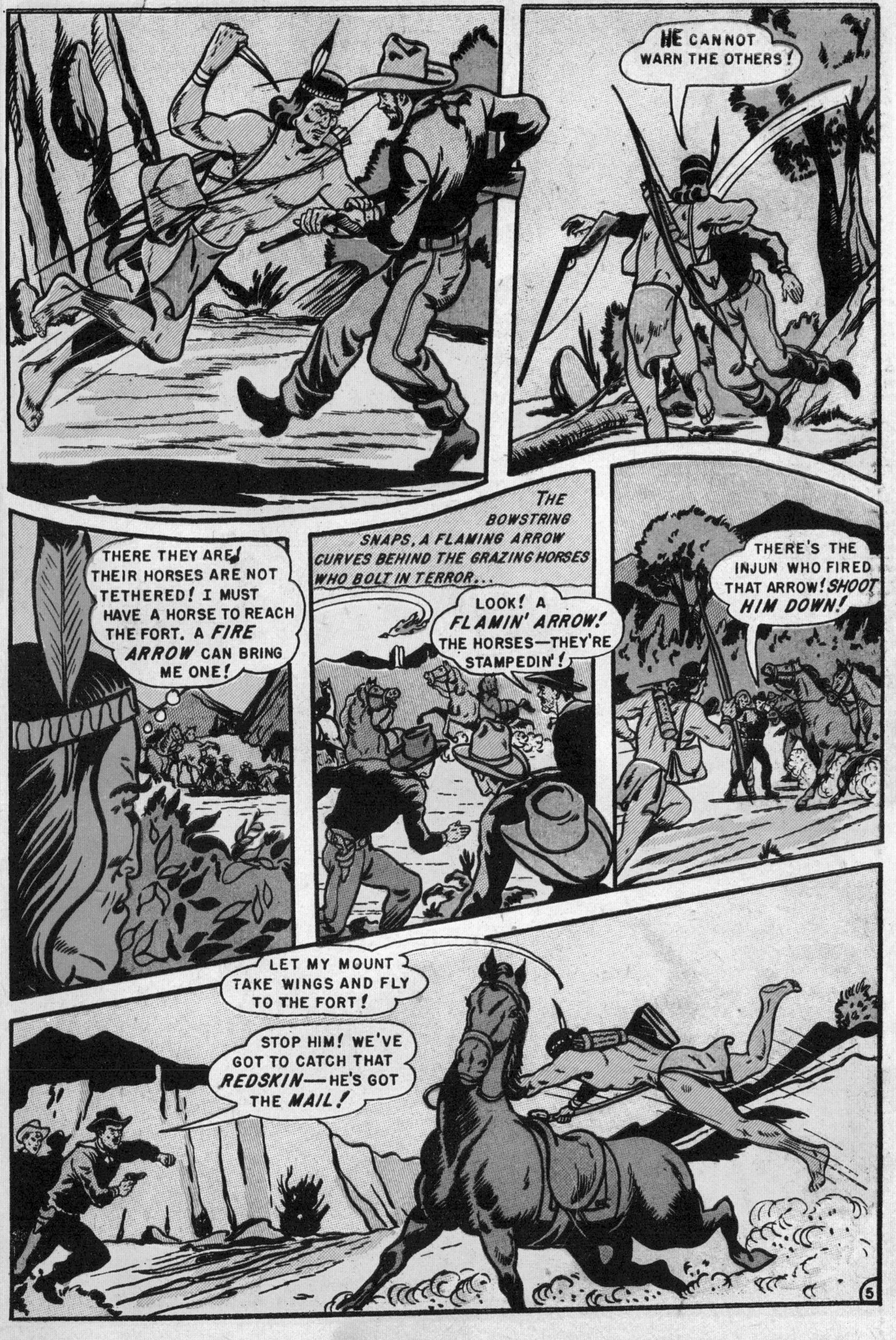

HE CANNOT WARN THE OTHERS!
THERE THEY ARE! THEIR HORSES ARE NOT TETHERED! I MUST HAVE A HORSE TO REACH THE FORT. A FIRE ARROW CAN BRING ME ONE!
THE BOWSTRING SNAPS, A FLAMING ARROW CURVES BEHIND THE GRAZING HORSES WHO BOLT IN TERROR...
LOOK! A FLAMIN' ARROW! THE HORSES—THEY'RE STAMPEDIN'!
THERE'S THE INJUN WHO FIRED THAT ARROW! SHOOT HIM DOWN!
LET MY MOUNT TAKE WINGS AND FLY TO THE FORT!
STOP HIM! WE'VE GOT TO CATCH THAT REDSKIN—HE'S GOT THE MAIL!
5

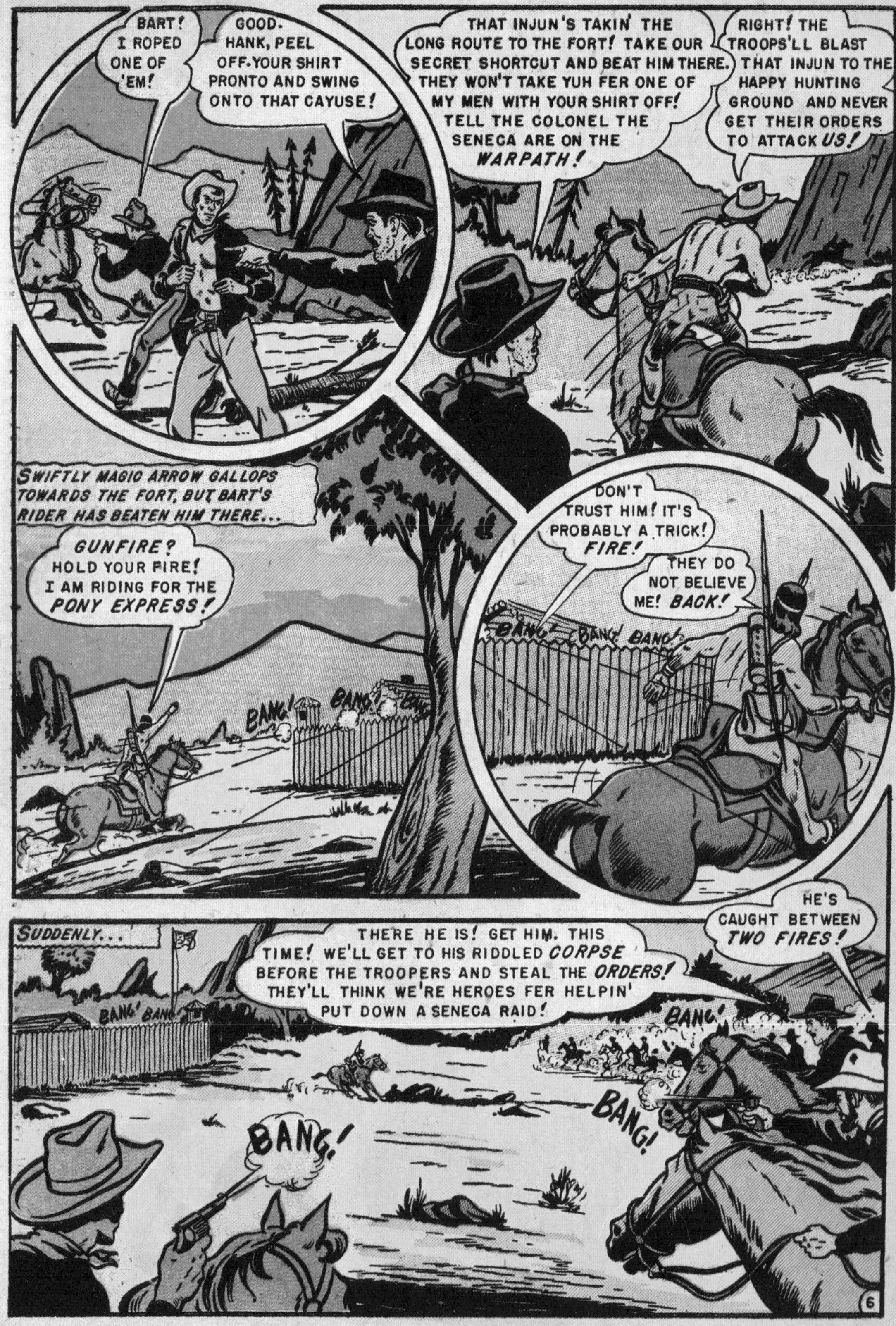
BART! I ROPED ONE OF 'EM!
GOOD. HANK, PEEL OFF YOUR SHIRT PRONTO AND SWING ONTO THAT CAYUSE!
THAT INJUN'S TAKIN' THE LONG ROUTE TO THE FORT! TAKE OUR SECRET SHORTCUT AND BEAT HIM THERE. THEY WON'T TAKE YUH FER ONE OF MY MEN WITH YOUR SHIRT OFF! TELL THE COLONEL THE SENECA ARE ON THE WARPATH!
RIGHT! THE TROOPS'LL BLAST THAT INJUN TO THE HAPPY HUNTING GROUND AND NEVER GET THEIR ORDERS TO ATTACK US!
SWIFTLY MAGIC ARROW GALLOPS TOWARDS THE FORT, BUT BART'S RIDER HAS BEATEN HIM THERE...
GUNFIRE? HOLD YOUR FIRE! I AM RIDING FOR THE PONY EXPRESS!
BANG! BANG! BANG!
DON'T TRUST HIM! IT'S PROBABLY A TRICK! FIRE!
THEY DO NOT BELIEVE ME! BACK!
BANG! BANG! BANG!
SUDDENLY...
THERE HE IS! GET HIM. THIS TIME! WE'LL GET TO HIS RIDDLED CORPSE BEFORE THE TROOPERS AND STEAL THE ORDERS! THEY'LL THINK WE'RE HEROES FER HELPIN' PUT DOWN A SENECA RAID!
HE'S CAUGHT BETWEEN TWO FIRES!
BANG! BANG!
BANG!
BANG!
BANG!
6

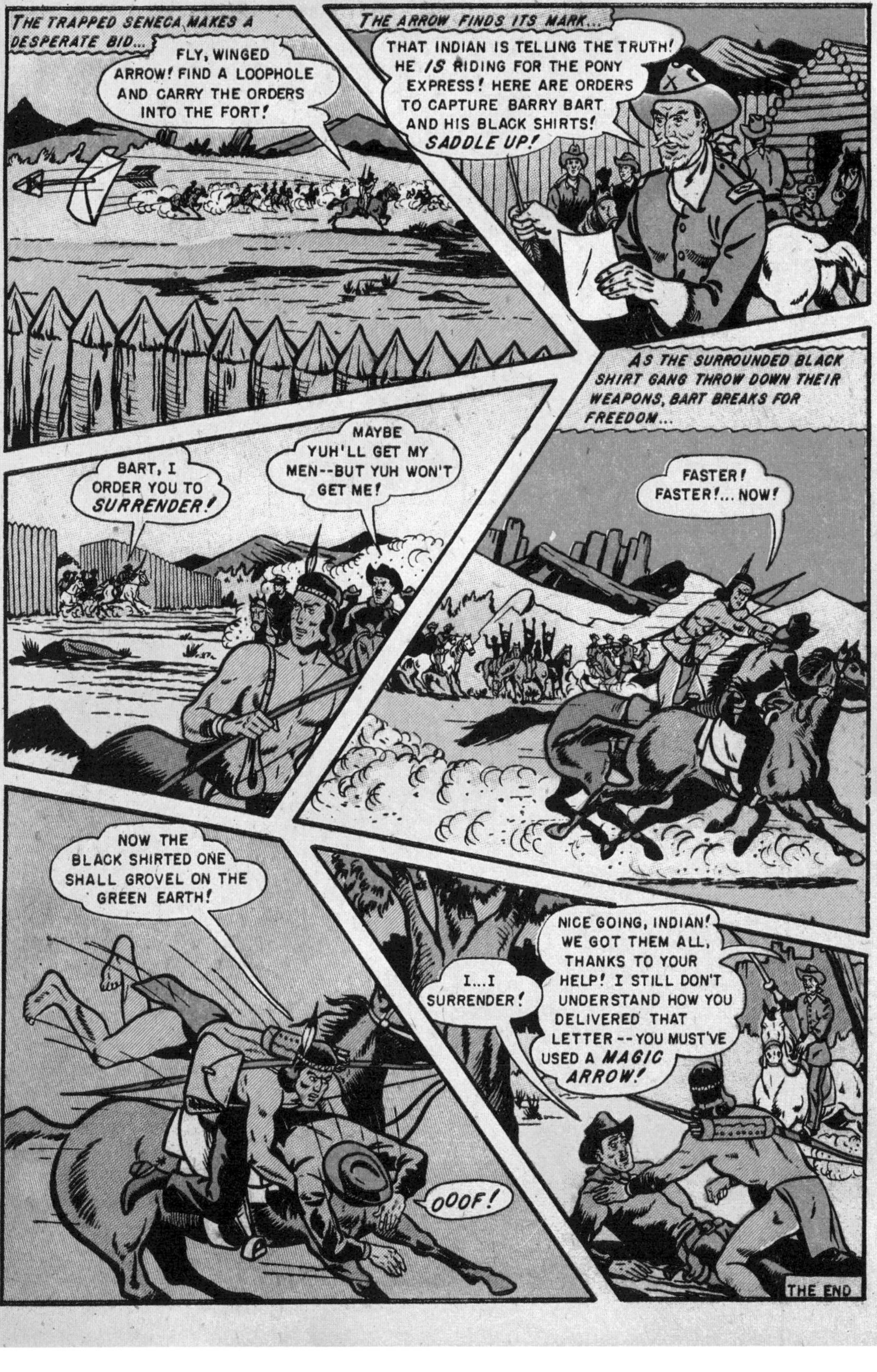
THE TRAPPED SENECA MAKES A DESPERATE BID...
FLY, WINGED ARROW! FIND A LOOPHOLE AND CARRY THE ORDERS INTO THE FORT!
THE ARROW FINDS ITS MARK...
THAT INDIAN IS TELLING THE TRUTH! HE IS RIDING FOR THE PONY EXPRESS! HERE ARE ORDERS TO CAPTURE BARRY BART AND HIS BLACK SHIRTS! SADDLE UP!
BART, I ORDER YOU TO SURRENDER!
MAYBE YUH'LL GET MY MEN--BUT YUH WON'T GET ME!
AS THE SURROUNDED BLACK SHIRT GANG THROW DOWN THEIR WEAPONS, BART BREAKS FOR FREEDOM...
FASTER! FASTER!... NOW!
NOW THE BLACK SHIRTED ONE SHALL GROVEL ON THE GREEN EARTH!
OOOF!
I...I SURRENDER!
NICE GOING, INDIAN! WE GOT THEM ALL, THANKS TO YOUR HELP! I STILL DON'T UNDERSTAND HOW YOU DELIVERED THAT LETTER--YOU MUST'VE USED A MAGIC ARROW!
THE END

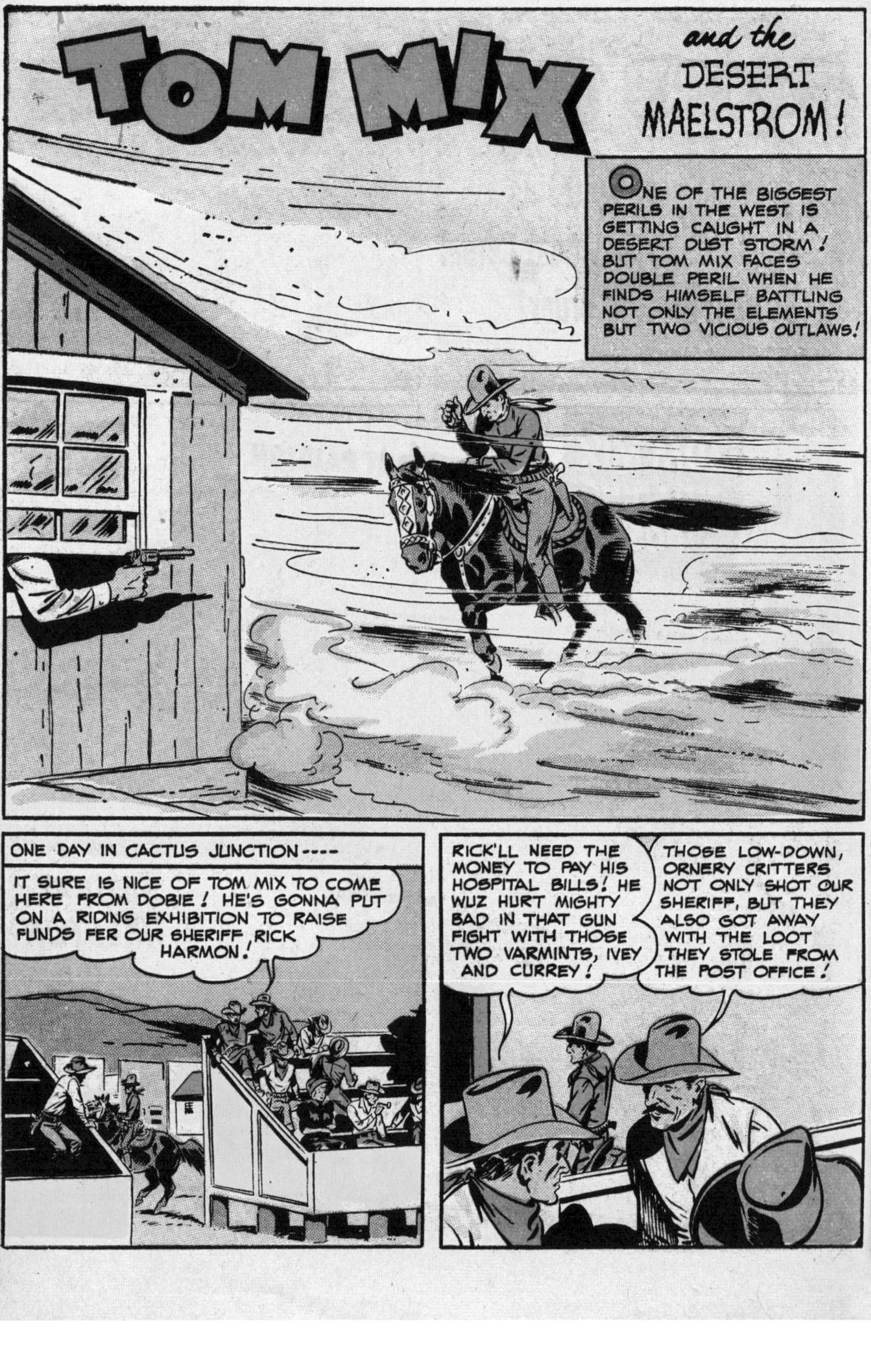
TOM MIX
and the DESERT MAELSTROM!
ONE OF THE BIGGEST PERILS IN THE WEST IS GETTING CAUGHT IN A DESERT DUST STORM! BUT TOM MIX FACES DOUBLE PERIL WHEN HE FINDS HIMSELF BATTLING NOT ONLY THE ELEMENTS BUT TWO VICIOUS OUTLAWS!
ONE DAY IN CACTUS JUNCTION----
IT SURE IS NICE OF TOM MIX TO COME HERE FROM DOBIE! HE'S GONNA PUT ON A RIDING EXHIBITION TO RAISE FUNDS FER OUR SHERIFF, RICK HARMON!
RICK'LL NEED THE MONEY TO PAY HIS HOSPITAL BILLS! HE WUZ HURT MIGHTY BAD IN THAT GUN FIGHT WITH THOSE TWO VARMINTS, IVEY AND CURREY!
THOSE LOW-DOWN, ORNERY CRITTERS NOT ONLY SHOT OUR SHERIFF, BUT THEY ALSO GOT AWAY WITH THE LOOT THEY STOLE FROM THE POST OFFICE!

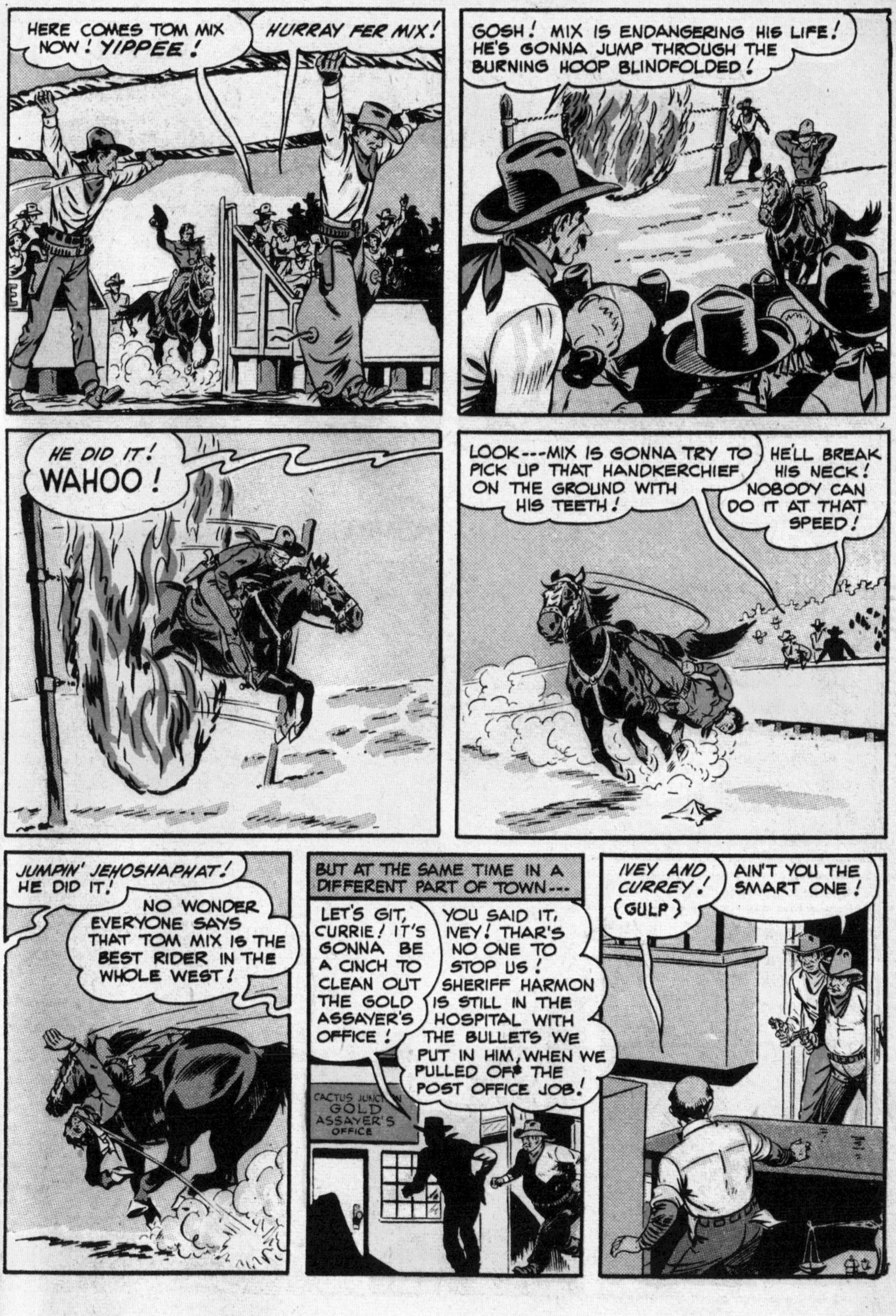
HERE COMES TOM MIX NOW! YIPPEE!
HURRAY FER MIX!
GOSH! MIX IS ENDANGERING HIS LIFE! HE'S GONNA JUMP THROUGH THE BURNING HOOP BLINDFOLDED!
HE DID IT! WAHOO!
LOOK---MIX IS GONNA TRY TO PICK UP THAT HANDKERCHIEF ON THE GROUND WITH HIS TEETH!
HE'LL BREAK HIS NECK! NOBODY CAN DO IT AT THAT SPEED!
JUMPIN' JEHOSHAPHAT! HE DID IT!
NO WONDER EVERYONE SAYS THAT TOM MIX IS THE BEST RIDER IN THE WHOLE WEST!
BUT AT THE SAME TIME IN A DIFFERENT PART OF TOWN---
LET'S GIT, CURRIE! IT'S GONNA BE A CINCH TO CLEAN OUT THE GOLD ASSAYER'S OFFICE!
YOU SAID IT, IVEY! THAR'S NO ONE TO STOP US! SHERIFF HARMON IS STILL IN THE HOSPITAL WITH THE BULLETS WE PUT IN HIM, WHEN WE PULLED OFF THE POST OFFICE JOB!
GOLD ASSAYER'S OFFICE
IVEY AND CURREY! (GULP)
AIN'T YOU THE SMART ONE!

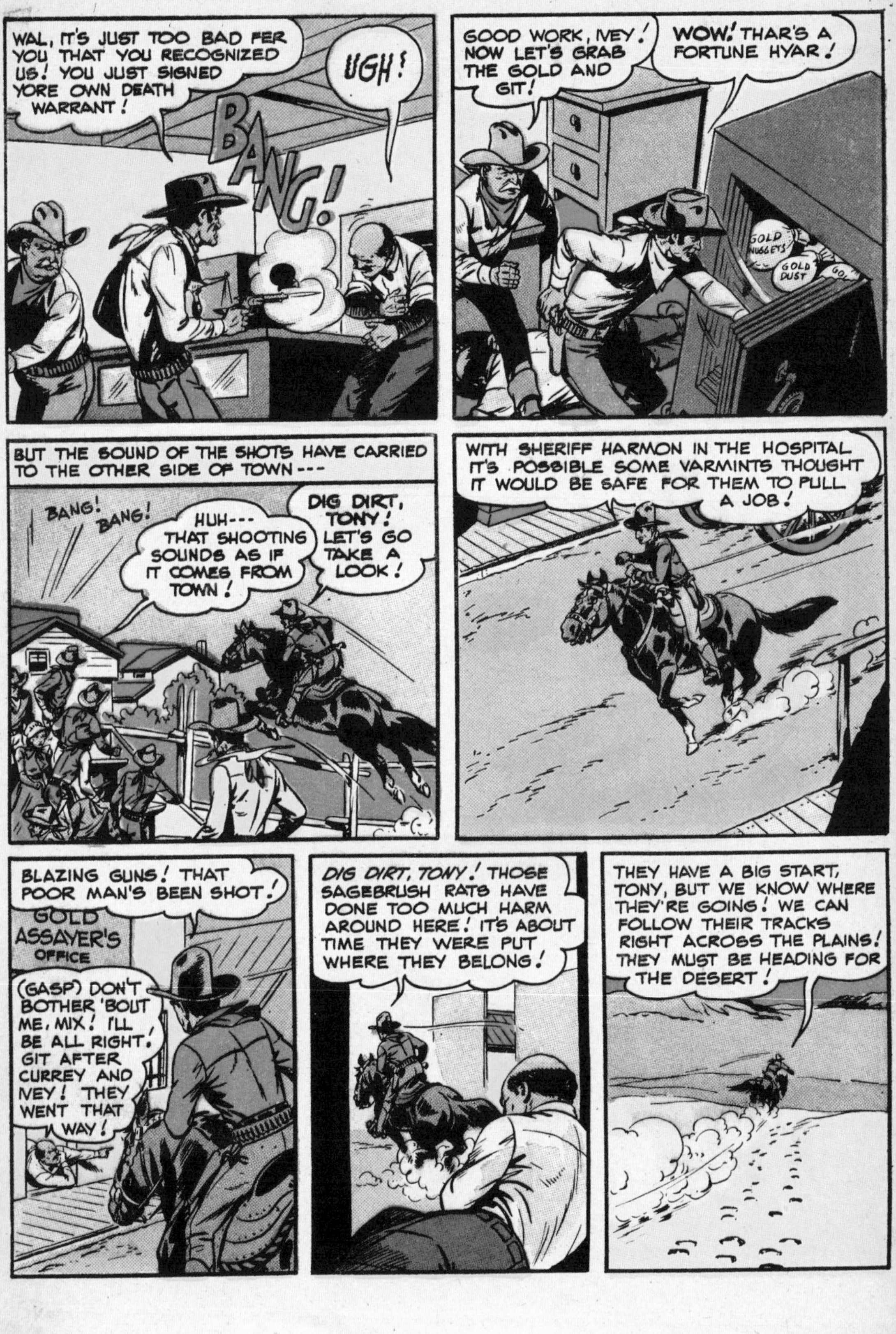
WAL, IT'S JUST TOO BAD FER YOU THAT YOU RECOGNIZED US! YOU JUST SIGNED YORE OWN DEATH WARRANT!
UGH!
BANG!
GOOD WORK, IVEY! NOW LET'S GRAB THE GOLD AND GIT!
WOW! THAR'S A FORTUNE HYAR!
GOLD NUGGETS
GOLD DUST
BUT THE SOUND OF THE SHOTS HAVE CARRIED TO THE OTHER SIDE OF TOWN---
BANG! BANG!
HUH--- THAT SHOOTING SOUNDS AS IF IT COMES FROM TOWN!
DIG DIRT, TONY! LET'S GO TAKE A LOOK!
WITH SHERIFF HARMON IN THE HOSPITAL IT'S POSSIBLE SOME VARMINTS THOUGHT IT WOULD BE SAFE FOR THEM TO PULL A JOB!
BLAZING GUNS! THAT POOR MAN'S BEEN SHOT!
GOLD ASSAYER'S OFFICE
(GASP) DON'T BOTHER 'BOUT ME, MIX! I'LL BE ALL RIGHT! GIT AFTER CURREY AND IVEY! THEY WENT THAT WAY!
DIG DIRT, TONY! THOSE SAGEBRUSH RATS HAVE DONE TOO MUCH HARM AROUND HERE! IT'S ABOUT TIME THEY WERE PUT WHERE THEY BELONG!
THEY HAVE A BIG START, TONY, BUT WE KNOW WHERE THEY'RE GOING! WE CAN FOLLOW THEIR TRACKS RIGHT ACROSS THE PLAINS! THEY MUST BE HEADING FOR THE DESERT!

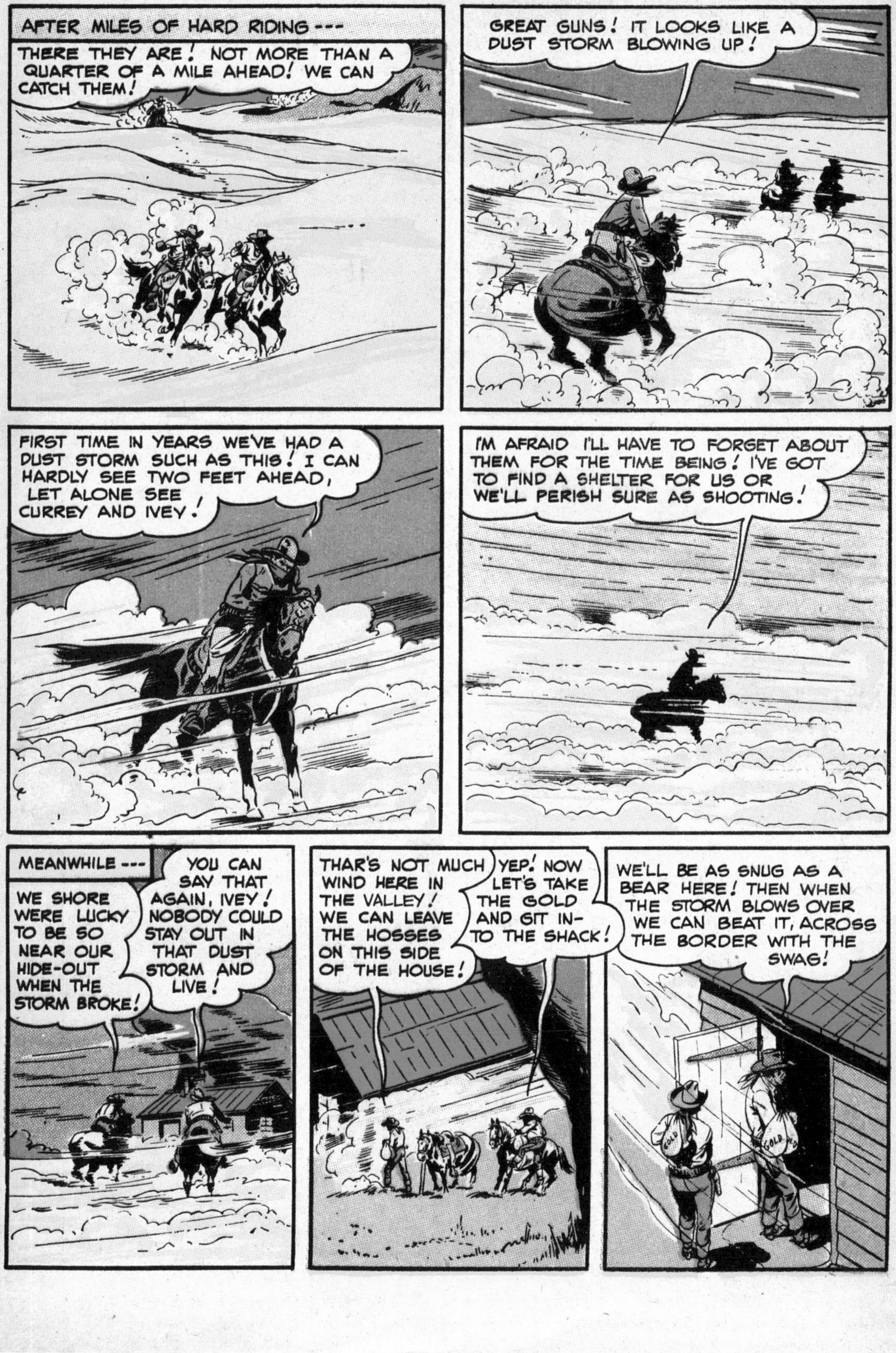
AFTER MILES OF HARD RIDING---
THERE THEY ARE! NOT MORE THAN A QUARTER OF A MILE AHEAD! WE CAN CATCH THEM!
GREAT GUNS! IT LOOKS LIKE A DUST STORM BLOWING UP!
FIRST TIME IN YEARS WE'VE HAD A DUST STORM SUCH AS THIS! I CAN HARDLY SEE TWO FEET AHEAD, LET ALONE SEE CURREY AND IVEY!
I'M AFRAID I'LL HAVE TO FORGET ABOUT THEM FOR THE TIME BEING! I'VE GOT TO FIND A SHELTER FOR US OR WE'LL PERISH SURE AS SHOOTING!
MEANWHILE---
WE SHORE WERE LUCKY TO BE SO NEAR OUR HIDE-OUT WHEN THE STORM BROKE!
YOU CAN SAY THAT AGAIN, IVEY! NOBODY COULD STAY OUT IN THAT DUST STORM AND LIVE!
THAR'S NOT MUCH WIND HERE IN THE VALLEY! WE CAN LEAVE THE HOSSES ON THIS SIDE OF THE HOUSE!
YEP! NOW LET'S TAKE THE GOLD AND GIT IN-TO THE SHACK!
WE'LL BE AS SNUG AS A BEAR HERE! THEN WHEN THE STORM BLOWS OVER WE CAN BEAT IT, ACROSS THE BORDER WITH THE SWAG!
GOLD
GOLD

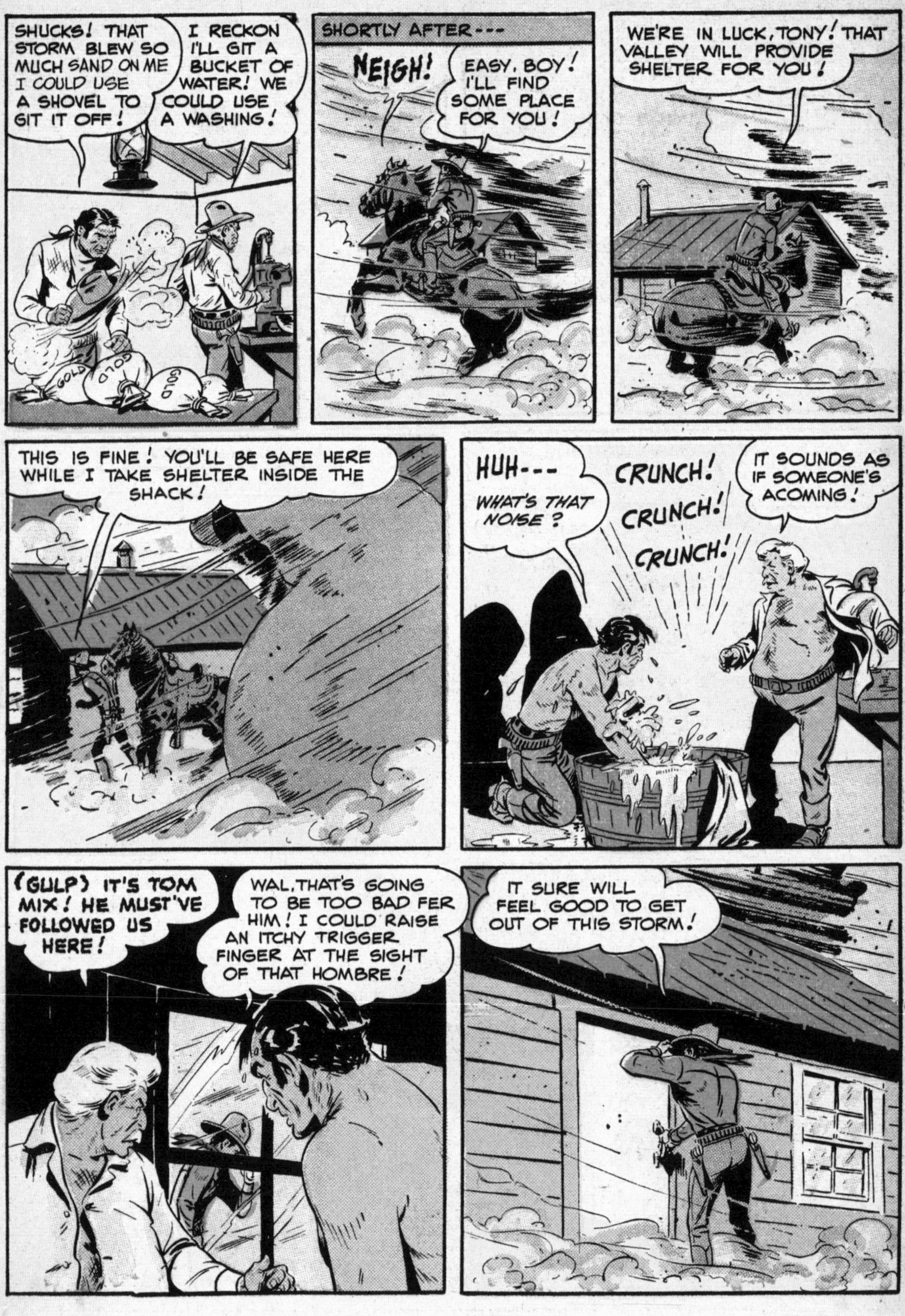
SHUCKS! THAT STORM BLEW SO MUCH SAND ON ME I COULD USE A SHOVEL TO GIT IT OFF!
I RECKON I'LL GIT A BUCKET OF WATER! WE COULD USE A WASHING!
GOLD
GOLD
GOLD
SHORTLY AFTER---
NEIGH!
EASY, BOY! I'LL FIND SOME PLACE FOR YOU!
WE'RE IN LUCK, TONY! THAT VALLEY WILL PROVIDE SHELTER FOR YOU!
THIS IS FINE! YOU'LL BE SAFE HERE WHILE I TAKE SHELTER INSIDE THE SHACK!
HUH--- WHAT'S THAT NOISE?
CRUNCH!
CRUNCH!
CRUNCH!
IT SOUNDS AS IF SOMEONE'S ACOMING!
(GULP) IT'S TOM MIX! HE MUST'VE FOLLOWED US HERE!
WAL, THAT'S GOING TO BE TOO BAD FER HIM! I COULD RAISE AN ITCHY TRIGGER FINGER AT THE SIGHT OF THAT HOMBRE!
IT SURE WILL FEEL GOOD TO GET OUT OF THIS STORM!

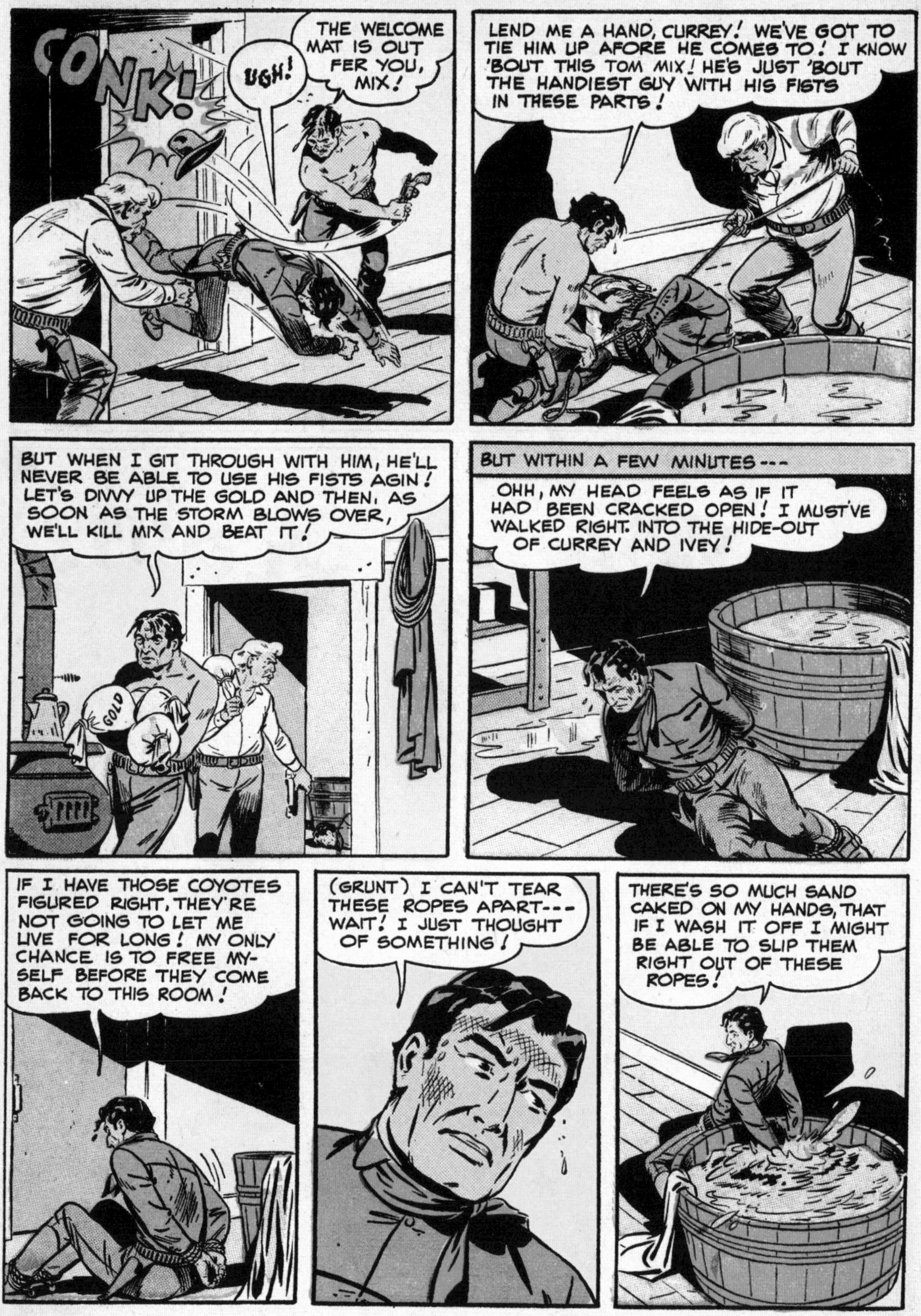
CONK!
THE WELCOME MAT IS OUT FER YOU, MIX!
UGH!
LEND ME A HAND, CURREY! WE'VE GOT TO TIE HIM UP AFORE HE COMES TO! I KNOW 'BOUT THIS TOM MIX! HE'S JUST 'BOUT THE HANDIEST GUY WITH HIS FISTS IN THESE PARTS!
BUT WHEN I GIT THROUGH WITH HIM, HE'LL NEVER BE ABLE TO USE HIS FISTS AGIN! LET'S DIVVY UP THE GOLD AND THEN, AS SOON AS THE STORM BLOWS OVER, WE'LL KILL MIX AND BEAT IT!
GOLD
BUT WITHIN A FEW MINUTES---
OHH, MY HEAD FEELS AS IF IT HAD BEEN CRACKED OPEN! I MUST'VE WALKED RIGHT INTO THE HIDE-OUT OF CURREY AND IVEY!
IF I HAVE THOSE COYOTES FIGURED RIGHT, THEY'RE NOT GOING TO LET ME LIVE FOR LONG! MY ONLY CHANCE IS TO FREE MY-SELF BEFORE THEY COME BACK TO THIS ROOM!
(GRUNT) I CAN'T TEAR THESE ROPES APART--- WAIT! I JUST THOUGHT OF SOMETHING!
THERE'S SO MUCH SAND CAKED ON MY HANDS, THAT IF I WASH IT OFF I MIGHT BE ABLE TO SLIP THEM RIGHT OUT OF THESE ROPES!

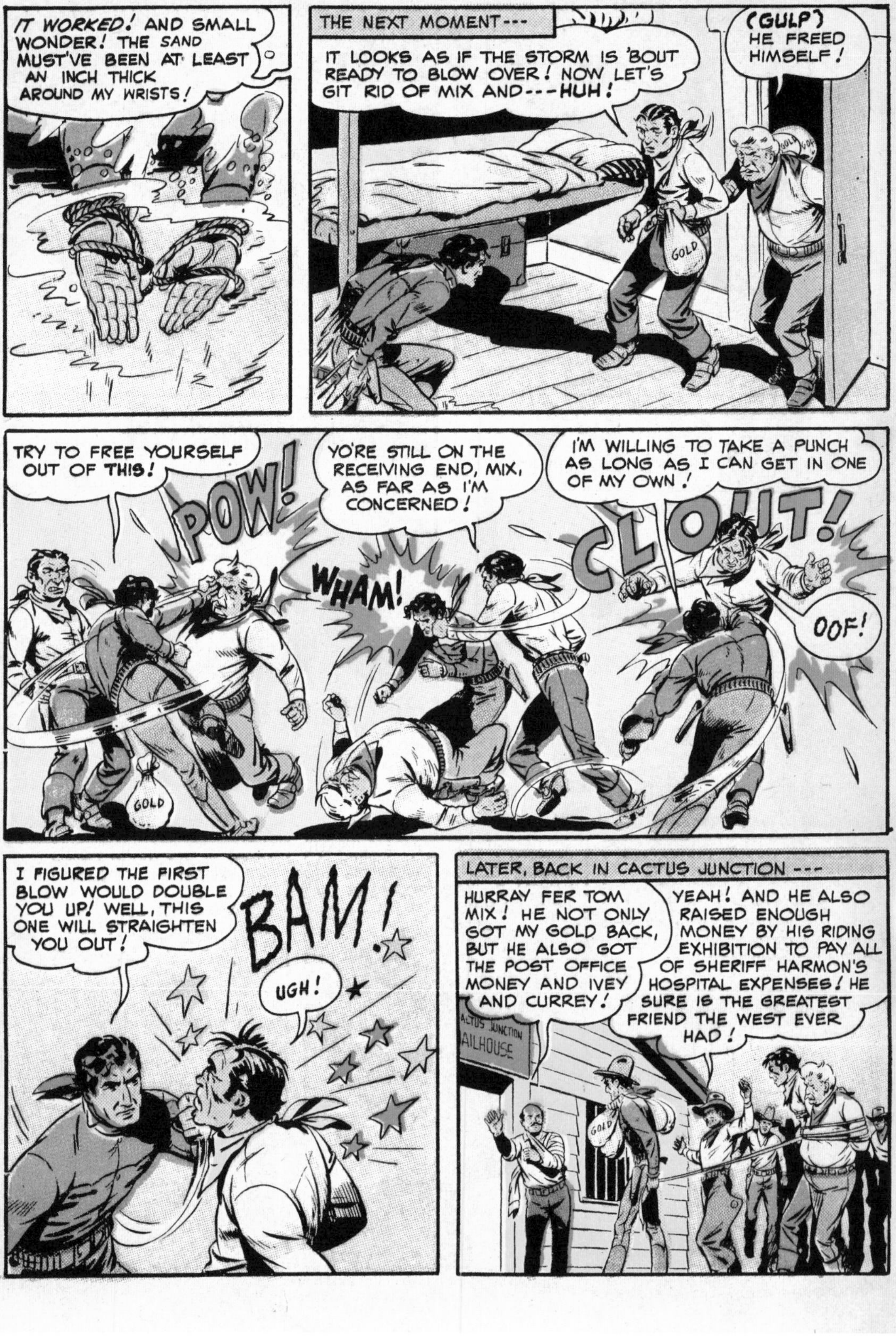
IT WORKED! AND SMALL WONDER! THE SAND MUST'VE BEEN AT LEAST AN INCH THICK AROUND MY WRISTS!
THE NEXT MOMENT---
IT LOOKS AS IF THE STORM IS 'BOUT READY TO BLOW OVER! NOW LET'S GIT RID OF MIX AND---HUH!
(GULP) HE FREED HIMSELF!
GOLD
TRY TO FREE YOURSELF OUT OF THIS!
POW!
YO'RE STILL ON THE RECEIVING END, MIX, AS FAR AS I'M CONCERNED!
WHAM!
I'M WILLING TO TAKE A PUNCH AS LONG AS I CAN GET IN ONE OF MY OWN!
CLOUT!
OOF!
GOLD
I FIGURED THE FIRST BLOW WOULD DOUBLE YOU UP! WELL, THIS ONE WILL STRAIGHTEN YOU OUT!
BAM!
UGH!
LATER, BACK IN CACTUS JUNCTION ---
HURRAY FER TOM MIX! HE NOT ONLY GOT MY GOLD BACK, BUT HE ALSO GOT THE POST OFFICE MONEY AND IVEY AND CURREY!
YEAH! AND HE ALSO RAISED ENOUGH MONEY BY HIS RIDING EXHIBITION TO PAY ALL OF SHERIFF HARMON'S HOSPITAL EXPENSES! HE SURE IS THE GREATEST FRIEND THE WEST EVER HAD!
ACTUS JUNCTION JAILHOUSE
GOLD

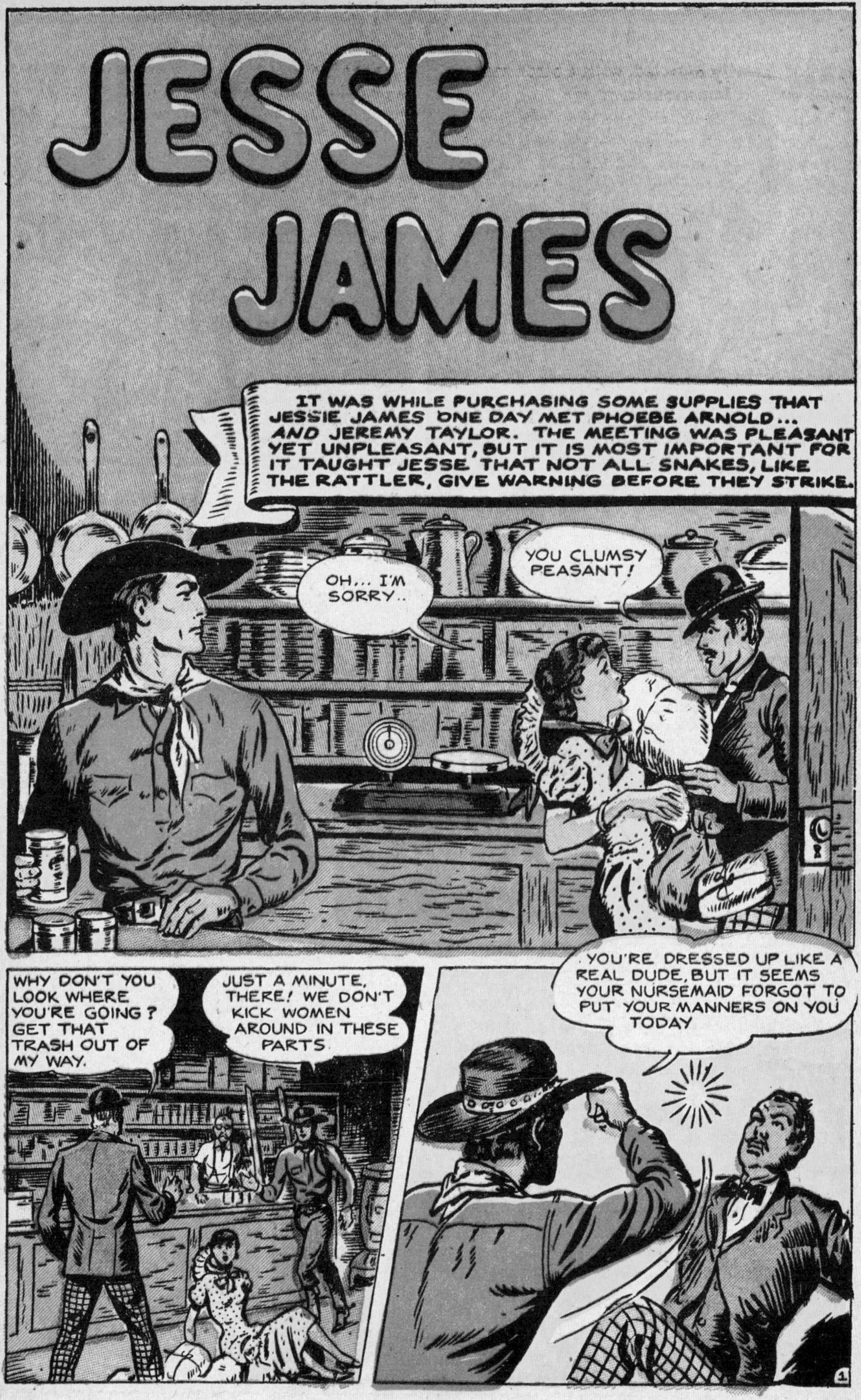
JESSE JAMES
IT WAS WHILE PURCHASING SOME SUPPLIES THAT JESSIE JAMES ONE DAY MET PHOEBE ARNOLD... AND JEREMY TAYLOR. THE MEETING WAS PLEASANT YET UNPLEASANT, BUT IT IS MOST IMPORTANT FOR IT TAUGHT JESSE THAT NOT ALL SNAKES, LIKE THE RATTLER, GIVE WARNING BEFORE THEY STRIKE.
OH,... I'M SORRY..
YOU CLUMSY PEASANT!
WHY DON'T YOU LOOK WHERE YOU'RE GOING? GET THAT TRASH OUT OF MY WAY.
JUST A MINUTE, THERE! WE DON'T KICK WOMEN AROUND IN THESE PARTS.
YOU'RE DRESSED UP LIKE A REAL DUDE, BUT IT SEEMS YOUR NURSEMAID FORGOT TO PUT YOUR MANNERS ON YOU TODAY
1

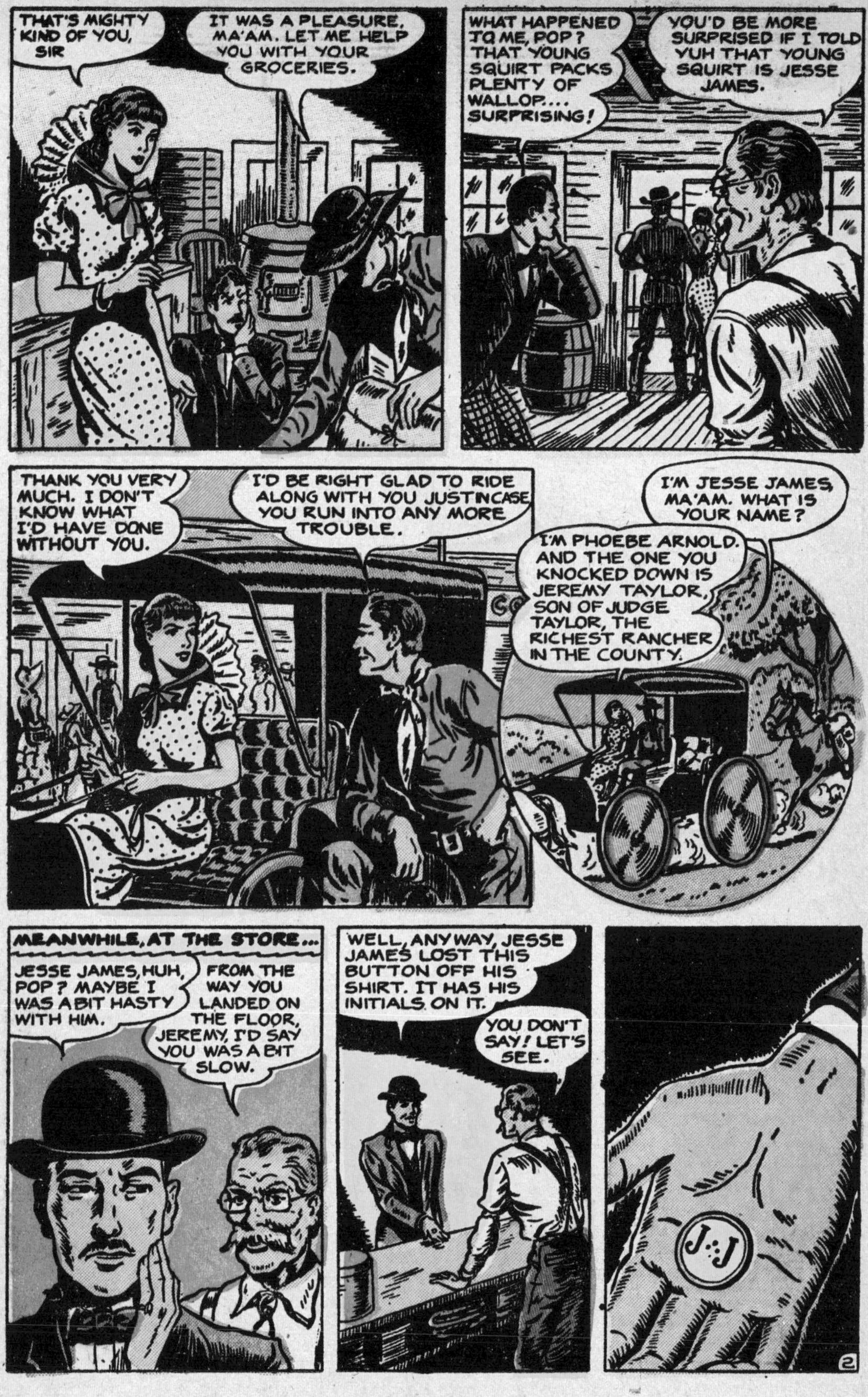
THAT'S MIGHTY KIND OF YOU, SIR
IT WAS A PLEASURE, MA'AM. LET ME HELP YOU WITH YOUR GROCERIES.
WHAT HAPPENED TO ME, POP? THAT YOUNG SQUIRT PACKS PLENTY OF WALLOP.... SURPRISING!
YOU'D BE MORE SURPRISED IF I TOLD YUH THAT YOUNG SQUIRT IS JESSE JAMES.
THANK YOU VERY MUCH. I DON'T KNOW WHAT I'D HAVE DONE WITHOUT YOU.
I'D BE RIGHT GLAD TO RIDE ALONG WITH YOU JUSTINCASE YOU RUN INTO ANY MORE TROUBLE.
I'M JESSE JAMES, MA'AM. WHAT IS YOUR NAME?
I'M PHOEBE ARNOLD. AND THE ONE YOU KNOCKED DOWN IS JEREMY TAYLOR, SON OF JUDGE TAYLOR, THE RICHEST RANCHER IN THE COUNTY.
MEANWHILE, AT THE STORE...
JESSE JAMES, HUH, POP? MAYBE I WAS A BIT HASTY WITH HIM.
FROM THE WAY YOU LANDED ON THE FLOOR, JEREMY, I'D SAY YOU WAS A BIT SLOW.
WELL, ANYWAY, JESSE JAMES LOST THIS BUTTON OFF HIS SHIRT. IT HAS HIS INITIALS ON IT.
YOU DON'T SAY! LET'S SEE.
J:J
2

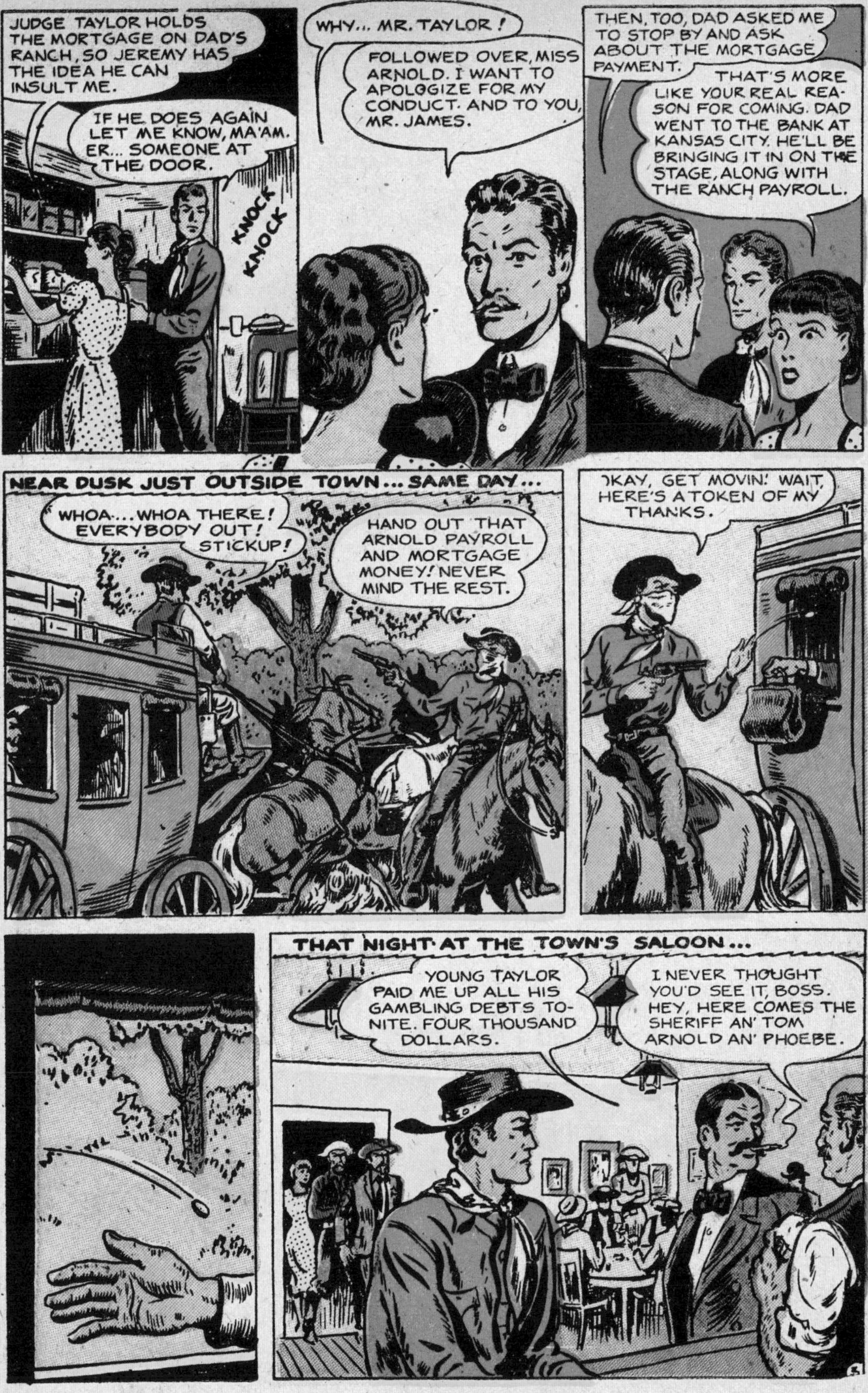
JUDGE TAYLOR HOLDS THE MORTGAGE ON DAD'S RANCH, SO JEREMY HAS THE IDEA HE CAN INSULT ME.
IF HE DOES AGAIN LET ME KNOW, MA'AM. ER... SOMEONE AT THE DOOR.
KNOCK KNOCK
WHY... MR. TAYLOR!
FOLLOWED OVER, MISS ARNOLD. I WANT TO APOLOGIZE FOR MY CONDUCT. AND TO YOU, MR. JAMES.
THEN, TOO, DAD ASKED ME TO STOP BY AND ASK ABOUT THE MORTGAGE PAYMENT.
THAT'S MORE LIKE YOUR REAL REASON FOR COMING. DAD WENT TO THE BANK AT KANSAS CITY. HE'LL BE BRINGING IT IN ON THE STAGE, ALONG WITH THE RANCH PAYROLL.
NEAR DUSK JUST OUTSIDE TOWN... SAME DAY...
WHOA... WHOA THERE! EVERYBODY OUT! STICKUP!
HAND OUT THAT ARNOLD PAYROLL AND MORTGAGE MONEY! NEVER MIND THE REST.
OKAY, GET MOVIN'. WAIT, HERE'S A TOKEN OF MY THANKS.
THAT NIGHT AT THE TOWN'S SALOON...
YOUNG TAYLOR PAID ME UP ALL HIS GAMBLING DEBTS TONITE. FOUR THOUSAND DOLLARS.
I NEVER THOUGHT YOU'D SEE IT, BOSS. HEY, HERE COMES THE SHERIFF AN' TOM ARNOLD AN' PHOEBE.
3

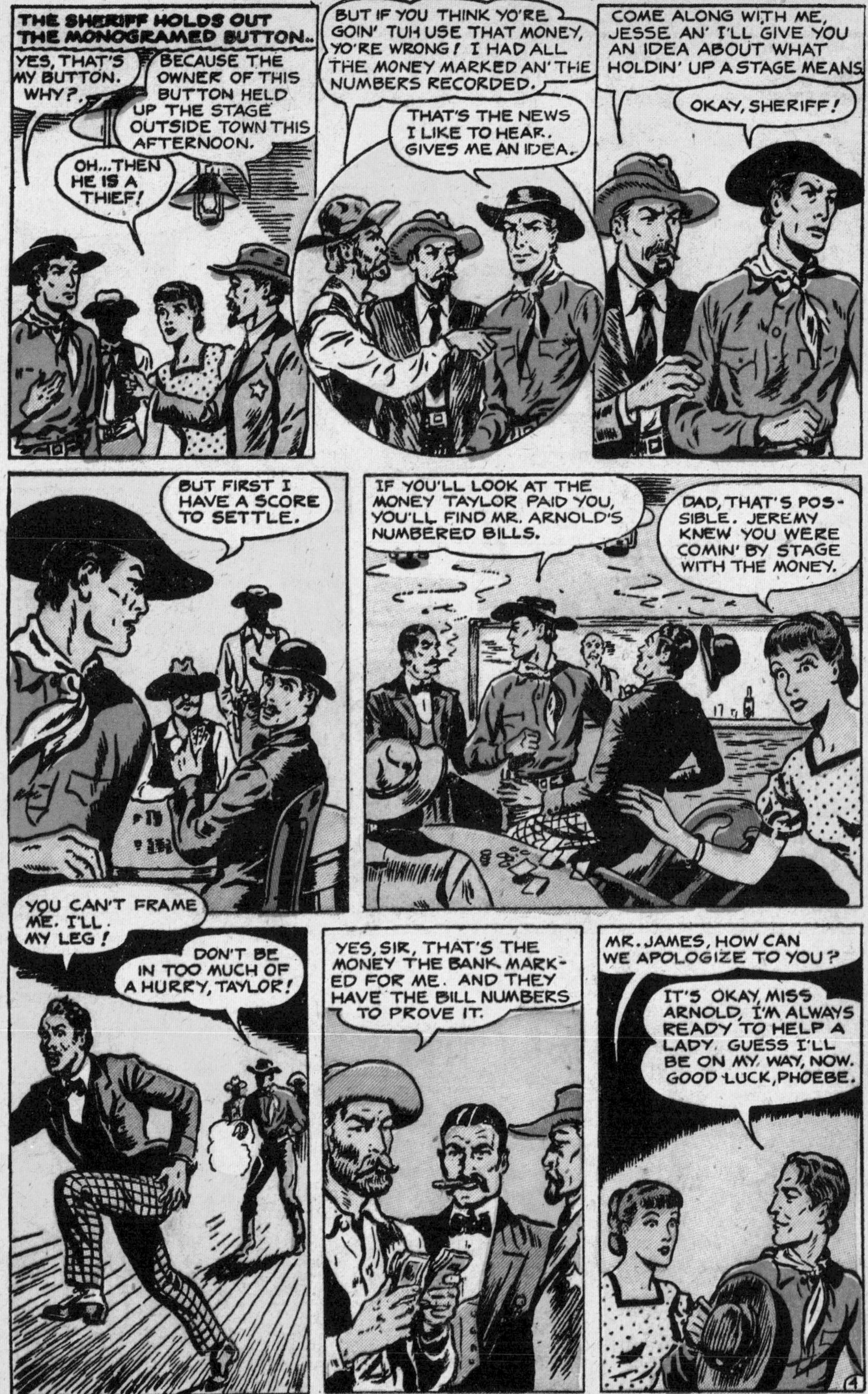
THE SHERIFF HOLDS OUT THE MONOGRAMED BUTTON..
YES, THAT'S MY BUTTON. WHY?
BECAUSE THE OWNER OF THIS BUTTON HELD UP THE STAGE OUTSIDE TOWN THIS AFTERNOON.
OH...THEN HE IS A THIEF!
BUT IF YOU THINK YO'RE GOIN' TUH USE THAT MONEY, YO'RE WRONG! I HAD ALL THE MONEY MARKED AN' THE NUMBERS RECORDED.
THAT'S THE NEWS I LIKE TO HEAR. GIVES ME AN IDEA.
COME ALONG WITH ME, JESSE AN' I'LL GIVE YOU AN IDEA ABOUT WHAT HOLDIN' UP A STAGE MEANS.
OKAY, SHERIFF!
BUT FIRST I HAVE A SCORE TO SETTLE.
IF YOU'LL LOOK AT THE MONEY TAYLOR PAID YOU, YOU'LL FIND MR. ARNOLD'S NUMBERED BILLS.
DAD, THAT'S POS-SIBLE. JEREMY KNEW YOU WERE COMIN' BY STAGE WITH THE MONEY.
YOU CAN'T FRAME ME. I'LL... MY LEG!
DON'T BE IN TOO MUCH OF A HURRY, TAYLOR!
YES, SIR, THAT'S THE MONEY THE BANK MARK-ED FOR ME. AND THEY HAVE THE BILL NUMBERS TO PROVE IT.
MR. JAMES, HOW CAN WE APOLOGIZE TO YOU?
IT'S OKAY, MISS ARNOLD, I'M ALWAYS READY TO HELP A LADY. GUESS I'LL BE ON MY WAY, NOW. GOOD LUCK, PHOEBE.
4

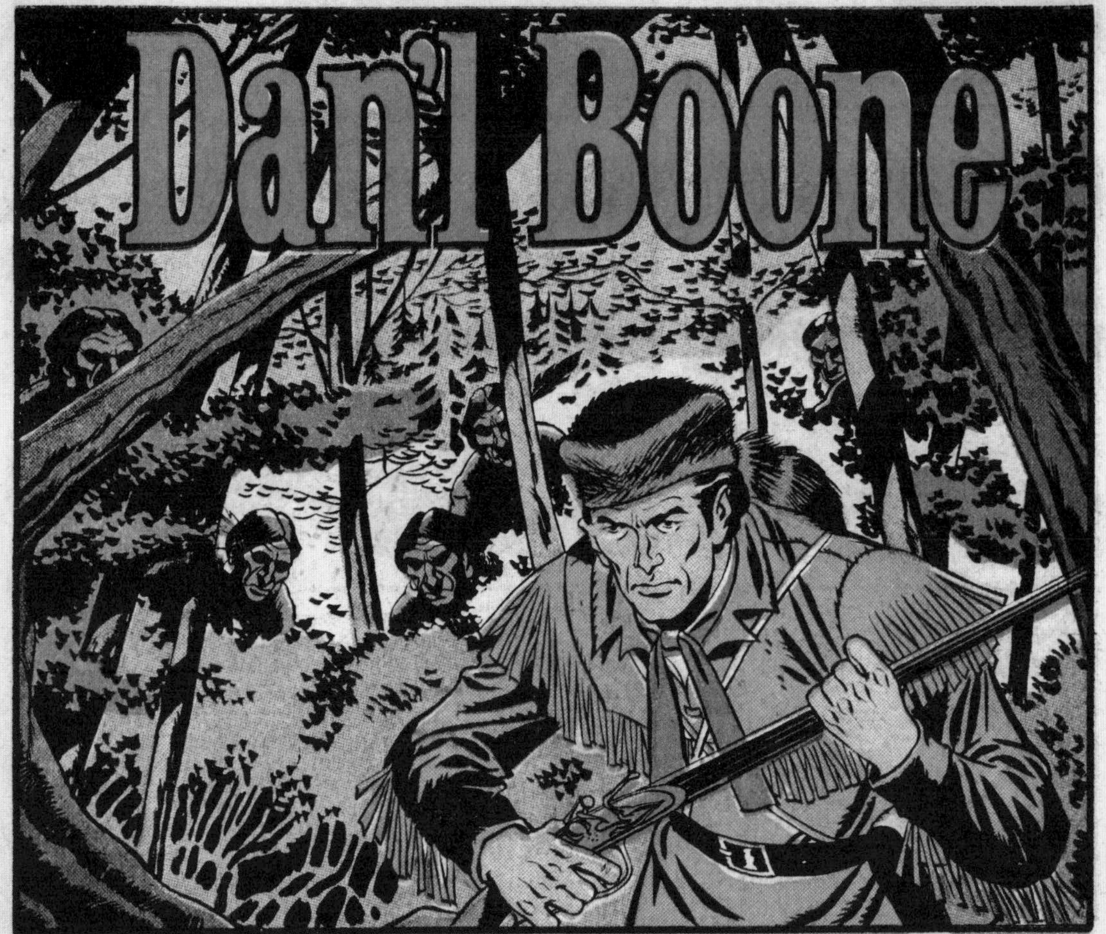
DAN'L BOONE

NO ONE KNOWS BETTER THAN **DAN'L BOONE** HOW CAREFUL A MAN HAS TO BE WHILE TRAIPSING THROUGH THE FOREST! NO ONE KNOWS BETTER THAN THE GREATEST FRONTIERSMAN OF THEM ALL THAT

"PERIL SHADOWS THE FOREST TRAIL"

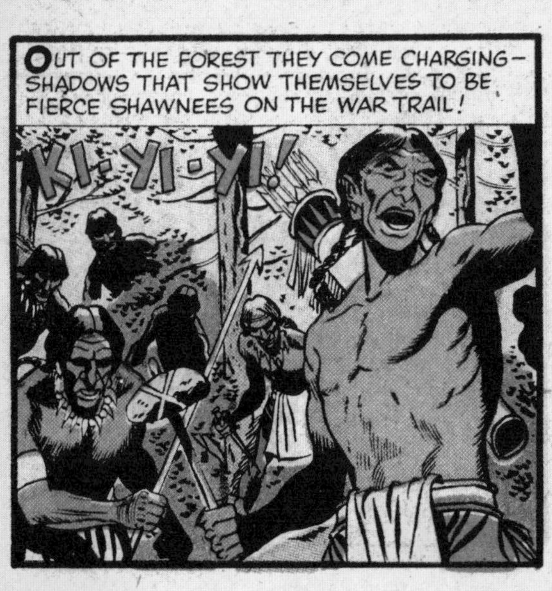
OUT OF THE FOREST THEY COME CHARGING— SHADOWS THAT SHOW THEMSELVES TO BE FIERCE SHAWNEES ON THE WAR TRAIL!
KI-YI-YI!

AND BEFORE THEY MELT BACK INTO THE FORESTS...

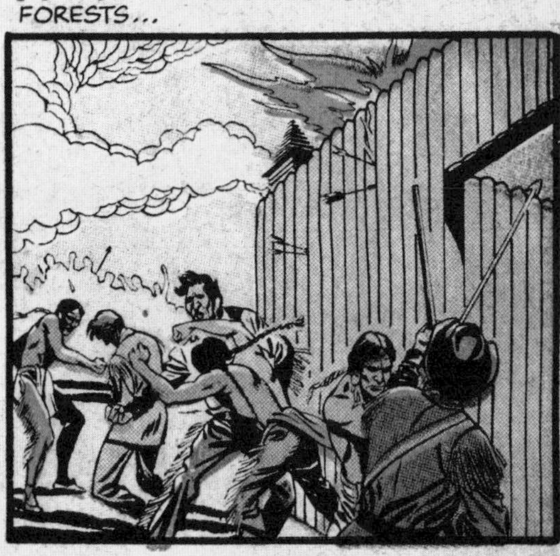

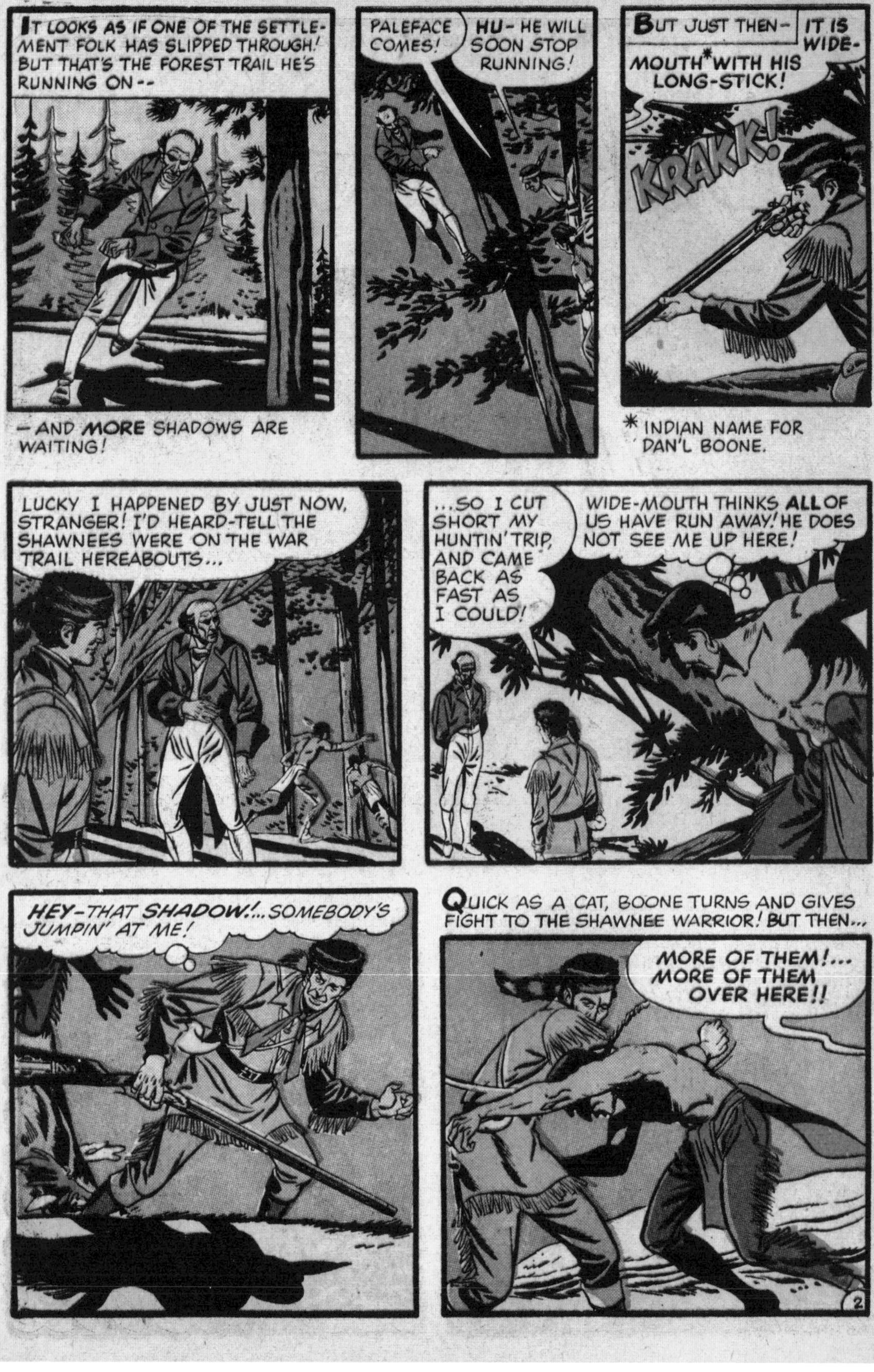
IT LOOKS AS IF ONE OF THE SETTLEMENT FOLK HAS SLIPPED THROUGH! BUT THAT'S THE FOREST TRAIL HE'S RUNNING ON --
-AND MORE SHADOWS ARE WAITING!
PALEFACE COMES!
HU- HE WILL SOON STOP RUNNING!
BUT JUST THEN-
IT IS WIDE-MOUTH* WITH HIS LONG-STICK!
KRAKK!
* INDIAN NAME FOR DAN'L BOONE.
LUCKY I HAPPENED BY JUST NOW, STRANGER! I'D HEARD-TELL THE SHAWNEES WERE ON THE WAR TRAIL HEREABOUTS...
...SO I CUT SHORT MY HUNTIN' TRIP, AND CAME BACK AS FAST AS I COULD!
WIDE-MOUTH THINKS ALL OF US HAVE RUN AWAY! HE DOES NOT SEE ME UP HERE!
HEY-THAT SHADOW!...SOMEBODY'S JUMPIN' AT ME!
QUICK AS A CAT, BOONE TURNS AND GIVES FIGHT TO THE SHAWNEE WARRIOR! BUT THEN...
MORE OF THEM!... MORE OF THEM OVER HERE!!
2

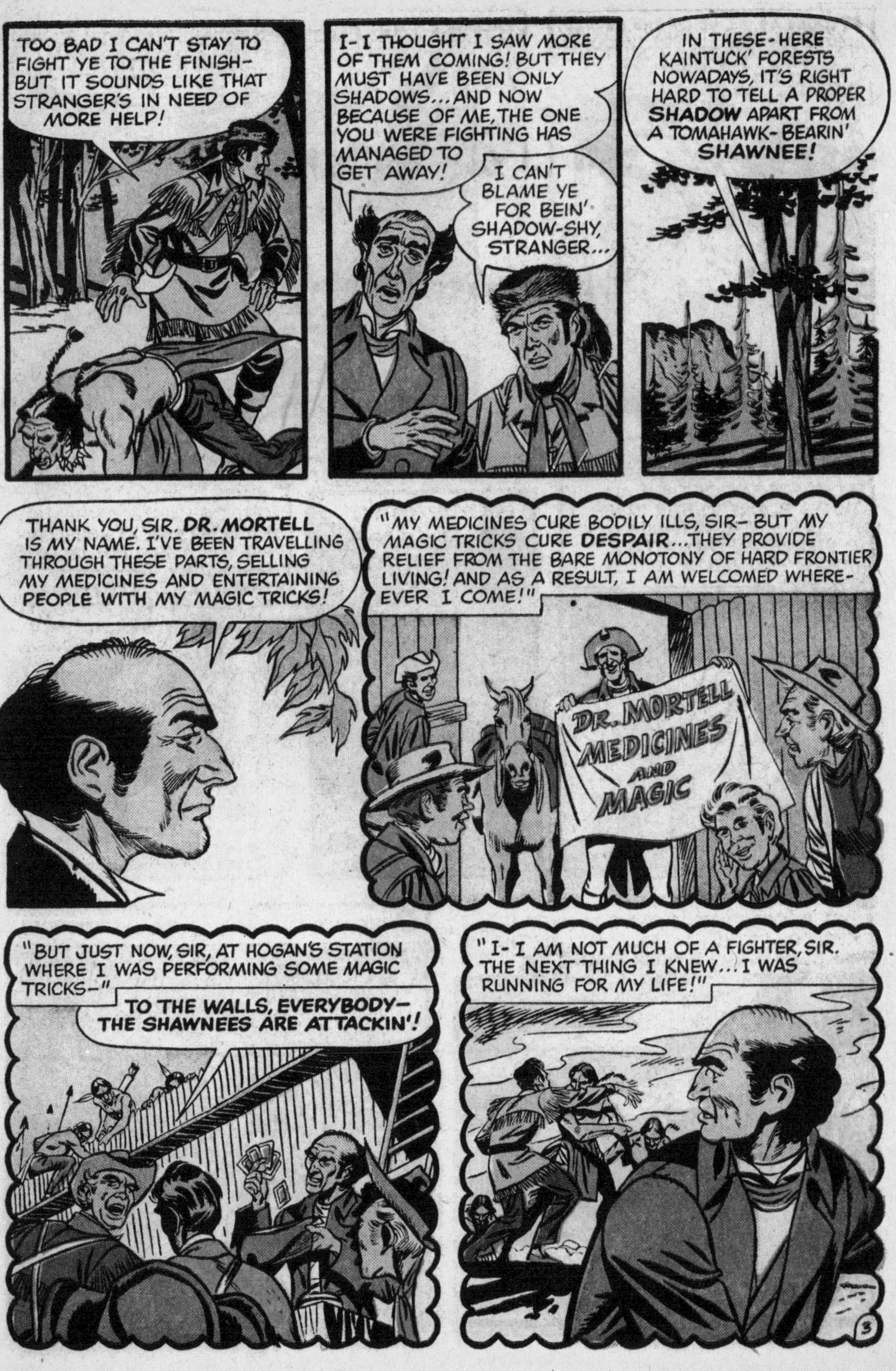
TOO BAD I CAN'T STAY TO FIGHT YE TO THE FINISH- BUT IT SOUNDS LIKE THAT STRANGER'S IN NEED OF MORE HELP!
I- I THOUGHT I SAW MORE OF THEM COMING! BUT THEY MUST HAVE BEEN ONLY SHADOWS... AND NOW BECAUSE OF ME, THE ONE YOU WERE FIGHTING HAS MANAGED TO GET AWAY!
I CAN'T BLAME YE FOR BEIN' SHADOW-SHY, STRANGER...
IN THESE-HERE KAINTUCK' FORESTS NOWADAYS, IT'S RIGHT HARD TO TELL A PROPER SHADOW APART FROM A TOMAHAWK-BEARIN' SHAWNEE!
THANK YOU, SIR. DR. MORTELL IS MY NAME. I'VE BEEN TRAVELLING THROUGH THESE PARTS, SELLING MY MEDICINES AND ENTERTAINING PEOPLE WITH MY MAGIC TRICKS!
"MY MEDICINES CURE BODILY ILLS, SIR- BUT MY MAGIC TRICKS CURE DESPAIR... THEY PROVIDE RELIEF FROM THE BARE MONOTONY OF HARD FRONTIER LIVING! AND AS A RESULT, I AM WELCOMED WHERE-EVER I COME!"
DR. MORTELL MEDICINES AND MAGIC
"BUT JUST NOW, SIR, AT HOGAN'S STATION WHERE I WAS PERFORMING SOME MAGIC TRICKS-"
TO THE WALLS, EVERYBODY- THE SHAWNEES ARE ATTACKIN'!
"I- I AM NOT MUCH OF A FIGHTER, SIR. THE NEXT THING I KNEW... I WAS RUNNING FOR MY LIFE!"
3

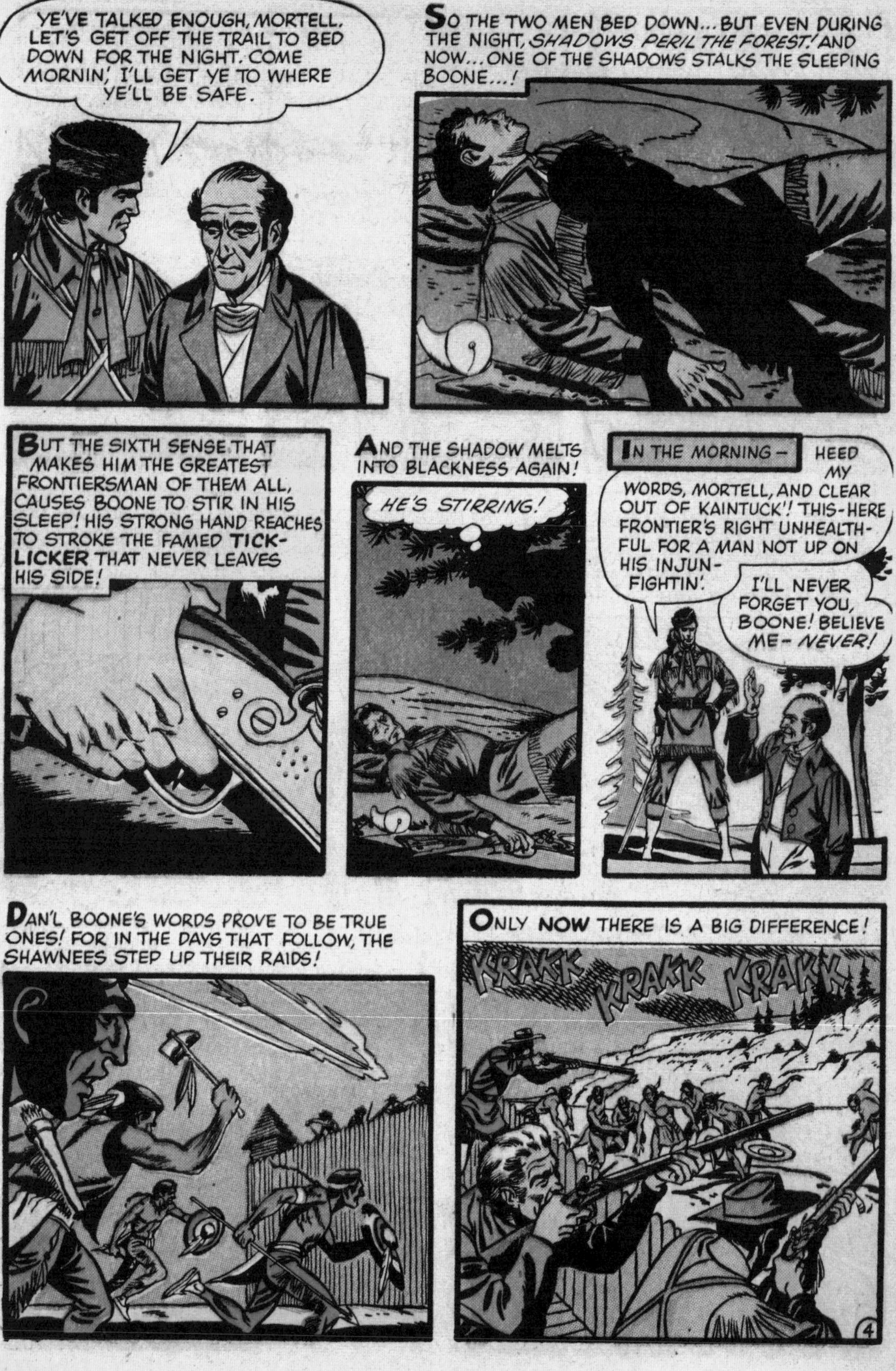
YE'VE TALKED ENOUGH, MORTELL. LET'S GET OFF THE TRAIL TO BED DOWN FOR THE NIGHT. COME MORNIN', I'LL GET YE TO WHERE YE'LL BE SAFE.
SO THE TWO MEN BED DOWN... BUT EVEN DURING THE NIGHT, SHADOWS PERIL THE FOREST! AND NOW... ONE OF THE SHADOWS STALKS THE SLEEPING BOONE...!
BUT THE SIXTH SENSE THAT MAKES HIM THE GREATEST FRONTIERSMAN OF THEM ALL, CAUSES BOONE TO STIR IN HIS SLEEP! HIS STRONG HAND REACHES TO STROKE THE FAMED TICK-LICKER THAT NEVER LEAVES HIS SIDE!
AND THE SHADOW MELTS INTO BLACKNESS AGAIN!
HE'S STIRRING!
IN THE MORNING—
HEED MY WORDS, MORTELL, AND CLEAR OUT OF KAINTUCK'! THIS-HERE FRONTIER'S RIGHT UNHEALTH-FUL FOR A MAN NOT UP ON HIS INJUN-FIGHTIN'.
I'LL NEVER FORGET YOU, BOONE! BELIEVE ME—NEVER!
DAN'L BOONE'S WORDS PROVE TO BE TRUE ONES! FOR IN THE DAYS THAT FOLLOW, THE SHAWNEES STEP UP THEIR RAIDS!
ONLY NOW THERE IS A BIG DIFFERENCE!
KRAKK KRAKK KRAKK
4

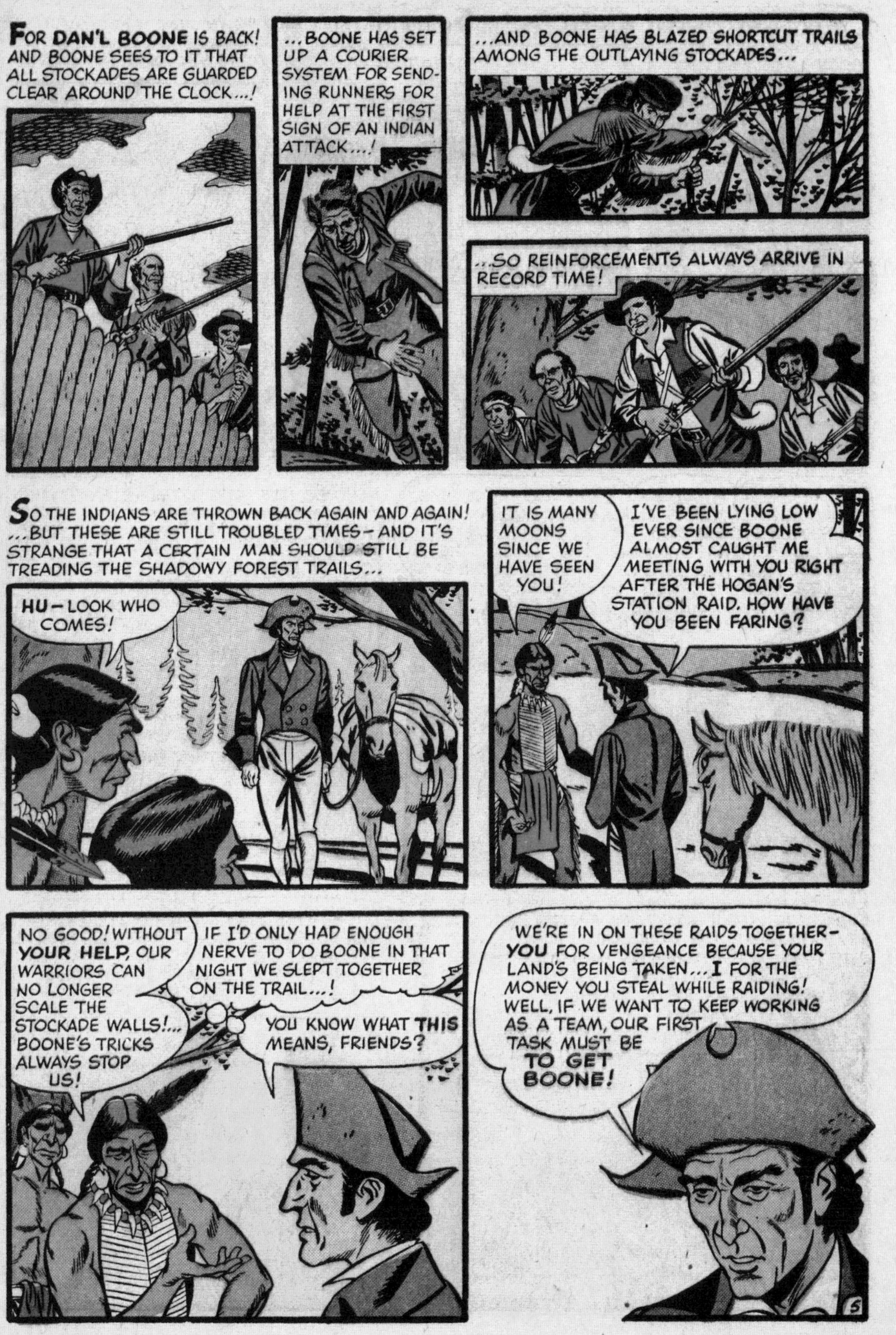

FOR DAN'L BOONE IS BACK! AND BOONE SEES TO IT THAT ALL STOCKADES ARE GUARDED CLEAR AROUND THE CLOCK...!
...BOONE HAS SET UP A COURIER SYSTEM FOR SENDING RUNNERS FOR HELP AT THE FIRST SIGN OF AN INDIAN ATTACK...!
...AND BOONE HAS BLAZED SHORTCUT TRAILS AMONG THE OUTLAYING STOCKADES...
...SO REINFORCEMENTS ALWAYS ARRIVE IN RECORD TIME!
SO THE INDIANS ARE THROWN BACK AGAIN AND AGAIN! ...BUT THESE ARE STILL TROUBLED TIMES— AND IT'S STRANGE THAT A CERTAIN MAN SHOULD STILL BE TREADING THE SHADOWY FOREST TRAILS...
HU—LOOK WHO COMES!
IT IS MANY MOONS SINCE WE HAVE SEEN YOU!
I'VE BEEN LYING LOW EVER SINCE BOONE ALMOST CAUGHT ME MEETING WITH YOU RIGHT AFTER THE HOGAN'S STATION RAID. HOW HAVE YOU BEEN FARING?
NO GOOD! WITHOUT YOUR HELP, OUR WARRIORS CAN NO LONGER SCALE THE STOCKADE WALLS!... BOONE'S TRICKS ALWAYS STOP US!
IF I'D ONLY HAD ENOUGH NERVE TO DO BOONE IN THAT NIGHT WE SLEPT TOGETHER ON THE TRAIL...!
YOU KNOW WHAT THIS MEANS, FRIENDS?
WE'RE IN ON THESE RAIDS TOGETHER— YOU FOR VENGEANCE BECAUSE YOUR LAND'S BEING TAKEN... I FOR THE MONEY YOU STEAL WHILE RAIDING! WELL, IF WE WANT TO KEEP WORKING AS A TEAM, OUR FIRST TASK MUST BE TO GET BOONE!
5

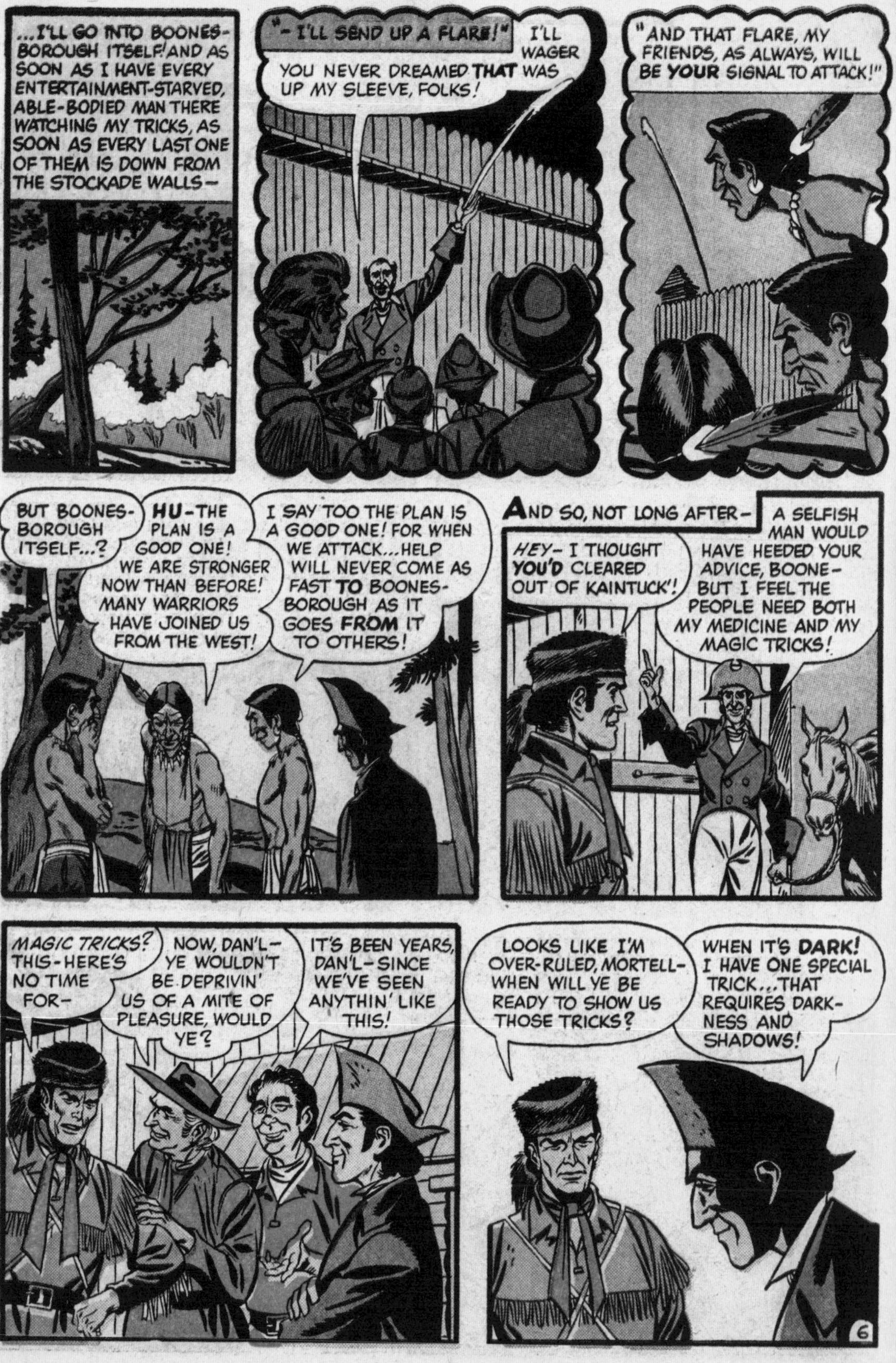
...I'LL GO INTO BOONES-BOROUGH ITSELF! AND AS SOON AS I HAVE EVERY ENTERTAINMENT-STARVED, ABLE-BODIED MAN THERE WATCHING MY TRICKS, AS SOON AS EVERY LAST ONE OF THEM IS DOWN FROM THE STOCKADE WALLS—
"—I'LL SEND UP A FLARE!"
I'LL WAGER YOU NEVER DREAMED THAT WAS UP MY SLEEVE, FOLKS!
"AND THAT FLARE, MY FRIENDS, AS ALWAYS, WILL BE YOUR SIGNAL TO ATTACK!"
BUT BOONES-BOROUGH ITSELF...?
HU—THE PLAN IS A GOOD ONE! WE ARE STRONGER NOW THAN BEFORE! MANY WARRIORS HAVE JOINED US FROM THE WEST!
I SAY TOO THE PLAN IS A GOOD ONE! FOR WHEN WE ATTACK... HELP WILL NEVER COME AS FAST TO BOONES-BOROUGH AS IT GOES FROM IT TO OTHERS!
AND SO, NOT LONG AFTER—
HEY—I THOUGHT YOU'D CLEARED OUT OF KAINTUCK'!
A SELFISH MAN WOULD HAVE HEEDED YOUR ADVICE, BOONE—BUT I FEEL THE PEOPLE NEED BOTH MY MEDICINE AND MY MAGIC TRICKS!
MAGIC TRICKS? THIS-HERE'S NO TIME FOR—
NOW, DAN'L—YE WOULDN'T BE DEPRIVIN' US OF A MITE OF PLEASURE, WOULD YE?
IT'S BEEN YEARS, DAN'L—SINCE WE'VE SEEN ANYTHIN' LIKE THIS!
LOOKS LIKE I'M OVER-RULED, MORTELL—WHEN WILL YE BE READY TO SHOW US THOSE TRICKS?
WHEN IT'S DARK! I HAVE ONE SPECIAL TRICK... THAT REQUIRES DARK-NESS AND SHADOWS!
6

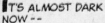

IT'S ALMOST DARK NOW --

I HAVE BAD NEWS FOR YE, MORTELL...

NONE OF THE WOMEN-FOLK CAN COME TO YOUR SHOW. THERE'S MEASLES SPREAD AMONGST THE YOUNG 'UNS...AND THEY HAVE TO BE TENDIN''EM!

AS IF I CARED! IT'S THE ABLE-BODIED MEN I WANT WATCHING ME!

THAT'S TOO BAD, BOONE!

IT'S DARK NOW! AND DR. MORTELL IS ABOUT TO START... KNOWING FULL WELL THAT HIS SHAWNEE FRIENDS LIE WAITING IN THE FOREST!

PICK A CARD! SOMEBODY PICK A CARD!

ONLY OLD MEN IN THE FRONT ROW -- BUT THOSE FILING IN BEHIND THEM MUST BE THE YOUNGER ABLE-BODIED MEN! THAT'S TWELVE SO FAR....THIRTEEN... FOURTEEN....

DR. MORTELL KEEPS CAREFUL COUNT, AND WHEN HE'S CERTAIN EVERY ABLE-BODIED MAN IN THE STOCKADE HAS EYES ONLY FOR HIM...

I'LL WAGER YOU NEVER DREAMED THAT WAS UP MY SLEEVE, FOLKS!

THE SIGNAL!... FORWARD, WARRIORS!

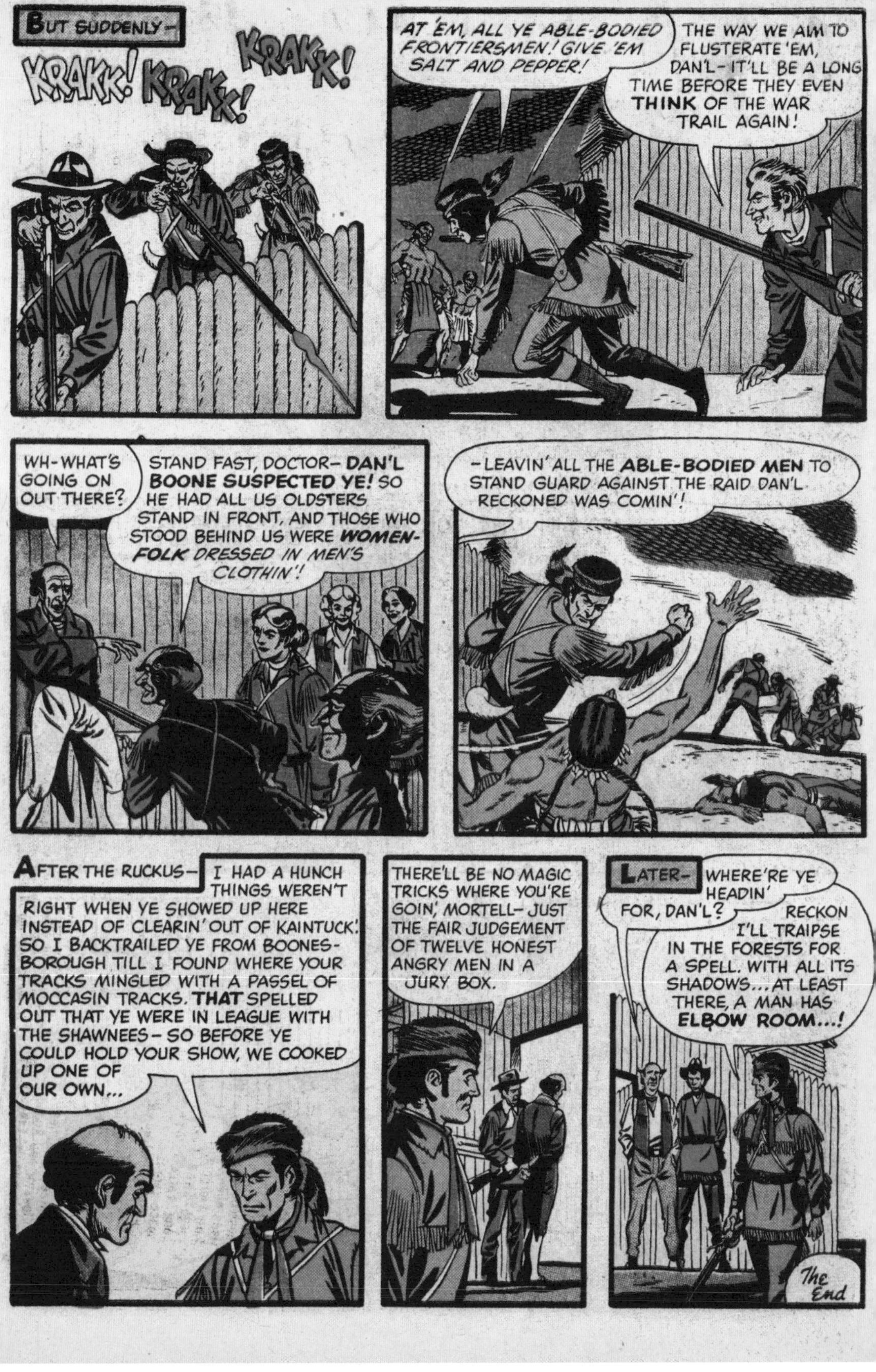
BUT SUDDENLY—
KRAKK! KRAKK! KRAKK!
AT 'EM, ALL YE ABLE-BODIED FRONTIERSMEN! GIVE 'EM SALT AND PEPPER!
THE WAY WE AIM TO FLUSTERATE 'EM, DAN'L— IT'LL BE A LONG TIME BEFORE THEY EVEN THINK OF THE WAR TRAIL AGAIN!
WH-WHAT'S GOING ON OUT THERE?
STAND FAST, DOCTOR— DAN'L BOONE SUSPECTED YE! SO HE HAD ALL US OLDSTERS STAND IN FRONT, AND THOSE WHO STOOD BEHIND US WERE WOMEN-FOLK DRESSED IN MEN'S CLOTHIN'!
—LEAVIN' ALL THE ABLE-BODIED MEN TO STAND GUARD AGAINST THE RAID DAN'L RECKONED WAS COMIN'!
AFTER THE RUCKUS—
I HAD A HUNCH THINGS WEREN'T RIGHT WHEN YE SHOWED UP HERE INSTEAD OF CLEARIN' OUT OF KAINTUCK'. SO I BACKTRAILED YE FROM BOONES-BOROUGH TILL I FOUND WHERE YOUR TRACKS MINGLED WITH A PASSEL OF MOCCASIN TRACKS. THAT SPELLED OUT THAT YE WERE IN LEAGUE WITH THE SHAWNEES— SO BEFORE YE COULD HOLD YOUR SHOW, WE COOKED UP ONE OF OUR OWN...
THERE'LL BE NO MAGIC TRICKS WHERE YOU'RE GOIN', MORTELL— JUST THE FAIR JUDGEMENT OF TWELVE HONEST ANGRY MEN IN A JURY BOX.
LATER—
WHERE'RE YE HEADIN' FOR, DAN'L?
RECKON I'LL TRAIPSE IN THE FORESTS FOR A SPELL. WITH ALL ITS SHADOWS... AT LEAST THERE, A MAN HAS ELBOW ROOM...!
The End

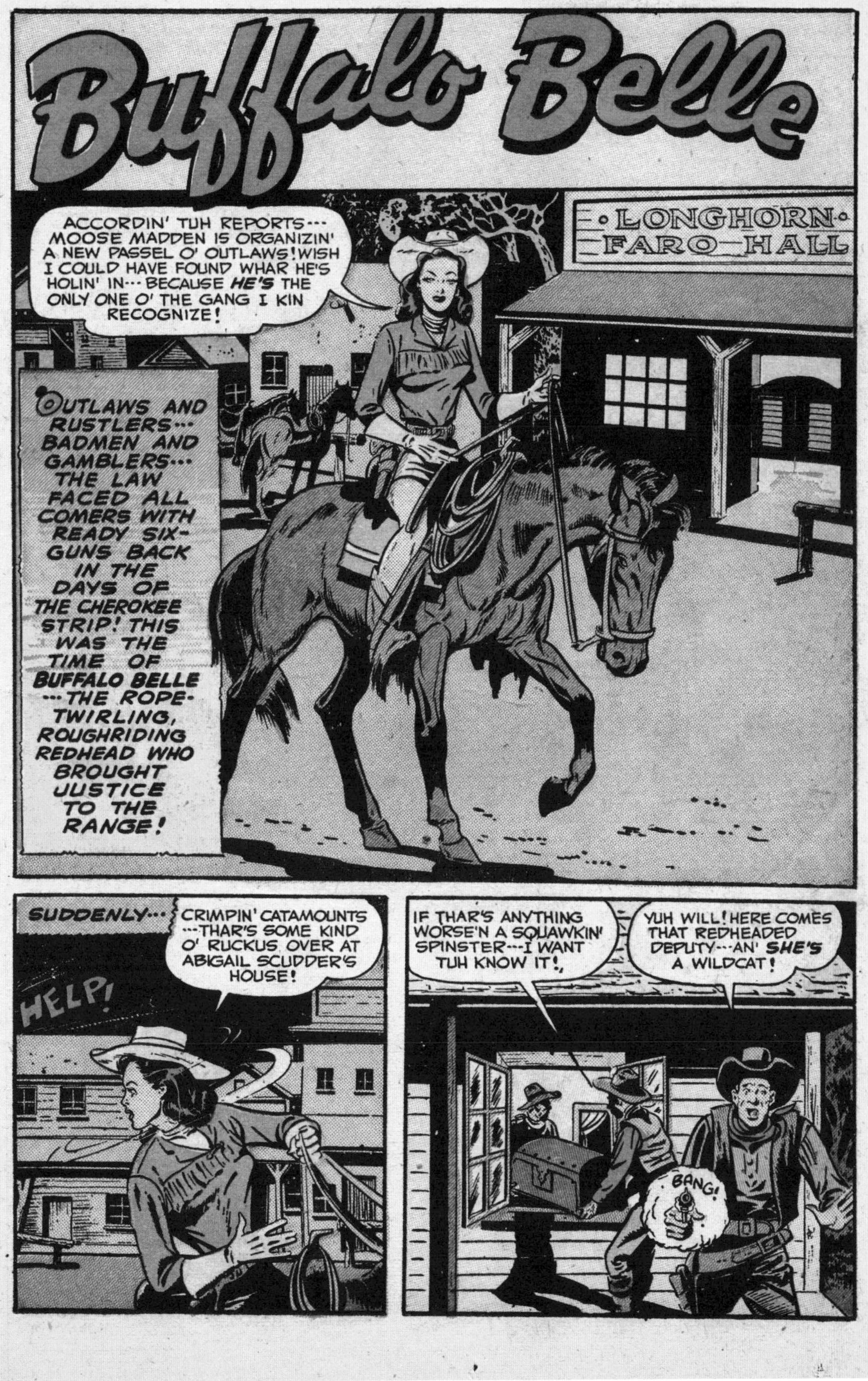

Buffalo Belle
LONGHORN FARO HALL
ACCORDIN' TUH REPORTS--- MOOSE MADDEN IS ORGANIZIN' A NEW PASSEL O' OUTLAWS! WISH I COULD HAVE FOUND WHAR HE'S HOLIN' IN--- BECAUSE HE'S THE ONLY ONE O' THE GANG I KIN RECOGNIZE!
OUTLAWS AND RUSTLERS--- BADMEN AND GAMBLERS--- THE LAW FACED ALL COMERS WITH READY SIX-GUNS BACK IN THE DAYS OF THE CHEROKEE STRIP! THIS WAS THE TIME OF BUFFALO BELLE --- THE ROPE-TWIRLING, ROUGHRIDING REDHEAD WHO BROUGHT JUSTICE TO THE RANGE!
SUDDENLY---
CRIMPIN' CATAMOUNTS ---THAR'S SOME KIND O' RUCKUS OVER AT ABIGAIL SCUDDER'S HOUSE!
HELP!
IF THAR'S ANYTHING WORSE'N A SQUAWKIN' SPINSTER---I WANT TUH KNOW IT!,
YUH WILL! HERE COMES THAT REDHEADED DEPUTY---AN' SHE'S A WILDCAT!
BANG!

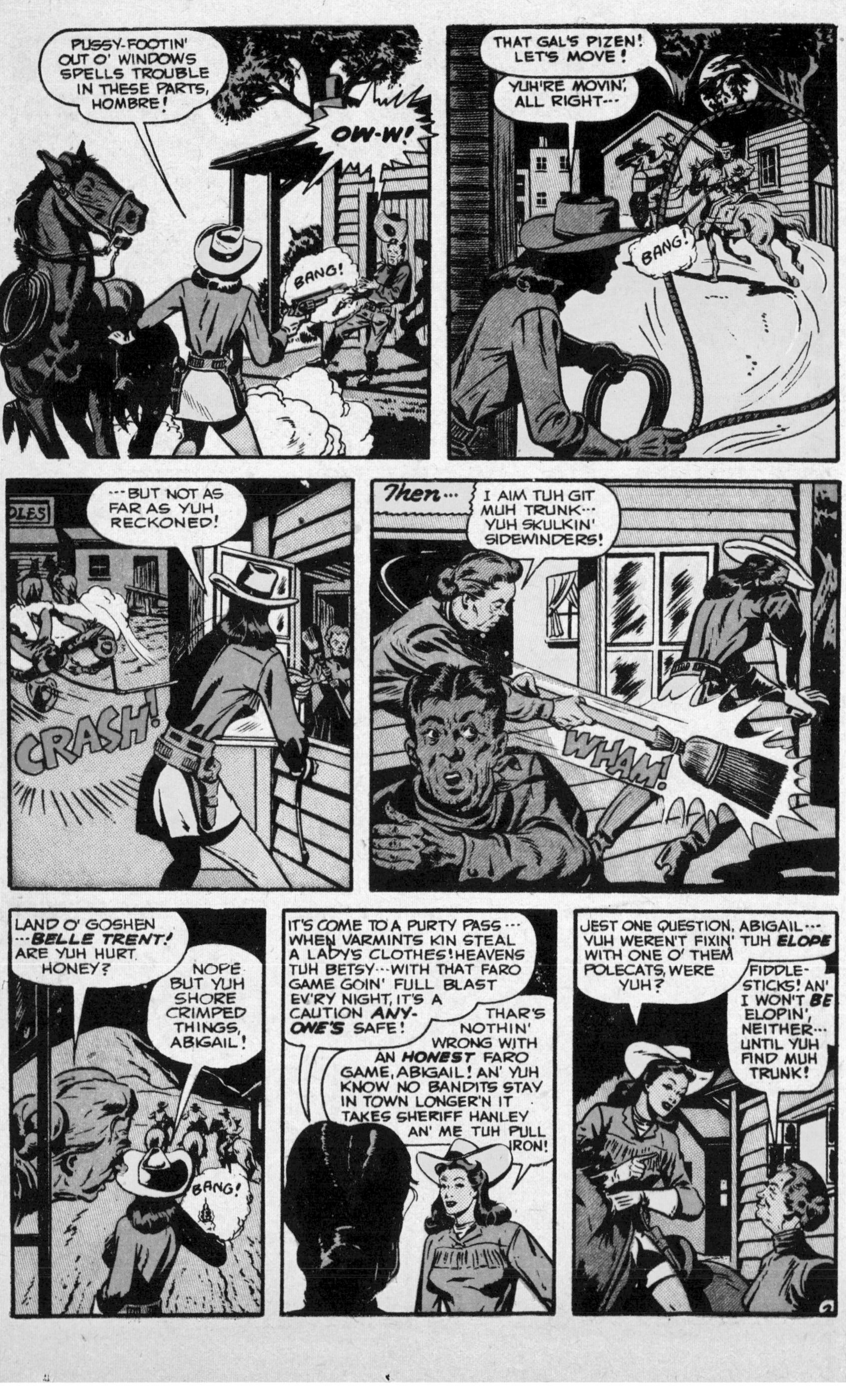

PUSSY-FOOTIN' OUT O' WINDOWS SPELLS TROUBLE IN THESE PARTS, HOMBRE!
OW-W!
BANG!
THAT GAL'S PIZEN! LET'S MOVE!
YUH'RE MOVIN', ALL RIGHT---
BANG!
---BUT NOT AS FAR AS YUH RECKONED!
CRASH!
Then...
I AIM TUH GIT MUH TRUNK--- YUH SKULKIN' SIDEWINDERS!
WHAM!
LAND O' GOSHEN ---BELLE TRENT! ARE YUH HURT, HONEY?
NOPE BUT YUH SHORE CRIMPED THINGS, ABIGAIL!
BANG!
IT'S COME TO A PURTY PASS --- WHEN VARMINTS KIN STEAL A LADY'S CLOTHES! HEAVENS TUH BETSY --- WITH THAT FARO GAME GOIN' FULL BLAST EV'RY NIGHT, IT'S A CAUTION ANY-ONE'S SAFE!
THAR'S NOTHIN' WRONG WITH AN HONEST FARO GAME, ABIGAIL! AN' YUH KNOW NO BANDITS STAY IN TOWN LONGER'N IT TAKES SHERIFF HANLEY AN' ME TUH PULL IRON!
JEST ONE QUESTION, ABIGAIL--- YUH WEREN'T FIXIN' TUH ELOPE WITH ONE O' THEM POLECATS, WERE YUH?
FIDDLE-STICKS! AN' I WON'T BE ELOPIN', NEITHER--- UNTIL YUH FIND MUH TRUNK!

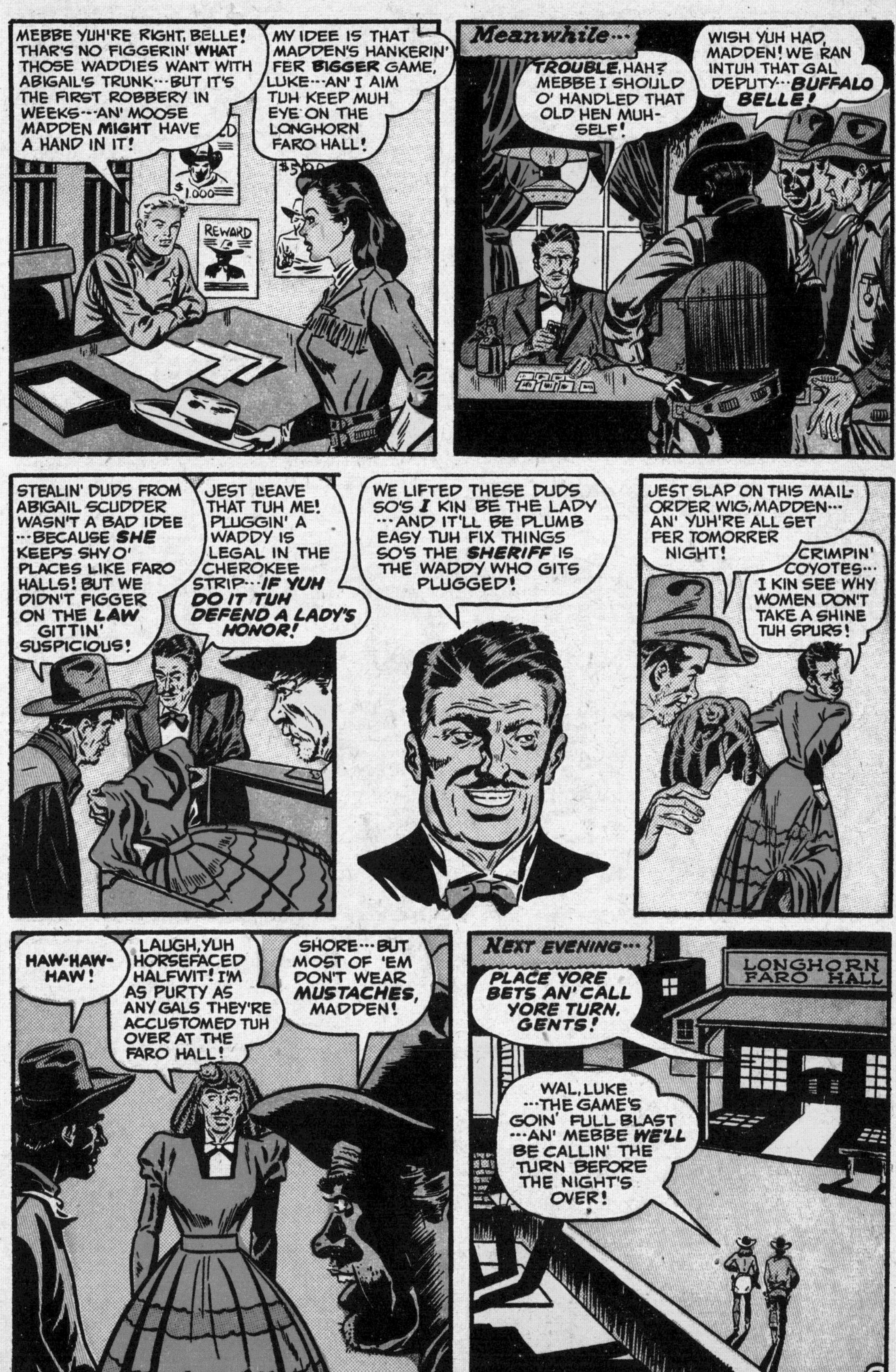
MEBBE YUH'RE RIGHT, BELLE! THAR'S NO FIGGERIN' WHAT THOSE WADDIES WANT WITH ABIGAIL'S TRUNK... BUT IT'S THE FIRST ROBBERY IN WEEKS... AN' MOOSE MADDEN MIGHT HAVE A HAND IN IT!
MY IDEE IS THAT MADDEN'S HANKERIN' FER BIGGER GAME, LUKE... AN' I AIM TUH KEEP MUH EYE ON THE LONGHORN FARO HALL!
REWARD
$1,000
Meanwhile...
TROUBLE, HAH? MEBBE I SHOULD O' HANDLED THAT OLD HEN MUH-SELF!
WISH YUH HAD, MADDEN! WE RAN INTUH THAT GAL DEPUTY... BUFFALO BELLE!
STEALIN' DUDS FROM ABIGAIL SCUDDER WASN'T A BAD IDEE ...BECAUSE SHE KEEPS SHY O' PLACES LIKE FARO HALLS! BUT WE DIDN'T FIGGER ON THE LAW GITTIN' SUSPICIOUS!
JEST LEAVE THAT TUH ME! PLUGGIN' A WADDY IS LEGAL IN THE CHEROKEE STRIP... IF YUH DO IT TUH DEFEND A LADY'S HONOR!
WE LIFTED THESE DUDS SO'S I KIN BE THE LADY ...AND IT'LL BE PLUMB EASY TUH FIX THINGS SO'S THE SHERIFF IS THE WADDY WHO GITS PLUGGED!
JEST SLAP ON THIS MAIL-ORDER WIG, MADDEN... AN' YUH'RE ALL SET FER TOMORRER NIGHT!
CRIMPIN' COYOTES... I KIN SEE WHY WOMEN DON'T TAKE A SHINE TUH SPURS!
HAW-HAW-HAW!
LAUGH, YUH HORSEFACED HALFWIT! I'M AS PURTY AS ANY GALS THEY'RE ACCUSTOMED TUH OVER AT THE FARO HALL!
SHORE... BUT MOST OF 'EM DON'T WEAR MUSTACHES, MADDEN!
NEXT EVENING...
LONGHORN FARO HALL
PLACE YORE BETS AN' CALL YORE TURN, GENTS!
WAL, LUKE ...THE GAME'S GOIN' FULL BLAST ...AN' MEBBE WE'LL BE CALLIN' THE TURN BEFORE THE NIGHT'S OVER!
3

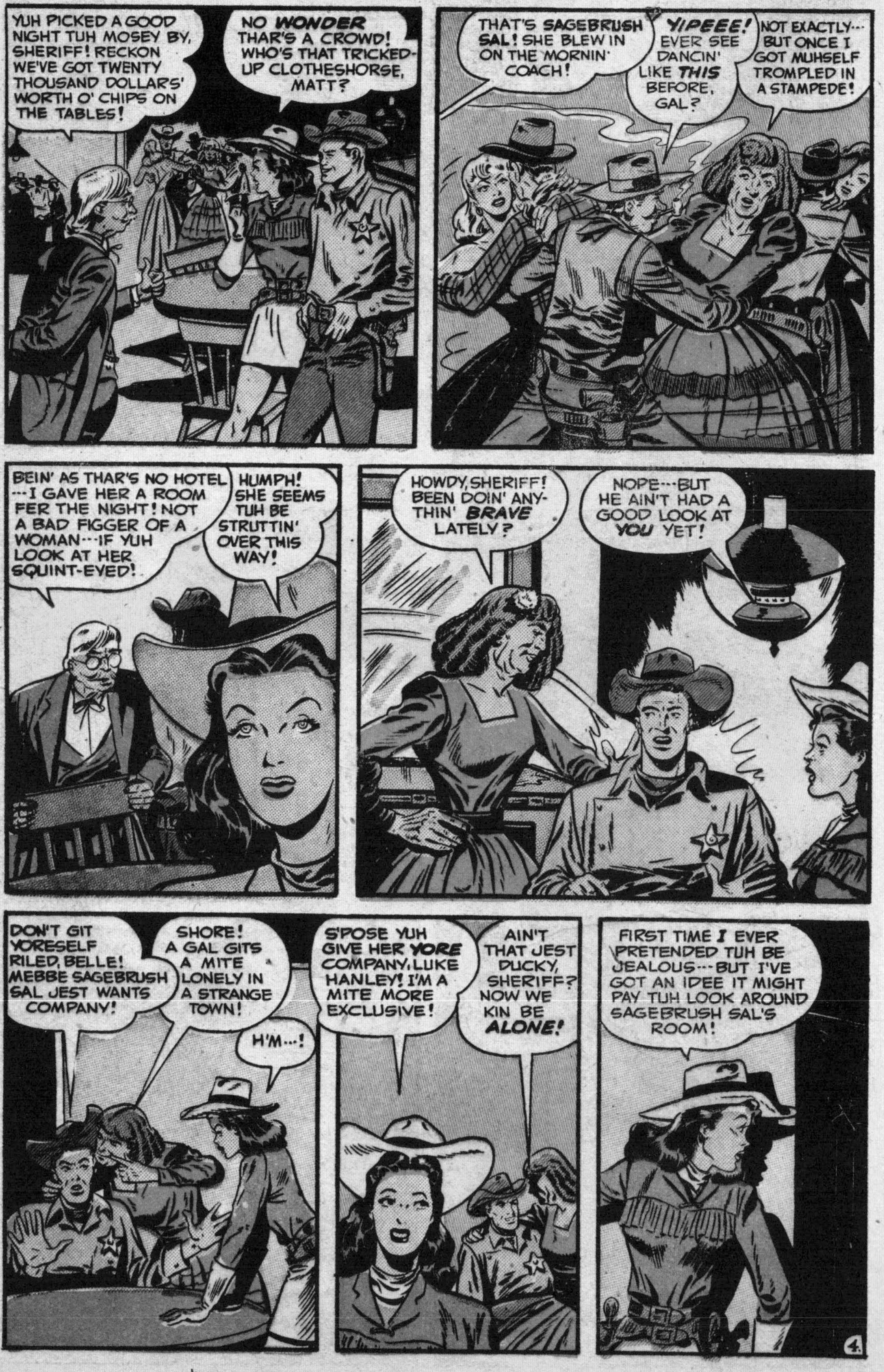
YUH PICKED A GOOD NIGHT TUH MOSEY BY, SHERIFF! RECKON WE'VE GOT TWENTY THOUSAND DOLLARS' WORTH O' CHIPS ON THE TABLES!
NO WONDER THAR'S A CROWD! WHO'S THAT TRICKED-UP CLOTHESHORSE, MATT?
THAT'S SAGEBRUSH SAL! SHE BLEW IN ON THE MORNIN' COACH!
YIPEEE! EVER SEE DANCIN' LIKE THIS BEFORE, GAL?
NOT EXACTLY... BUT ONCE I GOT MUHSELF TROMPLED IN A STAMPEDE!
BEIN' AS THAR'S NO HOTEL ...I GAVE HER A ROOM FER THE NIGHT! NOT A BAD FIGGER OF A WOMAN...IF YUH LOOK AT HER SQUINT-EYED!
HUMPH! SHE SEEMS TUH BE STRUTTIN' OVER THIS WAY!
HOWDY, SHERIFF! BEEN DOIN' ANYTHIN' BRAVE LATELY?
NOPE...BUT HE AIN'T HAD A GOOD LOOK AT YOU YET!
DON'T GIT YORESELF RILED, BELLE! MEBBE SAGEBRUSH SAL JEST WANTS COMPANY!
SHORE! A GAL GITS A MITE LONELY IN A STRANGE TOWN!
H'M...!
S'POSE YUH GIVE HER YORE COMPANY, LUKE HANLEY! I'M A MITE MORE EXCLUSIVE!
AIN'T THAT JEST DUCKY, SHERIFF? NOW WE KIN BE ALONE!
FIRST TIME I EVER PRETENDED TUH BE JEALOUS...BUT I'VE GOT AN IDEE IT MIGHT PAY TUH LOOK AROUND SAGEBRUSH SAL'S ROOM!
4.

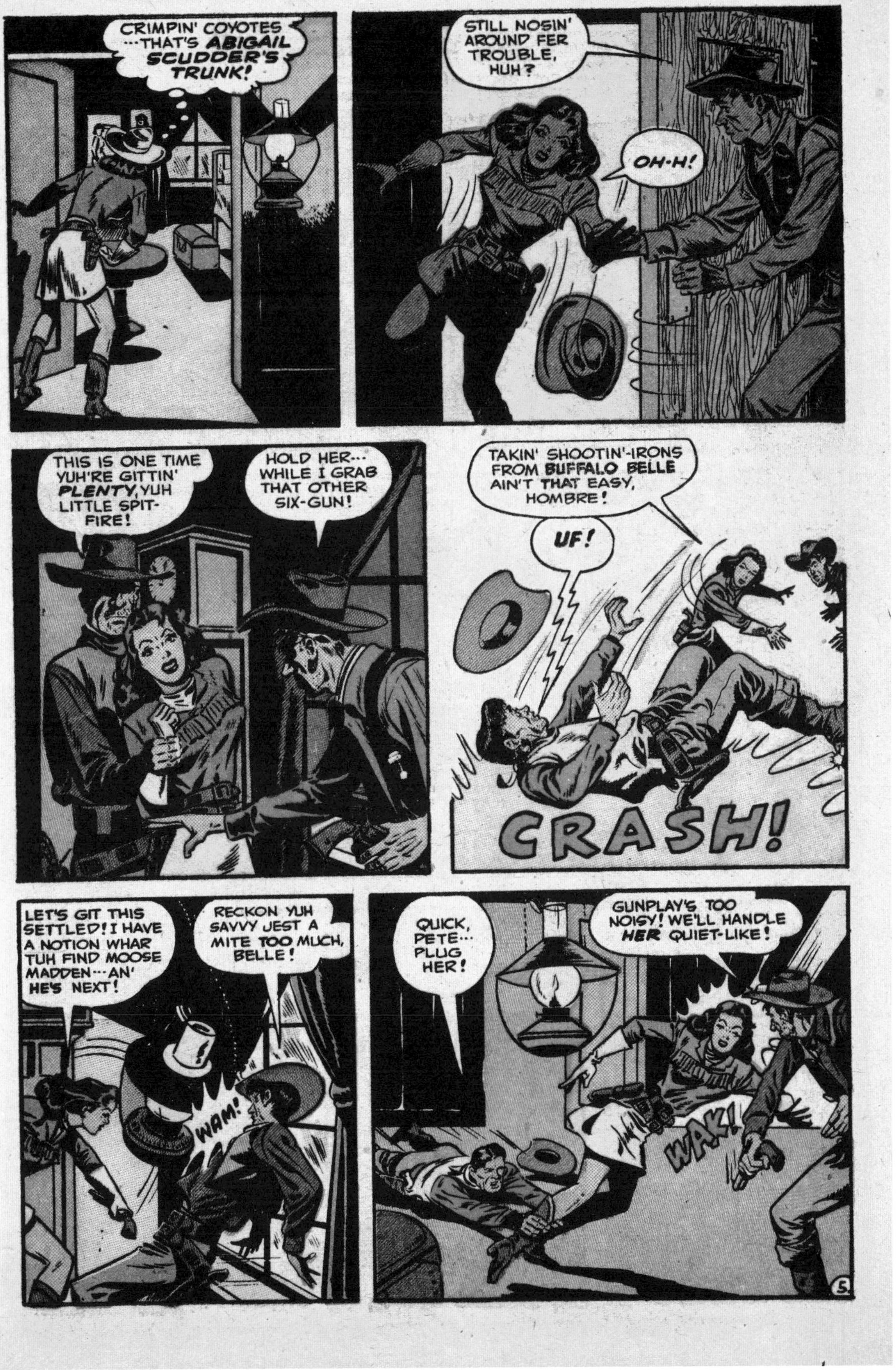
CRIMPIN' COYOTES ...THAT'S ABIGAIL SCUDDER'S TRUNK!
STILL NOSIN' AROUND FER TROUBLE, HUH?
OH-H!
THIS IS ONE TIME YUH'RE GITTIN' PLENTY, YUH LITTLE SPIT-FIRE!
HOLD HER... WHILE I GRAB THAT OTHER SIX-GUN!
TAKIN' SHOOTIN'-IRONS FROM BUFFALO BELLE AIN'T THAT EASY, HOMBRE!
UF!
CRASH!
LET'S GIT THIS SETTLED! I HAVE A NOTION WHAR TUH FIND MOOSE MADDEN... AN' HE'S NEXT!
RECKON YUH SAVVY JEST A MITE TOO MUCH, BELLE!
WAM!
QUICK, PETE... PLUG HER!
GUNPLAY'S TOO NOISY! WE'LL HANDLE HER QUIET-LIKE!
WAK!
5

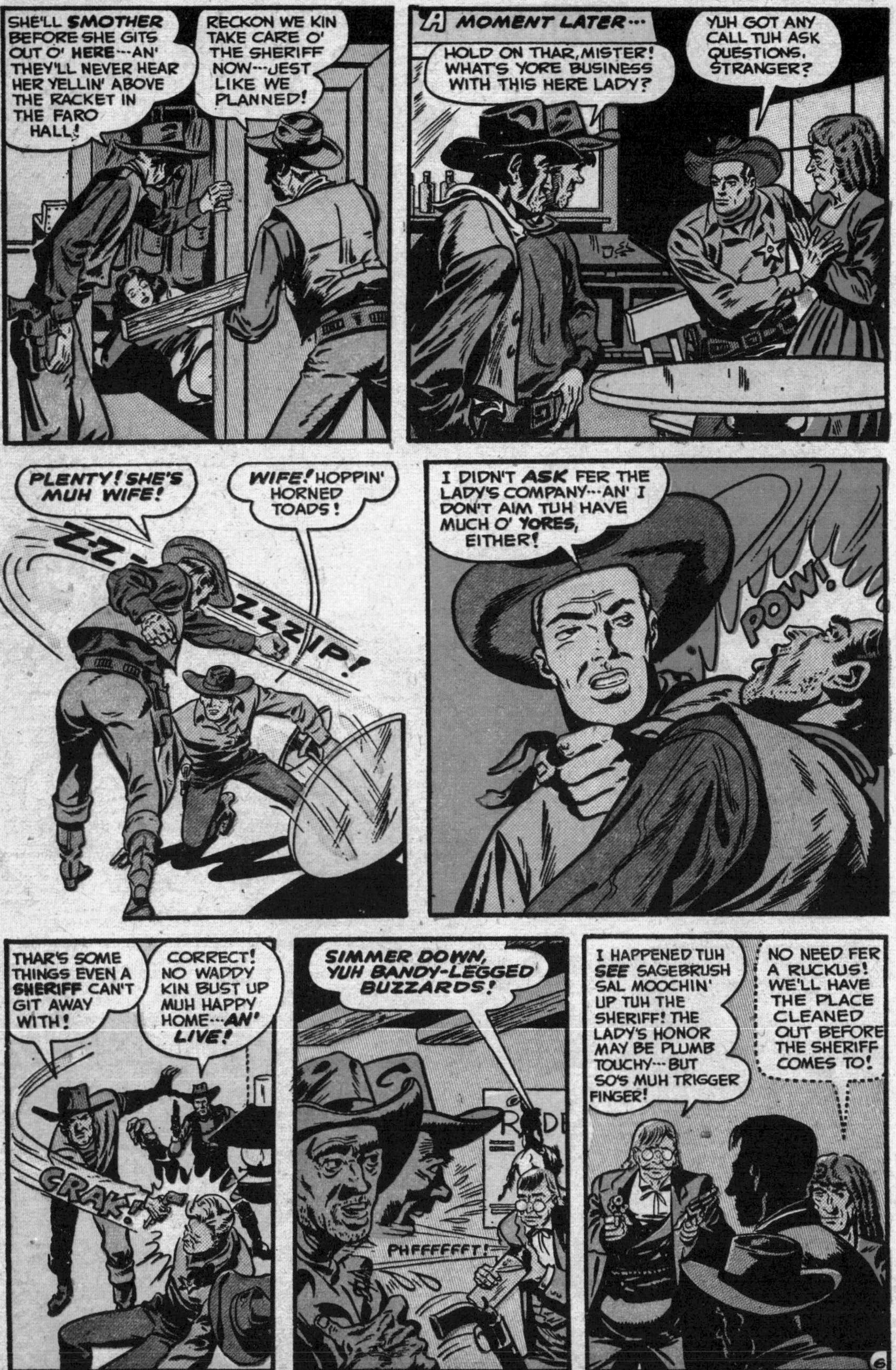

SHE'LL SMOTHER BEFORE SHE GITS OUT O' HERE---AN' THEY'LL NEVER HEAR HER YELLIN' ABOVE THE RACKET IN THE FARO HALL!
RECKON WE KIN TAKE CARE O' THE SHERIFF NOW---JEST LIKE WE PLANNED!
A MOMENT LATER---
HOLD ON THAR, MISTER! WHAT'S YORE BUSINESS WITH THIS HERE LADY?
YUH GOT ANY CALL TUH ASK QUESTIONS, STRANGER?
PLENTY! SHE'S MUH WIFE!
WIFE! HOPPIN' HORNED TOADS!
Z-Z-ZZZZIP!
I DIDN'T ASK FER THE LADY'S COMPANY---AN' I DON'T AIM TUH HAVE MUCH O' YORES, EITHER!
POW!
THAR'S SOME THINGS EVEN A SHERIFF CAN'T GIT AWAY WITH!
CORRECT! NO WADDY KIN BUST UP MUH HAPPY HOME---AN' LIVE!
CRAK!
SIMMER DOWN, YUH BANDY-LEGGED BUZZARDS!
PHFFFFFFT!
I HAPPENED TUH SEE SAGEBRUSH SAL MOOCHIN' UP TUH THE SHERIFF! THE LADY'S HONOR MAY BE PLUMB TOUCHY---BUT SO'S MUH TRIGGER FINGER!
NO NEED FER A RUCKUS! WE'LL HAVE THE PLACE CLEANED OUT BEFORE THE SHERIFF COMES TO!
6

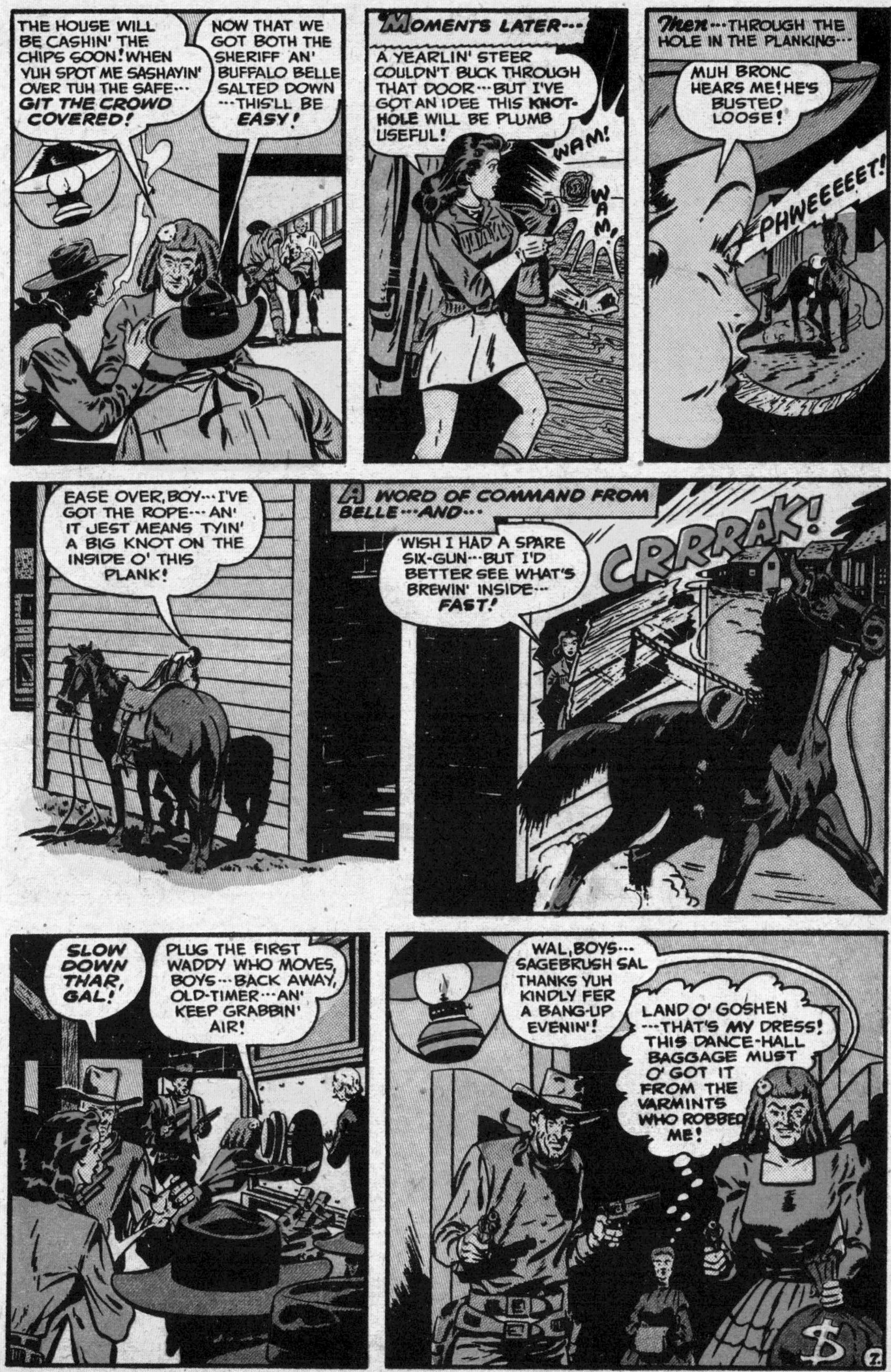
THE HOUSE WILL BE CASHIN' THE CHIPS SOON! WHEN YUH SPOT ME SASHAYIN' OVER TUH THE SAFE--- GIT THE CROWD COVERED!
NOW THAT WE GOT BOTH THE SHERIFF AN' BUFFALO BELLE SALTED DOWN ---THIS'LL BE EASY!
MOMENTS LATER---
A YEARLIN' STEER COULDN'T BUCK THROUGH THAT DOOR---BUT I'VE GOT AN IDEE THIS KNOT-HOLE WILL BE PLUMB USEFUL!
WAM!
WAM!
THEN---THROUGH THE HOLE IN THE PLANKING---
MUH BRONC HEARS ME! HE'S BUSTED LOOSE!
PHWEEEEEET!
EASE OVER, BOY---I'VE GOT THE ROPE---AN' IT JEST MEANS TYIN' A BIG KNOT ON THE INSIDE O' THIS PLANK!
A WORD OF COMMAND FROM BELLE---AND---
CRRRAK!
WISH I HAD A SPARE SIX-GUN---BUT I'D BETTER SEE WHAT'S BREWIN' INSIDE--- FAST!
SLOW DOWN THAR, GAL!
PLUG THE FIRST WADDY WHO MOVES, BOYS---BACK AWAY, OLD-TIMER---AN' KEEP GRABBIN' AIR!
WAL, BOYS--- SAGEBRUSH SAL THANKS YUH KINDLY FER A BANG-UP EVENIN'!
LAND O' GOSHEN ---THAT'S MY DRESS! THIS DANCE-HALL BAGGAGE MUST O' GOT IT FROM THE VARMINTS WHO ROBBED ME!
$
7.

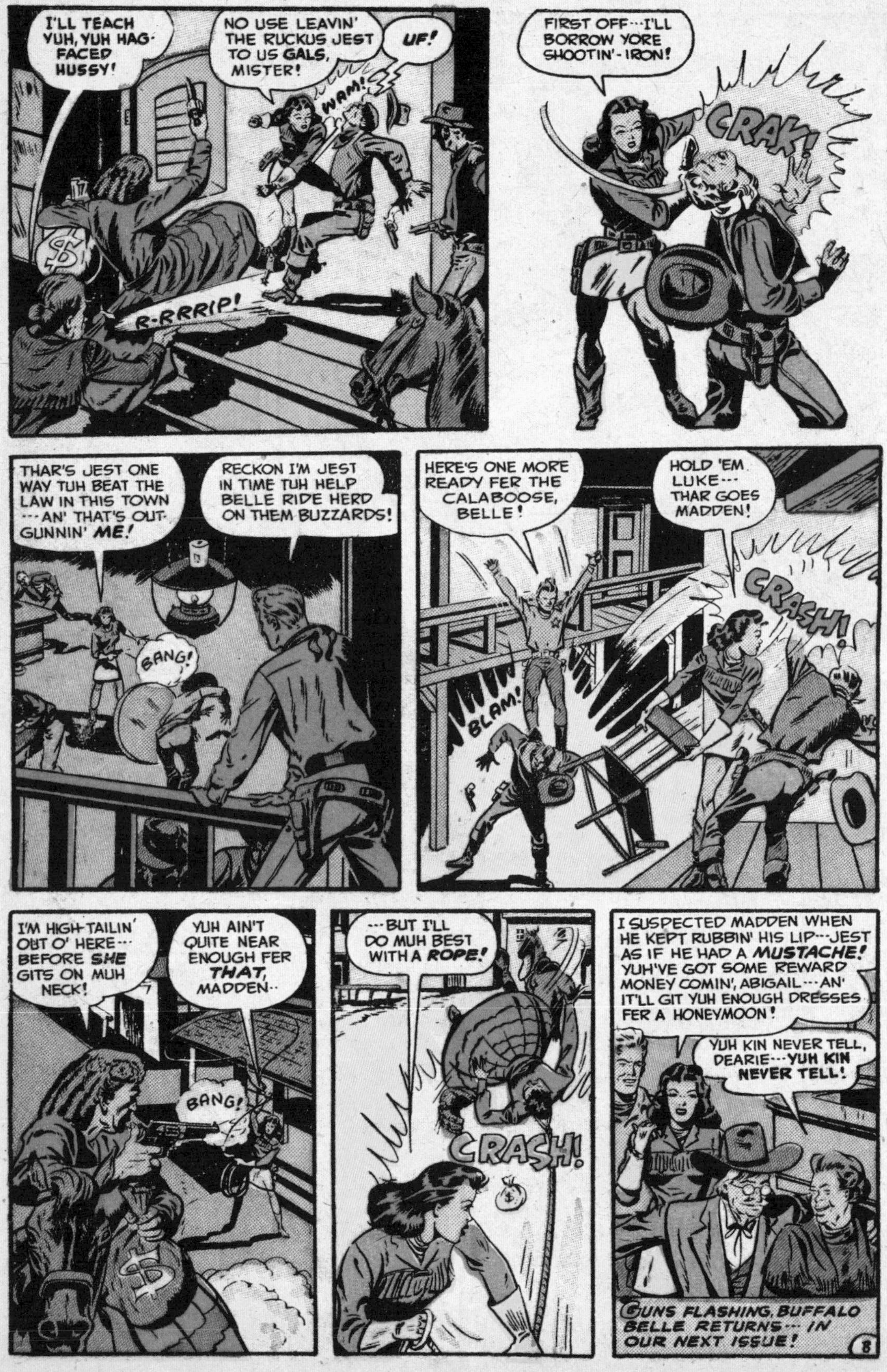

I'LL TEACH YUH, YUH HAG-FACED HUSSY!
NO USE LEAVIN' THE RUCKUS JEST TO US GALS, MISTER!
UF!
WAM!
R-RRRIP!
FIRST OFF---I'LL BORROW YORE SHOOTIN'-IRON!
CRAK!
THAR'S JEST ONE WAY TUH BEAT THE LAW IN THIS TOWN ---AN' THAT'S OUT-GUNNIN' ME!
RECKON I'M JEST IN TIME TUH HELP BELLE RIDE HERD ON THEM BUZZARDS!
BANG!
HERE'S ONE MORE READY FER THE CALABOOSE, BELLE!
HOLD 'EM LUKE--- THAR GOES MADDEN!
CRASH!
BLAM!
I'M HIGH-TAILIN' OUT O' HERE--- BEFORE SHE GITS ON MUH NECK!
YUH AIN'T QUITE NEAR ENOUGH FER THAT, MADDEN--
BANG!
---BUT I'LL DO MUH BEST WITH A ROPE!
CRASH!
I SUSPECTED MADDEN WHEN HE KEPT RUBBIN' HIS LIP---JEST AS IF HE HAD A MUSTACHE! YUH'VE GOT SOME REWARD MONEY COMIN', ABIGAIL---AN' IT'LL GIT YUH ENOUGH DRESSES FER A HONEYMOON!
YUH KIN NEVER TELL, DEARIE---YUH KIN NEVER TELL!
GUNS FLASHING, BUFFALO BELLE RETURNS--- IN OUR NEXT ISSUE!
8

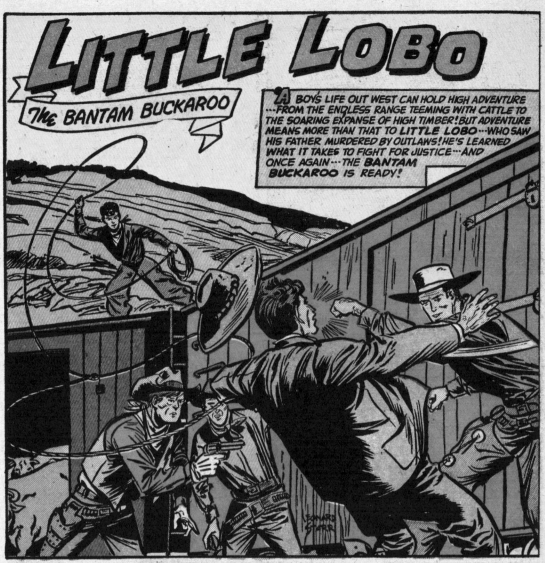

LITTLE LOBO

The BANTAM BUCKAROO

A BOYS LIFE OUT WEST CAN HOLD HIGH ADVENTURE ---FROM THE ENDLESS RANGE TEEMING WITH CATTLE TO THE SOARING EXPANSE OF HIGH TIMBER! BUT ADVENTURE MEANS MORE THAN THAT TO *LITTLE LOBO*---WHO SAW HIS FATHER MURDERED BY OUTLAWS! HE'S LEARNED WHAT IT TAKES TO FIGHT FOR JUSTICE---AND ONCE AGAIN---THE *BANTAM BUCKAROO* IS READY!

I GOT A MITE O' BUYIN' TUH DO! MIND YUH DON'T KICK UP ANY RUCKUS, LOBO!

YUH KNOW I NEVER **START** NOTHIN', MIKE! I'LL JEST MOSEY AROUND AN' TAKE IN THE SIGHTS!

SILVER

MINUTES LATER---

CRIMPERS! THAT WADDY IS SHORE SCORCHIN' THE DUST!

FLOOD WATER'S BUSTED LOOSE UP THAR! GIT TUH HIGH GROUND!

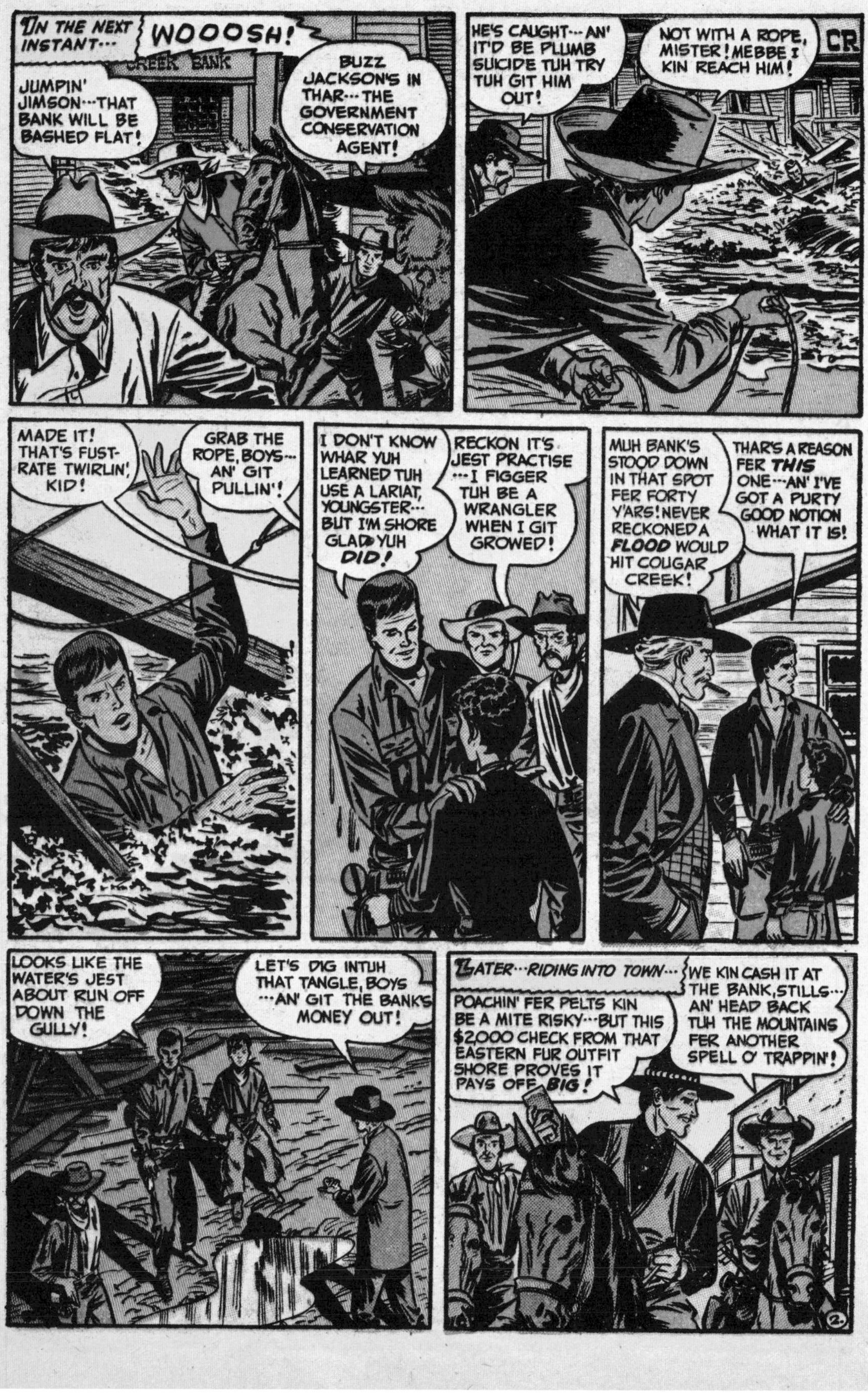

IN THE NEXT INSTANT...
WOOOSH!
CREEK BANK
JUMPIN' JIMSON...THAT BANK WILL BE BASHED FLAT!
BUZZ JACKSON'S IN THAR... THE GOVERNMENT CONSERVATION AGENT!
HE'S CAUGHT... AN' IT'D BE PLUMB SUICIDE TUH TRY TUH GIT HIM OUT!
NOT WITH A ROPE, MISTER! MEBBE I KIN REACH HIM!
CR
MADE IT! THAT'S FUST-RATE TWIRLIN', KID!
GRAB THE ROPE, BOYS... AN' GIT PULLIN'!
I DON'T KNOW WHAR YUH LEARNED TUH USE A LARIAT, YOUNGSTER... BUT I'M SHORE GLAD YUH DID!
RECKON IT'S JEST PRACTISE... I FIGGER TUH BE A WRANGLER WHEN I GIT GROWED!
MUH BANK'S STOOD DOWN IN THAT SPOT FER FORTY Y'ARS! NEVER RECKONED A FLOOD WOULD HIT COUGAR CREEK!
THAR'S A REASON FER THIS ONE... AN' I'VE GOT A PURTY GOOD NOTION WHAT IT IS!
LOOKS LIKE THE WATER'S JEST ABOUT RUN OFF DOWN THE GULLY!
LET'S DIG INTUH THAT TANGLE, BOYS ...AN' GIT THE BANK'S MONEY OUT!
LATER...RIDING INTO TOWN...
POACHIN' FER PELTS KIN BE A MITE RISKY...BUT THIS $2,000 CHECK FROM THAT EASTERN FUR OUTFIT SHORE PROVES IT PAYS OFF BIG!
WE KIN CASH IT AT THE BANK, STILLS... AN' HEAD BACK TUH THE MOUNTAINS FER ANOTHER SPELL O' TRAPPIN'!
2.

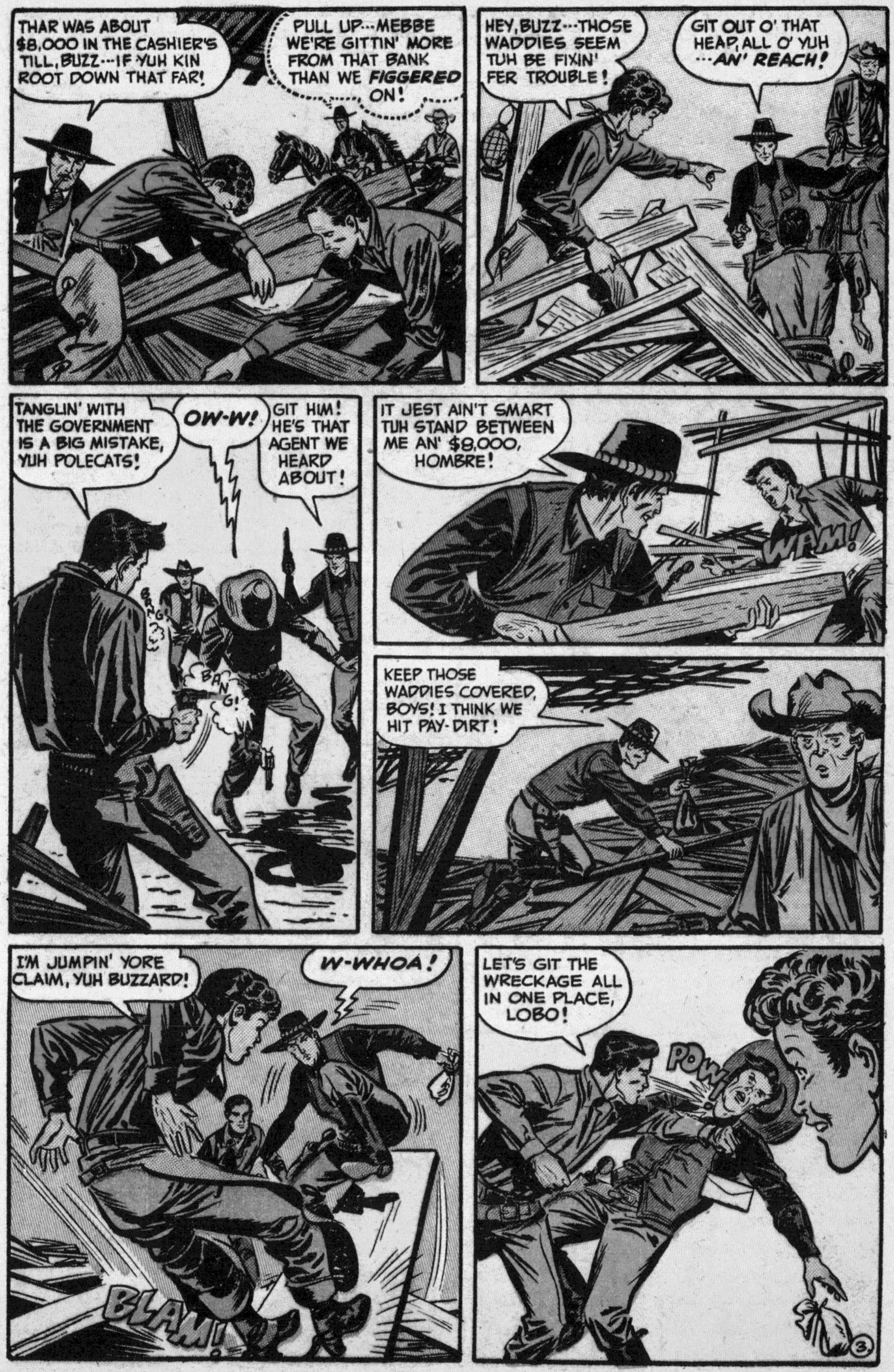
THAR WAS ABOUT $8,000 IN THE CASHIER'S TILL, BUZZ---IF YUH KIN ROOT DOWN THAT FAR!
PULL UP---MEBBE WE'RE GITTIN' MORE FROM THAT BANK THAN WE FIGGERED ON!
HEY, BUZZ---THOSE WADDIES SEEM TUH BE FIXIN' FER TROUBLE!
GIT OUT O' THAT HEAP, ALL O' YUH ---AN' REACH!
TANGLIN' WITH THE GOVERNMENT IS A BIG MISTAKE, YUH POLECATS!
OW-W!
GIT HIM! HE'S THAT AGENT WE HEARD ABOUT!
BANG!
BANG!
IT JEST AIN'T SMART TUH STAND BETWEEN ME AN' $8,000, HOMBRE!
WAM!
KEEP THOSE WADDIES COVERED, BOYS! I THINK WE HIT PAY-DIRT!
I'M JUMPIN' YORE CLAIM, YUH BUZZARD!
W-WHOA!
BLAM!
LET'S GIT THE WRECKAGE ALL IN ONE PLACE, LOBO!
POW!
3

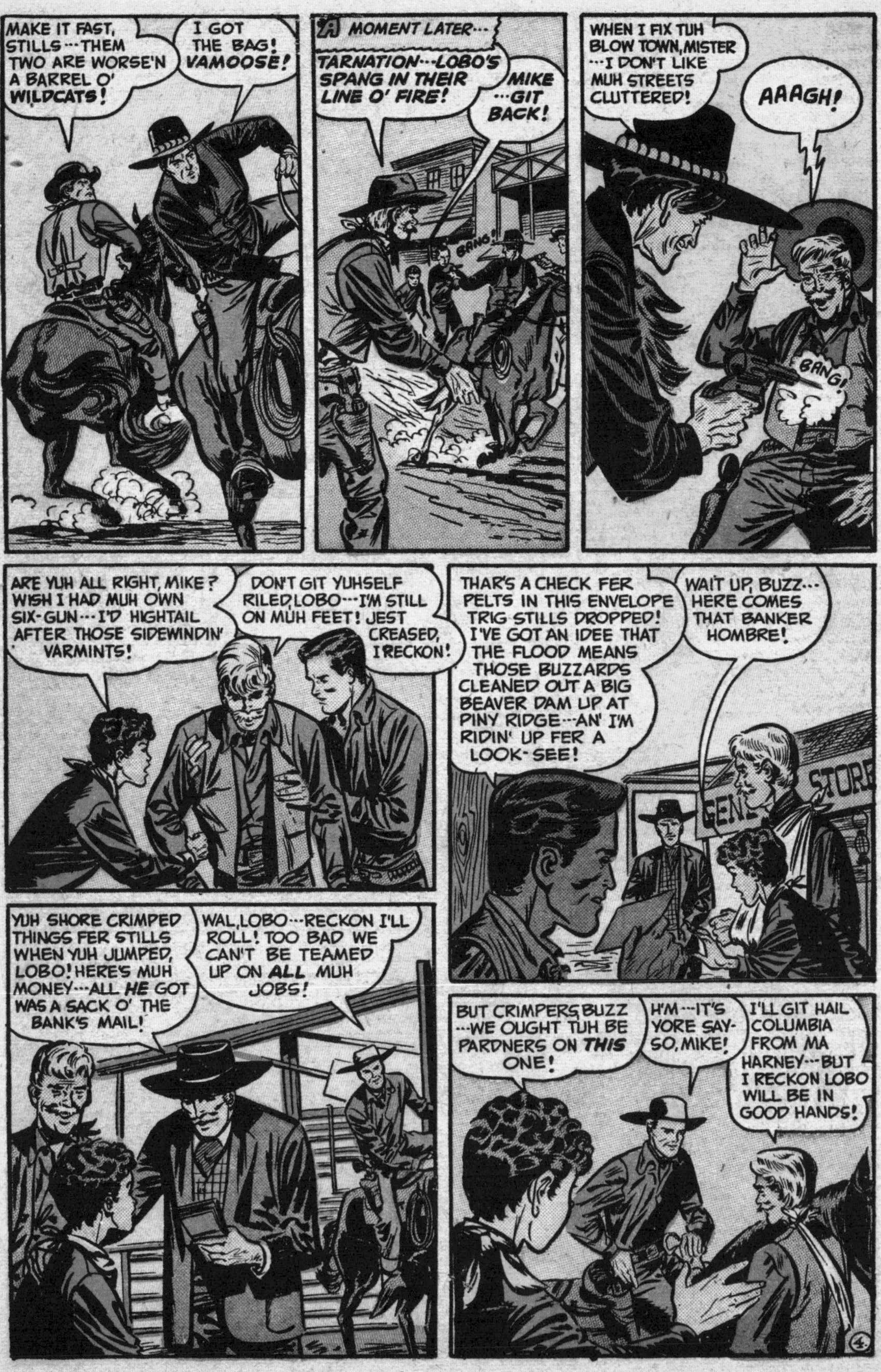

MAKE IT FAST, STILLS---THEM TWO ARE WORSE'N A BARREL O' WILDCATS!
I GOT THE BAG! VAMOOSE!
A MOMENT LATER---
TARNATION---LOBO'S SPANG IN THEIR LINE O' FIRE!
MIKE ---GIT BACK!
BANG
WHEN I FIX TUH BLOW TOWN, MISTER ---I DON'T LIKE MUH STREETS CLUTTERED!
AAAGH!
BANG!
ARE YUH ALL RIGHT, MIKE? WISH I HAD MUH OWN SIX-GUN---I'D HIGHTAIL AFTER THOSE SIDEWINDIN' VARMINTS!
DON'T GIT YUHSELF RILED, LOBO---I'M STILL ON MUH FEET! JEST CREASED, I RECKON!
THAR'S A CHECK FER PELTS IN THIS ENVELOPE TRIG STILLS DROPPED! I'VE GOT AN IDEE THAT THE FLOOD MEANS THOSE BUZZARDS CLEANED OUT A BIG BEAVER DAM UP AT PINY RIDGE---AN' I'M RIDIN' UP FER A LOOK-SEE!
WAIT UP, BUZZ--- HERE COMES THAT BANKER HOMBRE!
STORE
YUH SHORE CRIMPED THINGS FER STILLS WHEN YUH JUMPED, LOBO! HERE'S MUH MONEY---ALL HE GOT WAS A SACK O' THE BANK'S MAIL!
WAL, LOBO---RECKON I'LL ROLL! TOO BAD WE CAN'T BE TEAMED UP ON ALL MUH JOBS!
BUT CRIMPERS, BUZZ ---WE OUGHT TUH BE PARDNERS ON THIS ONE!
H'M---IT'S YORE SAY-SO, MIKE!
I'LL GIT HAIL COLUMBIA FROM MA HARNEY---BUT I RECKON LOBO WILL BE IN GOOD HANDS!
4.

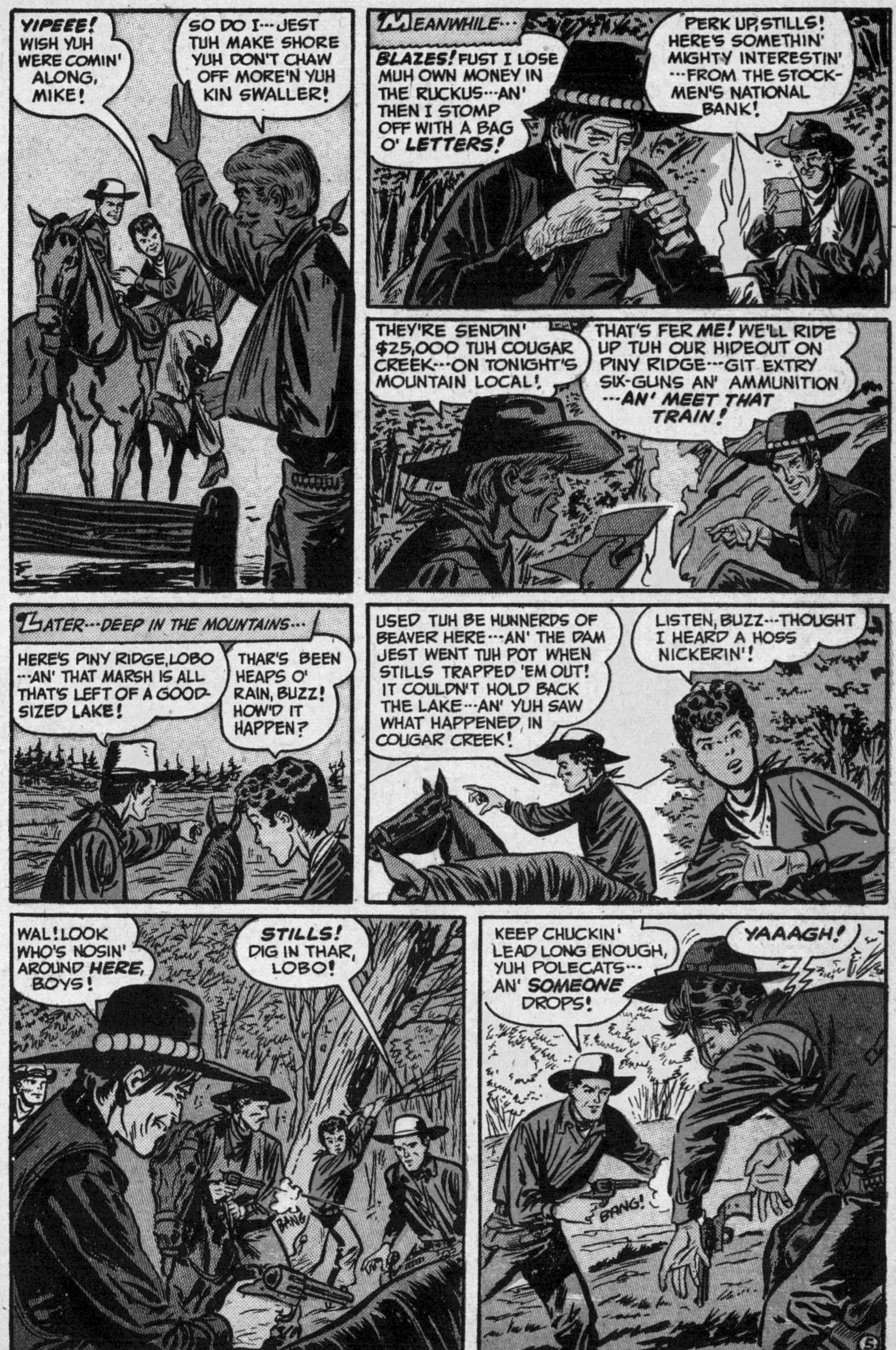
YIPEEE! WISH YUH WERE COMIN' ALONG, MIKE!
SO DO I---JEST TUH MAKE SHORE YUH DON'T CHAW OFF MORE'N YUH KIN SWALLER!
MEANWHILE---
BLAZES! FUST I LOSE MUH OWN MONEY IN THE RUCKUS---AN' THEN I STOMP OFF WITH A BAG O' LETTERS!
PERK UP, STILLS! HERE'S SOMETHIN' MIGHTY INTERESTIN' ---FROM THE STOCKMEN'S NATIONAL BANK!
THEY'RE SENDIN' $25,000 TUH COUGAR CREEK---ON TONIGHT'S MOUNTAIN LOCAL!
THAT'S FER ME! WE'LL RIDE UP TUH OUR HIDEOUT ON PINY RIDGE---GIT EXTRY SIX-GUNS AN' AMMUNITION ---AN' MEET THAT TRAIN!
LATER---DEEP IN THE MOUNTAINS---
HERE'S PINY RIDGE, LOBO ---AN' THAT MARSH IS ALL THAT'S LEFT OF A GOOD-SIZED LAKE!
THAR'S BEEN HEAPS O' RAIN, BUZZ! HOW'D IT HAPPEN?
USED TUH BE HUNNERDS OF BEAVER HERE---AN' THE DAM JEST WENT TUH POT WHEN STILLS TRAPPED 'EM OUT! IT COULDN'T HOLD BACK THE LAKE---AN' YUH SAW WHAT HAPPENED IN COUGAR CREEK!
LISTEN, BUZZ---THOUGHT I HEARD A HOSS NICKERIN'!
WAL! LOOK WHO'S NOSIN' AROUND HERE, BOYS!
STILLS! DIG IN THAR, LOBO!
BANG
KEEP CHUCKIN' LEAD LONG ENOUGH, YUH POLECATS--- AN' SOMEONE DROPS!
YAAAGH!
BANG!
5

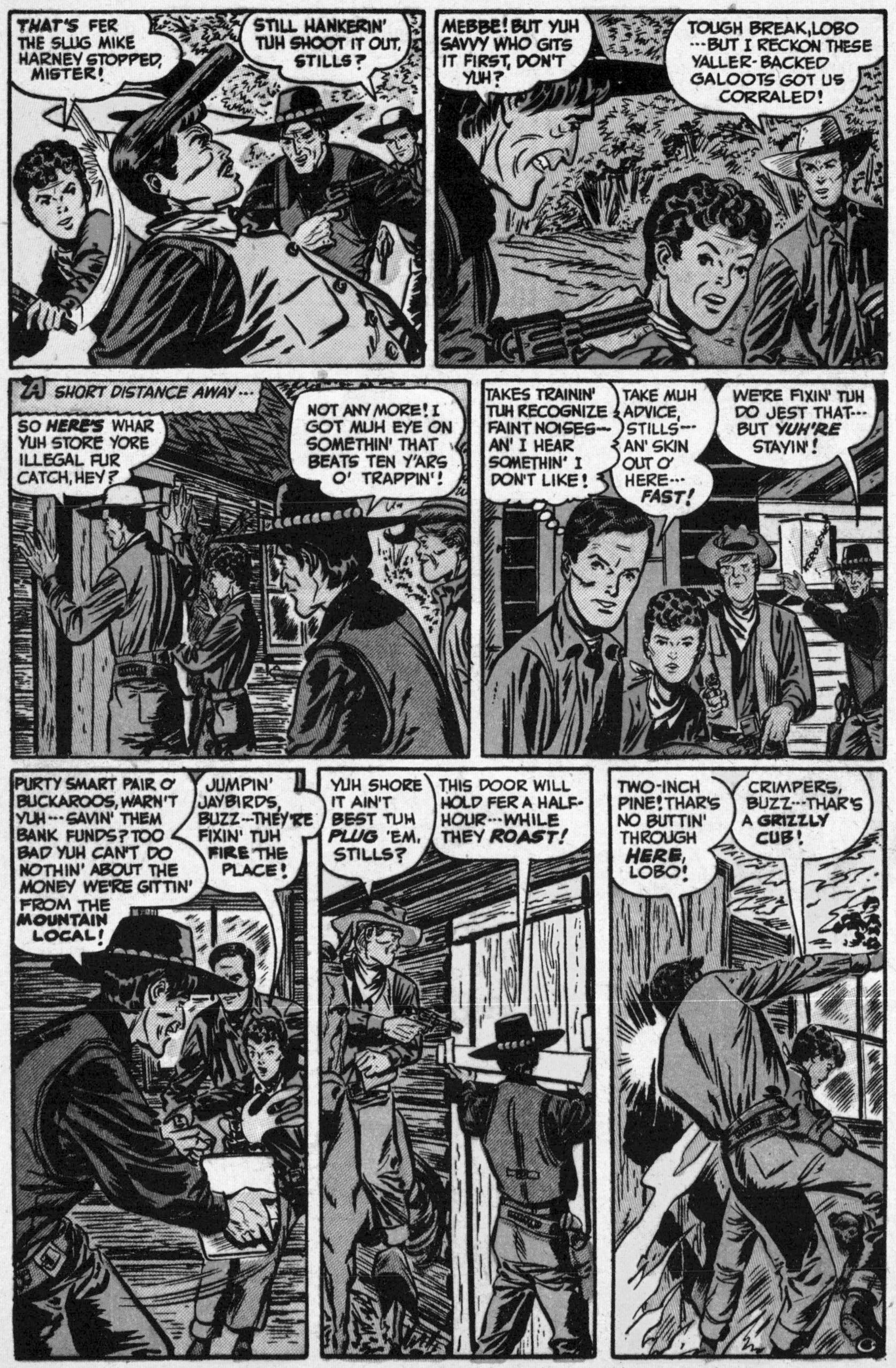
THAT'S FER THE SLUG MIKE HARNEY STOPPED, MISTER!
STILL HANKERIN' TUH SHOOT IT OUT, STILLS?
MEBBE! BUT YUH SAVVY WHO GITS IT FIRST, DON'T YUH?
TOUGH BREAK, LOBO ---BUT I RECKON THESE YALLER-BACKED GALOOTS GOT US CORRALED!
A SHORT DISTANCE AWAY---
SO HERE'S WHAR YUH STORE YORE ILLEGAL FUR CATCH, HEY?
NOT ANY MORE! I GOT MUH EYE ON SOMETHIN' THAT BEATS TEN Y'ARS O' TRAPPIN'!
TAKES TRAININ' TUH RECOGNIZE FAINT NOISES--- AN' I HEAR SOMETHIN' I DON'T LIKE!
TAKE MUH ADVICE, STILLS--- AN' SKIN OUT O' HERE--- FAST!
WE'RE FIXIN' TUH DO JEST THAT--- BUT YUH'RE STAYIN'!
PURTY SMART PAIR O' BUCKAROOS, WARN'T YUH---SAVIN' THEM BANK FUNDS? TOO BAD YUH CAN'T DO NOTHIN' ABOUT THE MONEY WE'RE GITTIN' FROM THE MOUNTAIN LOCAL!
JUMPIN' JAYBIRDS, BUZZ--THEY'RE FIXIN' TUH FIRE THE PLACE!
YUH SHORE IT AIN'T BEST TUH PLUG 'EM, STILLS?
THIS DOOR WILL HOLD FER A HALF-HOUR---WHILE THEY ROAST!
TWO-INCH PINE! THAR'S NO BUTTIN' THROUGH HERE, LOBO!
CRIMPERS, BUZZ---THAR'S A GRIZZLY CUB!

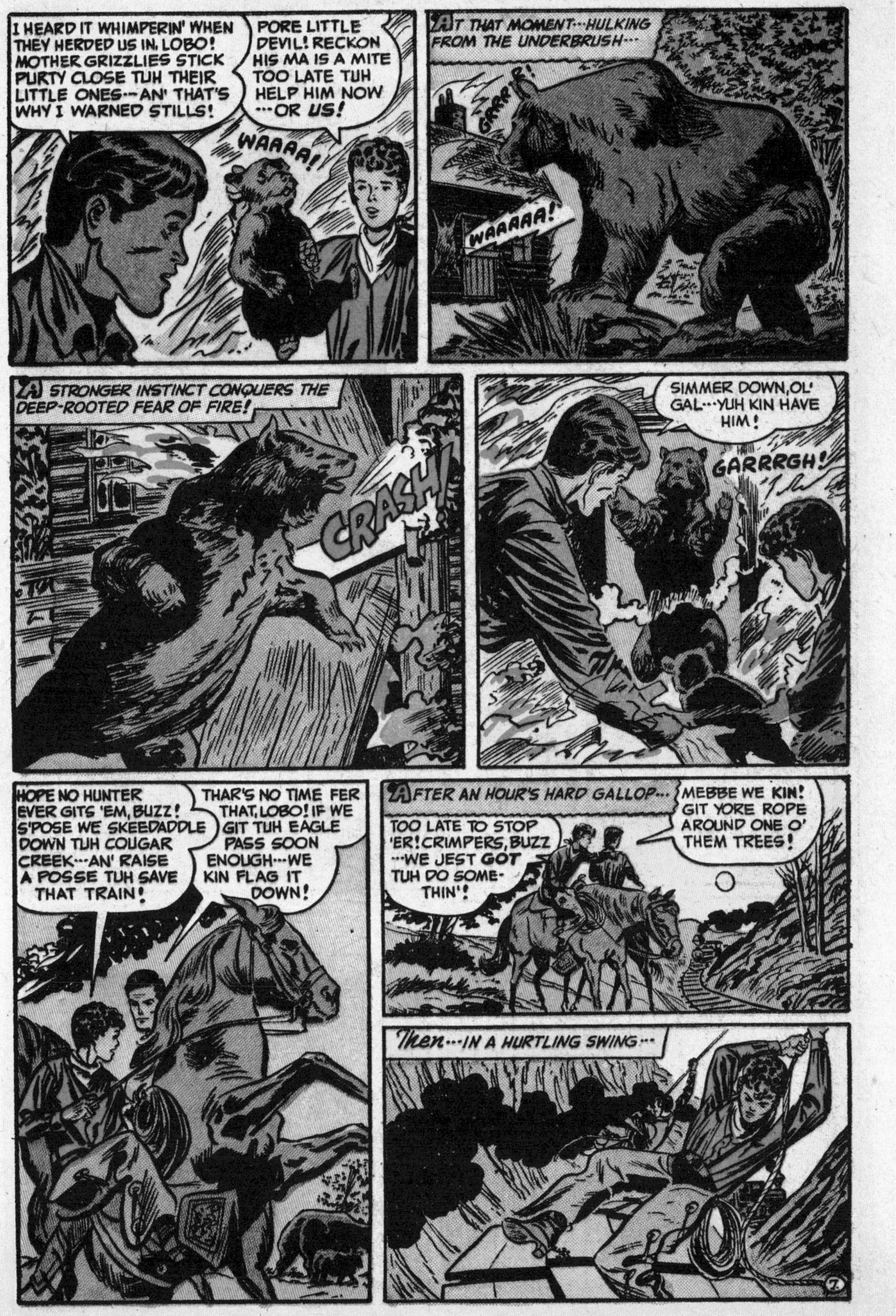
I HEARD IT WHIMPERIN' WHEN THEY HERDED US IN, LOBO! MOTHER GRIZZLIES STICK PURTY CLOSE TUH THEIR LITTLE ONES--AN' THAT'S WHY I WARNED STILLS!
PORE LITTLE DEVIL! RECKON HIS MA IS A MITE TOO LATE TUH HELP HIM NOW ...OR US!
WAAAA!
AT THAT MOMENT...HULKING FROM THE UNDERBRUSH...
GRRR-R!
WAAAAA!
A STRONGER INSTINCT CONQUERS THE DEEP-ROOTED FEAR OF FIRE!
CRASH!
SIMMER DOWN, OL' GAL...YUH KIN HAVE HIM!
GARRRGH!
HOPE NO HUNTER EVER GITS 'EM, BUZZ! S'POSE WE SKEEDADDLE DOWN TUH COUGAR CREEK...AN' RAISE A POSSE TUH SAVE THAT TRAIN!
THAR'S NO TIME FER THAT, LOBO! IF WE GIT TUH EAGLE PASS SOON ENOUGH...WE KIN FLAG IT DOWN!
AFTER AN HOUR'S HARD GALLOP...
TOO LATE TO STOP 'ER! CRIMPERS, BUZZ ...WE JEST GOT TUH DO SOME-THIN'!
MEBBE WE KIN! GIT YORE ROPE AROUND ONE O' THEM TREES!
Then...IN A HURTLING SWING...
7

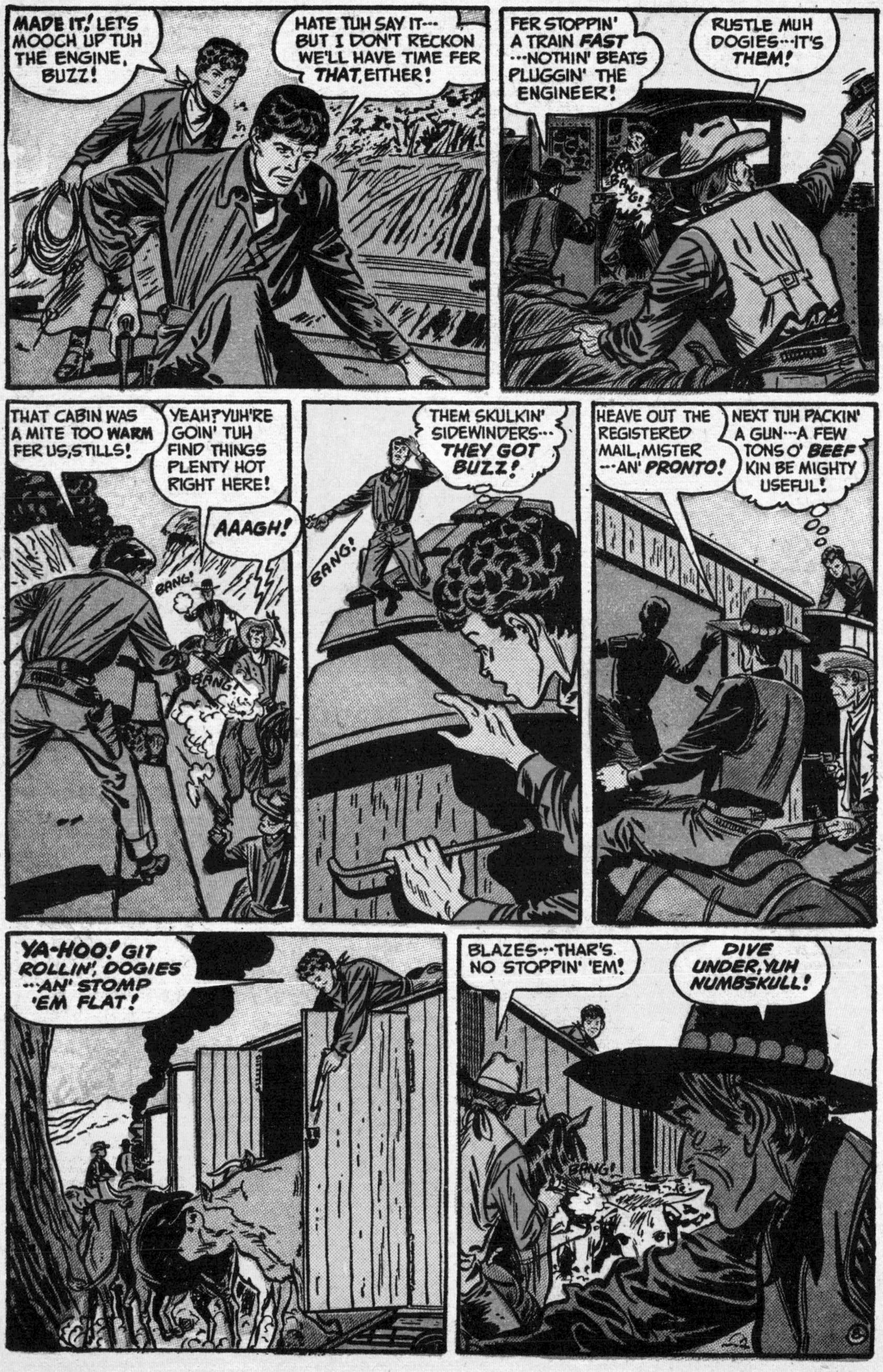
MADE IT! LET'S MOOCH UP TUH THE ENGINE, BUZZ!
HATE TUH SAY IT--- BUT I DON'T RECKON WE'LL HAVE TIME FER THAT, EITHER!
FER STOPPIN' A TRAIN FAST ---NOTHIN' BEATS PLUGGIN' THE ENGINEER!
RUSTLE MUH DOGIES---IT'S THEM!
BANG!
THAT CABIN WAS A MITE TOO WARM FER US, STILLS!
YEAH? YUH'RE GOIN' TUH FIND THINGS PLENTY HOT RIGHT HERE!
AAAGH!
BANG!
BANG!
THEM SKULKIN' SIDEWINDERS--- THEY GOT BUZZ!
BANG!
HEAVE OUT THE REGISTERED MAIL, MISTER ---AN' PRONTO!
NEXT TUH PACKIN' A GUN---A FEW TONS O' BEEF KIN BE MIGHTY USEFUL!
YA-HOO! GIT ROLLIN', DOGIES ---AN' STOMP 'EM FLAT!
BLAZES---THAR'S NO STOPPIN' 'EM!
DIVE UNDER, YUH NUMBSKULL!
BANG!

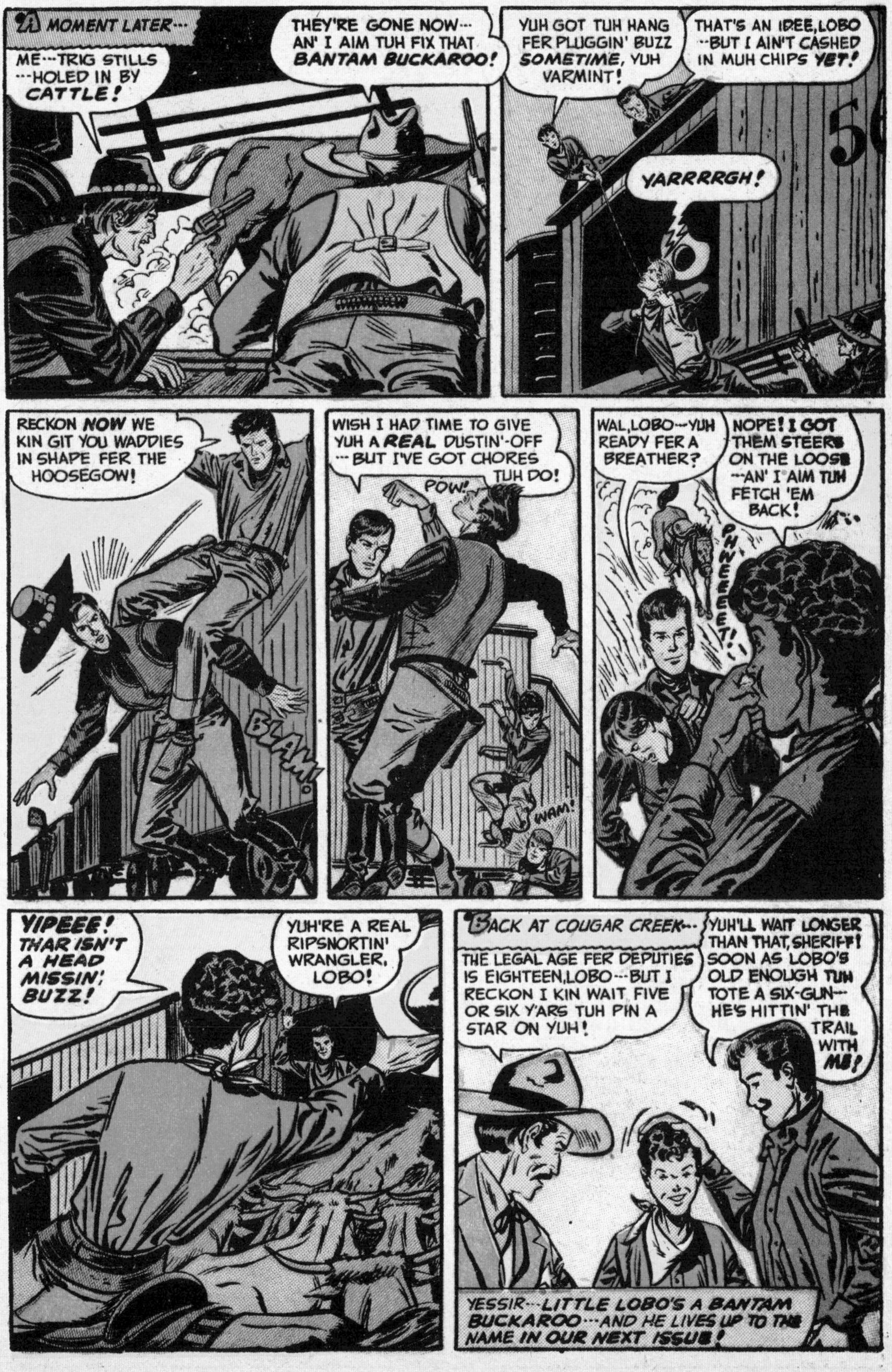
A MOMENT LATER---
ME---TRIG STILLS ---HOLED IN BY CATTLE!
THEY'RE GONE NOW--- AN' I AIM TUH FIX THAT BANTAM BUCKAROO!
YUH GOT TUH HANG FER PLUGGIN' BUZZ SOMETIME, YUH VARMINT!
THAT'S AN IDEE, LOBO --BUT I AIN'T CASHED IN MUH CHIPS YET!
YARRRRGH!
RECKON NOW WE KIN GIT YOU WADDIES IN SHAPE FER THE HOOSEGOW!
BLAM!
WISH I HAD TIME TO GIVE YUH A REAL DUSTIN'-OFF --- BUT I'VE GOT CHORES TUH DO!
POW!
WAM!
WAL, LOBO---YUH READY FER A BREATHER?
NOPE! I GOT THEM STEERS ON THE LOOSE --AN' I AIM TUH FETCH 'EM BACK!
PHWEEEEET!
YIPEEE! THAR ISN'T A HEAD MISSIN', BUZZ!
YUH'RE A REAL RIPSNORTIN' WRANGLER, LOBO!
BACK AT COUGAR CREEK---
THE LEGAL AGE FER DEPUTIES IS EIGHTEEN, LOBO---BUT I RECKON I KIN WAIT FIVE OR SIX Y'ARS TUH PIN A STAR ON YUH!
YUH'LL WAIT LONGER THAN THAT, SHERIFF! SOON AS LOBO'S OLD ENOUGH TUH TOTE A SIX-GUN--- HE'S HITTIN' THE TRAIL WITH ME!
YESSIR---LITTLE LOBO'S A BANTAM BUCKAROO---AND HE LIVES UP TO THE NAME IN OUR NEXT ISSUE!

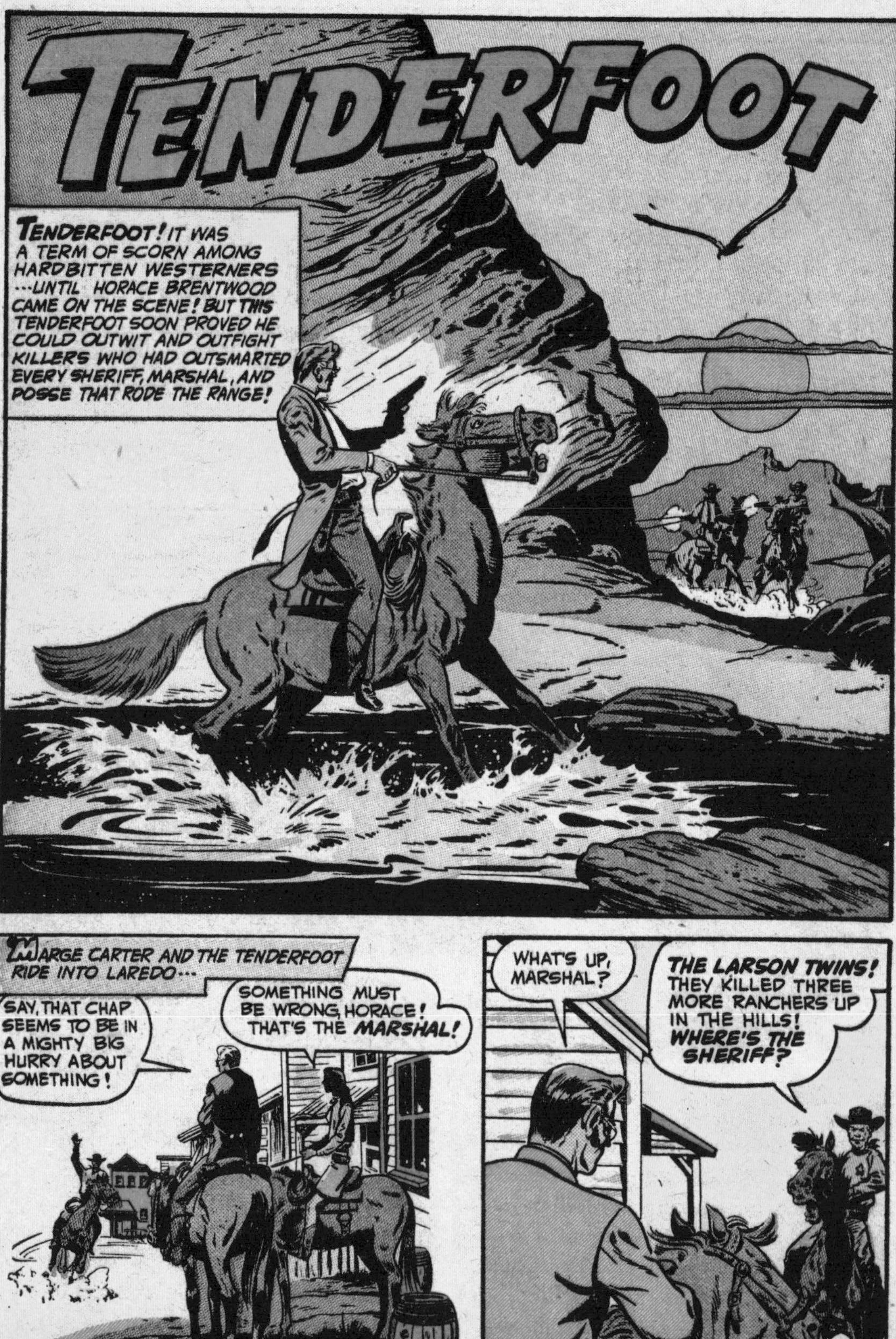

TENDERFOOT
TENDERFOOT! IT WAS A TERM OF SCORN AMONG HARDBITTEN WESTERNERS ...UNTIL HORACE BRENTWOOD CAME ON THE SCENE! BUT THIS TENDERFOOT SOON PROVED HE COULD OUTWIT AND OUTFIGHT KILLERS WHO HAD OUTSMARTED EVERY SHERIFF, MARSHAL, AND POSSE THAT RODE THE RANGE!
MARGE CARTER AND THE TENDERFOOT RIDE INTO LAREDO...
SAY, THAT CHAP SEEMS TO BE IN A MIGHTY BIG HURRY ABOUT SOMETHING!
SOMETHING MUST BE WRONG, HORACE! THAT'S THE MARSHAL!
WHAT'S UP, MARSHAL?
THE LARSON TWINS! THEY KILLED THREE MORE RANCHERS UP IN THE HILLS! WHERE'S THE SHERIFF?

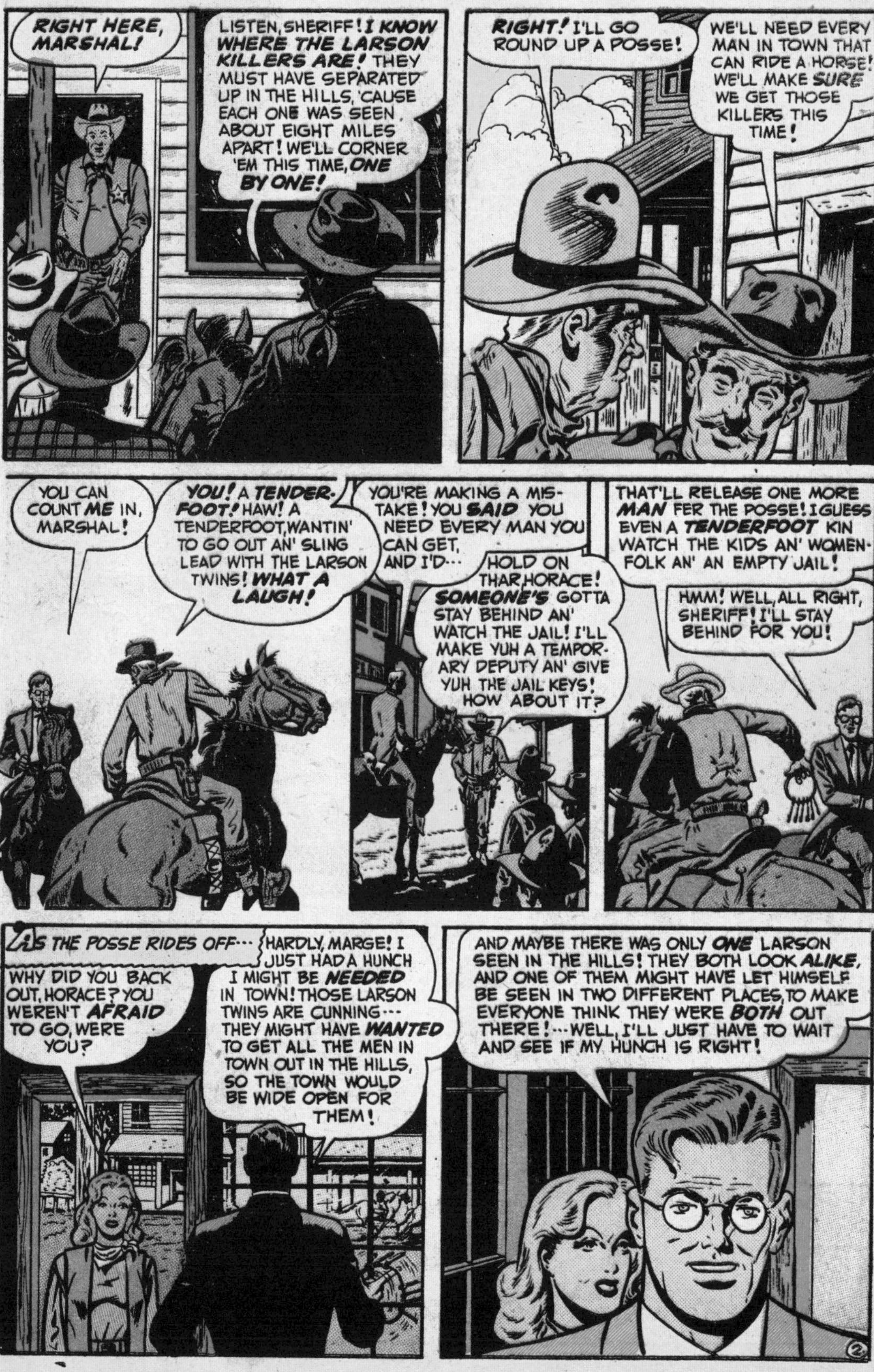
RIGHT HERE, MARSHAL!
LISTEN, SHERIFF! I KNOW WHERE THE LARSON KILLERS ARE! THEY MUST HAVE SEPARATED UP IN THE HILLS, 'CAUSE EACH ONE WAS SEEN ABOUT EIGHT MILES APART! WE'LL CORNER 'EM THIS TIME, ONE BY ONE!
RIGHT! I'LL GO ROUND UP A POSSE!
WE'LL NEED EVERY MAN IN TOWN THAT CAN RIDE A HORSE! WE'LL MAKE SURE WE GET THOSE KILLERS THIS TIME!
YOU CAN COUNT ME IN, MARSHAL!
YOU! A TENDERFOOT! HAW! A TENDERFOOT, WANTIN' TO GO OUT AN' SLING LEAD WITH THE LARSON TWINS! WHAT A LAUGH!
YOU'RE MAKING A MISTAKE! YOU SAID YOU NEED EVERY MAN YOU CAN GET, AND I'D---
HOLD ON THAR, HORACE! SOMEONE'S GOTTA STAY BEHIND AN' WATCH THE JAIL! I'LL MAKE YUH A TEMPORARY DEPUTY AN' GIVE YUH THE JAIL KEYS! HOW ABOUT IT?
THAT'LL RELEASE ONE MORE MAN FER THE POSSE! I GUESS EVEN A TENDERFOOT KIN WATCH THE KIDS AN' WOMENFOLK AN' AN EMPTY JAIL!
HMM! WELL, ALL RIGHT, SHERIFF! I'LL STAY BEHIND FOR YOU!
AS THE POSSE RIDES OFF---
WHY DID YOU BACK OUT, HORACE? YOU WEREN'T AFRAID TO GO, WERE YOU?
HARDLY, MARGE! I JUST HAD A HUNCH I MIGHT BE NEEDED IN TOWN! THOSE LARSON TWINS ARE CUNNING--- THEY MIGHT HAVE WANTED TO GET ALL THE MEN IN TOWN OUT IN THE HILLS, SO THE TOWN WOULD BE WIDE OPEN FOR THEM!
AND MAYBE THERE WAS ONLY ONE LARSON SEEN IN THE HILLS! THEY BOTH LOOK ALIKE, AND ONE OF THEM MIGHT HAVE LET HIMSELF BE SEEN IN TWO DIFFERENT PLACES, TO MAKE EVERYONE THINK THEY WERE BOTH OUT THERE! --- WELL, I'LL JUST HAVE TO WAIT AND SEE IF MY HUNCH IS RIGHT!
2

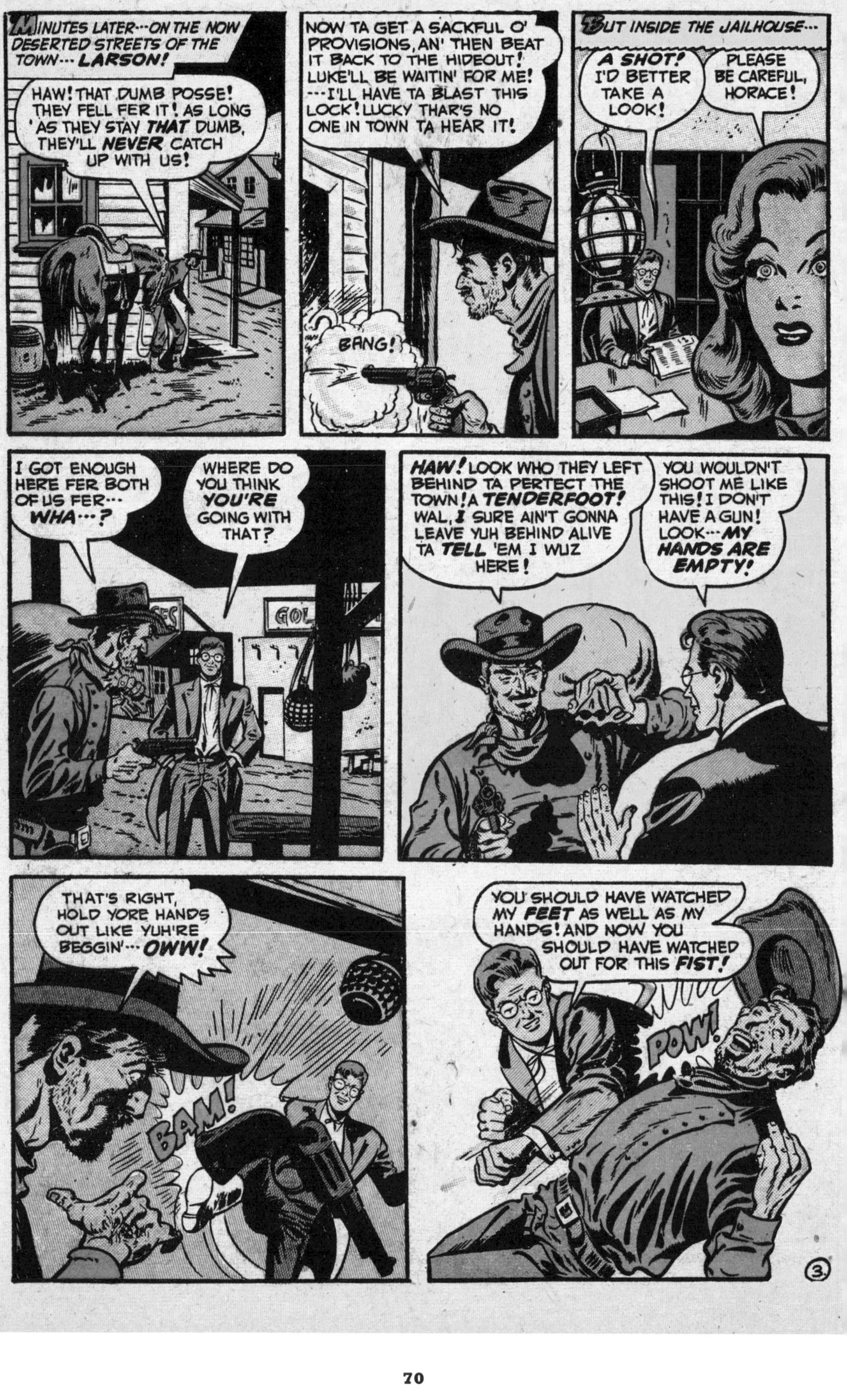
MINUTES LATER --- ON THE NOW DESERTED STREETS OF THE TOWN --- LARSON!
HAW! THAT DUMB POSSE! THEY FELL FER IT! AS LONG AS THEY STAY THAT DUMB, THEY'LL NEVER CATCH UP WITH US!
NOW TA GET A SACKFUL O' PROVISIONS, AN' THEN BEAT IT BACK TO THE HIDEOUT! LUKE'LL BE WAITIN' FOR ME! --- I'LL HAVE TA BLAST THIS LOCK! LUCKY THAR'S NO ONE IN TOWN TA HEAR IT!
BANG!
BUT INSIDE THE JAILHOUSE ---
A SHOT! I'D BETTER TAKE A LOOK!
PLEASE BE CAREFUL, HORACE!
I GOT ENOUGH HERE FER BOTH OF US FER --- WHA ---?
WHERE DO YOU THINK YOU'RE GOING WITH THAT?
HAW! LOOK WHO THEY LEFT BEHIND TA PERTECT THE TOWN! A TENDERFOOT! WAL, I SURE AIN'T GONNA LEAVE YUH BEHIND ALIVE TA TELL 'EM I WUZ HERE!
YOU WOULDN'T SHOOT ME LIKE THIS! I DON'T HAVE A GUN! LOOK --- MY HANDS ARE EMPTY!
THAT'S RIGHT, HOLD YORE HANDS OUT LIKE YUH'RE BEGGIN' --- OWW!
BAM!
YOU SHOULD HAVE WATCHED MY FEET AS WELL AS MY HANDS! AND NOW YOU SHOULD HAVE WATCHED OUT FOR THIS FIST!
POW!
3

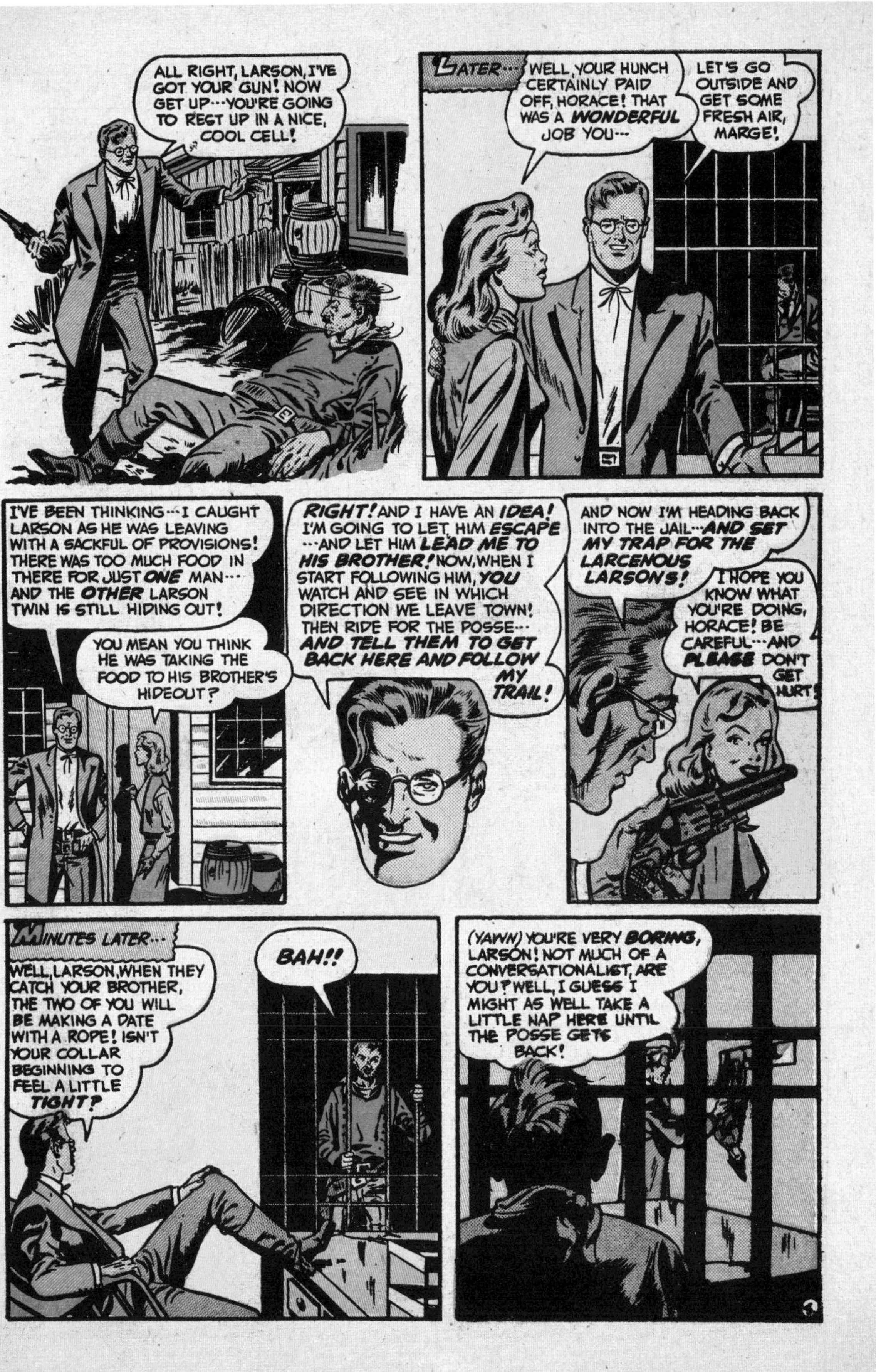
ALL RIGHT, LARSON, I'VE GOT YOUR GUN! NOW GET UP---YOU'RE GOING TO REST UP IN A NICE, COOL CELL!
LATER---
WELL, YOUR HUNCH CERTAINLY PAID OFF, HORACE! THAT WAS A WONDERFUL JOB YOU---
LET'S GO OUTSIDE AND GET SOME FRESH AIR, MARGE!
I'VE BEEN THINKING---I CAUGHT LARSON AS HE WAS LEAVING WITH A SACKFUL OF PROVISIONS! THERE WAS TOO MUCH FOOD IN THERE FOR JUST ONE MAN---AND THE OTHER LARSON TWIN IS STILL HIDING OUT!
YOU MEAN YOU THINK HE WAS TAKING THE FOOD TO HIS BROTHER'S HIDEOUT?
RIGHT! AND I HAVE AN IDEA! I'M GOING TO LET HIM ESCAPE ---AND LET HIM LEAD ME TO HIS BROTHER! NOW, WHEN I START FOLLOWING HIM, YOU WATCH AND SEE IN WHICH DIRECTION WE LEAVE TOWN! THEN RIDE FOR THE POSSE---AND TELL THEM TO GET BACK HERE AND FOLLOW MY TRAIL!
AND NOW I'M HEADING BACK INTO THE JAIL---AND SET MY TRAP FOR THE LARCENOUS LARSONS!
I HOPE YOU KNOW WHAT YOU'RE DOING, HORACE! BE CAREFUL---AND PLEASE DON'T GET HURT!
MINUTES LATER---
WELL, LARSON, WHEN THEY CATCH YOUR BROTHER, THE TWO OF YOU WILL BE MAKING A DATE WITH A ROPE! ISN'T YOUR COLLAR BEGINNING TO FEEL A LITTLE TIGHT?
BAH!!
(YAWN) YOU'RE VERY BORING, LARSON! NOT MUCH OF A CONVERSATIONALIST, ARE YOU? WELL, I GUESS I MIGHT AS WELL TAKE A LITTLE NAP HERE UNTIL THE POSSE GETS BACK!

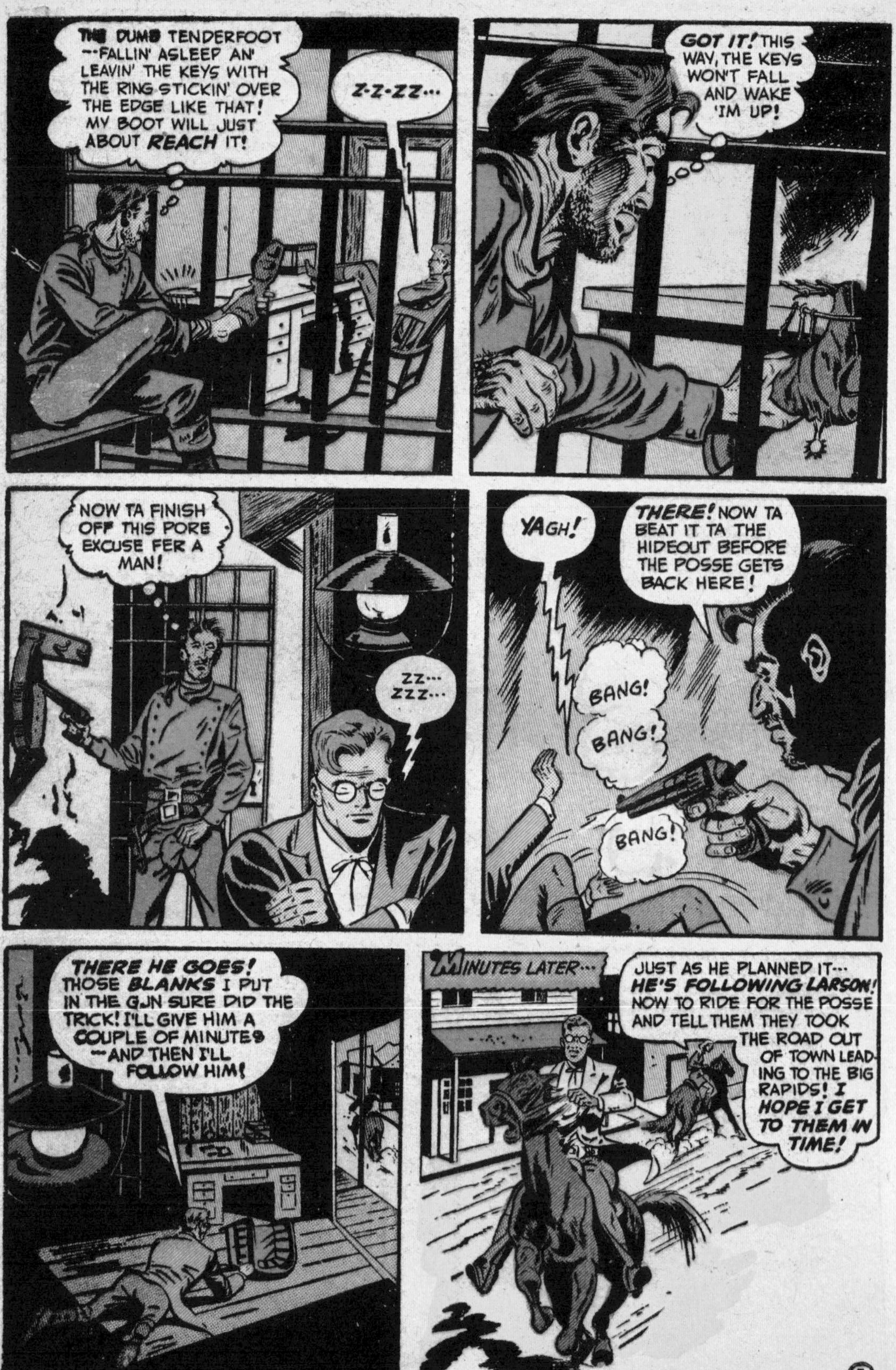
THE DUMB TENDERFOOT --FALLIN' ASLEEP AN' LEAVIN' THE KEYS WITH THE RING STICKIN' OVER THE EDGE LIKE THAT! MY BOOT WILL JUST ABOUT REACH IT!
Z-Z-ZZ...
GOT IT! THIS WAY, THE KEYS WON'T FALL AND WAKE 'IM UP!
NOW TA FINISH OFF THIS PORE EXCUSE FER A MAN!
ZZ... ZZZ...
YAGH!
THERE! NOW TA BEAT IT TA THE HIDEOUT BEFORE THE POSSE GETS BACK HERE!
BANG!
BANG!
BANG!
THERE HE GOES! THOSE BLANKS I PUT IN THE GUN SURE DID THE TRICK! I'LL GIVE HIM A COUPLE OF MINUTES --AND THEN I'LL FOLLOW HIM!
MINUTES LATER...
JUST AS HE PLANNED IT... HE'S FOLLOWING LARSON! NOW TO RIDE FOR THE POSSE AND TELL THEM THEY TOOK THE ROAD OUT OF TOWN LEADING TO THE BIG RAPIDS! I HOPE I GET TO THEM IN TIME!
5

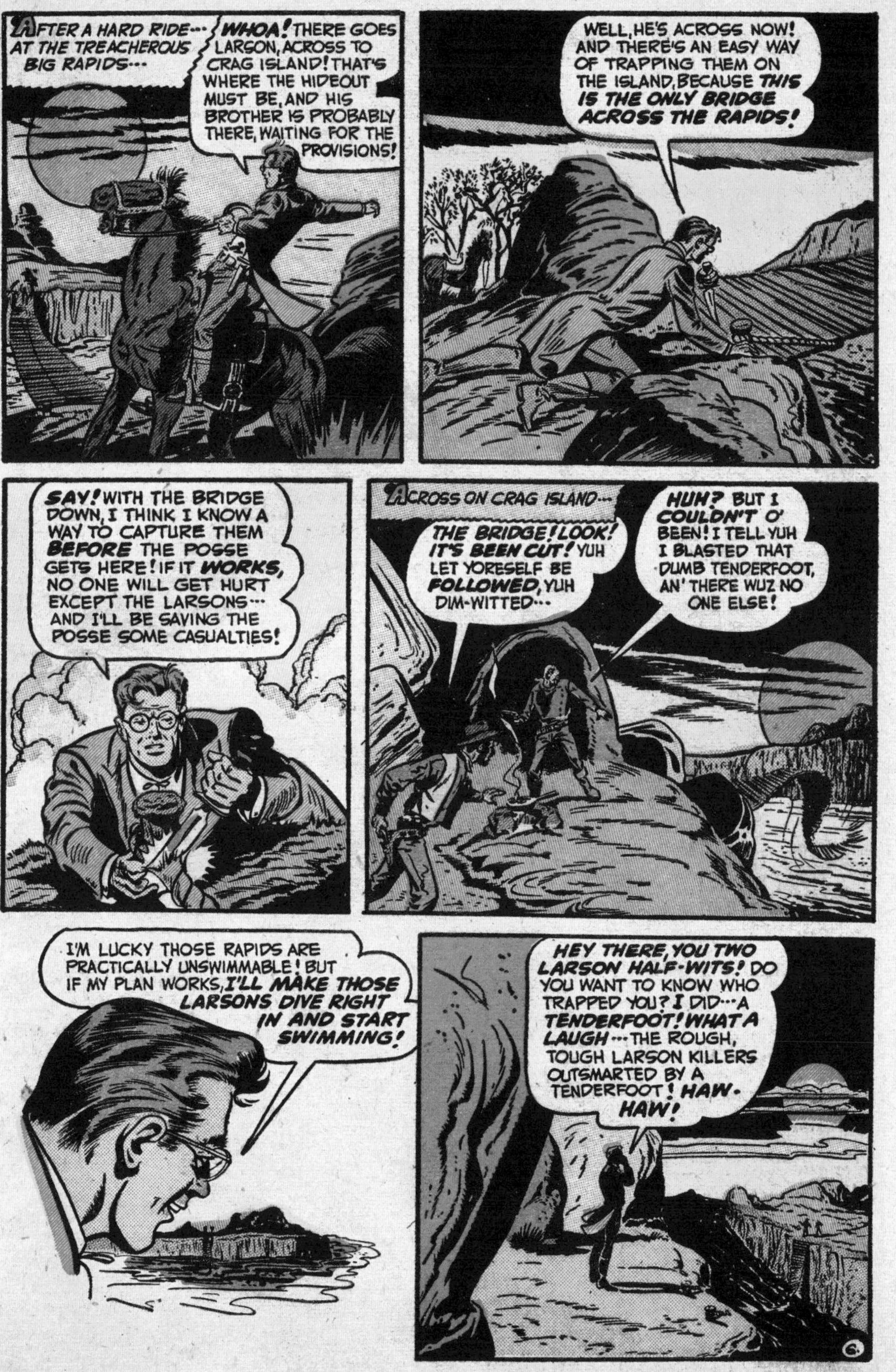
AFTER A HARD RIDE--- AT THE TREACHEROUS BIG RAPIDS---
WHOA! THERE GOES LARSON, ACROSS TO CRAG ISLAND! THAT'S WHERE THE HIDEOUT MUST BE, AND HIS BROTHER IS PROBABLY THERE, WAITING FOR THE PROVISIONS!
WELL, HE'S ACROSS NOW! AND THERE'S AN EASY WAY OF TRAPPING THEM ON THE ISLAND, BECAUSE THIS IS THE ONLY BRIDGE ACROSS THE RAPIDS!
SAY! WITH THE BRIDGE DOWN, I THINK I KNOW A WAY TO CAPTURE THEM BEFORE THE POSSE GETS HERE! IF IT WORKS, NO ONE WILL GET HURT EXCEPT THE LARSONS--- AND I'LL BE SAVING THE POSSE SOME CASUALTIES!
ACROSS ON CRAG ISLAND---
THE BRIDGE! LOOK! IT'S BEEN CUT! YUH LET YORESELF BE FOLLOWED, YUH DIM-WITTED---
HUH? BUT I COULDN'T O' BEEN! I TELL YUH I BLASTED THAT DUMB TENDERFOOT, AN' THERE WUZ NO ONE ELSE!
I'M LUCKY THOSE RAPIDS ARE PRACTICALLY UNSWIMMABLE! BUT IF MY PLAN WORKS, I'LL MAKE THOSE LARSONS DIVE RIGHT IN AND START SWIMMING!
HEY THERE, YOU TWO LARSON HALF-WITS! DO YOU WANT TO KNOW WHO TRAPPED YOU? I DID--- A TENDERFOOT! WHAT A LAUGH --- THE ROUGH, TOUGH LARSON KILLERS OUTSMARTED BY A TENDERFOOT! HAW-HAW!
6

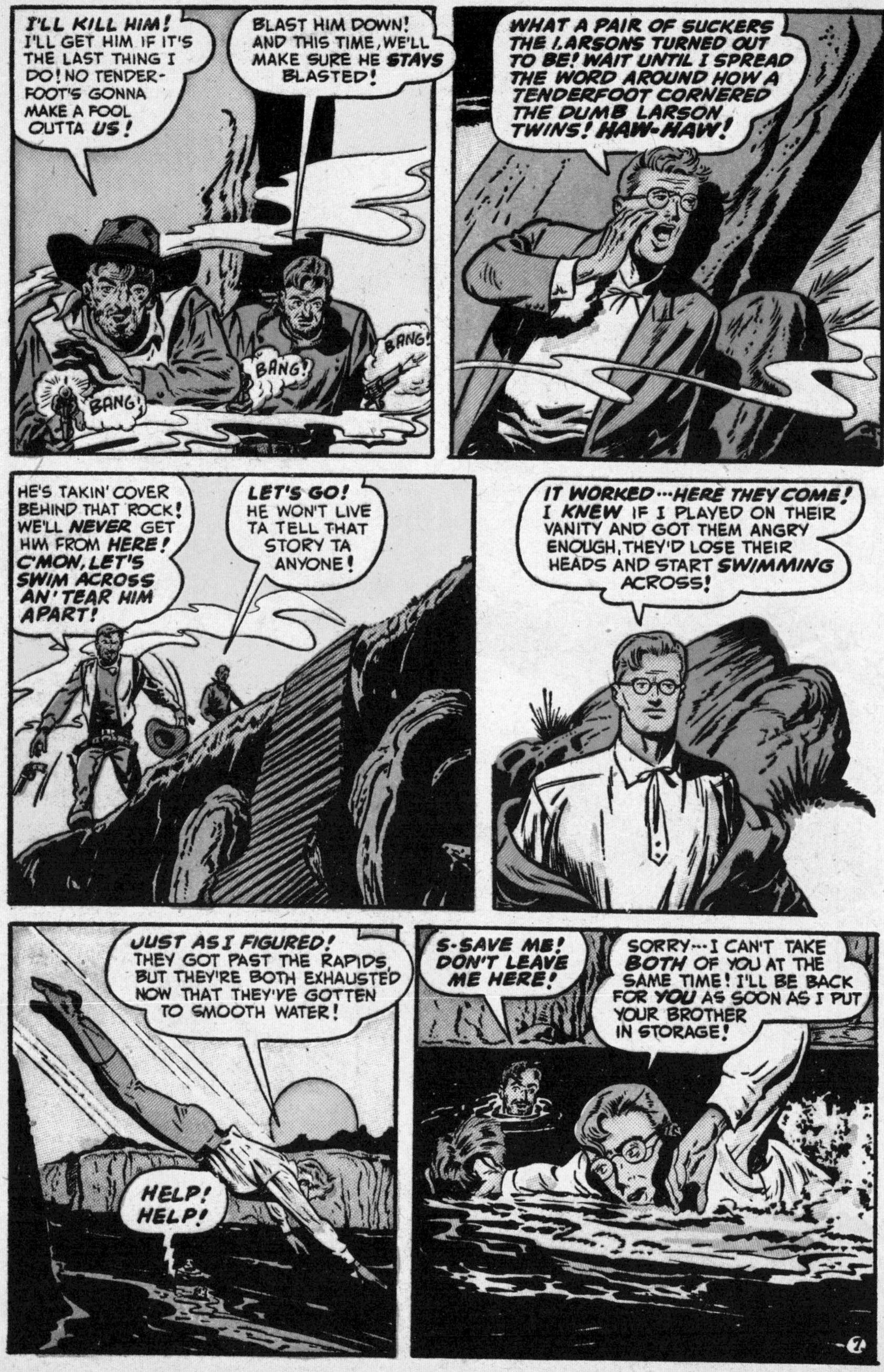
I'LL KILL HIM! I'LL GET HIM IF IT'S THE LAST THING I DO! NO TENDERFOOT'S GONNA MAKE A FOOL OUTTA US!
BLAST HIM DOWN! AND THIS TIME, WE'LL MAKE SURE HE STAYS BLASTED!
BANG!
BANG!
BANG!
WHAT A PAIR OF SUCKERS THE LARSONS TURNED OUT TO BE! WAIT UNTIL I SPREAD THE WORD AROUND HOW A TENDERFOOT CORNERED THE DUMB LARSON TWINS! HAW-HAW!
HE'S TAKIN' COVER BEHIND THAT ROCK! WE'LL NEVER GET HIM FROM HERE! C'MON, LET'S SWIM ACROSS AN' TEAR HIM APART!
LET'S GO! HE WON'T LIVE TA TELL THAT STORY TA ANYONE!
IT WORKED---HERE THEY COME! I KNEW IF I PLAYED ON THEIR VANITY AND GOT THEM ANGRY ENOUGH, THEY'D LOSE THEIR HEADS AND START SWIMMING ACROSS!
JUST AS I FIGURED! THEY GOT PAST THE RAPIDS, BUT THEY'RE BOTH EXHAUSTED NOW THAT THEY'VE GOTTEN TO SMOOTH WATER!
HELP! HELP!
S-SAVE ME! DON'T LEAVE ME HERE!
SORRY---I CAN'T TAKE BOTH OF YOU AT THE SAME TIME! I'LL BE BACK FOR YOU AS SOON AS I PUT YOUR BROTHER IN STORAGE!
7

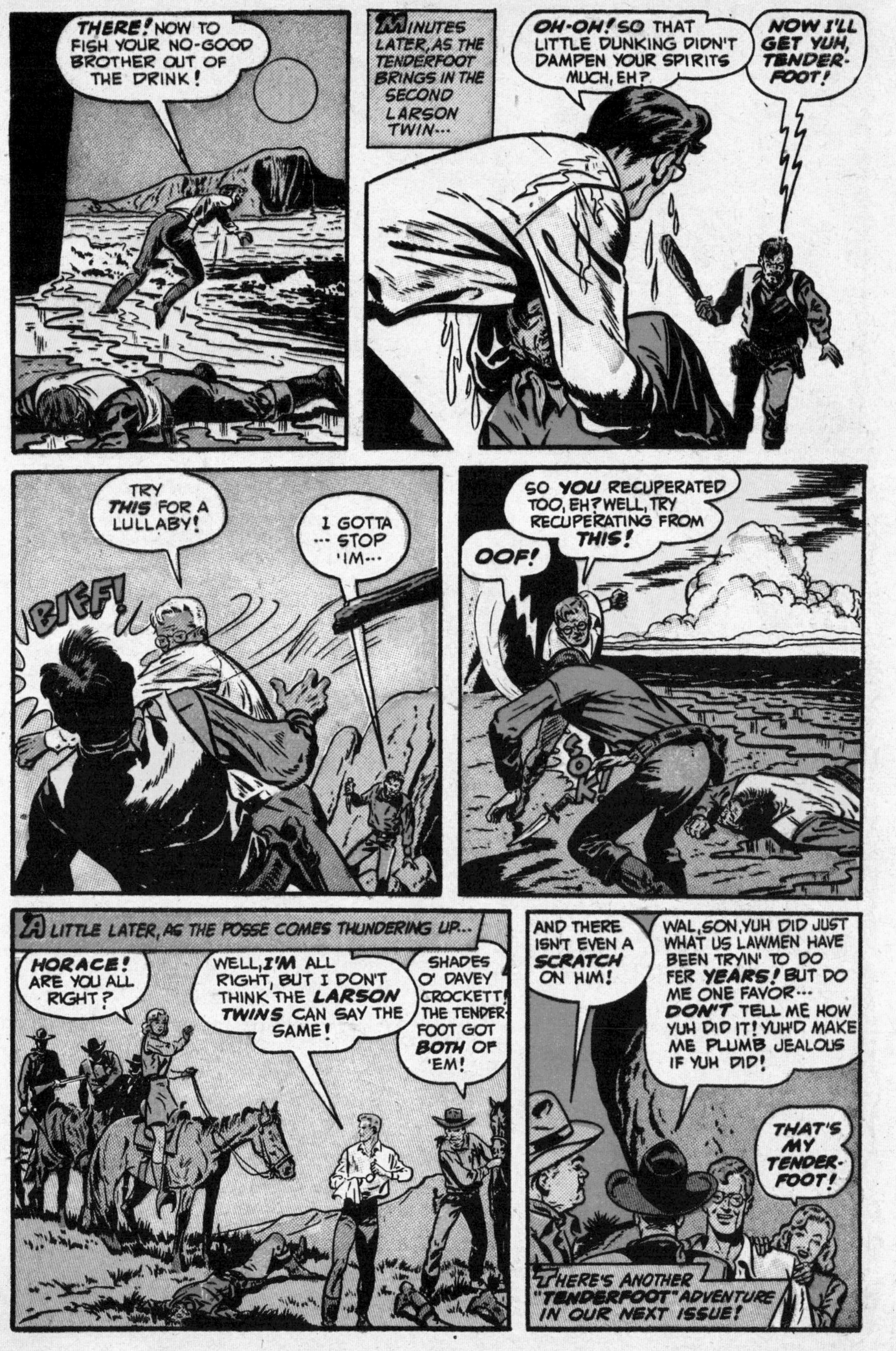
THERE! NOW TO FISH YOUR NO-GOOD BROTHER OUT OF THE DRINK!
MINUTES LATER, AS THE TENDERFOOT BRINGS IN THE SECOND LARSON TWIN...
OH-OH! SO THAT LITTLE DUNKING DIDN'T DAMPEN YOUR SPIRITS MUCH, EH?
NOW I'LL GET YUH, TENDER-FOOT!
TRY THIS FOR A LULLABY!
I GOTTA --- STOP 'IM---
BIFF!
SO YOU RECUPERATED TOO, EH? WELL, TRY RECUPERATING FROM THIS!
OOF!
SOK!
A LITTLE LATER, AS THE POSSE COMES THUNDERING UP...
HORACE! ARE YOU ALL RIGHT?
WELL, I'M ALL RIGHT, BUT I DON'T THINK THE LARSON TWINS CAN SAY THE SAME!
SHADES O' DAVEY CROCKETT! THE TENDER-FOOT GOT BOTH OF 'EM!
AND THERE ISN'T EVEN A SCRATCH ON HIM!
WAL, SON, YUH DID JUST WHAT US LAWMEN HAVE BEEN TRYIN' TO DO FER YEARS! BUT DO ME ONE FAVOR--- DON'T TELL ME HOW YUH DID IT! YUH'D MAKE ME PLUMB JEALOUS IF YUH DID!
THAT'S MY TENDER-FOOT!
THERE'S ANOTHER "TENDERFOOT" ADVENTURE IN OUR NEXT ISSUE!

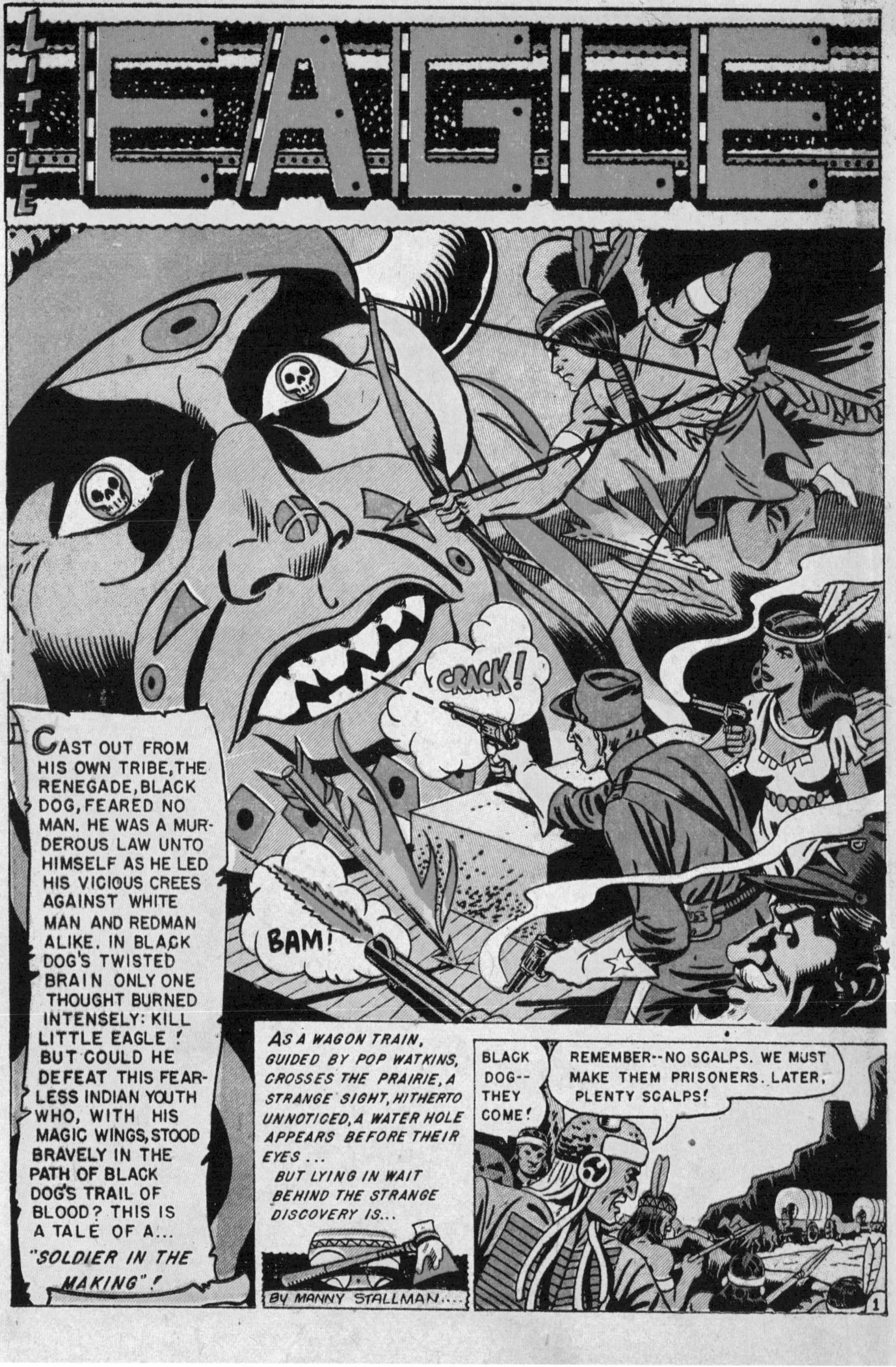
LITTLE EAGLE
CRACK!
BAM!
CAST OUT FROM HIS OWN TRIBE, THE RENEGADE, BLACK DOG, FEARED NO MAN. HE WAS A MURDEROUS LAW UNTO HIMSELF AS HE LED HIS VICIOUS CREES AGAINST WHITE MAN AND REDMAN ALIKE. IN BLACK DOG'S TWISTED BRAIN ONLY ONE THOUGHT BURNED INTENSELY: KILL LITTLE EAGLE! BUT COULD HE DEFEAT THIS FEARLESS INDIAN YOUTH WHO, WITH HIS MAGIC WINGS, STOOD BRAVELY IN THE PATH OF BLACK DOG'S TRAIL OF BLOOD? THIS IS A TALE OF A... "SOLDIER IN THE MAKING"!
AS A WAGON TRAIN, GUIDED BY POP WATKINS, CROSSES THE PRAIRIE, A STRANGE SIGHT, HITHERTO UNNOTICED, A WATER HOLE APPEARS BEFORE THEIR EYES ... BUT LYING IN WAIT BEHIND THE STRANGE DISCOVERY IS...
BY MANNY STALLMAN....
BLACK DOG-- THEY COME!
REMEMBER--NO SCALPS. WE MUST MAKE THEM PRISONERS. LATER, PLENTY SCALPS!
1

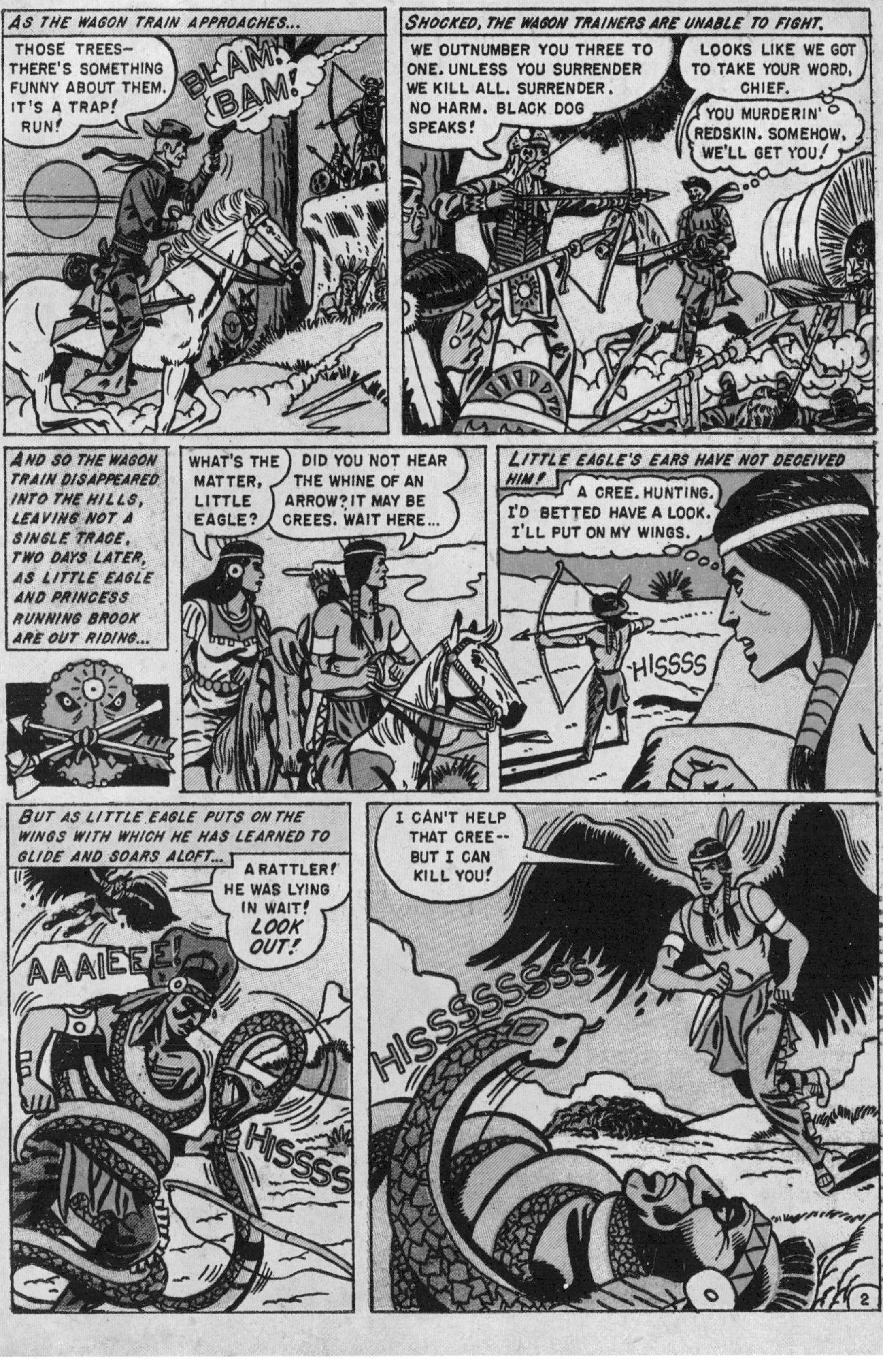

AS THE WAGON TRAIN APPROACHES...
THOSE TREES— THERE'S SOMETHING FUNNY ABOUT THEM. IT'S A TRAP! RUN!
BLAM! BAM!
SHOCKED, THE WAGON TRAINERS ARE UNABLE TO FIGHT.
WE OUTNUMBER YOU THREE TO ONE. UNLESS YOU SURRENDER WE KILL ALL. SURRENDER. NO HARM. BLACK DOG SPEAKS!
LOOKS LIKE WE GOT TO TAKE YOUR WORD, CHIEF.
YOU MURDERIN' REDSKIN. SOMEHOW, WE'LL GET YOU!
AND SO THE WAGON TRAIN DISAPPEARED INTO THE HILLS, LEAVING NOT A SINGLE TRACE. TWO DAYS LATER, AS LITTLE EAGLE AND PRINCESS RUNNING BROOK ARE OUT RIDING...
WHAT'S THE MATTER, LITTLE EAGLE?
DID YOU NOT HEAR THE WHINE OF AN ARROW? IT MAY BE CREES. WAIT HERE...
LITTLE EAGLE'S EARS HAVE NOT DECEIVED HIM!
A CREE. HUNTING. I'D BETTED HAVE A LOOK. I'LL PUT ON MY WINGS.
HISSSS
BUT AS LITTLE EAGLE PUTS ON THE WINGS WITH WHICH HE HAS LEARNED TO GLIDE AND SOARS ALOFT...
A RATTLER! HE WAS LYING IN WAIT! LOOK OUT!
AAAIEEE!
HISSSSS
I CAN'T HELP THAT CREE-- BUT I CAN KILL YOU!
HISSSSSSSSSS
2

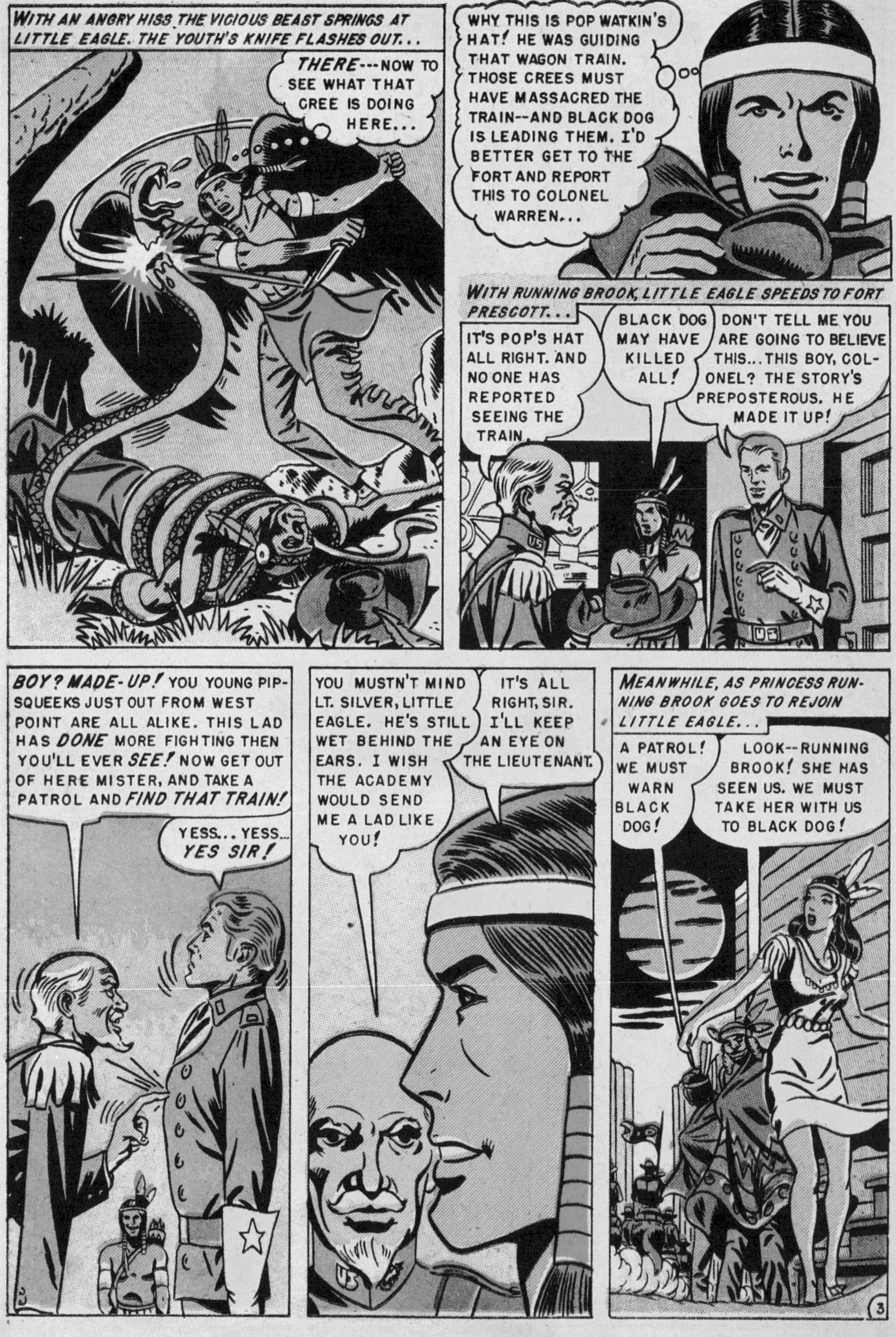
WITH AN ANGRY HISS THE VICIOUS BEAST SPRINGS AT LITTLE EAGLE. THE YOUTH'S KNIFE FLASHES OUT...
THERE---NOW TO SEE WHAT THAT CREE IS DOING HERE...
WHY THIS IS POP WATKIN'S HAT! HE WAS GUIDING THAT WAGON TRAIN. THOSE CREES MUST HAVE MASSACRED THE TRAIN--AND BLACK DOG IS LEADING THEM. I'D BETTER GET TO THE FORT AND REPORT THIS TO COLONEL WARREN...
WITH RUNNING BROOK, LITTLE EAGLE SPEEDS TO FORT PRESCOTT...
IT'S POP'S HAT ALL RIGHT. AND NO ONE HAS REPORTED SEEING THE TRAIN.
BLACK DOG MAY HAVE KILLED ALL!
DON'T TELL ME YOU ARE GOING TO BELIEVE THIS...THIS BOY, COLONEL? THE STORY'S PREPOSTEROUS. HE MADE IT UP!
BOY? MADE-UP! YOU YOUNG PIPSQUEEKS JUST OUT FROM WEST POINT ARE ALL ALIKE. THIS LAD HAS DONE MORE FIGHTING THEN YOU'LL EVER SEE! NOW GET OUT OF HERE MISTER, AND TAKE A PATROL AND FIND THAT TRAIN!
YESS... YESS... YES SIR!
YOU MUSTN'T MIND LT. SILVER, LITTLE EAGLE. HE'S STILL WET BEHIND THE EARS. I WISH THE ACADEMY WOULD SEND ME A LAD LIKE YOU!
IT'S ALL RIGHT, SIR. I'LL KEEP AN EYE ON THE LIEUTENANT.
MEANWHILE, AS PRINCESS RUNNING BROOK GOES TO REJOIN LITTLE EAGLE...
A PATROL! WE MUST WARN BLACK DOG!
LOOK--RUNNING BROOK! SHE HAS SEEN US. WE MUST TAKE HER WITH US TO BLACK DOG!
3

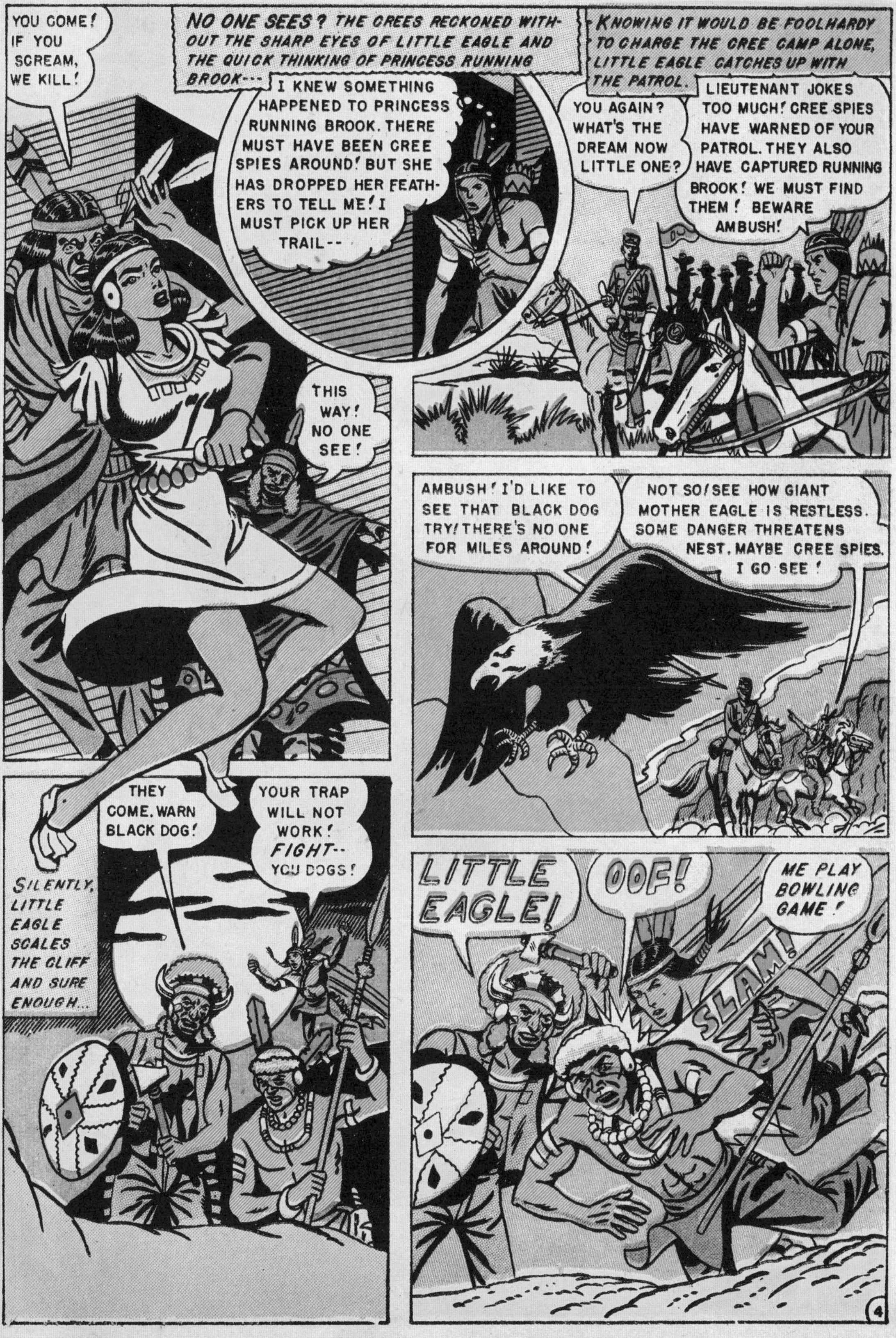
YOU COME! IF YOU SCREAM, WE KILL!
NO ONE SEES? THE CREES RECKONED WITHOUT THE SHARP EYES OF LITTLE EAGLE AND THE QUICK THINKING OF PRINCESS RUNNING BROOK---
THIS WAY! NO ONE SEE!
I KNEW SOMETHING HAPPENED TO PRINCESS RUNNING BROOK. THERE MUST HAVE BEEN CREE SPIES AROUND! BUT SHE HAS DROPPED HER FEATHERS TO TELL ME! I MUST PICK UP HER TRAIL--
KNOWING IT WOULD BE FOOLHARDY TO CHARGE THE CREE CAMP ALONE, LITTLE EAGLE CATCHES UP WITH THE PATROL.
YOU AGAIN? WHAT'S THE DREAM NOW LITTLE ONE?
LIEUTENANT JOKES TOO MUCH! CREE SPIES HAVE WARNED OF YOUR PATROL. THEY ALSO HAVE CAPTURED RUNNING BROOK! WE MUST FIND THEM! BEWARE AMBUSH!
AMBUSH! I'D LIKE TO SEE THAT BLACK DOG TRY! THERE'S NO ONE FOR MILES AROUND!
NOT SO! SEE HOW GIANT MOTHER EAGLE IS RESTLESS. SOME DANGER THREATENS NEST. MAYBE CREE SPIES. I GO SEE!
SILENTLY, LITTLE EAGLE SCALES THE CLIFF AND SURE ENOUGH..
THEY COME. WARN BLACK DOG!
YOUR TRAP WILL NOT WORK! FIGHT-- YOU DOGS!
LITTLE EAGLE!
OOF!
ME PLAY BOWLING GAME!
SLAM!
4

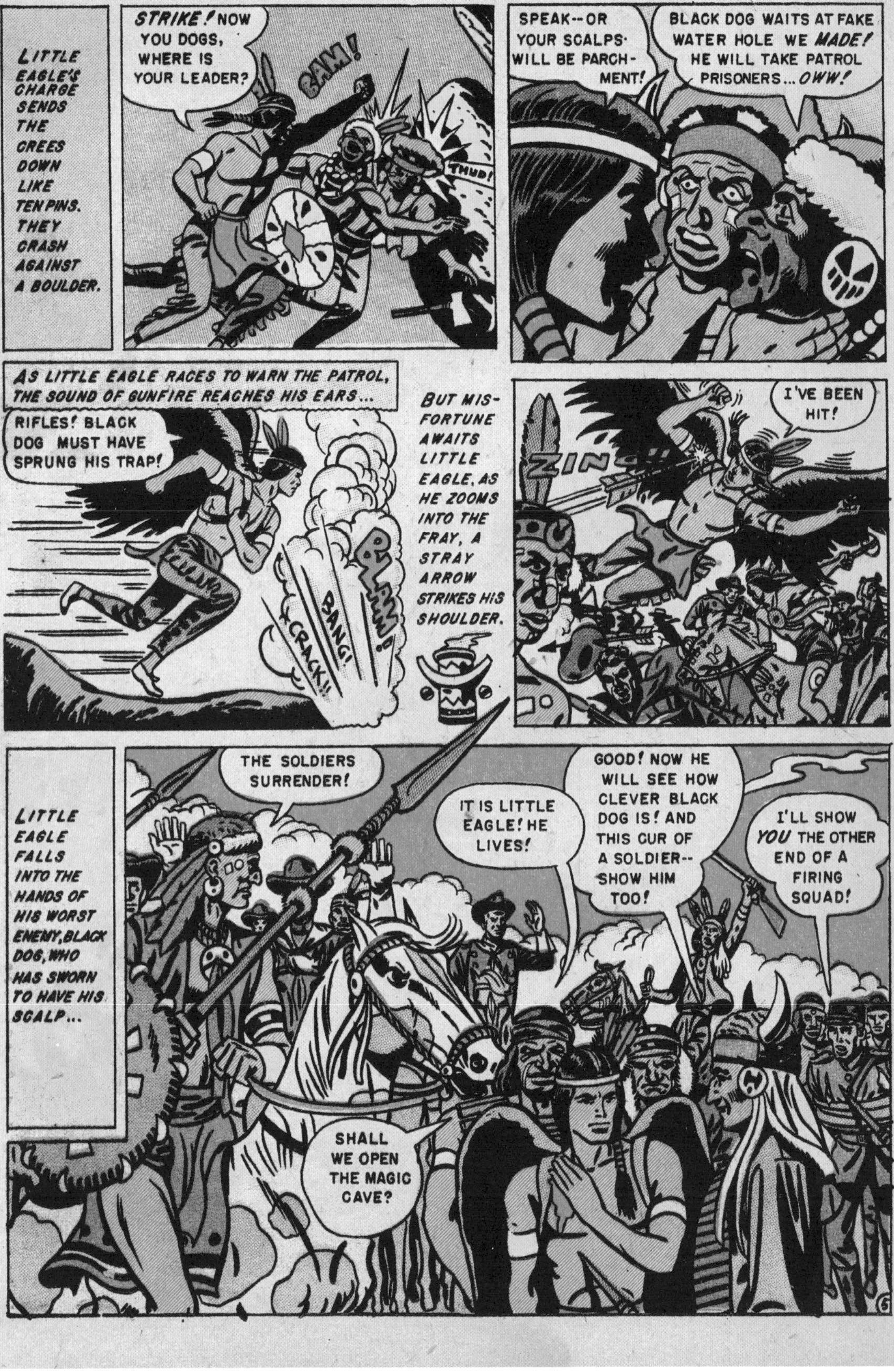

LITTLE EAGLE'S CHARGE SENDS THE CREES DOWN LIKE TEN PINS. THEY CRASH AGAINST A BOULDER.
STRIKE! NOW YOU DOGS, WHERE IS YOUR LEADER?
BAM!
THUD!
SPEAK--OR YOUR SCALPS WILL BE PARCHMENT!
BLACK DOG WAITS AT FAKE WATER HOLE WE MADE! HE WILL TAKE PATROL PRISONERS... OWW!
AS LITTLE EAGLE RACES TO WARN THE PATROL, THE SOUND OF GUNFIRE REACHES HIS EARS...
RIFLES! BLACK DOG MUST HAVE SPRUNG HIS TRAP!
BLAM!
BANG!
CRACK!!
BUT MISFORTUNE AWAITS LITTLE EAGLE, AS HE ZOOMS INTO THE FRAY, A STRAY ARROW STRIKES HIS SHOULDER.
I'VE BEEN HIT!
ZING
LITTLE EAGLE FALLS INTO THE HANDS OF HIS WORST ENEMY, BLACK DOG, WHO HAS SWORN TO HAVE HIS SCALP...
THE SOLDIERS SURRENDER!
IT IS LITTLE EAGLE! HE LIVES!
GOOD! NOW HE WILL SEE HOW CLEVER BLACK DOG IS! AND THIS CUR OF A SOLDIER--SHOW HIM TOO!
I'LL SHOW YOU THE OTHER END OF A FIRING SQUAD!
SHALL WE OPEN THE MAGIC CAVE?
5

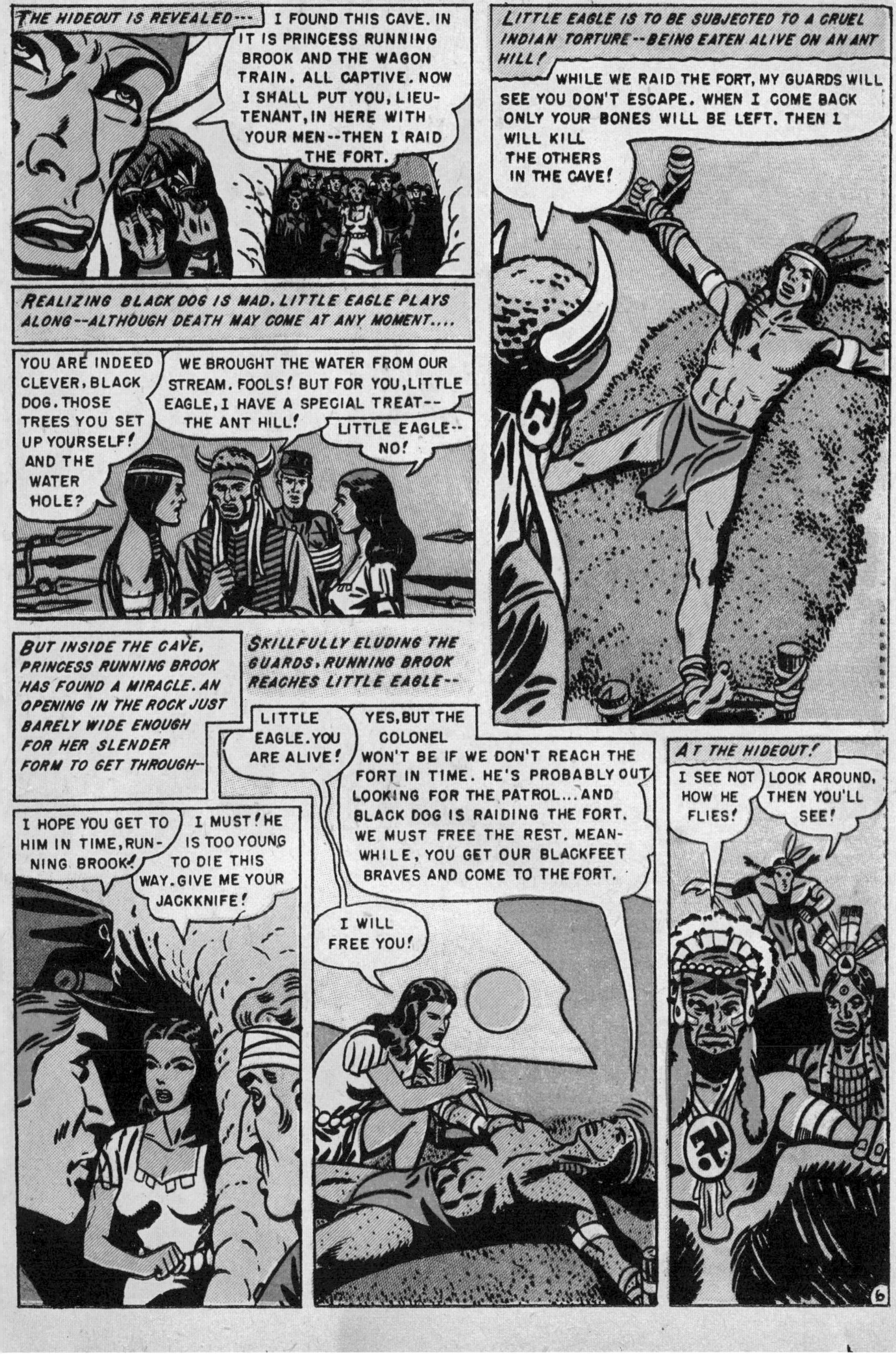
THE HIDEOUT IS REVEALED---
I FOUND THIS CAVE. IN IT IS PRINCESS RUNNING BROOK AND THE WAGON TRAIN. ALL CAPTIVE. NOW I SHALL PUT YOU, LIEU-TENANT, IN HERE WITH YOUR MEN--THEN I RAID THE FORT.
REALIZING BLACK DOG IS MAD, LITTLE EAGLE PLAYS ALONG--ALTHOUGH DEATH MAY COME AT ANY MOMENT....
YOU ARE INDEED CLEVER, BLACK DOG. THOSE TREES YOU SET UP YOURSELF! AND THE WATER HOLE?
WE BROUGHT THE WATER FROM OUR STREAM. FOOLS! BUT FOR YOU, LITTLE EAGLE, I HAVE A SPECIAL TREAT-- THE ANT HILL!
LITTLE EAGLE-- NO!
LITTLE EAGLE IS TO BE SUBJECTED TO A CRUEL INDIAN TORTURE--BEING EATEN ALIVE ON AN ANT HILL!
WHILE WE RAID THE FORT, MY GUARDS WILL SEE YOU DON'T ESCAPE. WHEN I COME BACK ONLY YOUR BONES WILL BE LEFT. THEN I WILL KILL THE OTHERS IN THE CAVE!
BUT INSIDE THE CAVE, PRINCESS RUNNING BROOK HAS FOUND A MIRACLE. AN OPENING IN THE ROCK JUST BARELY WIDE ENOUGH FOR HER SLENDER FORM TO GET THROUGH--
I HOPE YOU GET TO HIM IN TIME, RUN-NING BROOK!
I MUST! HE IS TOO YOUNG TO DIE THIS WAY. GIVE ME YOUR JACKKNIFE!
SKILLFULLY ELUDING THE GUARDS, RUNNING BROOK REACHES LITTLE EAGLE--
I WILL FREE YOU!
LITTLE EAGLE. YOU ARE ALIVE!
YES, BUT THE COLONEL WON'T BE IF WE DON'T REACH THE FORT IN TIME. HE'S PROBABLY OUT LOOKING FOR THE PATROL... AND BLACK DOG IS RAIDING THE FORT. WE MUST FREE THE REST. MEAN-WHILE, YOU GET OUR BLACKFEET BRAVES AND COME TO THE FORT.
AT THE HIDEOUT!
I SEE NOT HOW HE FLIES!
LOOK AROUND, THEN YOU'LL SEE!
6

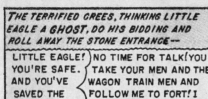

THE TERRIFIED CREES, THINKING LITTLE EAGLE A GHOST, DO HIS BIDDING AND ROLL AWAY THE STONE ENTRANCE--

LITTLE EAGLE! YOU'RE SAFE. AND YOU'VE SAVED THE WAGON TRAIN, TOO!

NO TIME FOR TALK! YOU TAKE YOUR MEN AND THE WAGON TRAIN MEN AND FOLLOW ME TO FORT! I TAKE SHORT CUT! HURRY!

MEANWHILE AT THE FORT, COLONEL WARREN AND HIS REMAINING SOLDIERS ARE ABOUT TO START IN SEARCH OF THE PATROL, WHEN SUDDENLY..

CREES!

HUNDREDS OF 'EM, SIR! THEY OUTNUMBER US PLENTY!

SHOW NO MERCY. KILL! KILL!

BAM!

THAT MACHINE-GUN. GET BLACK DOG!

TOO LATE, SIR-- NO--LOOK. IT'S --IT'S LITTLE EAGLE!

A-RAT-TAT-TAT

BAM!

INDEED IT IS! LIKE AN AVENGING ANGEL, LITTLE EAGLE HEADS FOR THE MURDEROUS BLACK DOG. HIS ARROW SINGS THROUGH THE AIR, AND....

DEATH TO THE RENEGADE!

WE ARE LOST! BLACKFEET COME. AND WHITE MEN!

UGH!

IN A FEW MOMENTS, AS RUNNING BROOK ARRIVES WITH HER BLACKFEET BRAVES, THE FIGHTING ENDS...

DEATH TO ALL CREES!

MERCY-- SPARE US! BLACK DOG IS DEAD!

MAKE THEM PRISONERS! WE SHALL HAVE THEM DO SQUAW'S WORK!

LATER

I APOLOGIZE, LITTLE EAGLE. I AGREE, WEST POINT COULD USE A LAD LIKE YOU!

AND IS GOING TO GET HIM! I'M RECOMMENDING LITTLE EAGLE FOR AN APPOINTMENT WHEN HE REACHES THE LEGAL AGE!

THE END

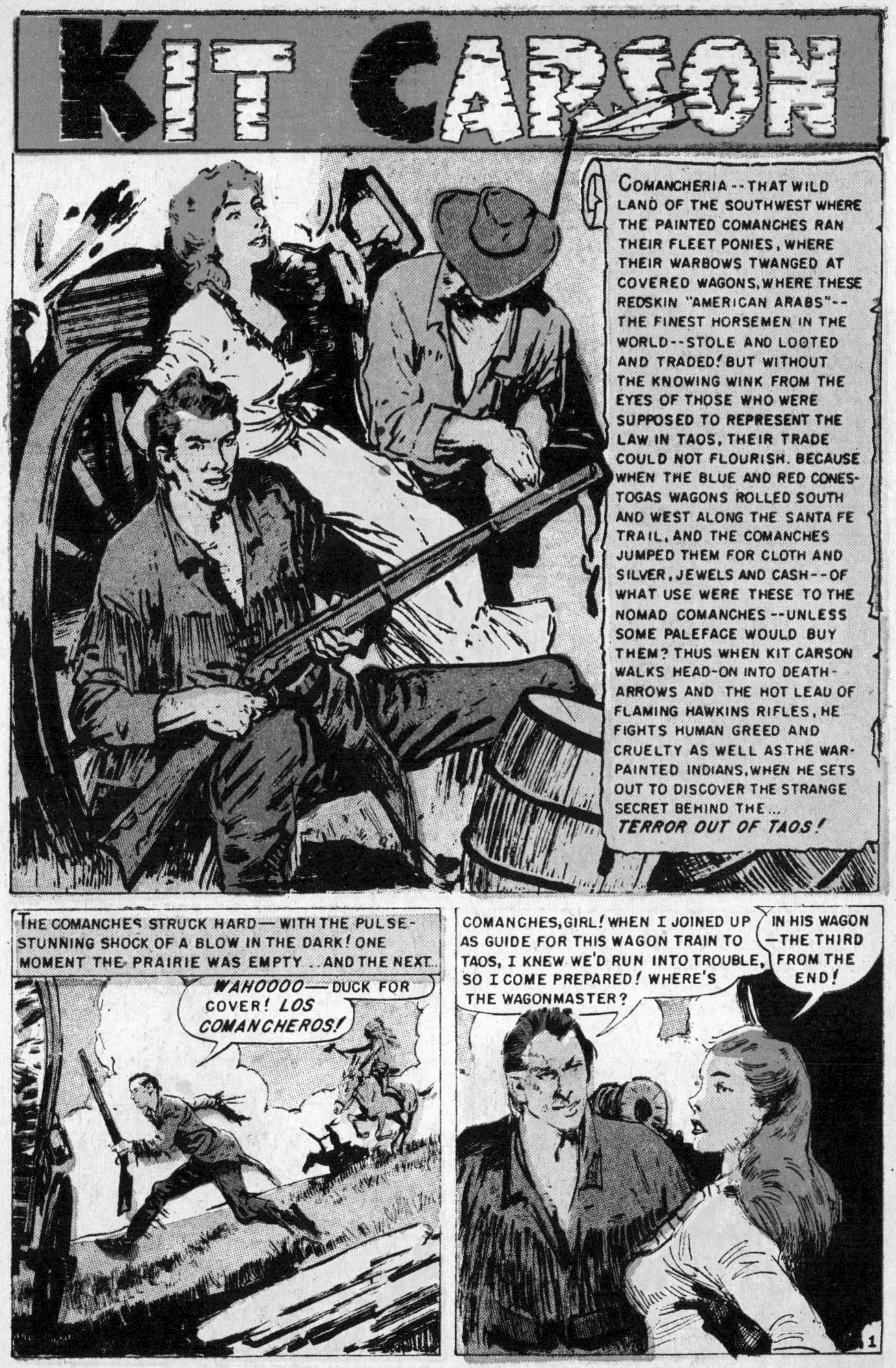
KIT CARSON
COMANCHERIA -- THAT WILD LAND OF THE SOUTHWEST WHERE THE PAINTED COMANCHES RAN THEIR FLEET PONIES, WHERE THEIR WARBOWS TWANGED AT COVERED WAGONS, WHERE THESE REDSKIN "AMERICAN ARABS" -- THE FINEST HORSEMEN IN THE WORLD -- STOLE AND LOOTED AND TRADED! BUT WITHOUT THE KNOWING WINK FROM THE EYES OF THOSE WHO WERE SUPPOSED TO REPRESENT THE LAW IN TAOS, THEIR TRADE COULD NOT FLOURISH. BECAUSE WHEN THE BLUE AND RED CONESTOGAS WAGONS ROLLED SOUTH AND WEST ALONG THE SANTA FE TRAIL, AND THE COMANCHES JUMPED THEM FOR CLOTH AND SILVER, JEWELS AND CASH -- OF WHAT USE WERE THESE TO THE NOMAD COMANCHES -- UNLESS SOME PALEFACE WOULD BUY THEM? THUS WHEN KIT CARSON WALKS HEAD-ON INTO DEATH-ARROWS AND THE HOT LEAD OF FLAMING HAWKINS RIFLES, HE FIGHTS HUMAN GREED AND CRUELTY AS WELL AS THE WAR-PAINTED INDIANS, WHEN HE SETS OUT TO DISCOVER THE STRANGE SECRET BEHIND THE...
TERROR OUT OF TAOS!
THE COMANCHES STRUCK HARD — WITH THE PULSE-STUNNING SHOCK OF A BLOW IN THE DARK! ONE MOMENT THE PRAIRIE WAS EMPTY .. AND THE NEXT..
WAHOOOO — DUCK FOR COVER! LOS COMANCHEROS!
COMANCHES, GIRL! WHEN I JOINED UP AS GUIDE FOR THIS WAGON TRAIN TO TAOS, I KNEW WE'D RUN INTO TROUBLE, SO I COME PREPARED! WHERE'S THE WAGONMASTER?
IN HIS WAGON — THE THIRD FROM THE END!
1

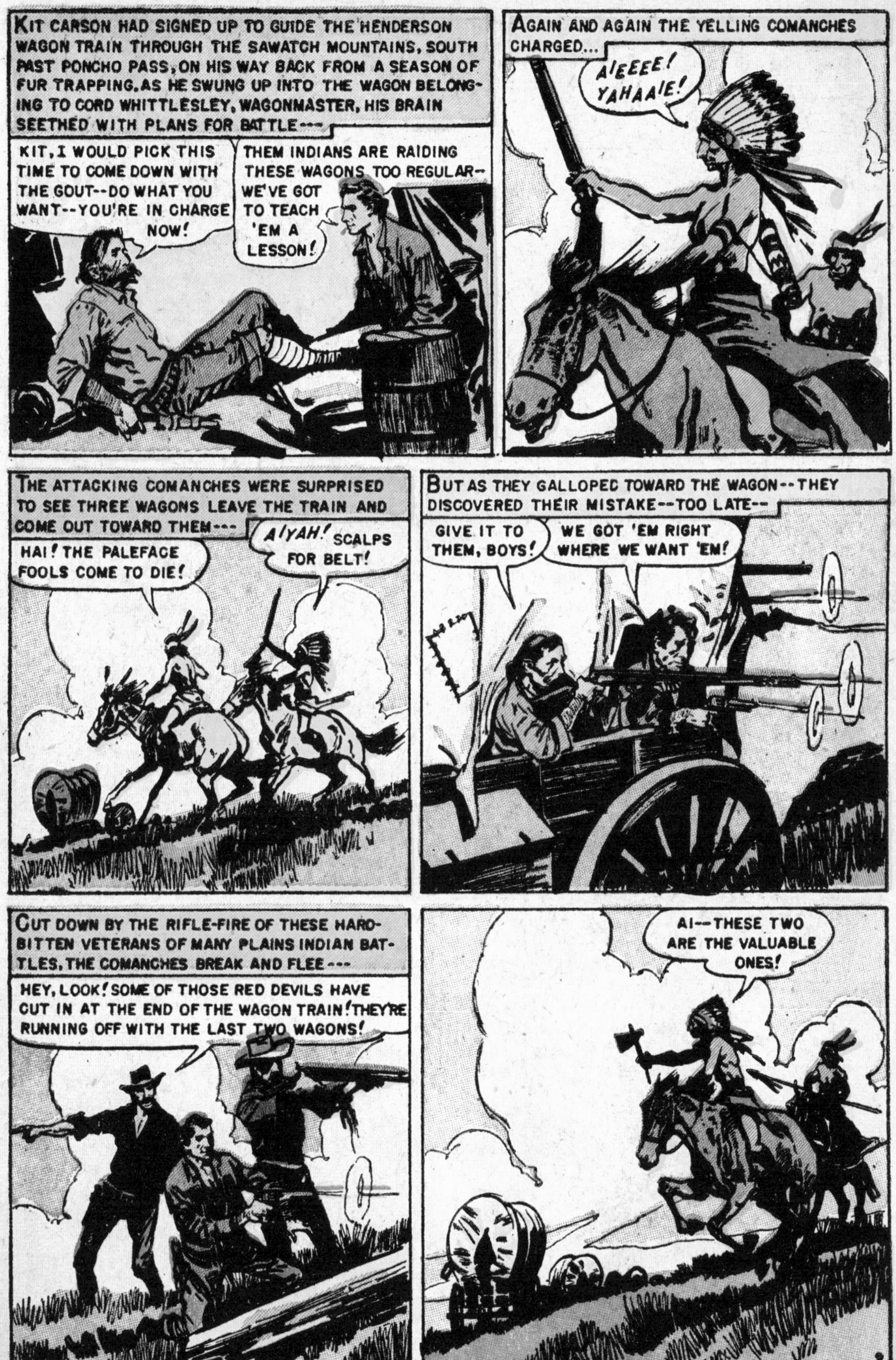
KIT CARSON HAD SIGNED UP TO GUIDE THE HENDERSON WAGON TRAIN THROUGH THE SAWATCH MOUNTAINS, SOUTH PAST PONCHO PASS, ON HIS WAY BACK FROM A SEASON OF FUR TRAPPING. AS HE SWUNG UP INTO THE WAGON BELONGING TO CORD WHITTLESLEY, WAGONMASTER, HIS BRAIN SEETHED WITH PLANS FOR BATTLE---
KIT, I WOULD PICK THIS TIME TO COME DOWN WITH THE GOUT--DO WHAT YOU WANT--YOU'RE IN CHARGE NOW!
THEM INDIANS ARE RAIDING THESE WAGONS TOO REGULAR--WE'VE GOT TO TEACH 'EM A LESSON!
AGAIN AND AGAIN THE YELLING COMANCHES CHARGED...
AIEEEE! YAHAAIE!
THE ATTACKING COMANCHES WERE SURPRISED TO SEE THREE WAGONS LEAVE THE TRAIN AND COME OUT TOWARD THEM---
HAI! THE PALEFACE FOOLS COME TO DIE!
AIYAH! SCALPS FOR BELT!
BUT AS THEY GALLOPED TOWARD THE WAGON--THEY DISCOVERED THEIR MISTAKE--TOO LATE--
GIVE IT TO THEM, BOYS!
WE GOT 'EM RIGHT WHERE WE WANT 'EM!
CUT DOWN BY THE RIFLE-FIRE OF THESE HARD-BITTEN VETERANS OF MANY PLAINS INDIAN BATTLES, THE COMANCHES BREAK AND FLEE---
HEY, LOOK! SOME OF THOSE RED DEVILS HAVE CUT IN AT THE END OF THE WAGON TRAIN! THEY'RE RUNNING OFF WITH THE LAST TWO WAGONS!
AI--THESE TWO ARE THE VALUABLE ONES!
2

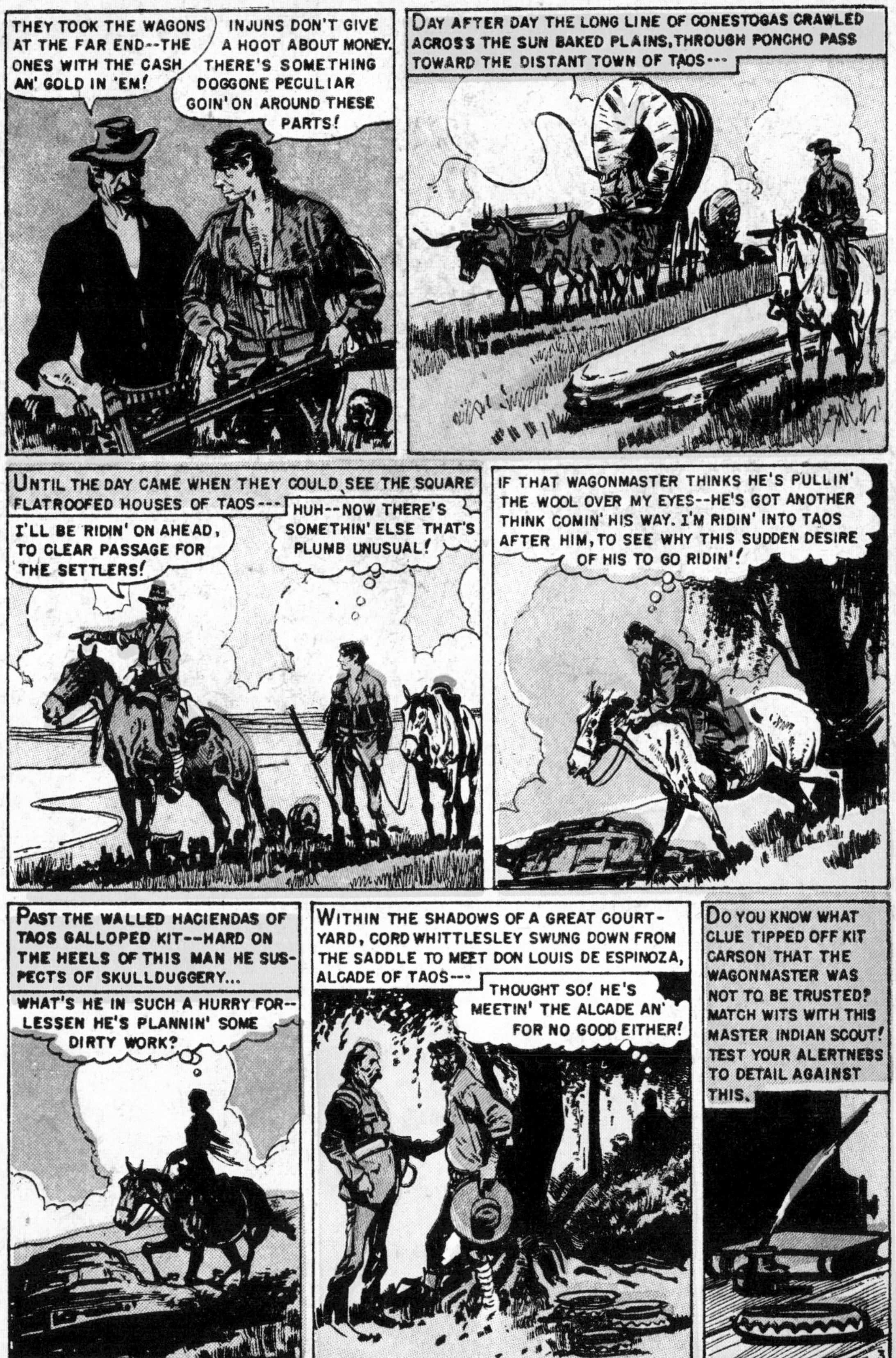
THEY TOOK THE WAGONS AT THE FAR END--THE ONES WITH THE CASH AN' GOLD IN 'EM!
INJUNS DON'T GIVE A HOOT ABOUT MONEY. THERE'S SOMETHING DOGGONE PECULIAR GOIN' ON AROUND THESE PARTS!
DAY AFTER DAY THE LONG LINE OF CONESTOGAS CRAWLED ACROSS THE SUN BAKED PLAINS, THROUGH PONCHO PASS TOWARD THE DISTANT TOWN OF TAOS---
UNTIL THE DAY CAME WHEN THEY COULD SEE THE SQUARE FLATROOFED HOUSES OF TAOS---
I'LL BE RIDIN' ON AHEAD, TO CLEAR PASSAGE FOR THE SETTLERS!
HUH--NOW THERE'S SOMETHIN' ELSE THAT'S PLUMB UNUSUAL!
IF THAT WAGONMASTER THINKS HE'S PULLIN' THE WOOL OVER MY EYES--HE'S GOT ANOTHER THINK COMIN' HIS WAY. I'M RIDIN' INTO TAOS AFTER HIM, TO SEE WHY THIS SUDDEN DESIRE OF HIS TO GO RIDIN'!
PAST THE WALLED HACIENDAS OF TAOS GALLOPED KIT--HARD ON THE HEELS OF THIS MAN HE SUSPECTS OF SKULLDUGGERY...
WHAT'S HE IN SUCH A HURRY FOR--LESSEN HE'S PLANNIN' SOME DIRTY WORK?
WITHIN THE SHADOWS OF A GREAT COURTYARD, CORD WHITTLESLEY SWUNG DOWN FROM THE SADDLE TO MEET DON LOUIS DE ESPINOZA, ALCADE OF TAOS---
THOUGHT SO! HE'S MEETIN' THE ALCADE AN' FOR NO GOOD EITHER!
DO YOU KNOW WHAT CLUE TIPPED OFF KIT CARSON THAT THE WAGONMASTER WAS NOT TO BE TRUSTED? MATCH WITS WITH THIS MASTER INDIAN SCOUT! TEST YOUR ALERTNESS TO DETAIL AGAINST THIS.
3

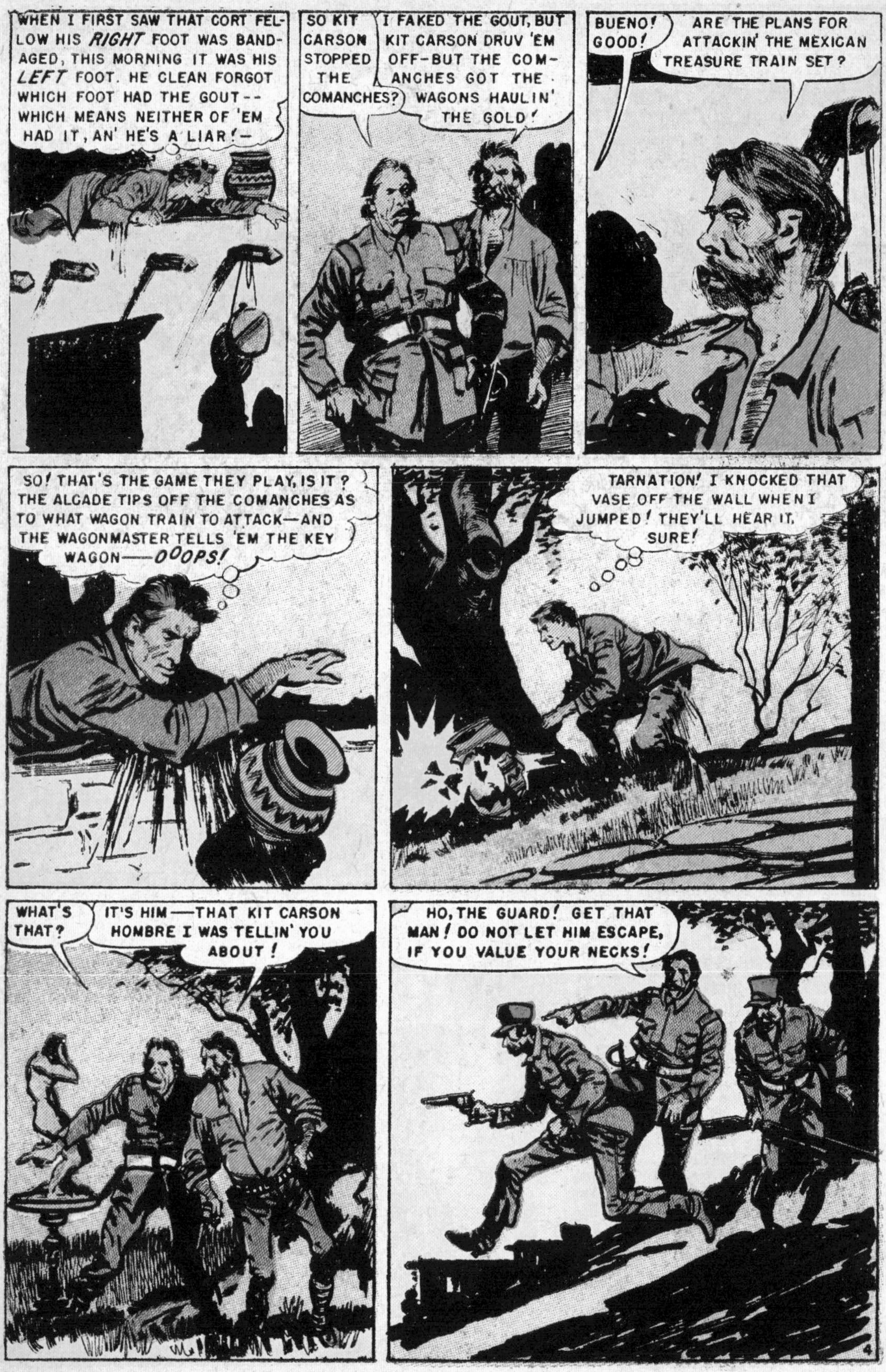
WHEN I FIRST SAW THAT CORT FELLOW HIS RIGHT FOOT WAS BANDAGED, THIS MORNING IT WAS HIS LEFT FOOT. HE CLEAN FORGOT WHICH FOOT HAD THE GOUT-- WHICH MEANS NEITHER OF 'EM HAD IT, AN' HE'S A LIAR!—
SO KIT CARSON STOPPED THE COMANCHES?
I FAKED THE GOUT, BUT KIT CARSON DRUV 'EM OFF-BUT THE COMANCHES GOT THE WAGONS HAULIN' THE GOLD!
BUENO! GOOD!
ARE THE PLANS FOR ATTACKIN' THE MEXICAN TREASURE TRAIN SET?
SO! THAT'S THE GAME THEY PLAY, IS IT? THE ALCADE TIPS OFF THE COMANCHES AS TO WHAT WAGON TRAIN TO ATTACK—AND THE WAGONMASTER TELLS 'EM THE KEY WAGON——OOOPS!
TARNATION! I KNOCKED THAT VASE OFF THE WALL WHEN I JUMPED! THEY'LL HEAR IT, SURE!
WHAT'S THAT?
IT'S HIM—THAT KIT CARSON HOMBRE I WAS TELLIN' YOU ABOUT!
HO, THE GUARD! GET THAT MAN! DO NOT LET HIM ESCAPE, IF YOU VALUE YOUR NECKS!
4

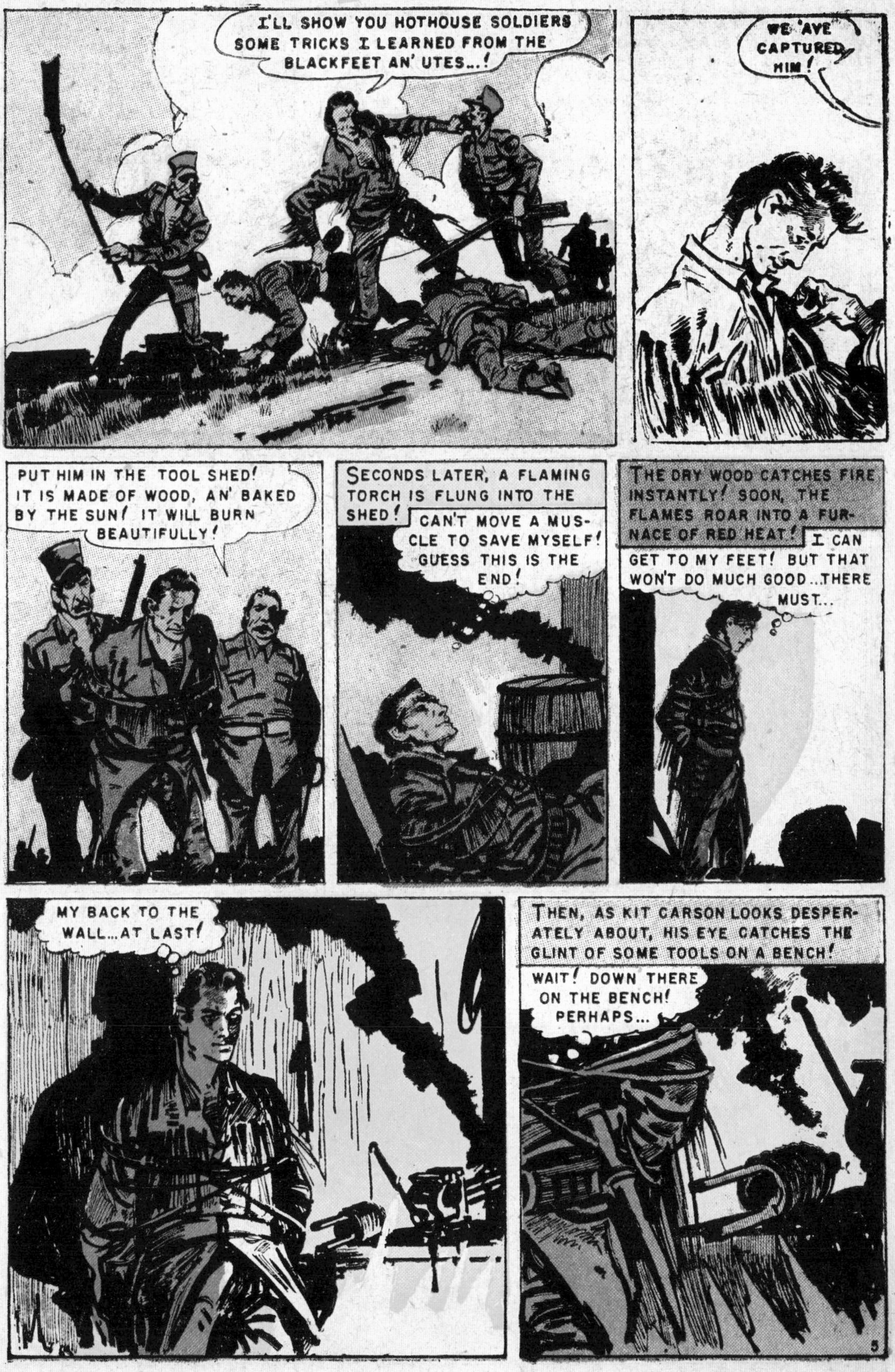

I'LL SHOW YOU HOTHOUSE SOLDIERS SOME TRICKS I LEARNED FROM THE BLACKFEET AN' UTES...!
WE 'AVE CAPTURED HIM!
PUT HIM IN THE TOOL SHED! IT IS MADE OF WOOD, AN' BAKED BY THE SUN! IT WILL BURN BEAUTIFULLY!
SECONDS LATER, A FLAMING TORCH IS FLUNG INTO THE SHED!
CAN'T MOVE A MUSCLE TO SAVE MYSELF! GUESS THIS IS THE END!
THE DRY WOOD CATCHES FIRE INSTANTLY! SOON, THE FLAMES ROAR INTO A FURNACE OF RED HEAT!
I CAN GET TO MY FEET! BUT THAT WON'T DO MUCH GOOD...THERE MUST...
MY BACK TO THE WALL...AT LAST!
THEN, AS KIT CARSON LOOKS DESPERATELY ABOUT, HIS EYE CATCHES THE GLINT OF SOME TOOLS ON A BENCH!
WAIT! DOWN THERE ON THE BENCH! PERHAPS...
5

KIT CARSON SAW A BIG MAGNET, AND HE THRUST HIS KNIFE—HAFT AGAINST IT, THEN LOWERED HIMSELF SLOWLY. THE POWERFUL MAGNET CAUGHT HIS KNIFE AND HELD IT...

THE MAGNET IS HEAVY ENOUGH TO HOLD MY HUNTIN' KNIFE—IT HAS TO BE!

GOT IT! THERE! KNIFE'S CUTTIN' THE ROPES—THEN TO GO AFTER A FEW FRIENDS OF MINE!

LESS THAN AN HOUR LATER AT A TRADING POST HIGH UP ALONG A BACK TRAIL...

BOYS, WE'RE RIDIN' AGAINST THE COMANCHES AN' THE ALCADE AN' HIS MEN!

TRADIN' WITH INJUNS IS HE? KIT, COUNT ME IN!

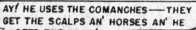

AY! HE USES THE COMANCHES—THEY GET THE SCALPS AN' HORSES AN' HE GETS THE GOLD!

ON THE SLOPES OF THE JEMEZ MOUNTAINS, THE ALCADE OF TAOS, WITH A FEW OF HIS GUARDS AND THE WARRIORS OF THE COMANCHE NATION, AWAIT THE MEXICAN TREASURE TRAIL...

HERE COMES THE TRAIN NOW, LOADED WITH SILVER AN' GOLD! HAI!

AIIEEE!

LOOK! MOUNTAIN MEN!

THEY SCALPED MY BROTHER!

THIS IS FOR KILLIN' MY PARTNER!

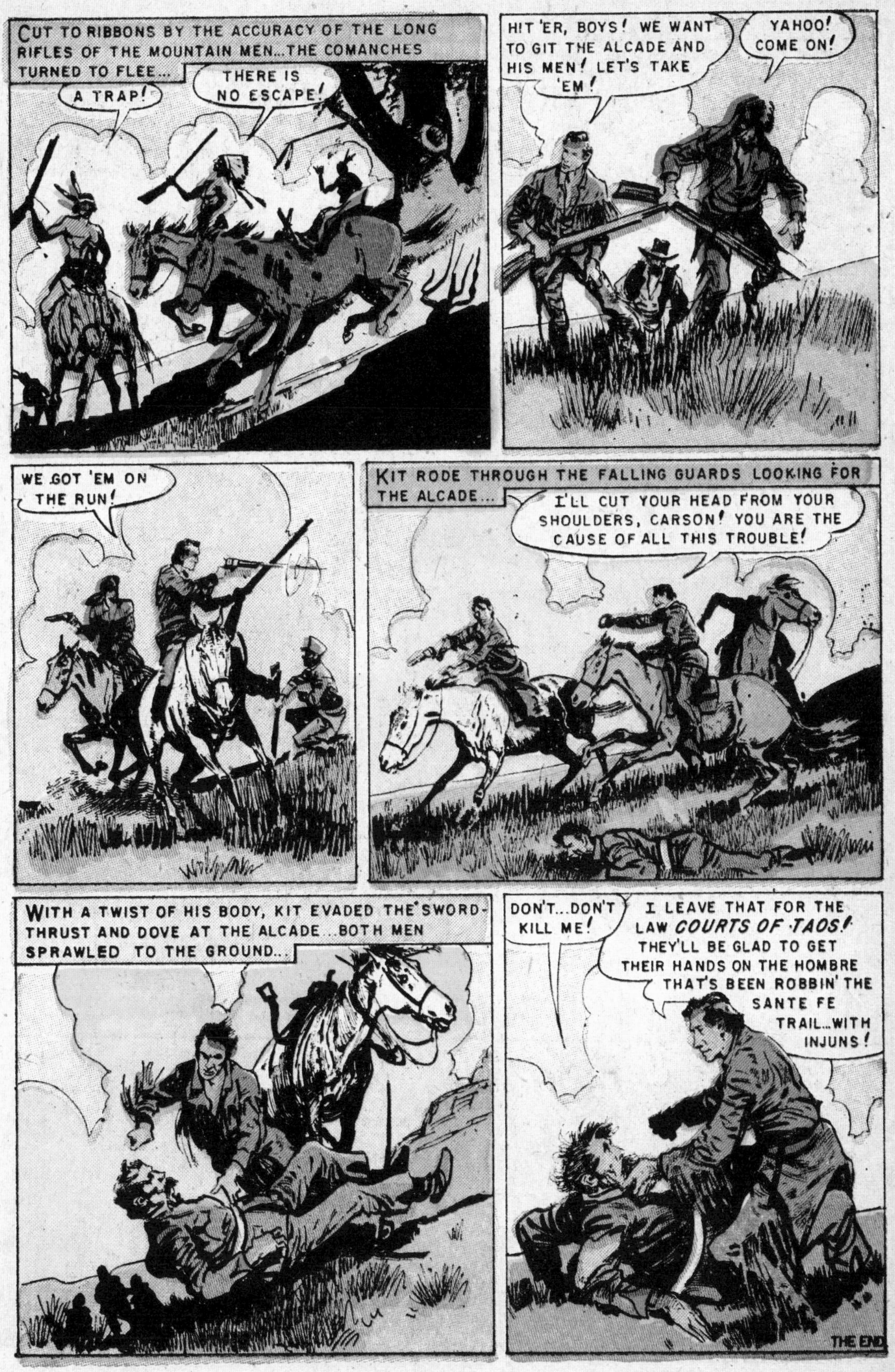
CUT TO RIBBONS BY THE ACCURACY OF THE LONG RIFLES OF THE MOUNTAIN MEN...THE COMANCHES TURNED TO FLEE...
A TRAP!
THERE IS NO ESCAPE!
HIT 'ER, BOYS! WE WANT TO GIT THE ALCADE AND HIS MEN! LET'S TAKE 'EM!
YAHOO! COME ON!
WE GOT 'EM ON THE RUN!
KIT RODE THROUGH THE FALLING GUARDS LOOKING FOR THE ALCADE...
I'LL CUT YOUR HEAD FROM YOUR SHOULDERS, CARSON! YOU ARE THE CAUSE OF ALL THIS TROUBLE!
WITH A TWIST OF HIS BODY, KIT EVADED THE SWORD-THRUST AND DOVE AT THE ALCADE...BOTH MEN SPRAWLED TO THE GROUND...
DON'T...DON'T KILL ME!
I LEAVE THAT FOR THE LAW COURTS OF TAOS! THEY'LL BE GLAD TO GET THEIR HANDS ON THE HOMBRE THAT'S BEEN ROBBIN' THE SANTE FE TRAIL...WITH INJUNS!
THE END

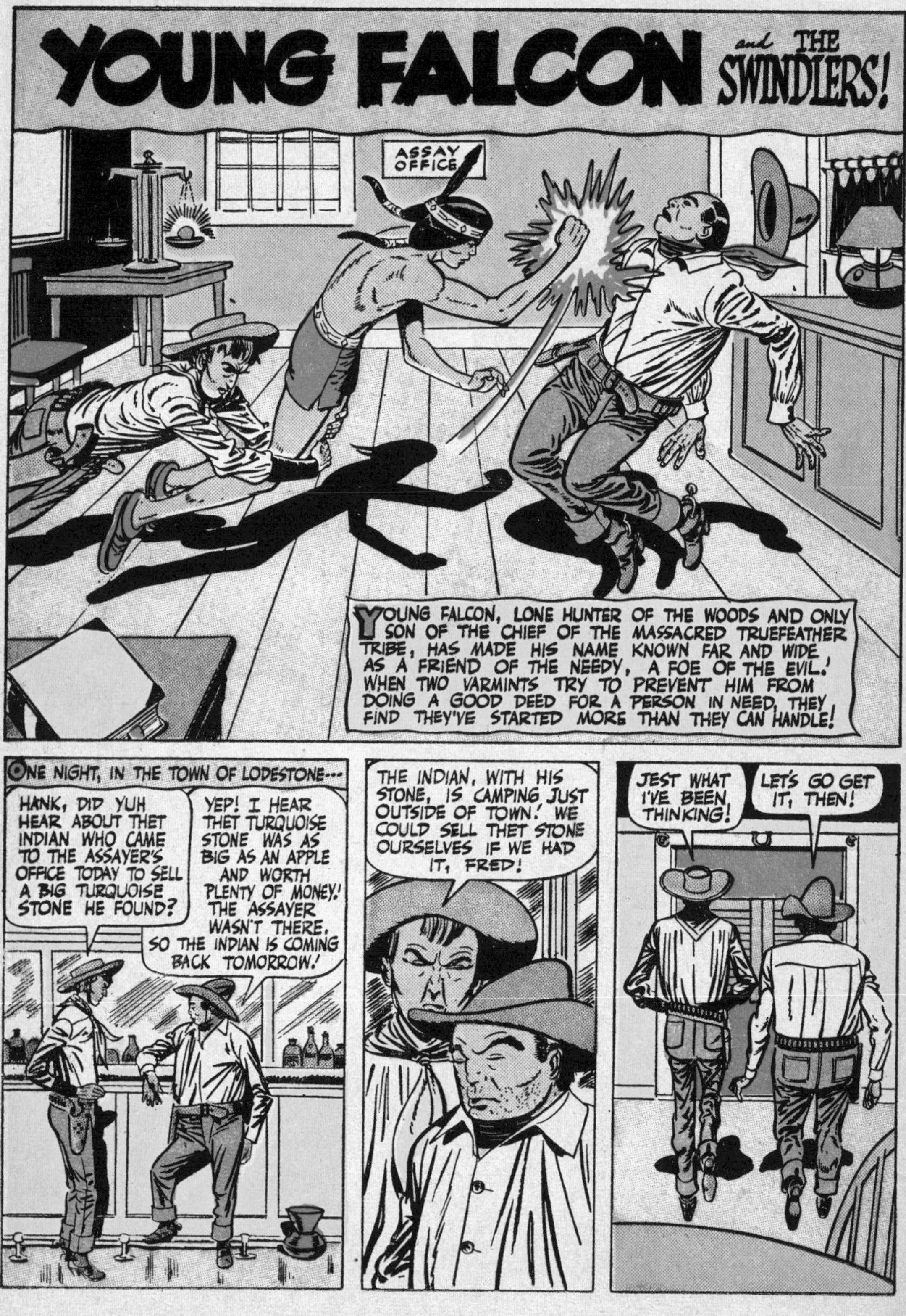
YOUNG FALCON and THE SWINDLERS!
ASSAY OFFICE
YOUNG FALCON, LONE HUNTER OF THE WOODS AND ONLY SON OF THE CHIEF OF THE MASSACRED TRUEFEATHER TRIBE, HAS MADE HIS NAME KNOWN FAR AND WIDE AS A FRIEND OF THE NEEDY, A FOE OF THE EVIL! WHEN TWO VARMINTS TRY TO PREVENT HIM FROM DOING A GOOD DEED FOR A PERSON IN NEED, THEY FIND THEY'VE STARTED MORE THAN THEY CAN HANDLE!
ONE NIGHT, IN THE TOWN OF LODESTONE---
HANK, DID YUH HEAR ABOUT THET INDIAN WHO CAME TO THE ASSAYER'S OFFICE TODAY TO SELL A BIG TURQUOISE STONE HE FOUND?
YEP! I HEAR THET TURQUOISE STONE WAS AS BIG AS AN APPLE AND WORTH PLENTY OF MONEY! THE ASSAYER WASN'T THERE, SO THE INDIAN IS COMING BACK TOMORROW!
THE INDIAN, WITH HIS STONE, IS CAMPING JUST OUTSIDE OF TOWN! WE COULD SELL THET STONE OURSELVES IF WE HAD IT, FRED!
JEST WHAT I'VE BEEN THINKING!
LET'S GO GET IT, THEN!

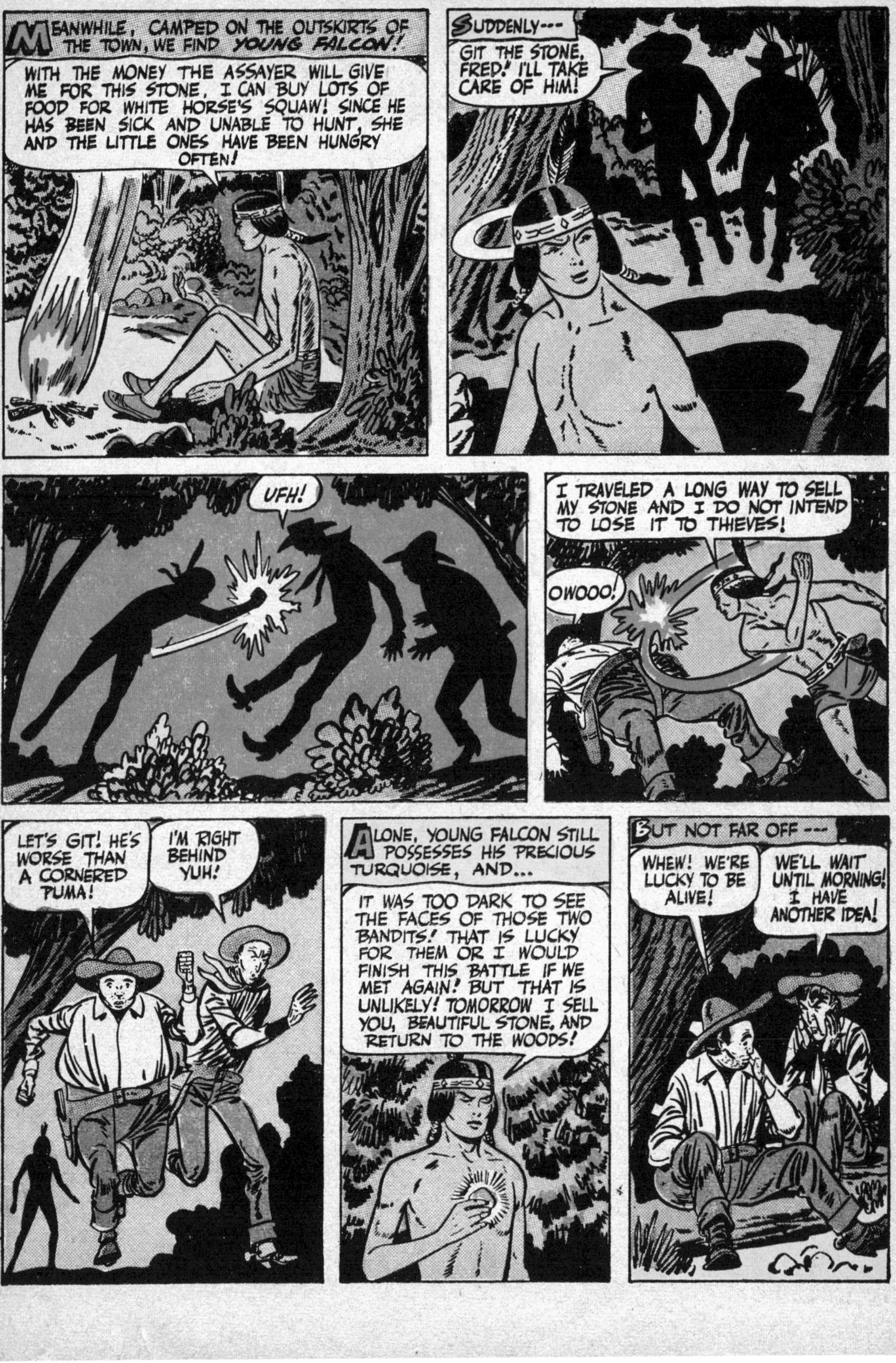
MEANWHILE, CAMPED ON THE OUTSKIRTS OF THE TOWN, WE FIND YOUNG FALCON!
WITH THE MONEY THE ASSAYER WILL GIVE ME FOR THIS STONE, I CAN BUY LOTS OF FOOD FOR WHITE HORSE'S SQUAW! SINCE HE HAS BEEN SICK AND UNABLE TO HUNT, SHE AND THE LITTLE ONES HAVE BEEN HUNGRY OFTEN!
SUDDENLY---
GIT THE STONE, FRED! I'LL TAKE CARE OF HIM!
UFH!
I TRAVELED A LONG WAY TO SELL MY STONE AND I DO NOT INTEND TO LOSE IT TO THIEVES!
OWOOO!
LET'S GIT! HE'S WORSE THAN A CORNERED PUMA!
I'M RIGHT BEHIND YUH!
ALONE, YOUNG FALCON STILL POSSESSES HIS PRECIOUS TURQUOISE, AND...
IT WAS TOO DARK TO SEE THE FACES OF THOSE TWO BANDITS! THAT IS LUCKY FOR THEM OR I WOULD FINISH THIS BATTLE IF WE MET AGAIN! BUT THAT IS UNLIKELY! TOMORROW I SELL YOU, BEAUTIFUL STONE, AND RETURN TO THE WOODS!
BUT NOT FAR OFF ---
WHEW! WE'RE LUCKY TO BE ALIVE!
WE'LL WAIT UNTIL MORNING! I HAVE ANOTHER IDEA!

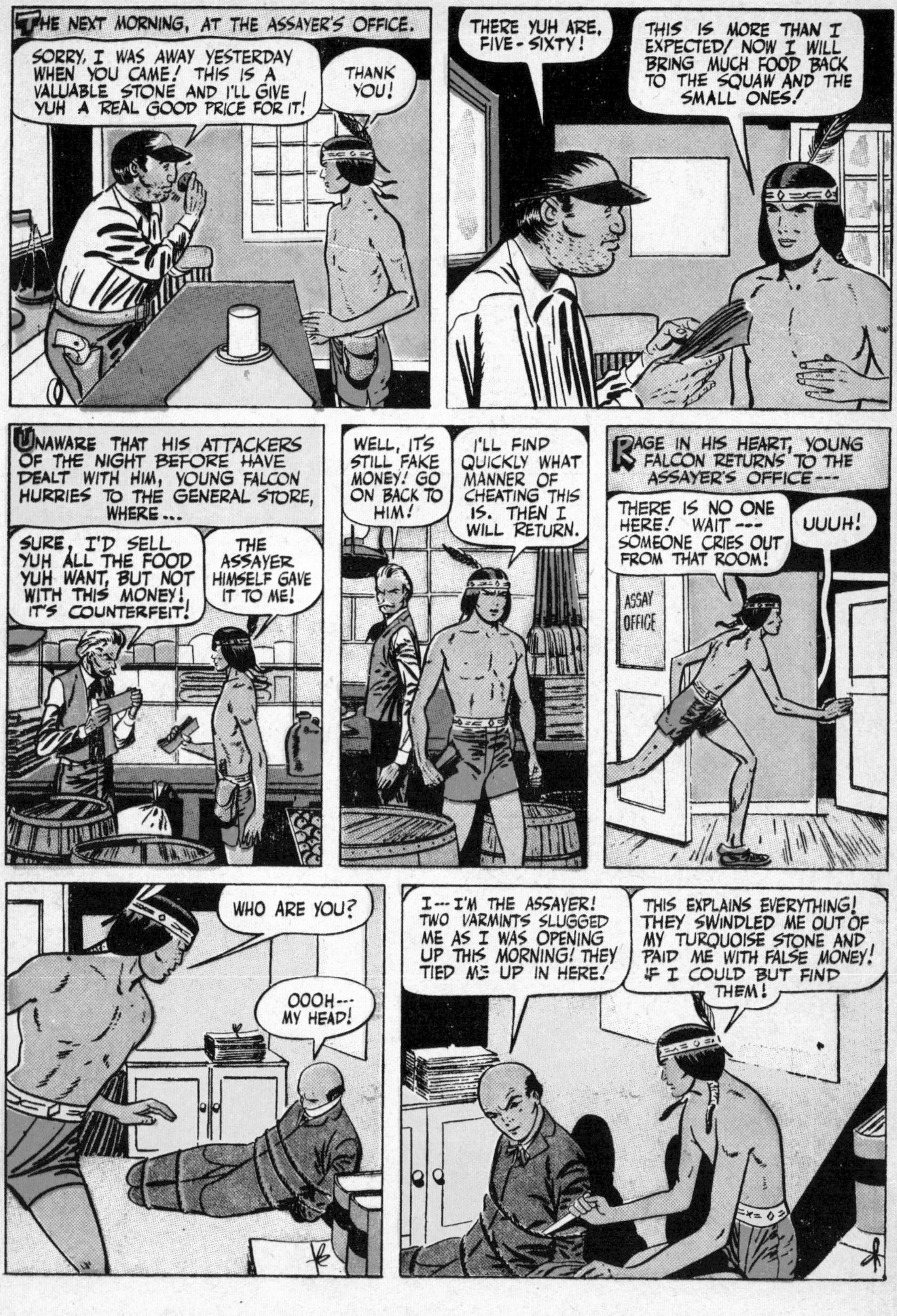
THE NEXT MORNING, AT THE ASSAYER'S OFFICE.
SORRY, I WAS AWAY YESTERDAY WHEN YOU CAME! THIS IS A VALUABLE STONE AND I'LL GIVE YUH A REAL GOOD PRICE FOR IT!
THANK YOU!
THERE YUH ARE. FIVE-SIXTY!
THIS IS MORE THAN I EXPECTED! NOW I WILL BRING MUCH FOOD BACK TO THE SQUAW AND THE SMALL ONES!
UNAWARE THAT HIS ATTACKERS OF THE NIGHT BEFORE HAVE DEALT WITH HIM, YOUNG FALCON HURRIES TO THE GENERAL STORE, WHERE...
SURE, I'D SELL YUH ALL THE FOOD YUH WANT, BUT NOT WITH THIS MONEY! IT'S COUNTERFEIT!
THE ASSAYER HIMSELF GAVE IT TO ME!
WELL, IT'S STILL FAKE MONEY! GO ON BACK TO HIM!
I'LL FIND QUICKLY WHAT MANNER OF CHEATING THIS IS. THEN I WILL RETURN.
RAGE IN HIS HEART, YOUNG FALCON RETURNS TO THE ASSAYER'S OFFICE---
THERE IS NO ONE HERE! WAIT--- SOMEONE CRIES OUT FROM THAT ROOM!
UUUH!
ASSAY OFFICE
WHO ARE YOU?
OOOH--- MY HEAD!
I--- I'M THE ASSAYER! TWO VARMINTS SLUGGED ME AS I WAS OPENING UP THIS MORNING! THEY TIED ME UP IN HERE!
THIS EXPLAINS EVERYTHING! THEY SWINDLED ME OUT OF MY TURQUOISE STONE AND PAID ME WITH FALSE MONEY! IF I COULD BUT FIND THEM!

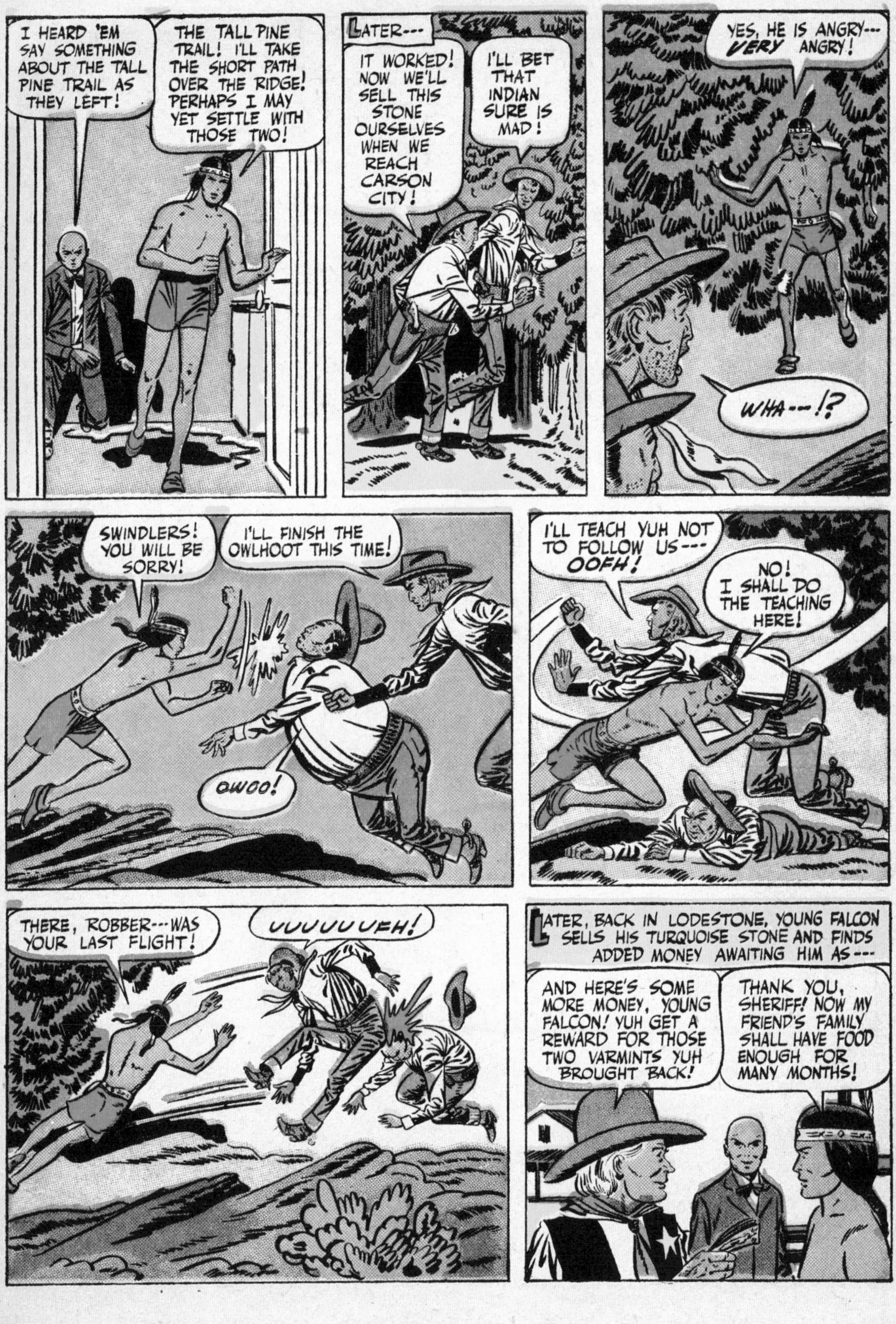
I HEARD 'EM SAY SOMETHING ABOUT THE TALL PINE TRAIL AS THEY LEFT!
THE TALL PINE TRAIL! I'LL TAKE THE SHORT PATH OVER THE RIDGE! PERHAPS I MAY YET SETTLE WITH THOSE TWO!
LATER---
IT WORKED! NOW WE'LL SELL THIS STONE OURSELVES WHEN WE REACH CARSON CITY!
I'LL BET THAT INDIAN SURE IS MAD!
YES, HE IS ANGRY--- VERY ANGRY!
WHA---!?
SWINDLERS! YOU WILL BE SORRY!
I'LL FINISH THE OWLHOOT THIS TIME!
OWOO!
I'LL TEACH YUH NOT TO FOLLOW US--- OOFH!
NO! I SHALL DO THE TEACHING HERE!
THERE, ROBBER---WAS YOUR LAST FLIGHT!
UUUUUUFH!
LATER, BACK IN LODESTONE, YOUNG FALCON SELLS HIS TURQUOISE STONE AND FINDS ADDED MONEY AWAITING HIM AS---
AND HERE'S SOME MORE MONEY, YOUNG FALCON! YUH GET A REWARD FOR THOSE TWO VARMINTS YUH BROUGHT BACK!
THANK YOU, SHERIFF! NOW MY FRIEND'S FAMILY SHALL HAVE FOOD ENOUGH FOR MANY MONTHS!

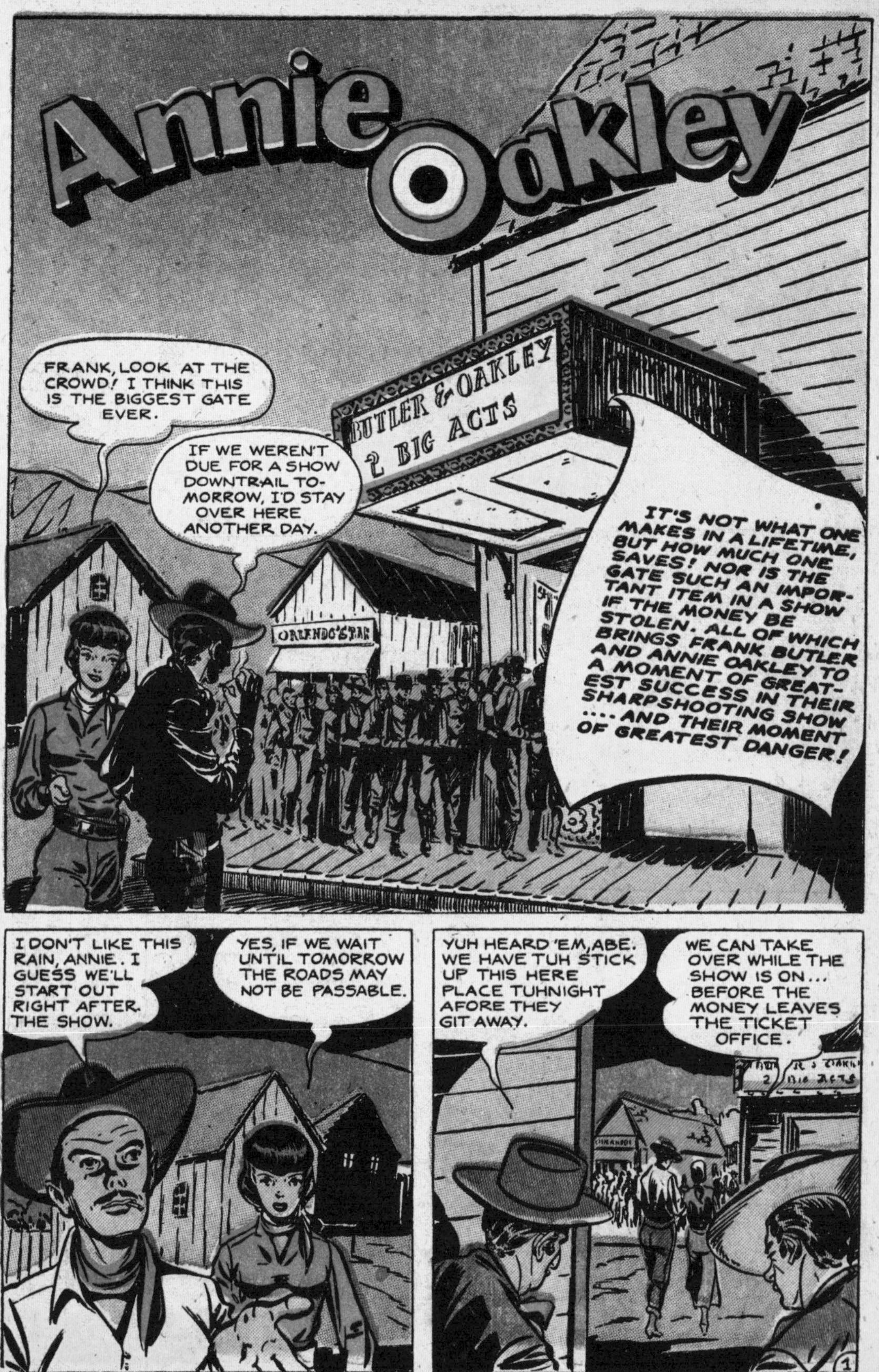
Annie Oakley
BUTLER & OAKLEY
2 BIG ACTS
FRANK, LOOK AT THE CROWD! I THINK THIS IS THE BIGGEST GATE EVER.
IF WE WEREN'T DUE FOR A SHOW DOWNTRAIL TO-MORROW, I'D STAY OVER HERE ANOTHER DAY.
IT'S NOT WHAT ONE MAKES IN A LIFETIME, BUT HOW MUCH ONE SAVES! NOR IS THE GATE SUCH AN IMPOR-TANT ITEM IN A SHOW IF THE MONEY BE STOLEN. ALL OF WHICH BRINGS FRANK BUTLER AND ANNIE OAKLEY TO A MOMENT OF GREAT-EST SUCCESS IN THEIR SHARPSHOOTING SHOW .... AND THEIR MOMENT OF GREATEST DANGER!
I DON'T LIKE THIS RAIN, ANNIE. I GUESS WE'LL START OUT RIGHT AFTER THE SHOW.
YES, IF WE WAIT UNTIL TOMORROW THE ROADS MAY NOT BE PASSABLE.
YUH HEARD 'EM, ABE. WE HAVE TUH STICK UP THIS HERE PLACE TUHNIGHT AFORE THEY GIT AWAY.
WE CAN TAKE OVER WHILE THE SHOW IS ON... BEFORE THE MONEY LEAVES THE TICKET OFFICE.
1

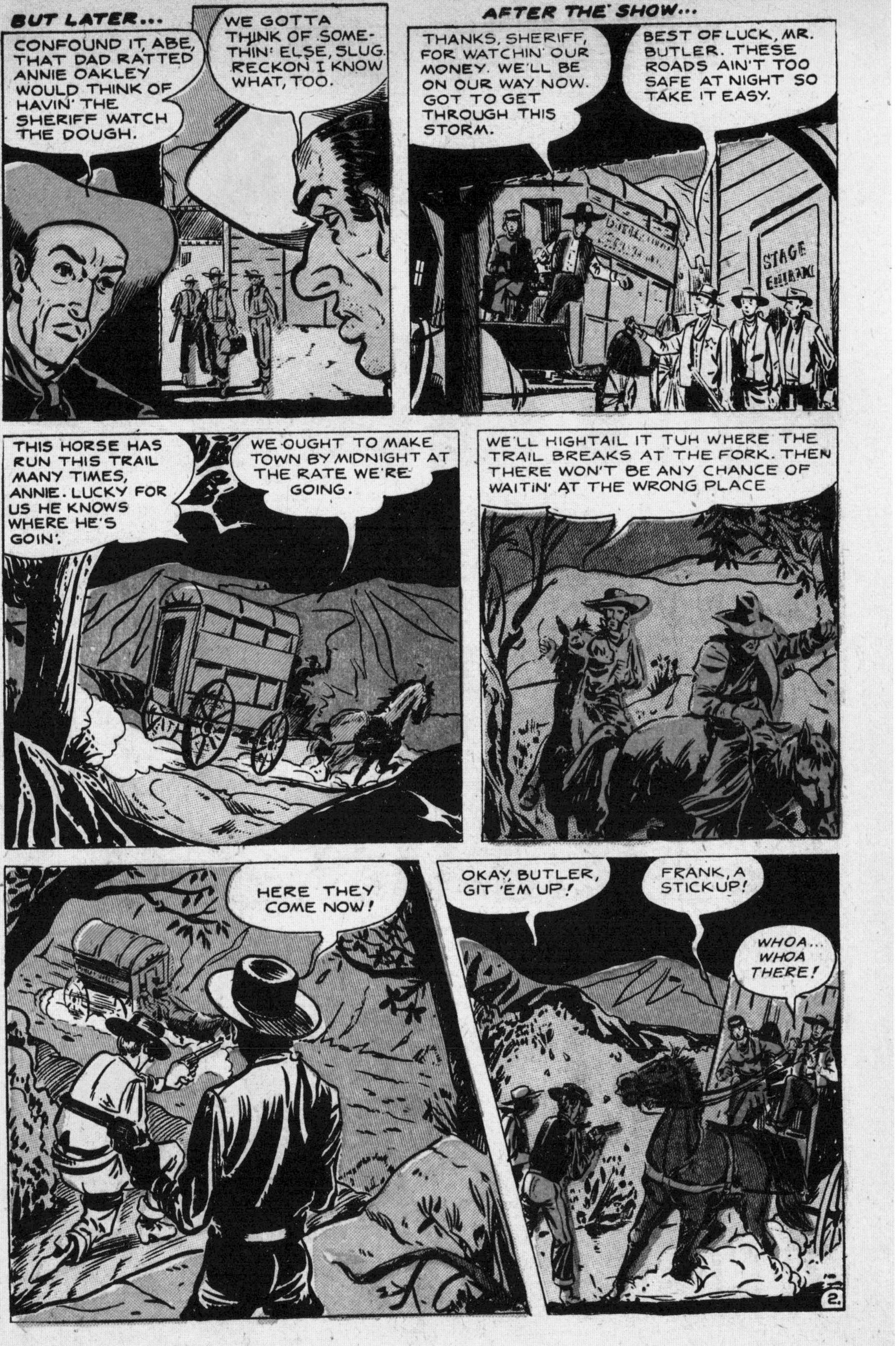
BUT LATER...
CONFOUND IT, ABE, THAT DAD RATTED ANNIE OAKLEY WOULD THINK OF HAVIN' THE SHERIFF WATCH THE DOUGH.
WE GOTTA THINK OF SOME-THIN' ELSE, SLUG. RECKON I KNOW WHAT, TOO.
AFTER THE SHOW...
THANKS, SHERIFF, FOR WATCHIN' OUR MONEY. WE'LL BE ON OUR WAY NOW. GOT TO GET THROUGH THIS STORM.
BEST OF LUCK, MR. BUTLER. THESE ROADS AIN'T TOO SAFE AT NIGHT SO TAKE IT EASY.
STAGE
THIS HORSE HAS RUN THIS TRAIL MANY TIMES, ANNIE. LUCKY FOR US HE KNOWS WHERE HE'S GOIN'.
WE OUGHT TO MAKE TOWN BY MIDNIGHT AT THE RATE WE'RE GOING.
WE'LL HIGHTAIL IT TUH WHERE THE TRAIL BREAKS AT THE FORK. THEN THERE WON'T BE ANY CHANCE OF WAITIN' AT THE WRONG PLACE
HERE THEY COME NOW!
OKAY, BUTLER, GIT 'EM UP!
FRANK, A STICKUP!
WHOA... WHOA THERE!
2.

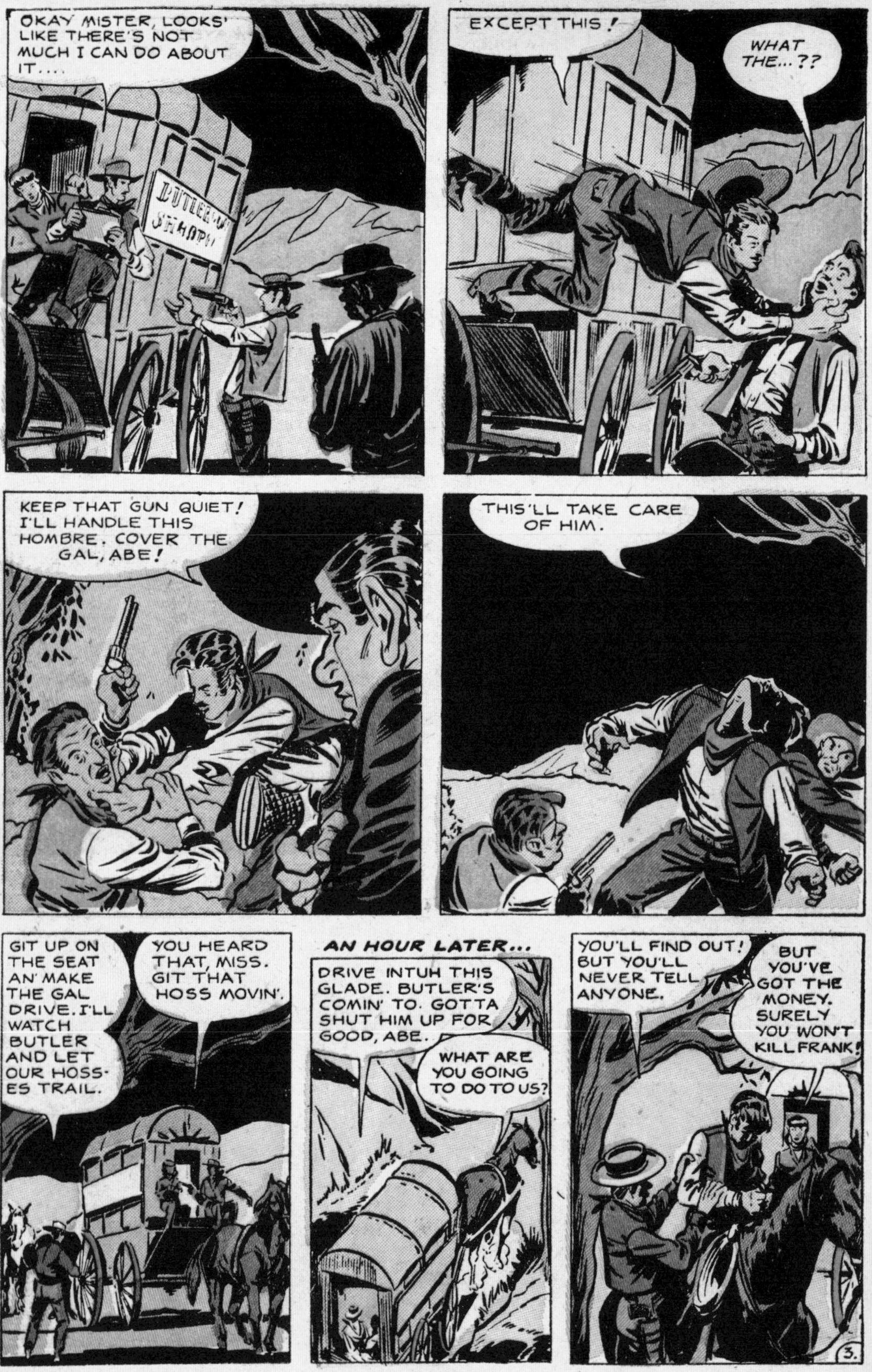
OKAY MISTER, LOOKS' LIKE THERE'S NOT MUCH I CAN DO ABOUT IT....
EXCEPT THIS!
WHAT THE...??
KEEP THAT GUN QUIET! I'LL HANDLE THIS HOMBRE. COVER THE GAL, ABE!
THIS'LL TAKE CARE OF HIM.
GIT UP ON THE SEAT AN' MAKE THE GAL DRIVE. I'LL WATCH BUTLER AND LET OUR HOSS-ES TRAIL.
YOU HEARD THAT, MISS. GIT THAT HOSS MOVIN'.
AN HOUR LATER...
DRIVE INTUH THIS GLADE. BUTLER'S COMIN' TO. GOTTA SHUT HIM UP FOR GOOD, ABE.
WHAT ARE YOU GOING TO DO TO US?
YOU'LL FIND OUT! BUT YOU'LL NEVER TELL ANYONE.
BUT YOU'VE GOT THE MONEY. SURELY YOU WON'T KILL FRANK!
3.

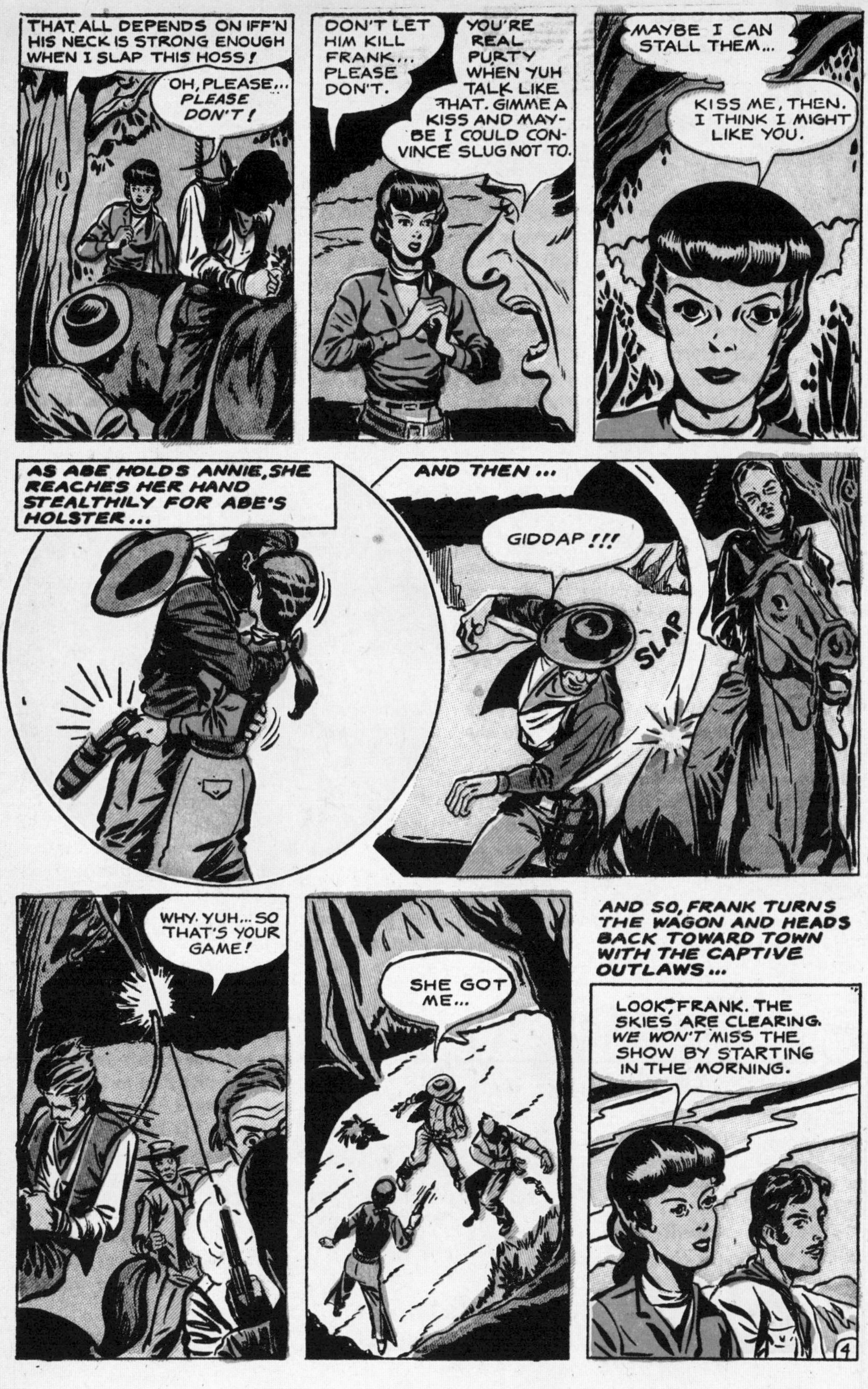
THAT ALL DEPENDS ON IFF'N HIS NECK IS STRONG ENOUGH WHEN I SLAP THIS HOSS!
OH, PLEASE... PLEASE DON'T!
DON'T LET HIM KILL FRANK... PLEASE DON'T.
YOU'RE REAL PURTY WHEN YUH TALK LIKE THAT. GIMME A KISS AND MAYBE I COULD CONVINCE SLUG NOT TO.
MAYBE I CAN STALL THEM...
KISS ME, THEN. I THINK I MIGHT LIKE YOU.
AS ABE HOLDS ANNIE, SHE REACHES HER HAND STEALTHILY FOR ABE'S HOLSTER...
AND THEN...
GIDDAP!!!
SLAP
WHY. YUH... SO THAT'S YOUR GAME!
SHE GOT ME...
AND SO, FRANK TURNS THE WAGON AND HEADS BACK TOWARD TOWN WITH THE CAPTIVE OUTLAWS...
LOOK, FRANK. THE SKIES ARE CLEARING. WE WON'T MISS THE SHOW BY STARTING IN THE MORNING.
4

DEATH VALLEY

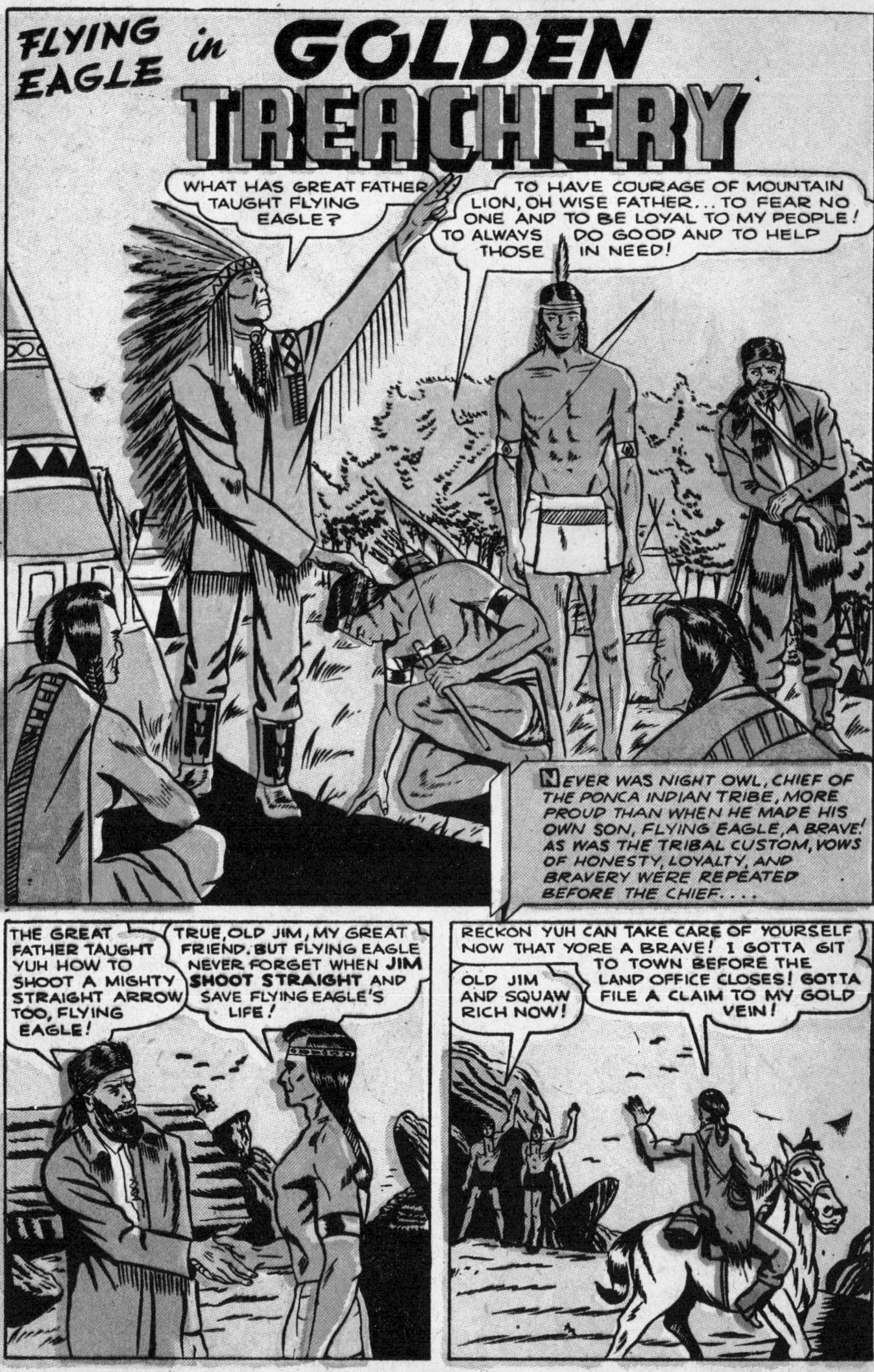

FLYING EAGLE in GOLDEN TREACHERY
WHAT HAS GREAT FATHER TAUGHT FLYING EAGLE?
TO HAVE COURAGE OF MOUNTAIN LION, OH WISE FATHER... TO FEAR NO ONE AND TO BE LOYAL TO MY PEOPLE! TO ALWAYS DO GOOD AND TO HELP THOSE IN NEED!
NEVER WAS NIGHT OWL, CHIEF OF THE PONCA INDIAN TRIBE, MORE PROUD THAN WHEN HE MADE HIS OWN SON, FLYING EAGLE, A BRAVE! AS WAS THE TRIBAL CUSTOM, VOWS OF HONESTY, LOYALTY, AND BRAVERY WERE REPEATED BEFORE THE CHIEF...
THE GREAT FATHER TAUGHT YUH HOW TO SHOOT A MIGHTY STRAIGHT ARROW TOO, FLYING EAGLE!
TRUE, OLD JIM, MY GREAT FRIEND. BUT FLYING EAGLE NEVER FORGET WHEN JIM SHOOT STRAIGHT AND SAVE FLYING EAGLE'S LIFE!
RECKON YUH CAN TAKE CARE OF YOURSELF NOW THAT YORE A BRAVE! I GOTTA GIT TO TOWN BEFORE THE LAND OFFICE CLOSES! GOTTA FILE A CLAIM TO MY GOLD VEIN!
OLD JIM AND SQUAW RICH NOW!

DEATH VALLEY

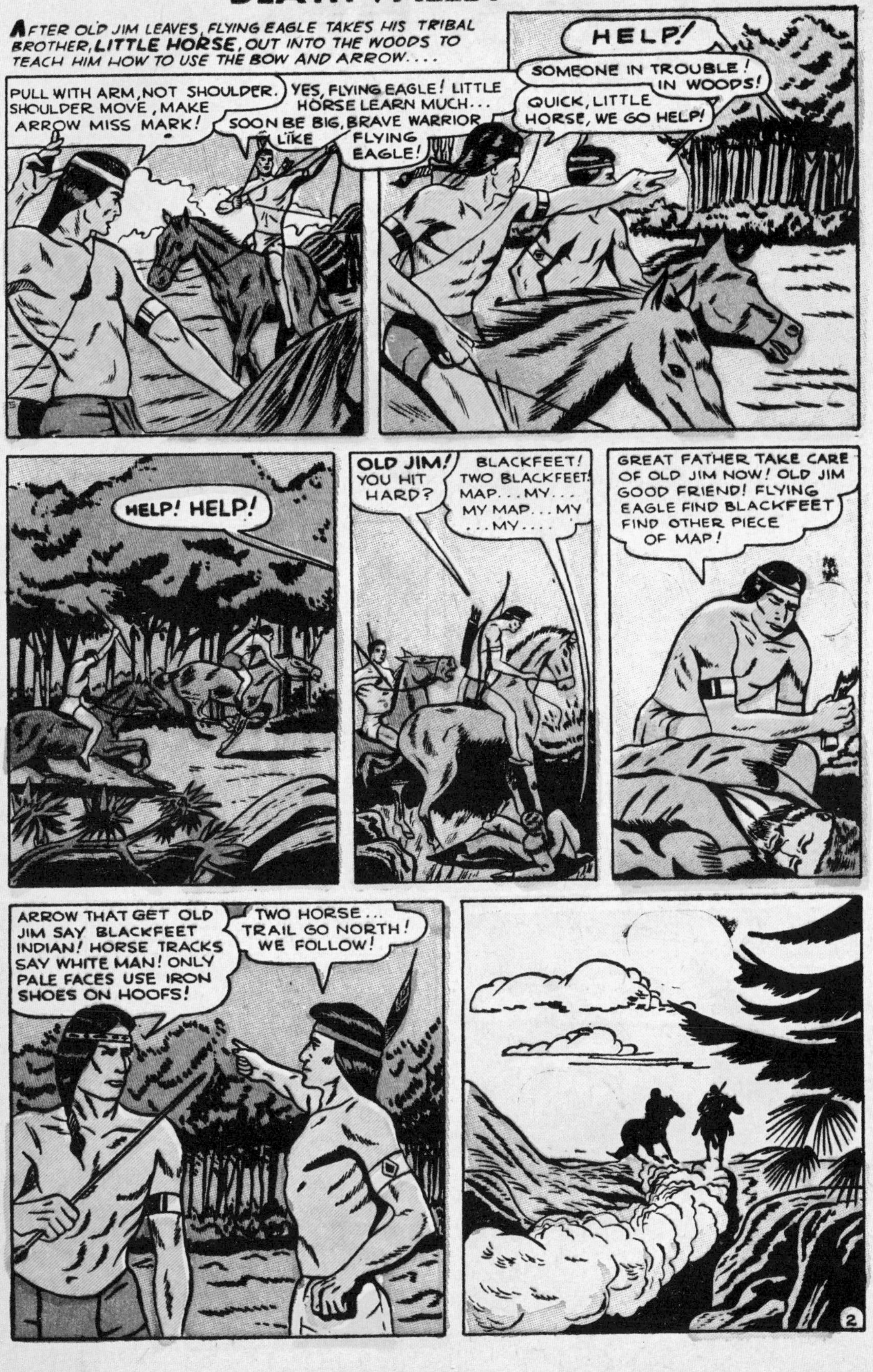
AFTER OLD JIM LEAVES, FLYING EAGLE TAKES HIS TRIBAL BROTHER, LITTLE HORSE, OUT INTO THE WOODS TO TEACH HIM HOW TO USE THE BOW AND ARROW....
PULL WITH ARM, NOT SHOULDER. SHOULDER MOVE, MAKE ARROW MISS MARK!
YES, FLYING EAGLE! LITTLE HORSE LEARN MUCH... SOON BE BIG, BRAVE WARRIOR LIKE FLYING EAGLE!
HELP!
SOMEONE IN TROUBLE! IN WOODS!
QUICK, LITTLE HORSE, WE GO HELP!
HELP! HELP!
OLD JIM! YOU HIT HARD?
BLACKFEET! TWO BLACKFEET! MAP... MY... MY MAP... MY ...MY....
GREAT FATHER TAKE CARE OF OLD JIM NOW! OLD JIM GOOD FRIEND! FLYING EAGLE FIND BLACKFEET FIND OTHER PIECE OF MAP!
ARROW THAT GET OLD JIM SAY BLACKFEET INDIAN! HORSE TRACKS SAY WHITE MAN! ONLY PALE FACES USE IRON SHOES ON HOOFS!
TWO HORSE... TRAIL GO NORTH! WE FOLLOW!
2

DEATH VALLEY

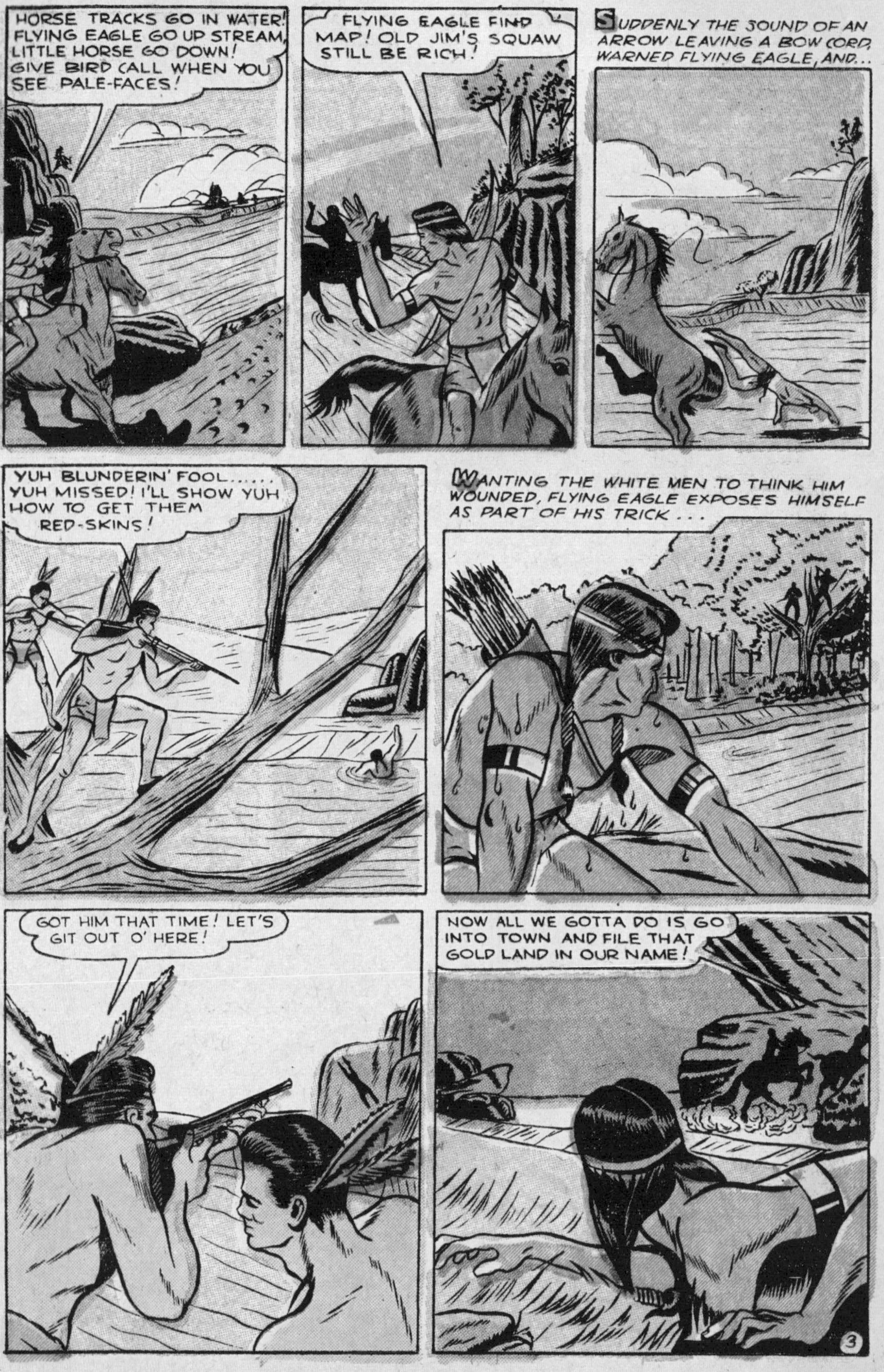

HORSE TRACKS GO IN WATER! FLYING EAGLE GO UP STREAM, LITTLE HORSE GO DOWN! GIVE BIRD CALL WHEN YOU SEE PALE-FACES!
FLYING EAGLE FIND MAP! OLD JIM'S SQUAW STILL BE RICH!
SUDDENLY THE SOUND OF AN ARROW LEAVING A BOW CORD, WARNED FLYING EAGLE, AND...
YUH BLUNDERIN' FOOL...... YUH MISSED! I'LL SHOW YUH HOW TO GET THEM RED-SKINS!
WANTING THE WHITE MEN TO THINK HIM WOUNDED, FLYING EAGLE EXPOSES HIMSELF AS PART OF HIS TRICK...
GOT HIM THAT TIME! LET'S GIT OUT O' HERE!
NOW ALL WE GOTTA DO IS GO INTO TOWN AND FILE THAT GOLD LAND IN OUR NAME!
3

DEATH VALLEY

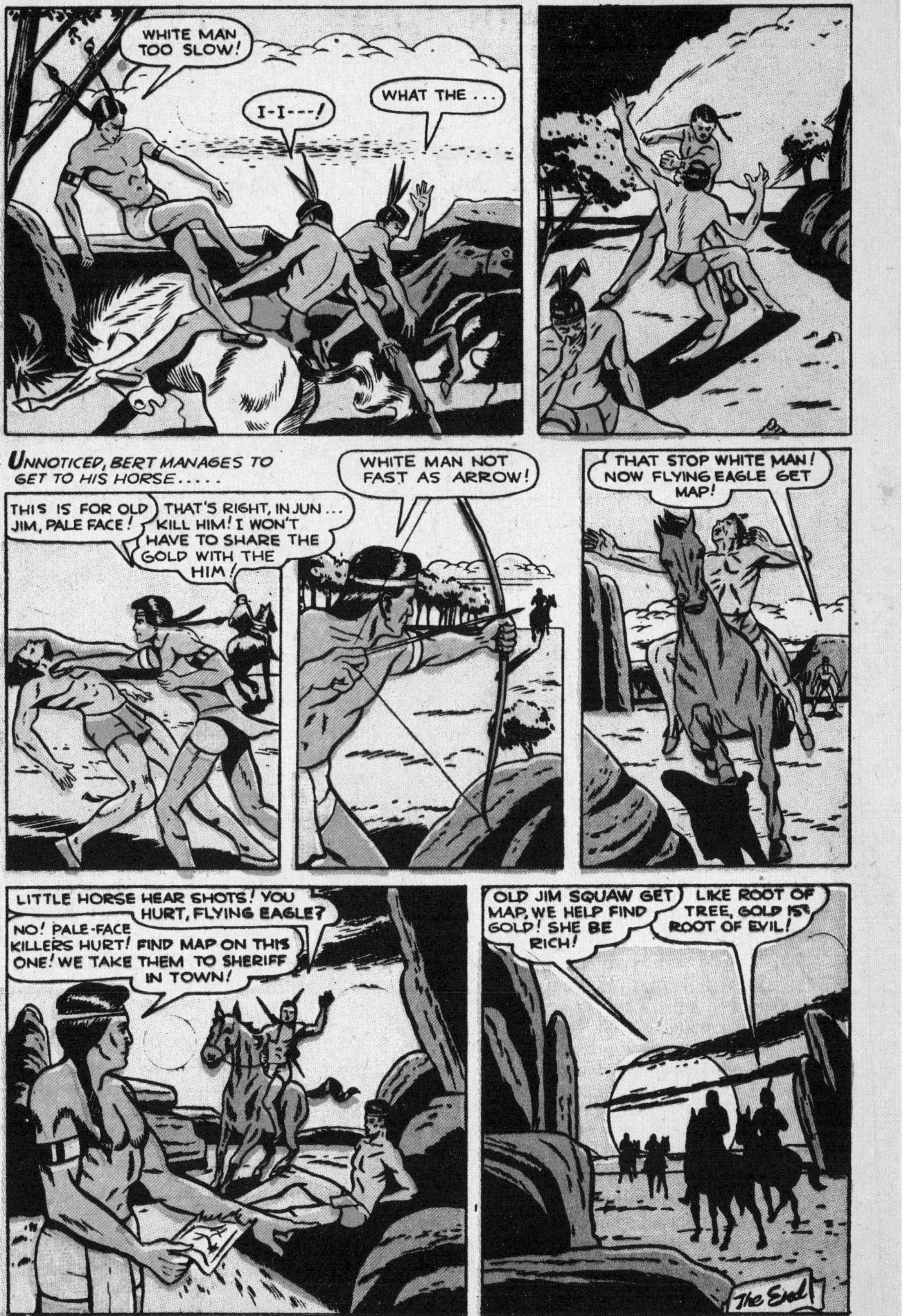
WHITE MAN TOO SLOW!
I-I---!
WHAT THE . . .
UNNOTICED, BERT MANAGES TO GET TO HIS HORSE.....
THIS IS FOR OLD JIM, PALE FACE!
THAT'S RIGHT, INJUN ... KILL HIM! I WON'T HAVE TO SHARE THE GOLD WITH THE HIM!
WHITE MAN NOT FAST AS ARROW!
THAT STOP WHITE MAN! NOW FLYING EAGLE GET MAP!
LITTLE HORSE HEAR SHOTS! YOU HURT, FLYING EAGLE?
NO! PALE-FACE KILLERS HURT! FIND MAP ON THIS ONE! WE TAKE THEM TO SHERIFF IN TOWN!
OLD JIM SQUAW GET MAP, WE HELP FIND GOLD! SHE BE RICH!
LIKE ROOT OF TREE, GOLD IS ROOT OF EVIL!
The End

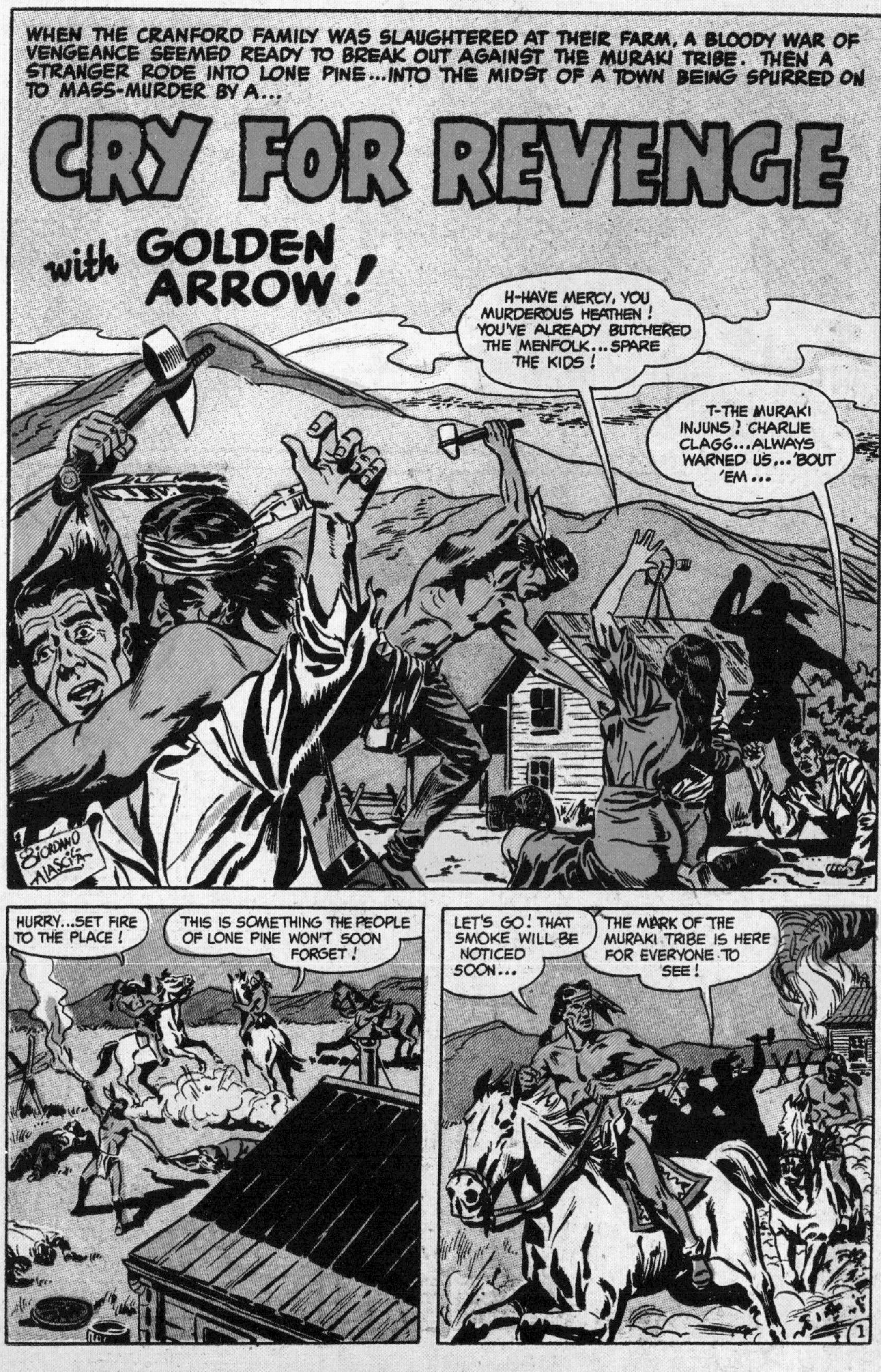
WHEN THE CRANFORD FAMILY WAS SLAUGHTERED AT THEIR FARM, A BLOODY WAR OF VENGEANCE SEEMED READY TO BREAK OUT AGAINST THE MURAKI TRIBE. THEN A STRANGER RODE INTO LONE PINE...INTO THE MIDST OF A TOWN BEING SPURRED ON TO MASS-MURDER BY A...
CRY FOR REVENGE
with GOLDEN ARROW!
H-HAVE MERCY, YOU MURDEROUS HEATHEN! YOU'VE ALREADY BUTCHERED THE MENFOLK...SPARE THE KIDS!
T-THE MURAKI INJUNS? CHARLIE CLAGG...ALWAYS WARNED US...'BOUT 'EM...
HURRY...SET FIRE TO THE PLACE!
THIS IS SOMETHING THE PEOPLE OF LONE PINE WON'T SOON FORGET!
LET'S GO! THAT SMOKE WILL BE NOTICED SOON...
THE MARK OF THE MURAKI TRIBE IS HERE FOR EVERYONE TO SEE!
1

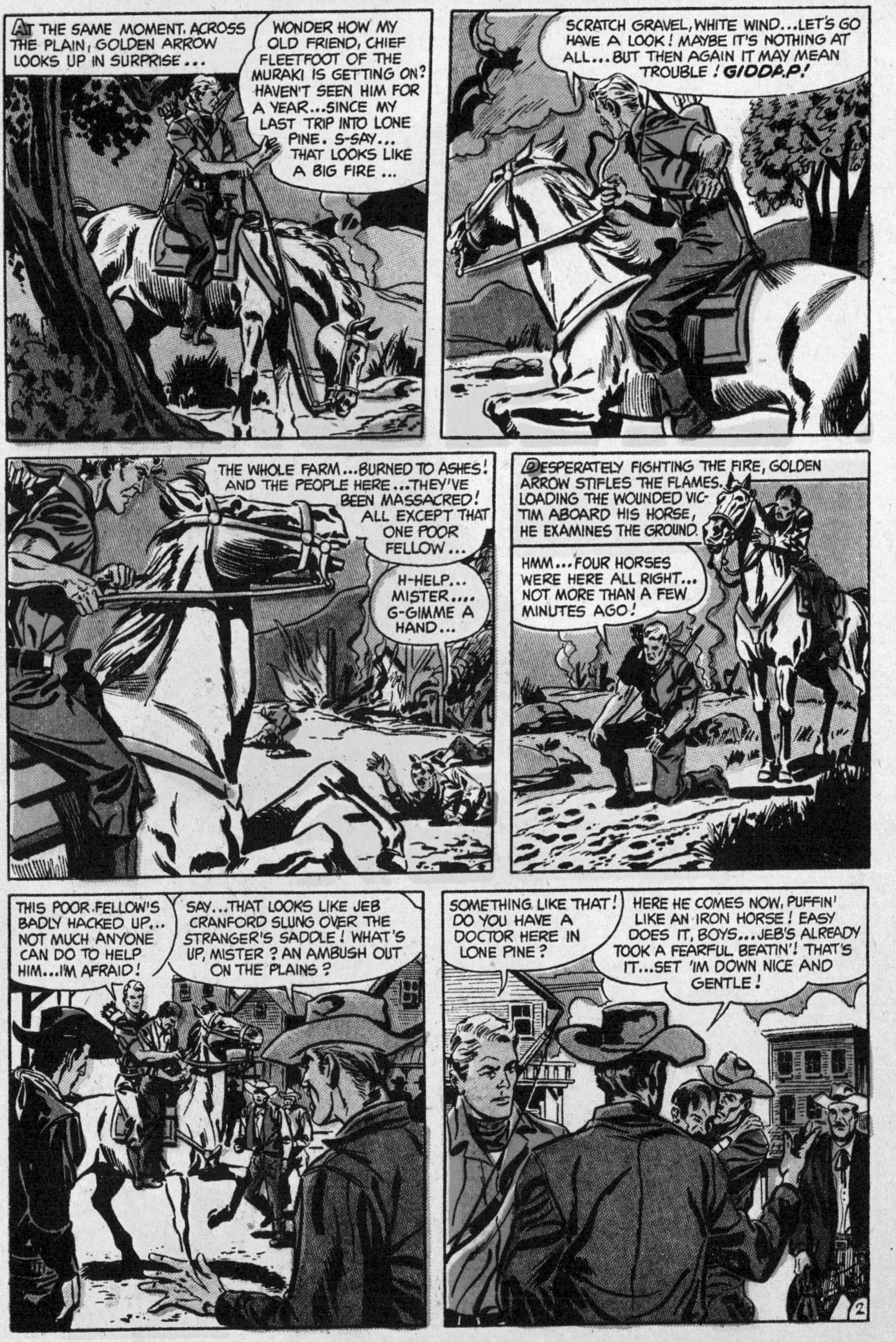
AT THE SAME MOMENT, ACROSS THE PLAIN, GOLDEN ARROW LOOKS UP IN SURPRISE...
WONDER HOW MY OLD FRIEND, CHIEF FLEETFOOT OF THE MURAKI IS GETTING ON? HAVEN'T SEEN HIM FOR A YEAR...SINCE MY LAST TRIP INTO LONE PINE. S-SAY... THAT LOOKS LIKE A BIG FIRE ...
SCRATCH GRAVEL, WHITE WIND...LET'S GO HAVE A LOOK! MAYBE IT'S NOTHING AT ALL...BUT THEN AGAIN IT MAY MEAN TROUBLE! GIDDAP!
THE WHOLE FARM...BURNED TO ASHES! AND THE PEOPLE HERE...THEY'VE BEEN MASSACRED! ALL EXCEPT THAT ONE POOR FELLOW...
H-HELP... MISTER.... G-GIMME A HAND...
DESPERATELY FIGHTING THE FIRE, GOLDEN ARROW STIFLES THE FLAMES. LOADING THE WOUNDED VICTIM ABOARD HIS HORSE, HE EXAMINES THE GROUND.
HMM...FOUR HORSES WERE HERE ALL RIGHT... NOT MORE THAN A FEW MINUTES AGO!
THIS POOR FELLOW'S BADLY HACKED UP... NOT MUCH ANYONE CAN DO TO HELP HIM...I'M AFRAID!
SAY...THAT LOOKS LIKE JEB CRANFORD SLUNG OVER THE STRANGER'S SADDLE! WHAT'S UP, MISTER? AN AMBUSH OUT ON THE PLAINS?
SOMETHING LIKE THAT! DO YOU HAVE A DOCTOR HERE IN LONE PINE?
HERE HE COMES NOW, PUFFIN' LIKE AN IRON HORSE! EASY DOES IT, BOYS...JEB'S ALREADY TOOK A FEARFUL BEATIN'! THAT'S IT...SET 'IM DOWN NICE AND GENTLE!
2

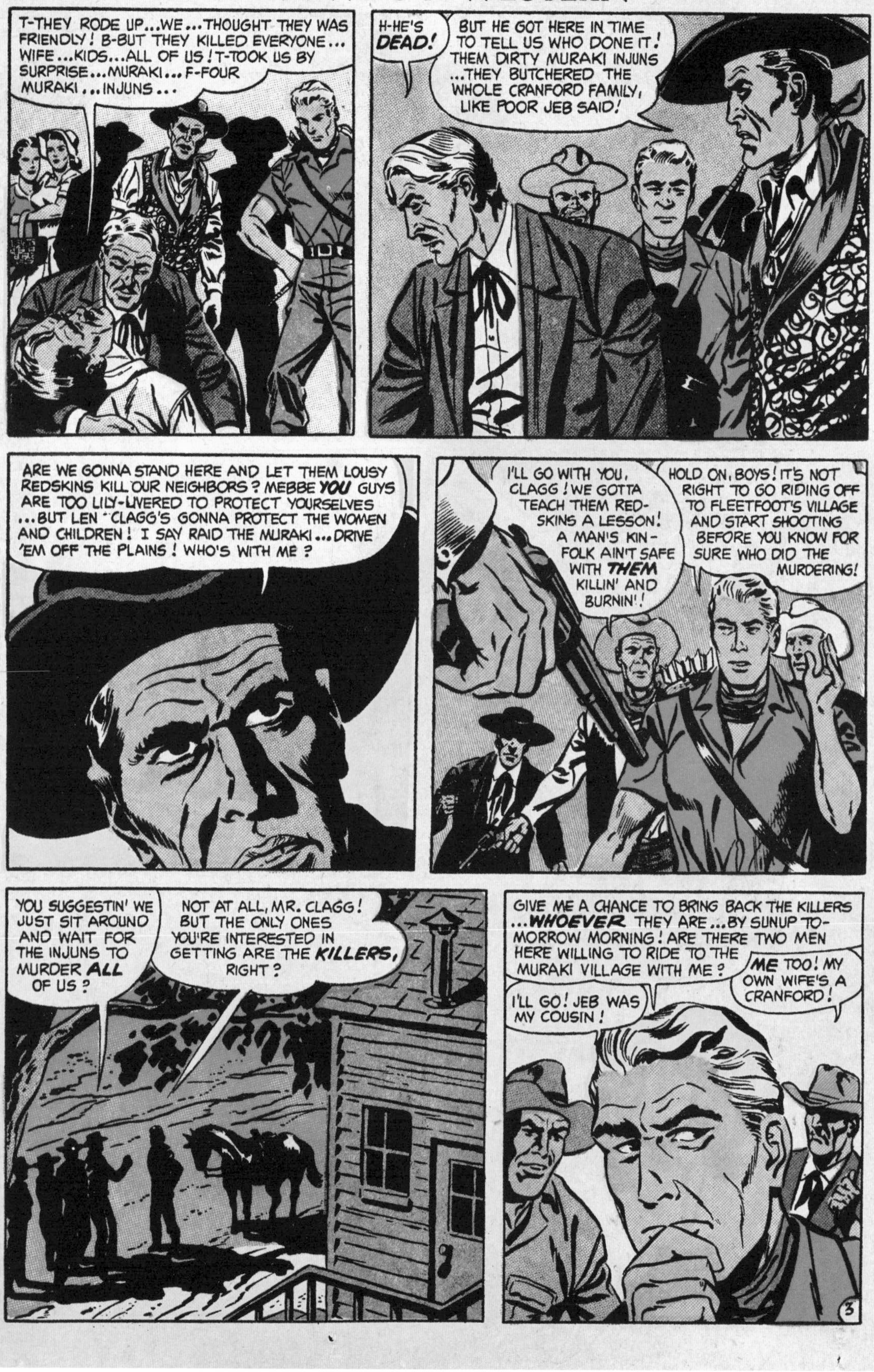
T-THEY RODE UP...WE...THOUGHT THEY WAS FRIENDLY! B-BUT THEY KILLED EVERYONE... WIFE...KIDS...ALL OF US! T-TOOK US BY SURPRISE...MURAKI...F-FOUR MURAKI...INJUNS...
H-HE'S DEAD!
BUT HE GOT HERE IN TIME TO TELL US WHO DONE IT! THEM DIRTY MURAKI INJUNS ...THEY BUTCHERED THE WHOLE CRANFORD FAMILY, LIKE POOR JEB SAID!
ARE WE GONNA STAND HERE AND LET THEM LOUSY REDSKINS KILL OUR NEIGHBORS? MEBBE YOU GUYS ARE TOO LILY-LIVERED TO PROTECT YOURSELVES ...BUT LEN CLAGG'S GONNA PROTECT THE WOMEN AND CHILDREN! I SAY RAID THE MURAKI...DRIVE 'EM OFF THE PLAINS! WHO'S WITH ME?
I'LL GO WITH YOU, CLAGG! WE GOTTA TEACH THEM RED-SKINS A LESSON! A MAN'S KIN-FOLK AIN'T SAFE WITH THEM KILLIN' AND BURNIN'!
HOLD ON, BOYS! IT'S NOT RIGHT TO GO RIDING OFF TO FLEETFOOT'S VILLAGE AND START SHOOTING BEFORE YOU KNOW FOR SURE WHO DID THE MURDERING!
YOU SUGGESTIN' WE JUST SIT AROUND AND WAIT FOR THE INJUNS TO MURDER ALL OF US?
NOT AT ALL, MR. CLAGG! BUT THE ONLY ONES YOU'RE INTERESTED IN GETTING ARE THE KILLERS, RIGHT?
GIVE ME A CHANCE TO BRING BACK THE KILLERS ...WHOEVER THEY ARE...BY SUNUP TO-MORROW MORNING! ARE THERE TWO MEN HERE WILLING TO RIDE TO THE MURAKI VILLAGE WITH ME?
I'LL GO! JEB WAS MY COUSIN!
ME TOO! MY OWN WIFE'S A CRANFORD!
3

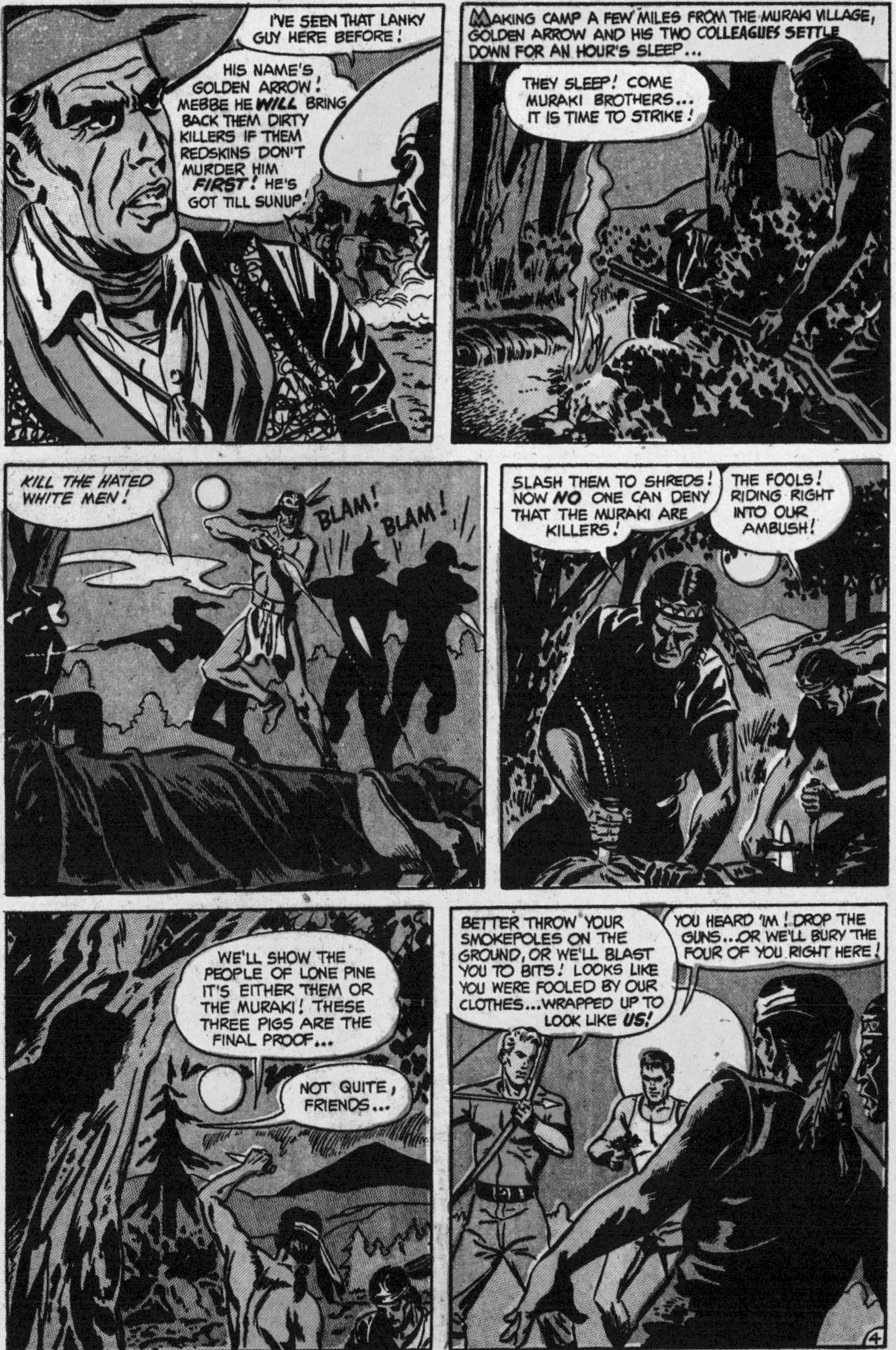
I'VE SEEN THAT LANKY GUY HERE BEFORE!
HIS NAME'S GOLDEN ARROW! MEBBE HE WILL BRING BACK THEM DIRTY KILLERS IF THEM REDSKINS DON'T MURDER HIM FIRST! HE'S GOT TILL SUNUP!
MAKING CAMP A FEW MILES FROM THE MURAKI VILLAGE, GOLDEN ARROW AND HIS TWO COLLEAGUES SETTLE DOWN FOR AN HOUR'S SLEEP...
THEY SLEEP! COME MURAKI BROTHERS... IT IS TIME TO STRIKE!
KILL THE HATED WHITE MEN!
BLAM!
BLAM!
SLASH THEM TO SHREDS! NOW NO ONE CAN DENY THAT THE MURAKI ARE KILLERS!
THE FOOLS! RIDING RIGHT INTO OUR AMBUSH!
WE'LL SHOW THE PEOPLE OF LONE PINE IT'S EITHER THEM OR THE MURAKI! THESE THREE PIGS ARE THE FINAL PROOF...
NOT QUITE, FRIENDS...
BETTER THROW YOUR SMOKEPOLES ON THE GROUND, OR WE'LL BLAST YOU TO BITS! LOOKS LIKE YOU WERE FOOLED BY OUR CLOTHES...WRAPPED UP TO LOOK LIKE US!
YOU HEARD 'IM! DROP THE GUNS...OR WE'LL BURY THE FOUR OF YOU RIGHT HERE!
4

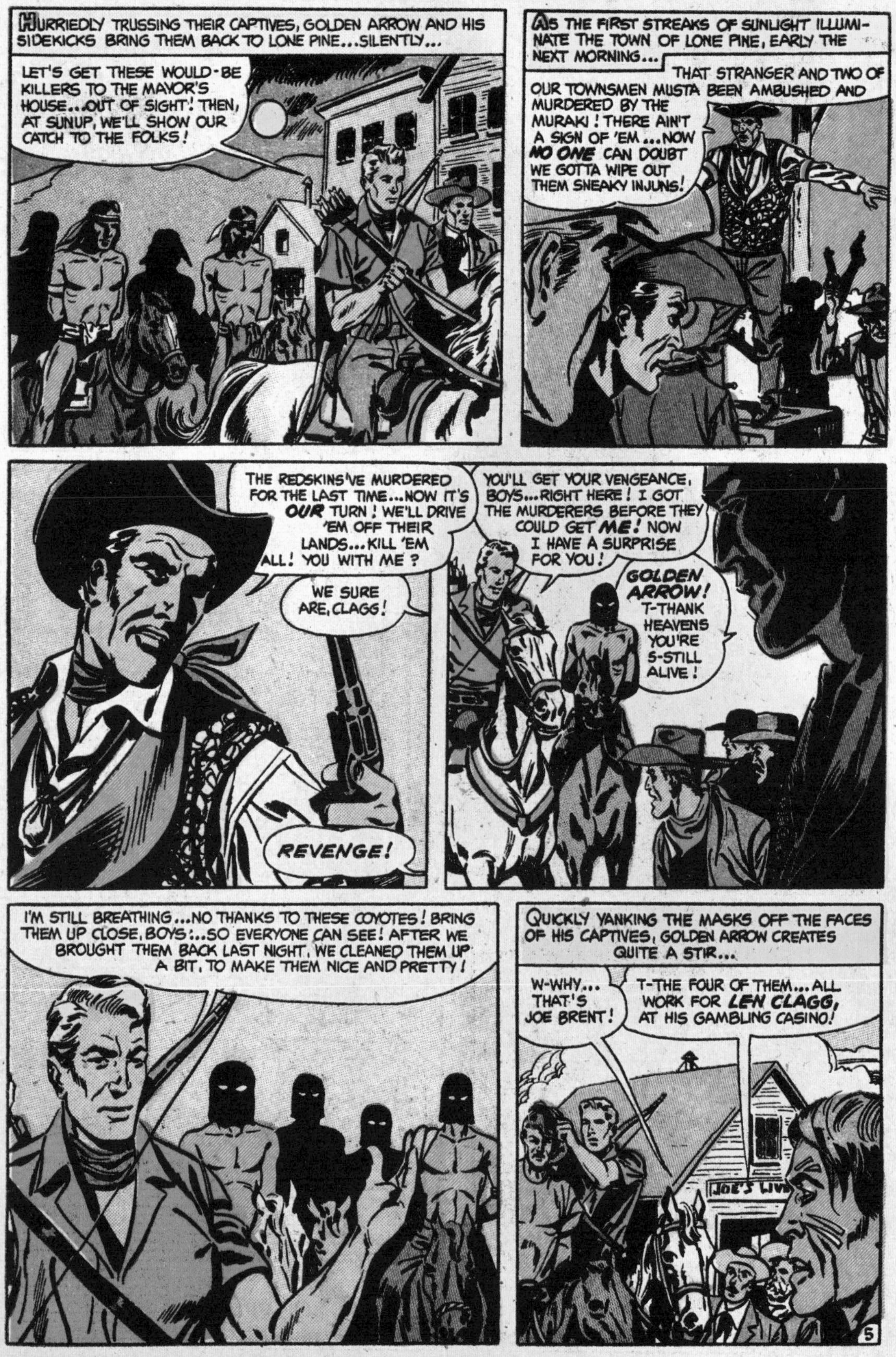
HURRIEDLY TRUSSING THEIR CAPTIVES, GOLDEN ARROW AND HIS SIDEKICKS BRING THEM BACK TO LONE PINE...SILENTLY...
LET'S GET THESE WOULD-BE KILLERS TO THE MAYOR'S HOUSE...OUT OF SIGHT! THEN, AT SUNUP, WE'LL SHOW OUR CATCH TO THE FOLKS!
AS THE FIRST STREAKS OF SUNLIGHT ILLUMINATE THE TOWN OF LONE PINE, EARLY THE NEXT MORNING...
THAT STRANGER AND TWO OF OUR TOWNSMEN MUSTA BEEN AMBUSHED AND MURDERED BY THE MURAKI! THERE AIN'T A SIGN OF 'EM...NOW NO ONE CAN DOUBT WE GOTTA WIPE OUT THEM SNEAKY INJUNS!
THE REDSKINS'VE MURDERED FOR THE LAST TIME...NOW IT'S OUR TURN! WE'LL DRIVE 'EM OFF THEIR LANDS...KILL 'EM ALL! YOU WITH ME?
WE SURE ARE, CLAGG!
REVENGE!
YOU'LL GET YOUR VENGEANCE, BOYS...RIGHT HERE! I GOT THE MURDERERS BEFORE THEY COULD GET ME! NOW I HAVE A SURPRISE FOR YOU!
GOLDEN ARROW! T-THANK HEAVENS YOU'RE S-STILL ALIVE!
I'M STILL BREATHING...NO THANKS TO THESE COYOTES! BRING THEM UP CLOSE, BOYS!...SO EVERYONE CAN SEE! AFTER WE BROUGHT THEM BACK LAST NIGHT, WE CLEANED THEM UP A BIT, TO MAKE THEM NICE AND PRETTY!
QUICKLY YANKING THE MASKS OFF THE FACES OF HIS CAPTIVES, GOLDEN ARROW CREATES QUITE A STIR...
W-WHY... THAT'S JOE BRENT!
T-THE FOUR OF THEM...ALL WORK FOR LEN CLAGG, AT HIS GAMBLING CASINO!
5

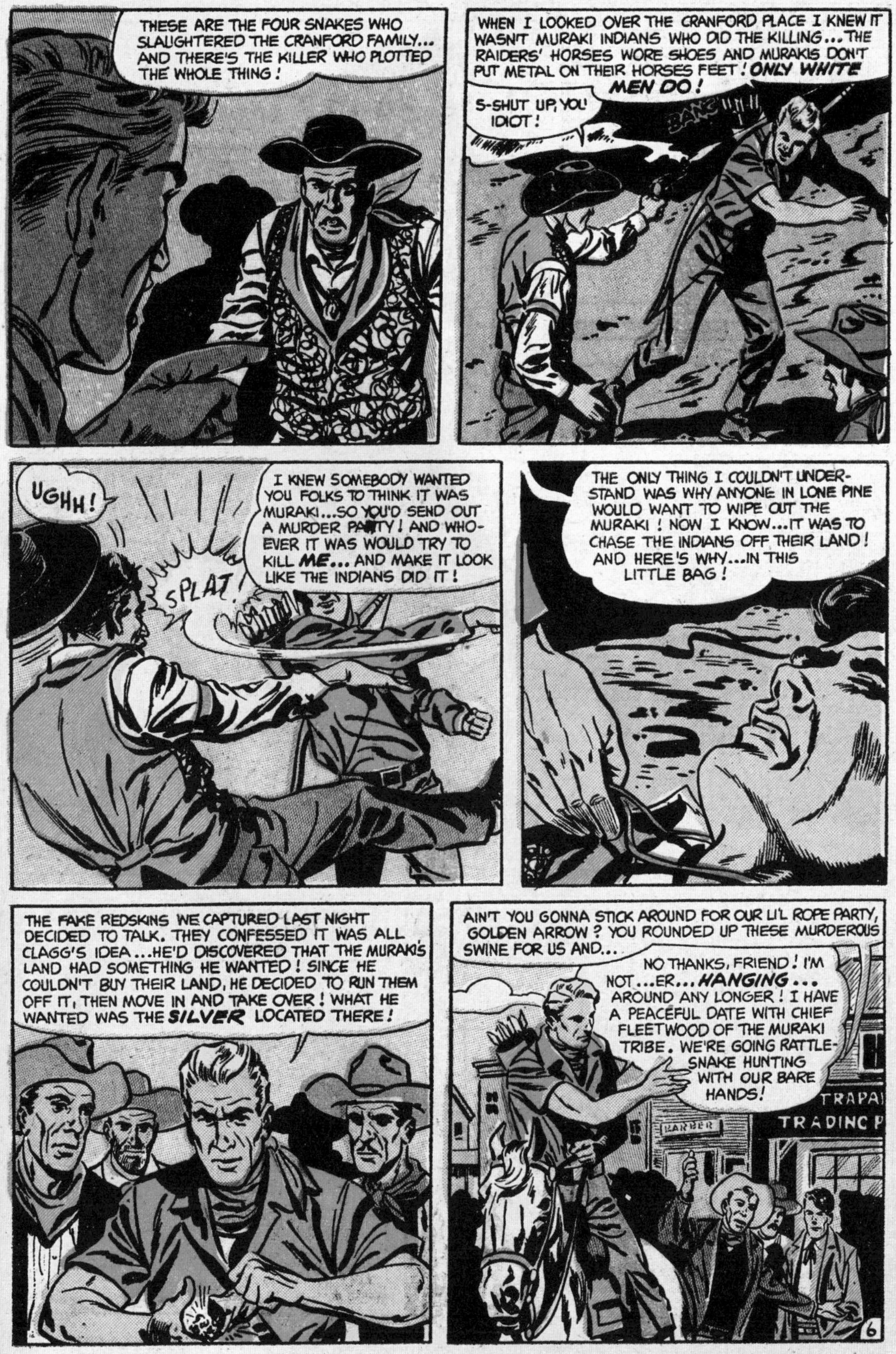
THESE ARE THE FOUR SNAKES WHO SLAUGHTERED THE CRANFORD FAMILY... AND THERE'S THE KILLER WHO PLOTTED THE WHOLE THING!
WHEN I LOOKED OVER THE CRANFORD PLACE I KNEW IT WASN'T MURAKI INDIANS WHO DID THE KILLING... THE RAIDERS' HORSES WORE SHOES AND MURAKIS DON'T PUT METAL ON THEIR HORSES FEET! ONLY WHITE MEN DO!
S-SHUT UP, YOU IDIOT!
BANG
UGHH!
I KNEW SOMEBODY WANTED YOU FOLKS TO THINK IT WAS MURAKI...SO YOU'D SEND OUT A MURDER PARTY! AND WHO-EVER IT WAS WOULD TRY TO KILL ME... AND MAKE IT LOOK LIKE THE INDIANS DID IT!
SPLAT!
THE ONLY THING I COULDN'T UNDER-STAND WAS WHY ANYONE IN LONE PINE WOULD WANT TO WIPE OUT THE MURAKI! NOW I KNOW...IT WAS TO CHASE THE INDIANS OFF THEIR LAND! AND HERE'S WHY...IN THIS LITTLE BAG!
THE FAKE REDSKINS WE CAPTURED LAST NIGHT DECIDED TO TALK. THEY CONFESSED IT WAS ALL CLAGG'S IDEA...HE'D DISCOVERED THAT THE MURAKI'S LAND HAD SOMETHING HE WANTED! SINCE HE COULDN'T BUY THEIR LAND, HE DECIDED TO RUN THEM OFF IT, THEN MOVE IN AND TAKE OVER! WHAT HE WANTED WAS THE SILVER LOCATED THERE!
AIN'T YOU GONNA STICK AROUND FOR OUR LI'L ROPE PARTY, GOLDEN ARROW? YOU ROUNDED UP THESE MURDEROUS SWINE FOR US AND...
NO THANKS, FRIEND! I'M NOT...ER...HANGING... AROUND ANY LONGER! I HAVE A PEACEFUL DATE WITH CHIEF FLEETWOOD OF THE MURAKI TRIBE. WE'RE GOING RATTLE-SNAKE HUNTING WITH OUR BARE HANDS!
BARBER
TRAPA
TRADING P
6

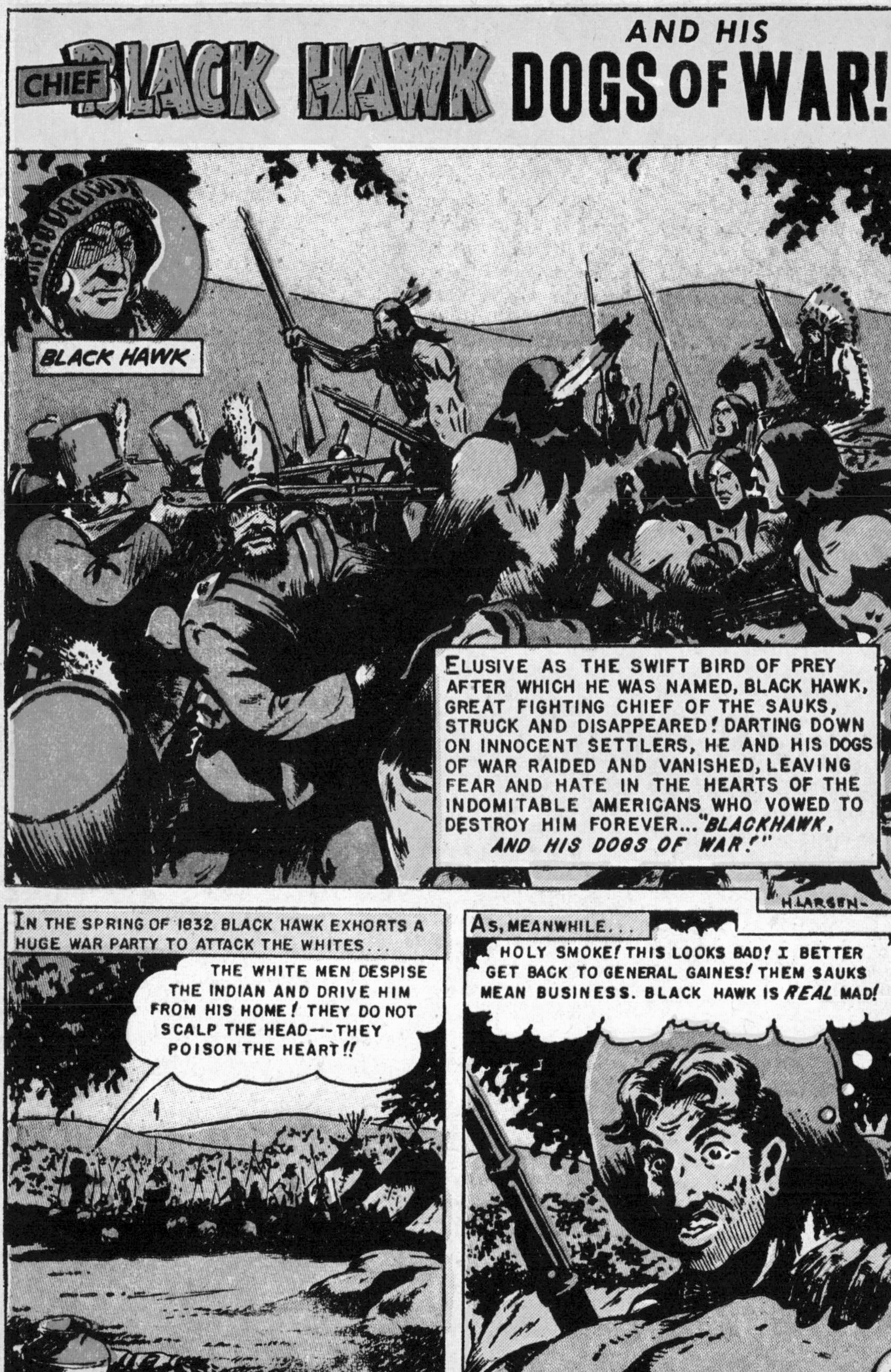
CHIEF BLACK HAWK AND HIS DOGS OF WAR!
BLACK HAWK
ELUSIVE AS THE SWIFT BIRD OF PREY AFTER WHICH HE WAS NAMED, BLACK HAWK, GREAT FIGHTING CHIEF OF THE SAUKS, STRUCK AND DISAPPEARED! DARTING DOWN ON INNOCENT SETTLERS, HE AND HIS DOGS OF WAR RAIDED AND VANISHED, LEAVING FEAR AND HATE IN THE HEARTS OF THE INDOMITABLE AMERICANS WHO VOWED TO DESTROY HIM FOREVER..."BLACKHAWK, AND HIS DOGS OF WAR!"
H. LARSEN
IN THE SPRING OF 1832 BLACK HAWK EXHORTS A HUGE WAR PARTY TO ATTACK THE WHITES...
THE WHITE MEN DESPISE THE INDIAN AND DRIVE HIM FROM HIS HOME! THEY DO NOT SCALP THE HEAD---THEY POISON THE HEART!!
AS, MEANWHILE...
HOLY SMOKE! THIS LOOKS BAD! I BETTER GET BACK TO GENERAL GAINES! THEM SAUKS MEAN BUSINESS. BLACK HAWK IS REAL MAD!
1

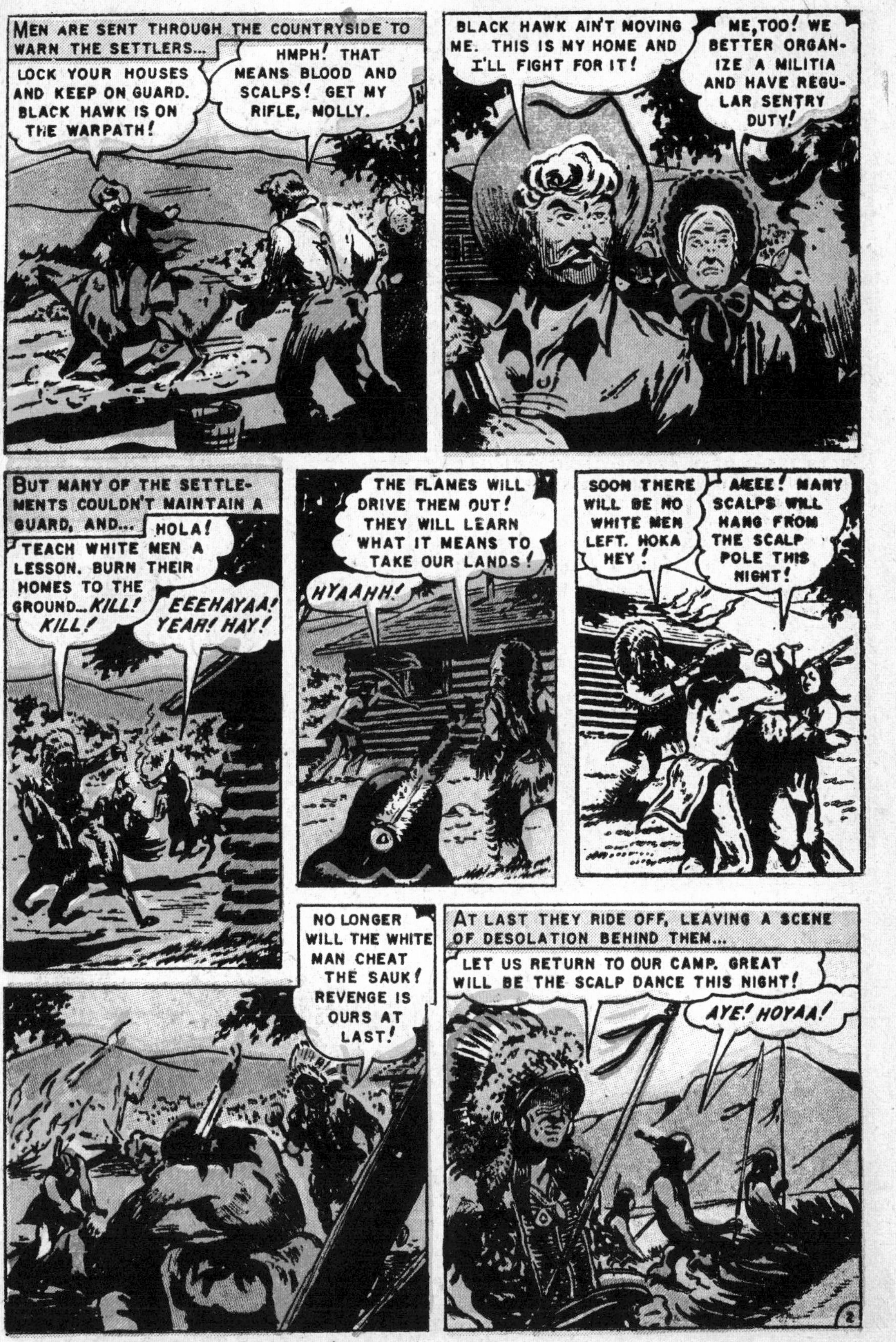
MEN ARE SENT THROUGH THE COUNTRYSIDE TO WARN THE SETTLERS...
LOCK YOUR HOUSES AND KEEP ON GUARD. BLACK HAWK IS ON THE WARPATH!
HMPH! THAT MEANS BLOOD AND SCALPS! GET MY RIFLE, MOLLY.
BLACK HAWK AIN'T MOVING ME. THIS IS MY HOME AND I'LL FIGHT FOR IT!
ME, TOO! WE BETTER ORGANIZE A MILITIA AND HAVE REGULAR SENTRY DUTY!
BUT MANY OF THE SETTLEMENTS COULDN'T MAINTAIN A GUARD, AND...
HOLA! TEACH WHITE MEN A LESSON. BURN THEIR HOMES TO THE GROUND...KILL! KILL!
EEEHAYAA! YEAH! HAY!
THE FLAMES WILL DRIVE THEM OUT! THEY WILL LEARN WHAT IT MEANS TO TAKE OUR LANDS!
HYAAHH!
SOON THERE WILL BE NO WHITE MEN LEFT. HOKA HEY!
AIEEE! MANY SCALPS WILL HANG FROM THE SCALP POLE THIS NIGHT!
NO LONGER WILL THE WHITE MAN CHEAT THE SAUK! REVENGE IS OURS AT LAST!
AT LAST THEY RIDE OFF, LEAVING A SCENE OF DESOLATION BEHIND THEM...
LET US RETURN TO OUR CAMP. GREAT WILL BE THE SCALP DANCE THIS NIGHT!
AYE! HOYAA!
2

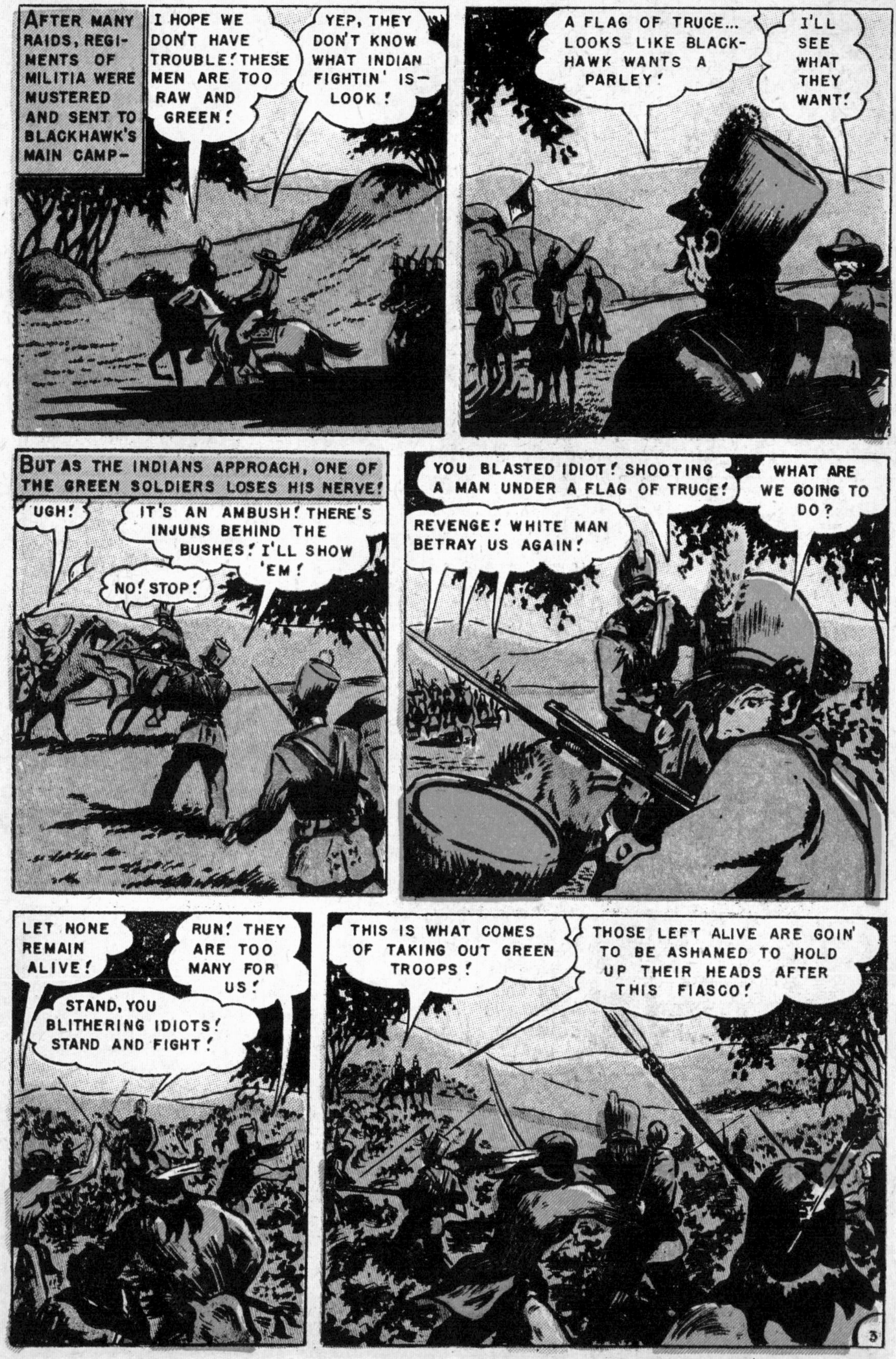
AFTER MANY RAIDS, REGIMENTS OF MILITIA WERE MUSTERED AND SENT TO BLACKHAWK'S MAIN CAMP-
I HOPE WE DON'T HAVE TROUBLE! THESE MEN ARE TOO RAW AND GREEN!
YEP, THEY DON'T KNOW WHAT INDIAN FIGHTIN' IS- LOOK!
A FLAG OF TRUCE... LOOKS LIKE BLACKHAWK WANTS A PARLEY!
I'LL SEE WHAT THEY WANT!
BUT AS THE INDIANS APPROACH, ONE OF THE GREEN SOLDIERS LOSES HIS NERVE!
UGH!
IT'S AN AMBUSH! THERE'S INJUNS BEHIND THE BUSHES! I'LL SHOW 'EM!
NO! STOP!
YOU BLASTED IDIOT! SHOOTING A MAN UNDER A FLAG OF TRUCE!
WHAT ARE WE GOING TO DO?
REVENGE! WHITE MAN BETRAY US AGAIN!
LET NONE REMAIN ALIVE!
RUN! THEY ARE TOO MANY FOR US!
STAND, YOU BLITHERING IDIOTS! STAND AND FIGHT!
THIS IS WHAT COMES OF TAKING OUT GREEN TROOPS!
THOSE LEFT ALIVE ARE GOIN' TO BE ASHAMED TO HOLD UP THEIR HEADS AFTER THIS FIASCO!
3

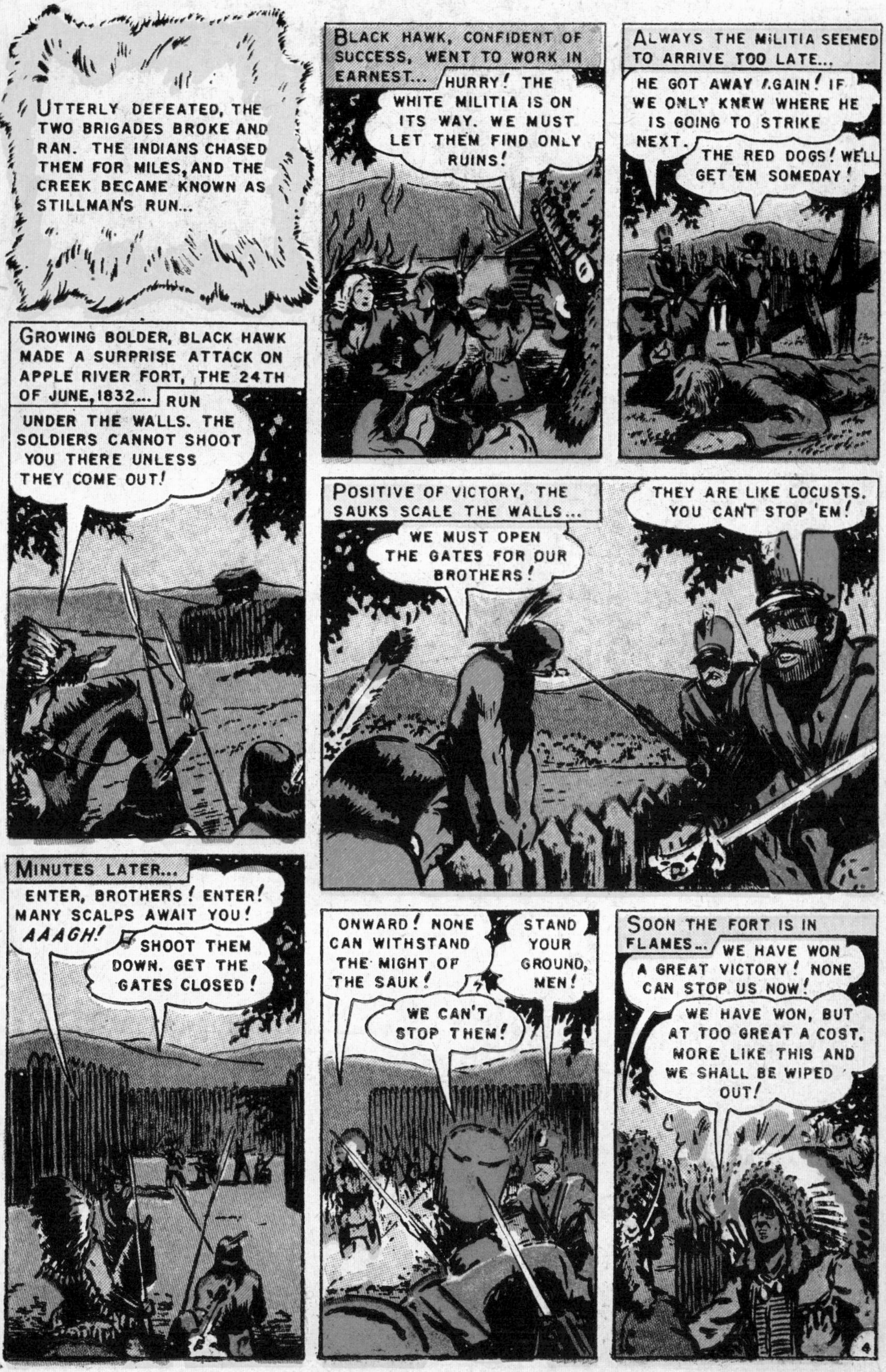
UTTERLY DEFEATED, THE TWO BRIGADES BROKE AND RAN. THE INDIANS CHASED THEM FOR MILES, AND THE CREEK BECAME KNOWN AS STILLMAN'S RUN...
BLACK HAWK, CONFIDENT OF SUCCESS, WENT TO WORK IN EARNEST...
HURRY! THE WHITE MILITIA IS ON ITS WAY. WE MUST LET THEM FIND ONLY RUINS!
ALWAYS THE MILITIA SEEMED TO ARRIVE TOO LATE...
HE GOT AWAY AGAIN! IF WE ONLY KNEW WHERE HE IS GOING TO STRIKE NEXT.
THE RED DOGS! WE'LL GET 'EM SOMEDAY!
GROWING BOLDER, BLACK HAWK MADE A SURPRISE ATTACK ON APPLE RIVER FORT, THE 24TH OF JUNE, 1832...
RUN UNDER THE WALLS. THE SOLDIERS CANNOT SHOOT YOU THERE UNLESS THEY COME OUT!
POSITIVE OF VICTORY, THE SAUKS SCALE THE WALLS...
WE MUST OPEN THE GATES FOR OUR BROTHERS!
THEY ARE LIKE LOCUSTS. YOU CAN'T STOP 'EM!
MINUTES LATER...
ENTER, BROTHERS! ENTER! MANY SCALPS AWAIT YOU! AAAGH!
SHOOT THEM DOWN. GET THE GATES CLOSED!
ONWARD! NONE CAN WITHSTAND THE MIGHT OF THE SAUK!
STAND YOUR GROUND, MEN!
WE CAN'T STOP THEM!
SOON THE FORT IS IN FLAMES...
WE HAVE WON A GREAT VICTORY! NONE CAN STOP US NOW!
WE HAVE WON, BUT AT TOO GREAT A COST. MORE LIKE THIS AND WE SHALL BE WIPED OUT!
4

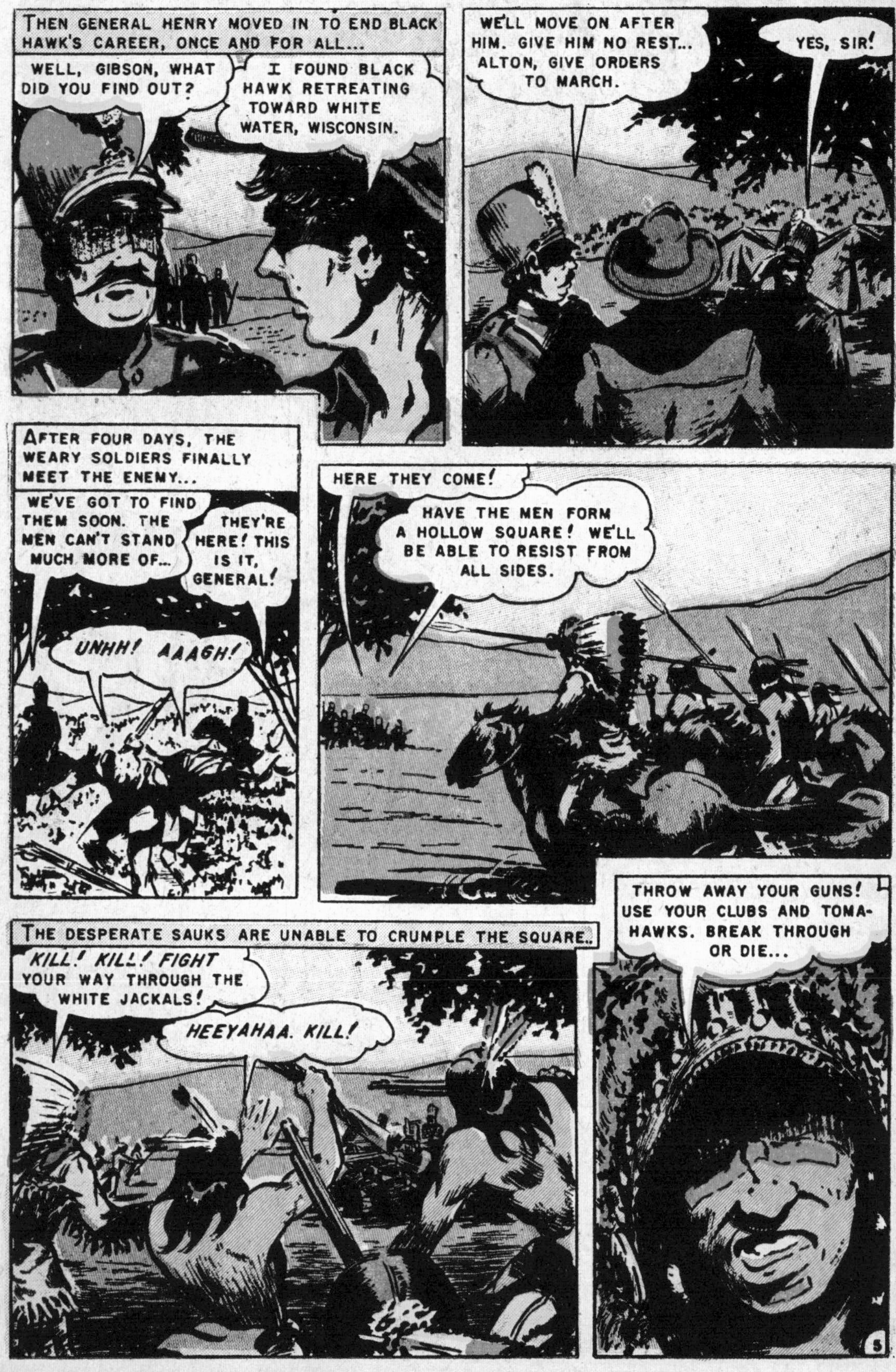
THEN GENERAL HENRY MOVED IN TO END BLACK HAWK'S CAREER, ONCE AND FOR ALL...
WELL, GIBSON, WHAT DID YOU FIND OUT?
I FOUND BLACK HAWK RETREATING TOWARD WHITE WATER, WISCONSIN.
WE'LL MOVE ON AFTER HIM. GIVE HIM NO REST... ALTON, GIVE ORDERS TO MARCH.
YES, SIR!
AFTER FOUR DAYS, THE WEARY SOLDIERS FINALLY MEET THE ENEMY...
WE'VE GOT TO FIND THEM SOON. THE MEN CAN'T STAND MUCH MORE OF...
THEY'RE HERE! THIS IS IT, GENERAL!
UNHH! AAAGH!
HERE THEY COME!
HAVE THE MEN FORM A HOLLOW SQUARE! WE'LL BE ABLE TO RESIST FROM ALL SIDES.
THE DESPERATE SAUKS ARE UNABLE TO CRUMPLE THE SQUARE..
KILL! KILL! FIGHT YOUR WAY THROUGH THE WHITE JACKALS!
HEEYAHAA. KILL!
THROW AWAY YOUR GUNS! USE YOUR CLUBS AND TOMAHAWKS. BREAK THROUGH OR DIE...
5

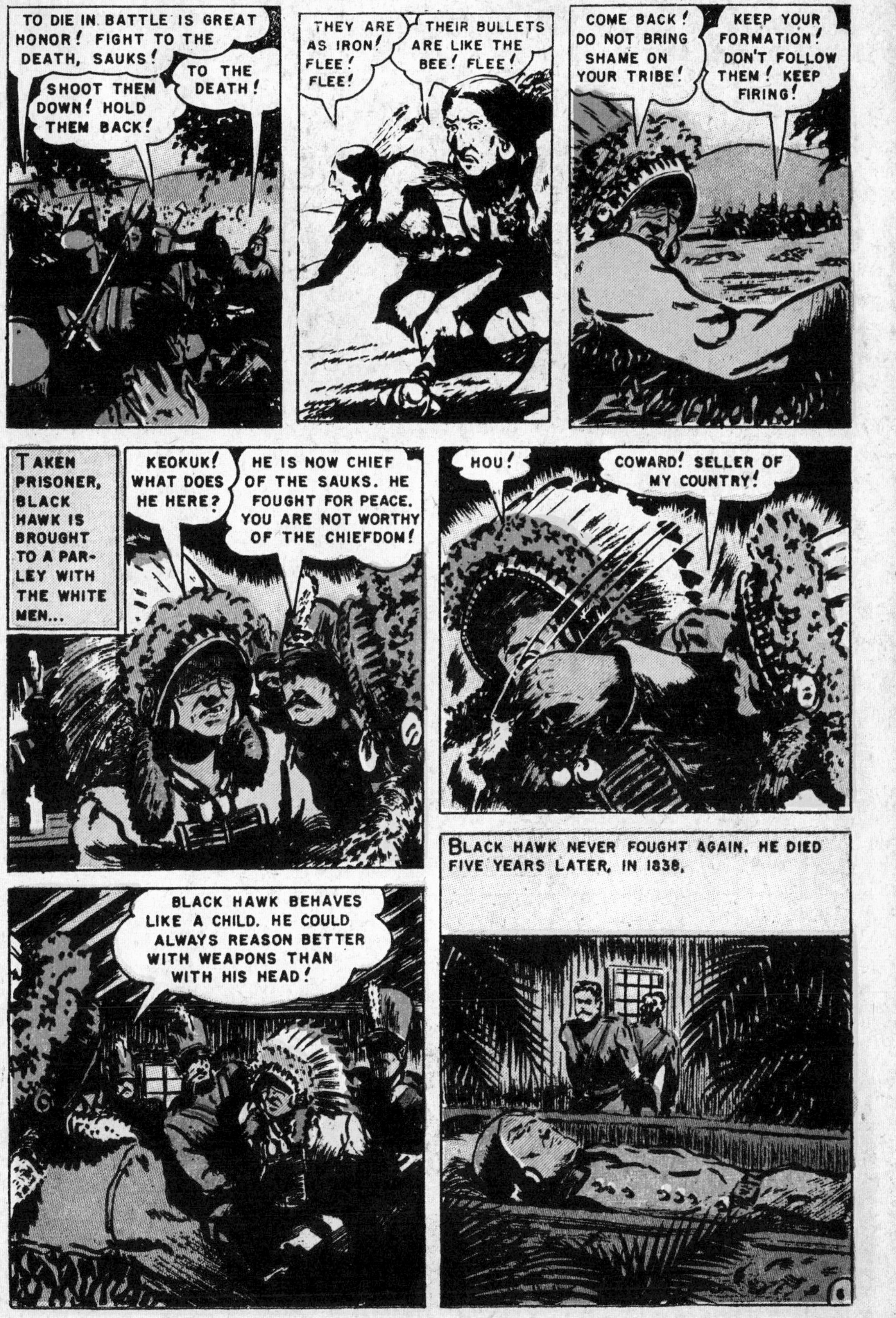

TO DIE IN BATTLE IS GREAT HONOR! FIGHT TO THE DEATH, SAUKS!
SHOOT THEM DOWN! HOLD THEM BACK!
TO THE DEATH!
THEY ARE AS IRON! FLEE! FLEE!
THEIR BULLETS ARE LIKE THE BEE! FLEE!
COME BACK! DO NOT BRING SHAME ON YOUR TRIBE!
KEEP YOUR FORMATION! DON'T FOLLOW THEM! KEEP FIRING!
TAKEN PRISONER, BLACK HAWK IS BROUGHT TO A PARLEY WITH THE WHITE MEN...
KEOKUK! WHAT DOES HE HERE?
HE IS NOW CHIEF OF THE SAUKS. HE FOUGHT FOR PEACE. YOU ARE NOT WORTHY OF THE CHIEFDOM!
HOU!
COWARD! SELLER OF MY COUNTRY!
BLACK HAWK BEHAVES LIKE A CHILD. HE COULD ALWAYS REASON BETTER WITH WEAPONS THAN WITH HIS HEAD!
BLACK HAWK NEVER FOUGHT AGAIN. HE DIED FIVE YEARS LATER, IN 1838.

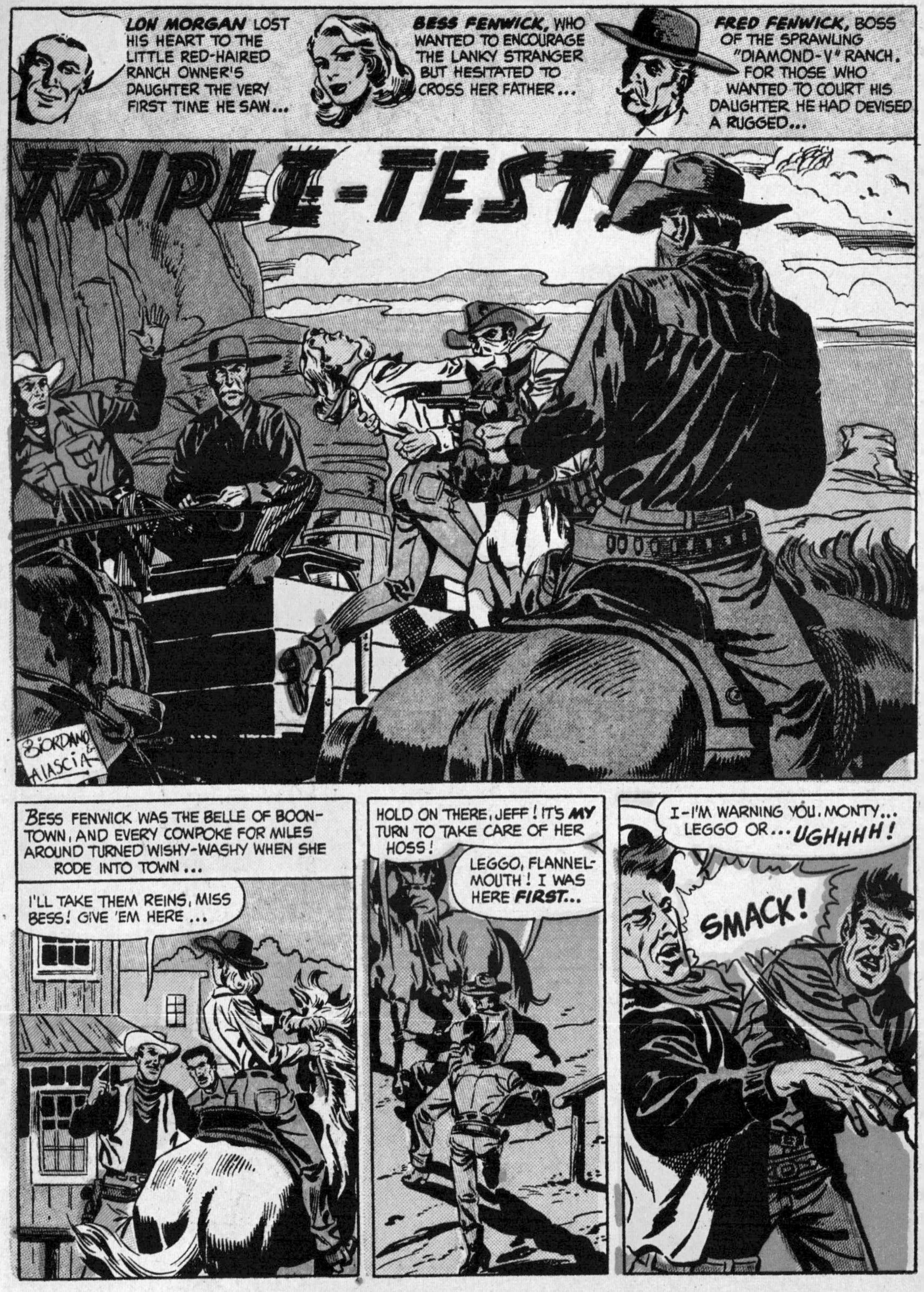

LON MORGAN LOST HIS HEART TO THE LITTLE RED-HAIRED RANCH OWNER'S DAUGHTER THE VERY FIRST TIME HE SAW...
BESS FENWICK, WHO WANTED TO ENCOURAGE THE LANKY STRANGER BUT HESITATED TO CROSS HER FATHER...
FRED FENWICK, BOSS OF THE SPRAWLING "DIAMOND-V" RANCH. FOR THOSE WHO WANTED TO COURT HIS DAUGHTER HE HAD DEVISED A RUGGED...
TRIPLE-TEST!
GIORDANO & ALASCIA
BESS FENWICK WAS THE BELLE OF BOON-TOWN, AND EVERY COWPOKE FOR MILES AROUND TURNED WISHY-WASHY WHEN SHE RODE INTO TOWN...
I'LL TAKE THEM REINS, MISS BESS! GIVE 'EM HERE...
HOLD ON THERE, JEFF! IT'S MY TURN TO TAKE CARE OF HER HOSS!
LEGGO, FLANNEL-MOUTH! I WAS HERE FIRST...
I-I'M WARNING YOU, MONTY... LEGGO OR... UGHHHH!
SMACK!

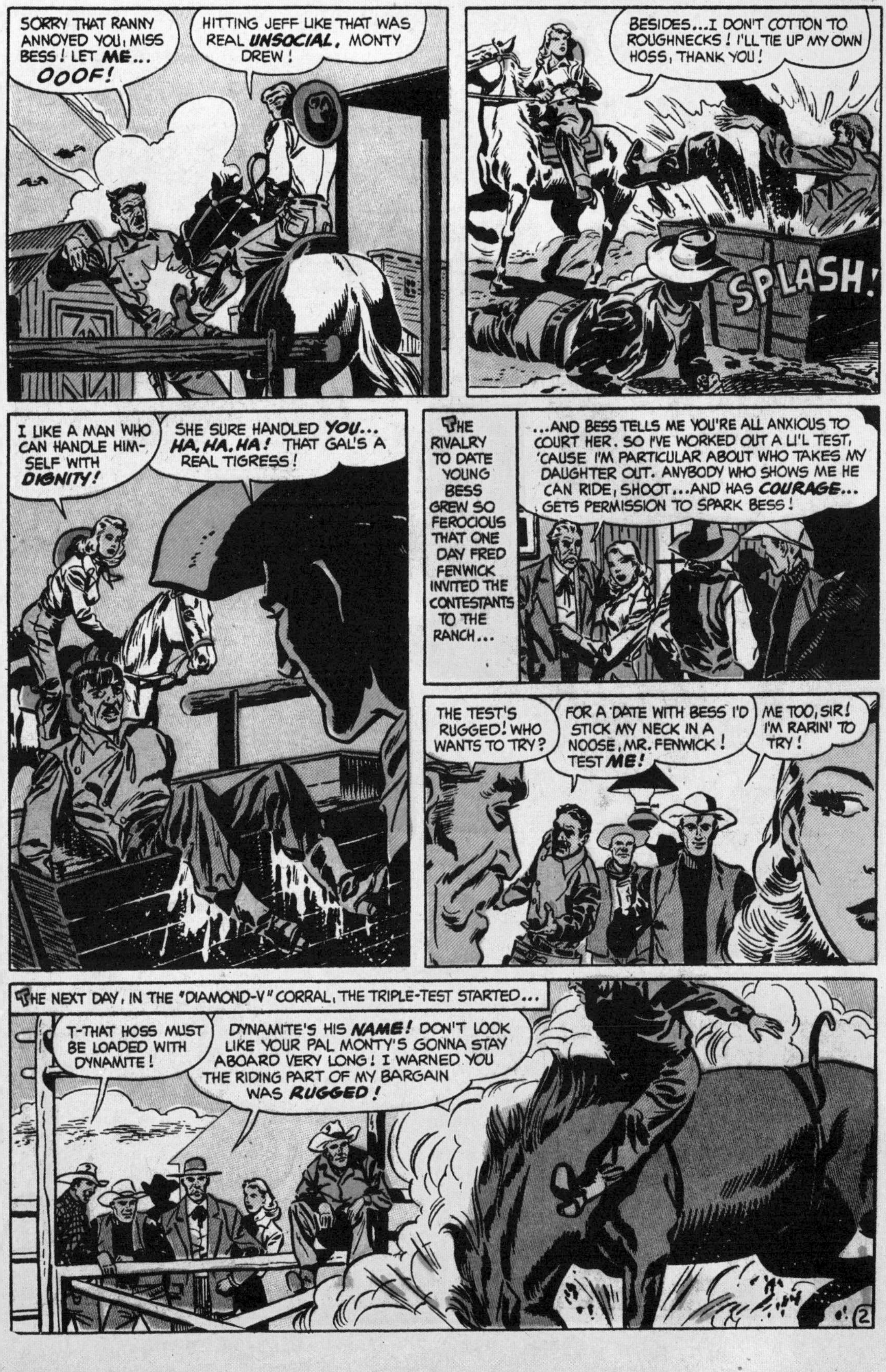
SORRY THAT RANNY ANNOYED YOU, MISS BESS! LET ME... OOOF!
HITTING JEFF LIKE THAT WAS REAL UNSOCIAL, MONTY DREW!
BESIDES...I DON'T COTTON TO ROUGHNECKS! I'LL TIE UP MY OWN HOSS, THANK YOU!
SPLASH!
I LIKE A MAN WHO CAN HANDLE HIMSELF WITH DIGNITY!
SHE SURE HANDLED YOU... HA, HA, HA! THAT GAL'S A REAL TIGRESS!
THE RIVALRY TO DATE YOUNG BESS GREW SO FEROCIOUS THAT ONE DAY FRED FENWICK INVITED THE CONTESTANTS TO THE RANCH...
...AND BESS TELLS ME YOU'RE ALL ANXIOUS TO COURT HER. SO I'VE WORKED OUT A LI'L TEST, 'CAUSE I'M PARTICULAR ABOUT WHO TAKES MY DAUGHTER OUT. ANYBODY WHO SHOWS ME HE CAN RIDE, SHOOT...AND HAS COURAGE... GETS PERMISSION TO SPARK BESS!
THE TEST'S RUGGED! WHO WANTS TO TRY?
FOR A DATE WITH BESS I'D STICK MY NECK IN A NOOSE, MR. FENWICK! TEST ME!
ME TOO, SIR! I'M RARIN' TO TRY!
THE NEXT DAY, IN THE "DIAMOND-V" CORRAL, THE TRIPLE-TEST STARTED...
T-THAT HOSS MUST BE LOADED WITH DYNAMITE!
DYNAMITE'S HIS NAME! DON'T LOOK LIKE YOUR PAL MONTY'S GONNA STAY ABOARD VERY LONG! I WARNED YOU THE RIDING PART OF MY BARGAIN WAS RUGGED!
2

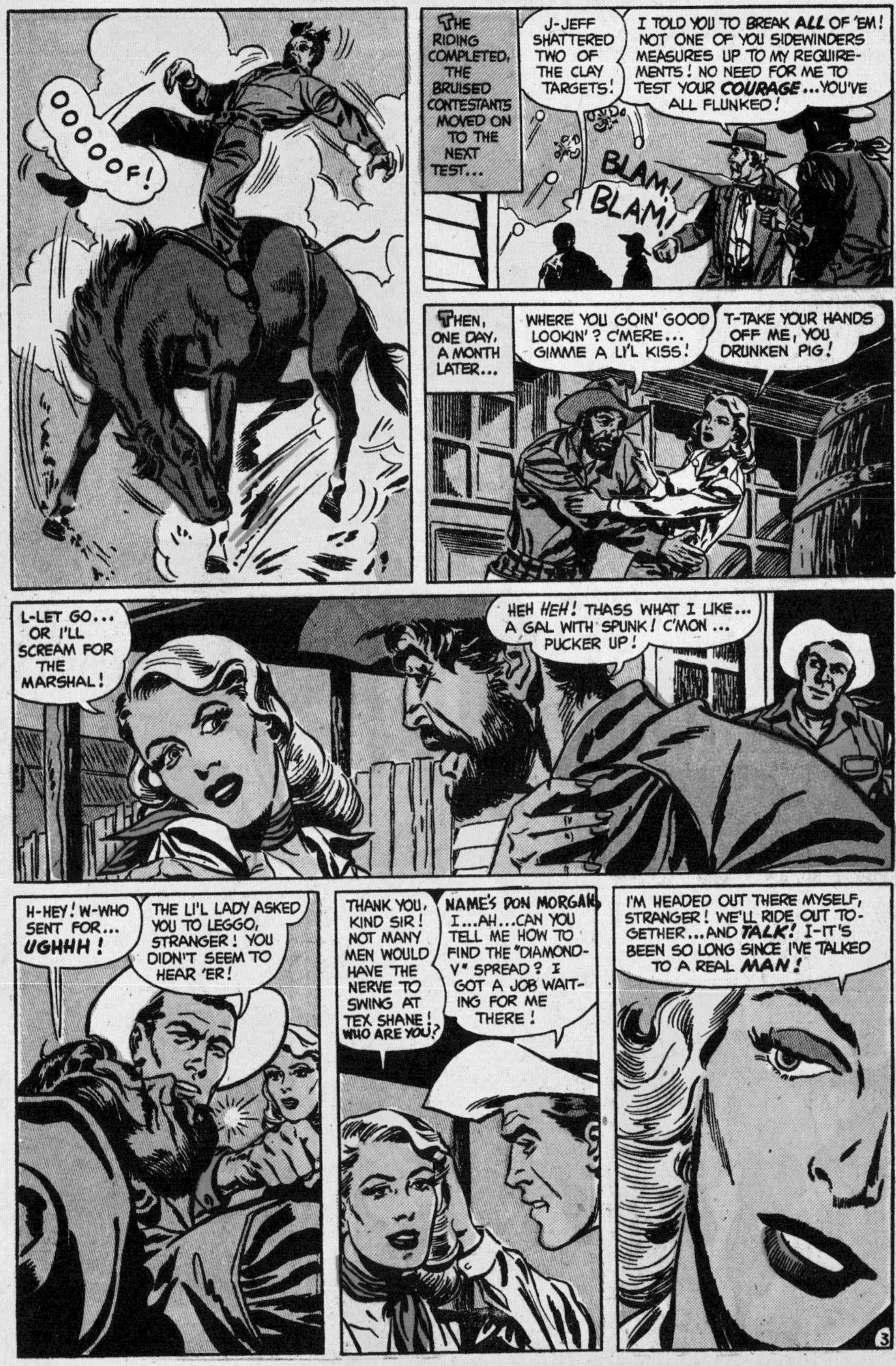
OOOOOF!
THE RIDING COMPLETED, THE BRUISED CONTESTANTS MOVED ON TO THE NEXT TEST...
J-JEFF SHATTERED TWO OF THE CLAY TARGETS!
I TOLD YOU TO BREAK ALL OF 'EM! NOT ONE OF YOU SIDEWINDERS MEASURES UP TO MY REQUIREMENTS! NO NEED FOR ME TO TEST YOUR COURAGE...YOU'VE ALL FLUNKED!
BLAM! BLAM!
THEN, ONE DAY, A MONTH LATER...
WHERE YOU GOIN' GOOD LOOKIN'? C'MERE... GIMME A LI'L KISS!
T-TAKE YOUR HANDS OFF ME, YOU DRUNKEN PIG!
L-LET GO... OR I'LL SCREAM FOR THE MARSHAL!
HEH HEH! THASS WHAT I LIKE... A GAL WITH SPUNK! C'MON ... PUCKER UP!
H-HEY! W-WHO SENT FOR... UGHHH!
THE LI'L LADY ASKED YOU TO LEGGO, STRANGER! YOU DIDN'T SEEM TO HEAR 'ER!
THANK YOU, KIND SIR! NOT MANY MEN WOULD HAVE THE NERVE TO SWING AT TEX SHANE! WHO ARE YOU?
NAME'S DON MORGAN. I...AH...CAN YOU TELL ME HOW TO FIND THE "DIAMOND-V" SPREAD? I GOT A JOB WAITING FOR ME THERE!
I'M HEADED OUT THERE MYSELF, STRANGER! WE'LL RIDE OUT TOGETHER...AND TALK! I-IT'S BEEN SO LONG SINCE I'VE TALKED TO A REAL MAN!
3

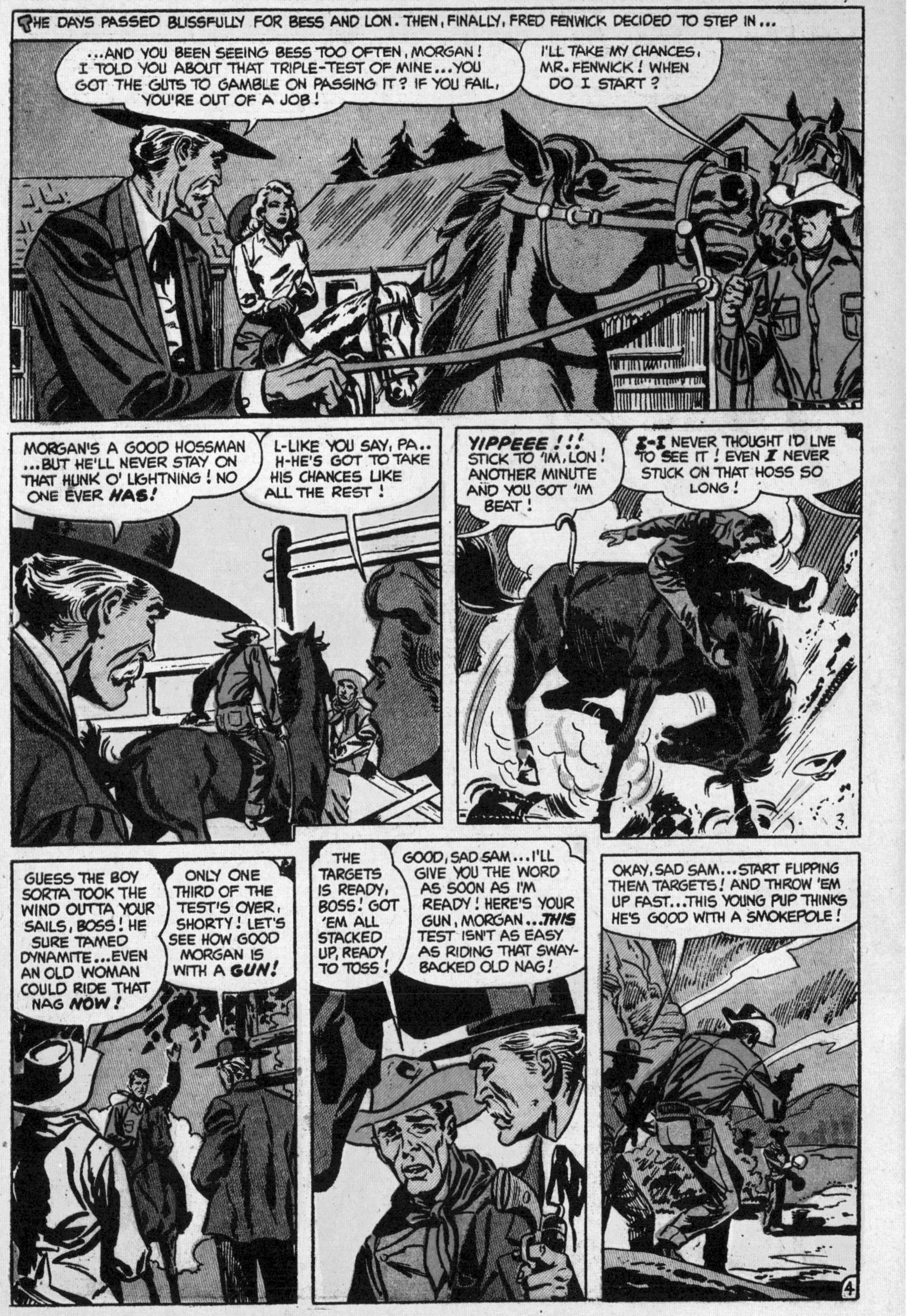
THE DAYS PASSED BLISSFULLY FOR BESS AND LON. THEN, FINALLY, FRED FENWICK DECIDED TO STEP IN...
...AND YOU BEEN SEEING BESS TOO OFTEN, MORGAN! I TOLD YOU ABOUT THAT TRIPLE-TEST OF MINE...YOU GOT THE GUTS TO GAMBLE ON PASSING IT? IF YOU FAIL, YOU'RE OUT OF A JOB!
I'LL TAKE MY CHANCES, MR. FENWICK! WHEN DO I START?
MORGAN'S A GOOD HOSSMAN ...BUT HE'LL NEVER STAY ON THAT HUNK O' LIGHTNING! NO ONE EVER HAS!
L-LIKE YOU SAY, PA.. H-HE'S GOT TO TAKE HIS CHANCES LIKE ALL THE REST!
YIPPEEE!!! STICK TO 'IM, LON! ANOTHER MINUTE AND YOU GOT 'IM BEAT!
I-I NEVER THOUGHT I'D LIVE TO SEE IT! EVEN I NEVER STUCK ON THAT HOSS SO LONG!
3
GUESS THE BOY SORTA TOOK THE WIND OUTTA YOUR SAILS, BOSS! HE SURE TAMED DYNAMITE...EVEN AN OLD WOMAN COULD RIDE THAT NAG NOW!
ONLY ONE THIRD OF THE TEST'S OVER, SHORTY! LET'S SEE HOW GOOD MORGAN IS WITH A GUN!
THE TARGETS IS READY, BOSS! GOT 'EM ALL STACKED UP, READY TO TOSS!
GOOD, SAD SAM...I'LL GIVE YOU THE WORD AS SOON AS I'M READY! HERE'S YOUR GUN, MORGAN...THIS TEST ISN'T AS EASY AS RIDING THAT SWAY-BACKED OLD NAG!
OKAY, SAD SAM...START FLIPPING THEM TARGETS! AND THROW 'EM UP FAST...THIS YOUNG PUP THINKS HE'S GOOD WITH A SMOKEPOLE!
4

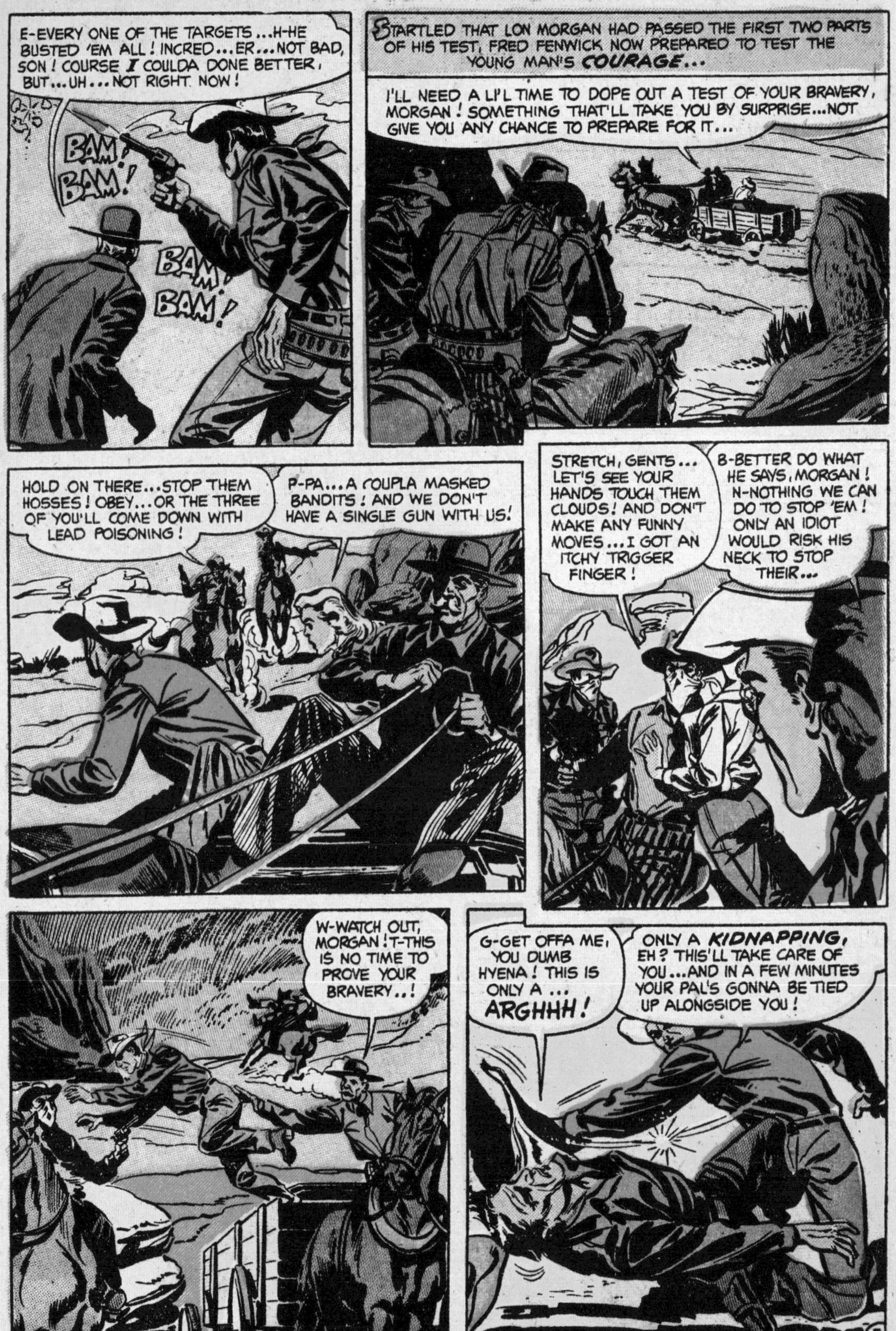
E-EVERY ONE OF THE TARGETS ...H-HE BUSTED 'EM ALL! INCRED...ER...NOT BAD, SON! COURSE I COULDA DONE BETTER, BUT...UH...NOT RIGHT NOW!
BAM! BAM!
BAM! BAM!
STARTLED THAT LON MORGAN HAD PASSED THE FIRST TWO PARTS OF HIS TEST, FRED FENWICK NOW PREPARED TO TEST THE YOUNG MAN'S COURAGE...
I'LL NEED A LI'L TIME TO DOPE OUT A TEST OF YOUR BRAVERY, MORGAN! SOMETHING THAT'LL TAKE YOU BY SURPRISE...NOT GIVE YOU ANY CHANCE TO PREPARE FOR IT...
HOLD ON THERE...STOP THEM HOSSES! OBEY...OR THE THREE OF YOU'LL COME DOWN WITH LEAD POISONING!
P-PA...A COUPLA MASKED BANDITS! AND WE DON'T HAVE A SINGLE GUN WITH US!
STRETCH, GENTS... LET'S SEE YOUR HANDS TOUCH THEM CLOUDS! AND DON'T MAKE ANY FUNNY MOVES...I GOT AN ITCHY TRIGGER FINGER!
B-BETTER DO WHAT HE SAYS, MORGAN! N-NOTHING WE CAN DO TO STOP 'EM! ONLY AN IDIOT WOULD RISK HIS NECK TO STOP THEIR...
W-WATCH OUT, MORGAN! T-THIS IS NO TIME TO PROVE YOUR BRAVERY..!
G-GET OFFA ME, YOU DUMB HYENA! THIS IS ONLY A ... ARGHHH!
ONLY A KIDNAPPING, EH? THIS'LL TAKE CARE OF YOU...AND IN A FEW MINUTES YOUR PAL'S GONNA BE TIED UP ALONGSIDE YOU!
5

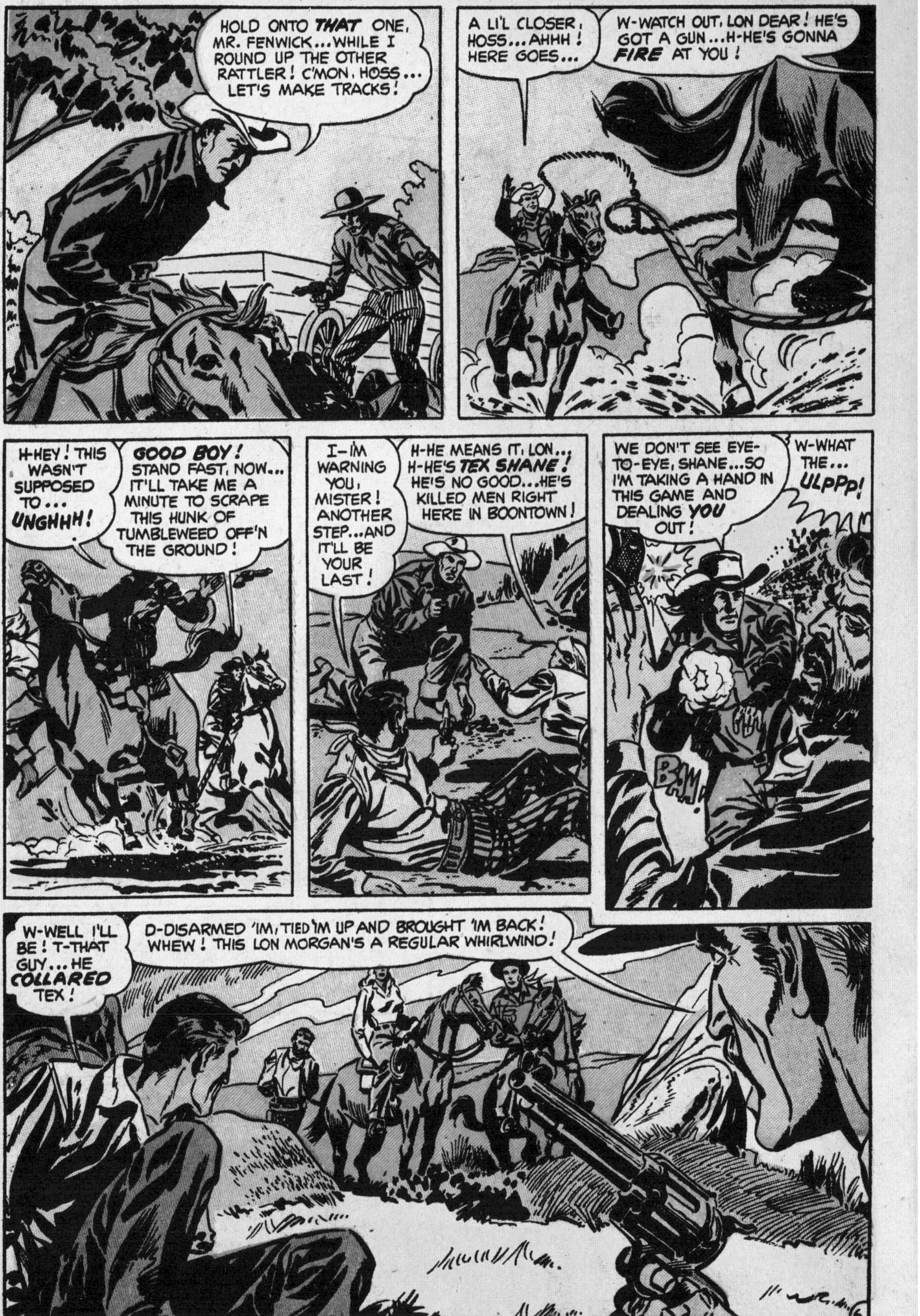
HOLD ONTO THAT ONE, MR. FENWICK... WHILE I ROUND UP THE OTHER RATTLER! C'MON, HOSS... LET'S MAKE TRACKS!
A LI'L CLOSER, HOSS... AHHH! HERE GOES...
W-WATCH OUT, LON DEAR! HE'S GOT A GUN... H-HE'S GONNA FIRE AT YOU!
H-HEY! THIS WASN'T SUPPOSED TO... UNGHHH!
GOOD BOY! STAND FAST, NOW... IT'LL TAKE ME A MINUTE TO SCRAPE THIS HUNK OF TUMBLEWEED OFF'N THE GROUND!
I-I'M WARNING YOU, MISTER! ANOTHER STEP...AND IT'LL BE YOUR LAST!
H-HE MEANS IT, LON... H-HE'S TEX SHANE! HE'S NO GOOD...HE'S KILLED MEN RIGHT HERE IN BOONTOWN!
WE DON'T SEE EYE-TO-EYE, SHANE...SO I'M TAKING A HAND IN THIS GAME AND DEALING YOU OUT!
W-WHAT THE... ULPPP!
BAM!
W-WELL I'LL BE! T-THAT GUY... HE COLLARED TEX!
D-DISARMED 'IM, TIED 'IM UP AND BROUGHT 'IM BACK! WHEW! THIS LON MORGAN'S A REGULAR WHIRLWIND!
6

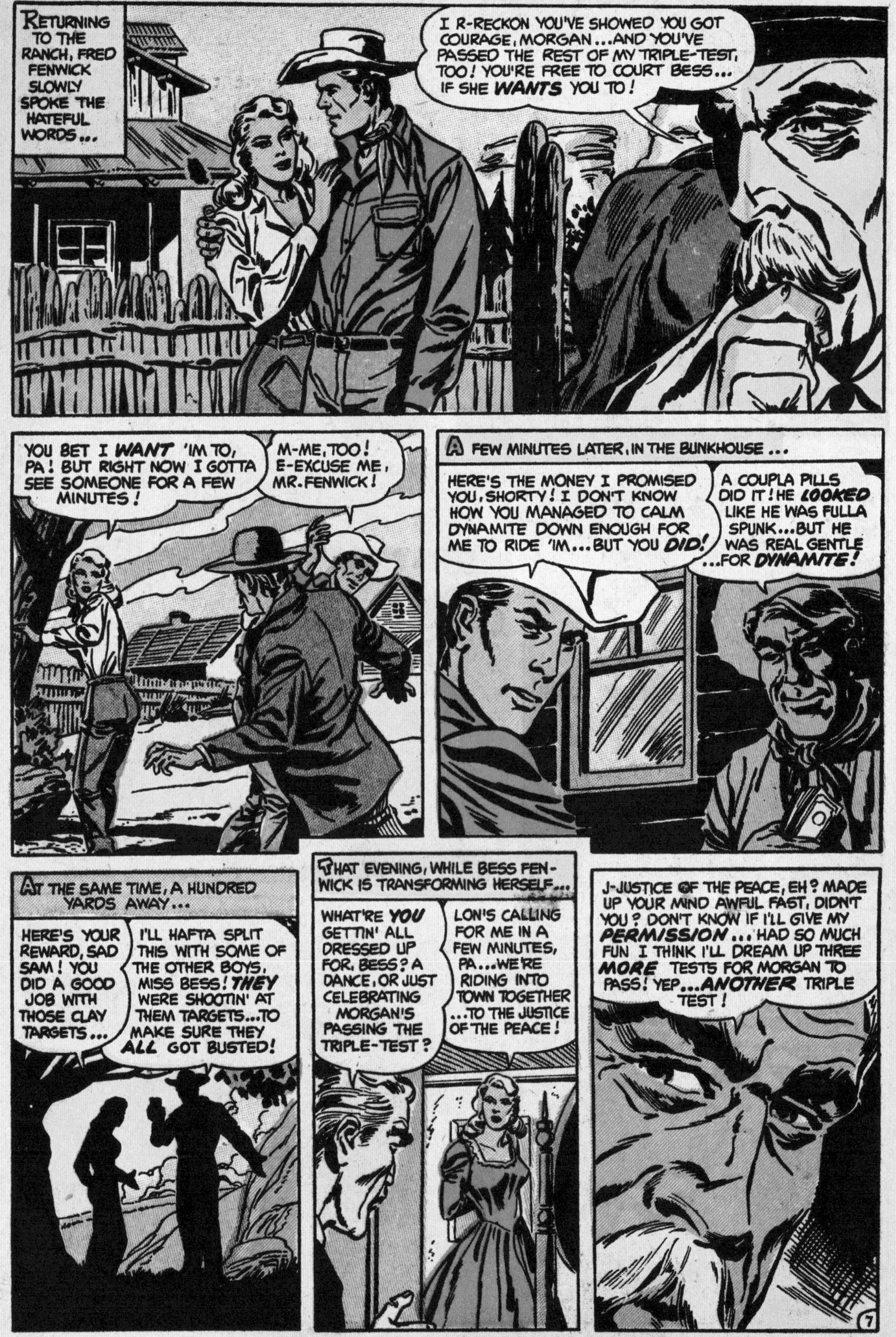
RETURNING TO THE RANCH, FRED FENWICK SLOWLY SPOKE THE HATEFUL WORDS...
I R-RECKON YOU'VE SHOWED YOU GOT COURAGE, MORGAN...AND YOU'VE PASSED THE REST OF MY TRIPLE-TEST, TOO! YOU'RE FREE TO COURT BESS... IF SHE WANTS YOU TO!
YOU BET I WANT 'IM TO, PA! BUT RIGHT NOW I GOTTA SEE SOMEONE FOR A FEW MINUTES!
M-ME, TOO! E-EXCUSE ME, MR. FENWICK!
A FEW MINUTES LATER, IN THE BUNKHOUSE...
HERE'S THE MONEY I PROMISED YOU, SHORTY! I DON'T KNOW HOW YOU MANAGED TO CALM DYNAMITE DOWN ENOUGH FOR ME TO RIDE 'IM...BUT YOU DID!
A COUPLA PILLS DID IT! HE LOOKED LIKE HE WAS FULLA SPUNK...BUT HE WAS REAL GENTLE ...FOR DYNAMITE!
AT THE SAME TIME, A HUNDRED YARDS AWAY...
HERE'S YOUR REWARD, SAD SAM! YOU DID A GOOD JOB WITH THOSE CLAY TARGETS...
I'LL HAFTA SPLIT THIS WITH SOME OF THE OTHER BOYS, MISS BESS! THEY WERE SHOOTIN' AT THEM TARGETS...TO MAKE SURE THEY ALL GOT BUSTED!
THAT EVENING, WHILE BESS FENWICK IS TRANSFORMING HERSELF...
WHAT'RE YOU GETTIN' ALL DRESSED UP FOR, BESS? A DANCE, OR JUST CELEBRATING MORGAN'S PASSING THE TRIPLE-TEST?
LON'S CALLING FOR ME IN A FEW MINUTES, PA...WE'RE RIDING INTO TOWN TOGETHER ...TO THE JUSTICE OF THE PEACE!
J-JUSTICE OF THE PEACE, EH? MADE UP YOUR MIND AWFUL FAST, DIDN'T YOU? DON'T KNOW IF I'LL GIVE MY PERMISSION...HAD SO MUCH FUN I THINK I'LL DREAM UP THREE MORE TESTS FOR MORGAN TO PASS! YEP...ANOTHER TRIPLE TEST!
7

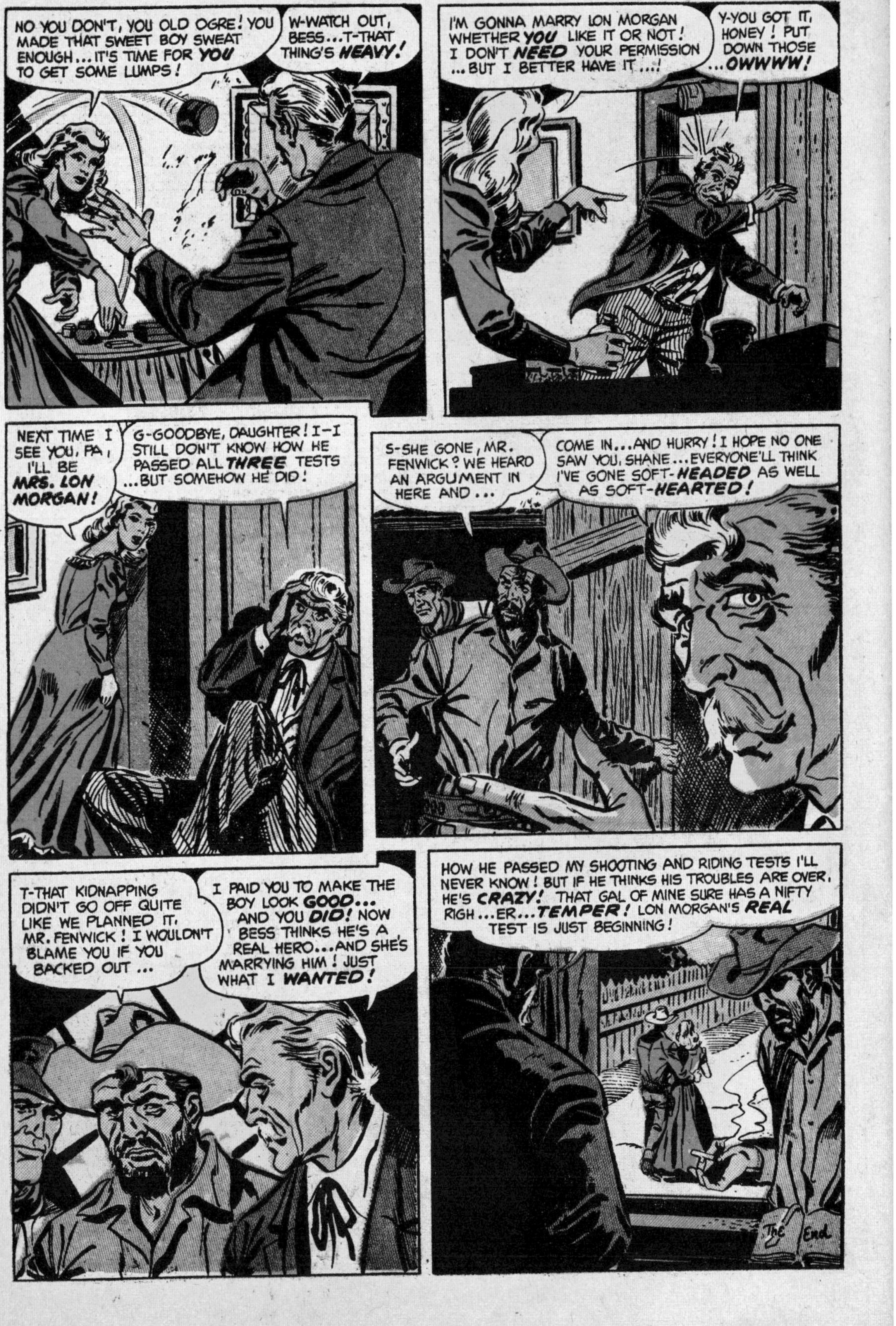
NO YOU DON'T, YOU OLD OGRE! YOU MADE THAT SWEET BOY SWEAT ENOUGH... IT'S TIME FOR YOU TO GET SOME LUMPS!
W-WATCH OUT, BESS...T-THAT THING'S HEAVY!
I'M GONNA MARRY LON MORGAN WHETHER YOU LIKE IT OR NOT! I DON'T NEED YOUR PERMISSION ...BUT I BETTER HAVE IT...!
Y-YOU GOT IT, HONEY! PUT DOWN THOSE ...OWWWW!
NEXT TIME I SEE YOU, PA, I'LL BE MRS. LON MORGAN!
G-GOODBYE, DAUGHTER! I-I STILL DON'T KNOW HOW HE PASSED ALL THREE TESTS ...BUT SOMEHOW HE DID!
S-SHE GONE, MR. FENWICK? WE HEARD AN ARGUMENT IN HERE AND...
COME IN...AND HURRY! I HOPE NO ONE SAW YOU, SHANE...EVERYONE'LL THINK I'VE GONE SOFT-HEADED AS WELL AS SOFT-HEARTED!
T-THAT KIDNAPPING DIDN'T GO OFF QUITE LIKE WE PLANNED IT, MR. FENWICK! I WOULDN'T BLAME YOU IF YOU BACKED OUT...
I PAID YOU TO MAKE THE BOY LOOK GOOD... AND YOU DID! NOW BESS THINKS HE'S A REAL HERO...AND SHE'S MARRYING HIM! JUST WHAT I WANTED!
HOW HE PASSED MY SHOOTING AND RIDING TESTS I'LL NEVER KNOW! BUT IF HE THINKS HIS TROUBLES ARE OVER, HE'S CRAZY! THAT GAL OF MINE SURE HAS A NIFTY RIGH...ER...TEMPER! LON MORGAN'S REAL TEST IS JUST BEGINNING!
THE END

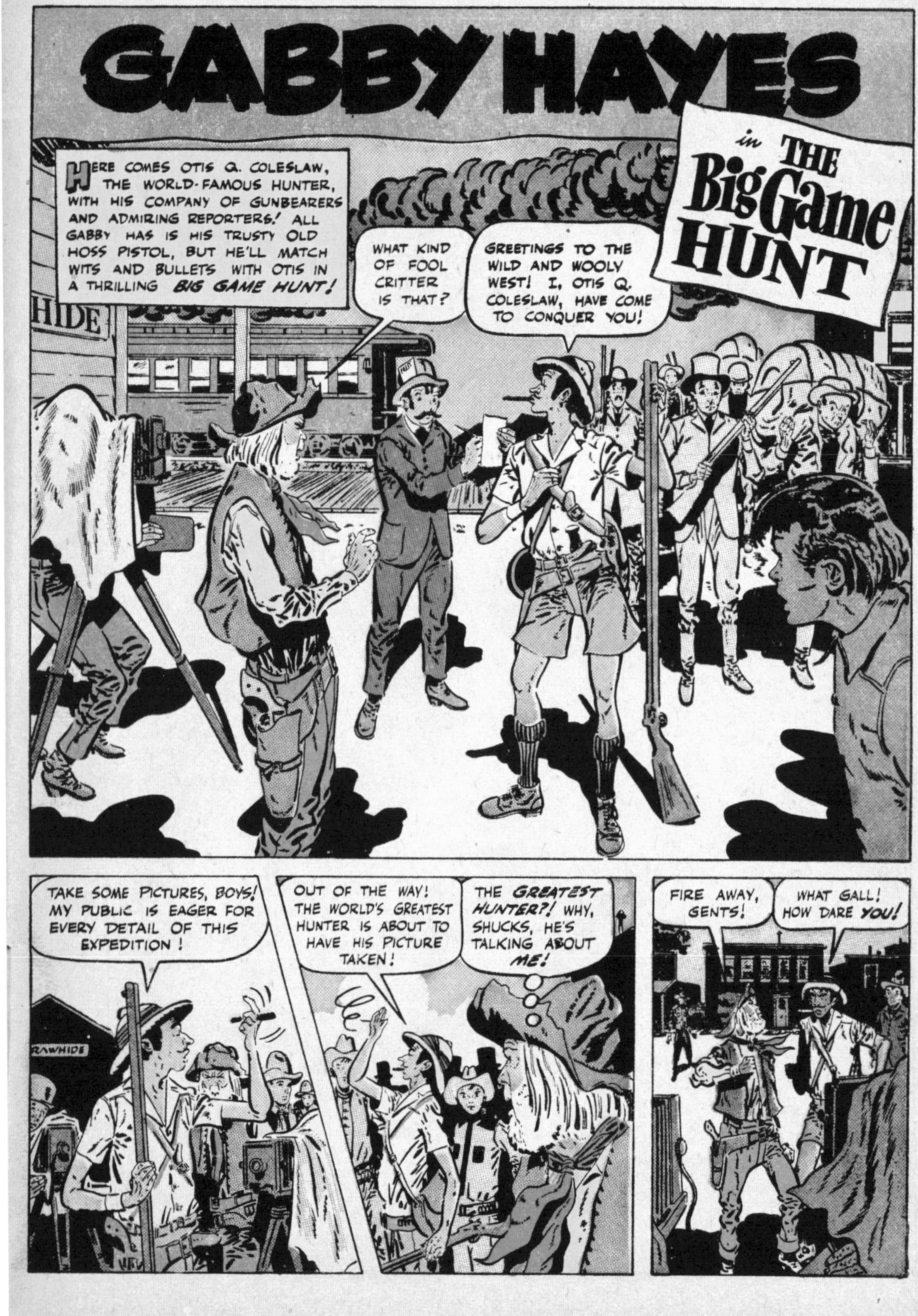
GABBY HAYES
in THE Big Game HUNT
HERE COMES OTIS Q. COLESLAW, THE WORLD-FAMOUS HUNTER, WITH HIS COMPANY OF GUNBEARERS AND ADMIRING REPORTERS! ALL GABBY HAS IS HIS TRUSTY OLD HOSS PISTOL, BUT HE'LL MATCH WITS AND BULLETS WITH OTIS IN A THRILLING BIG GAME HUNT!
WHAT KIND OF FOOL CRITTER IS THAT?
GREETINGS TO THE WILD AND WOOLY WEST! I, OTIS Q. COLESLAW, HAVE COME TO CONQUER YOU!
HIDE
TAKE SOME PICTURES, BOYS! MY PUBLIC IS EAGER FOR EVERY DETAIL OF THIS EXPEDITION!
RAWHIDE
OUT OF THE WAY! THE WORLD'S GREATEST HUNTER IS ABOUT TO HAVE HIS PICTURE TAKEN!
THE GREATEST HUNTER?! WHY, SHUCKS, HE'S TALKING ABOUT ME!
FIRE AWAY, GENTS!
WHAT GALL! HOW DARE YOU!

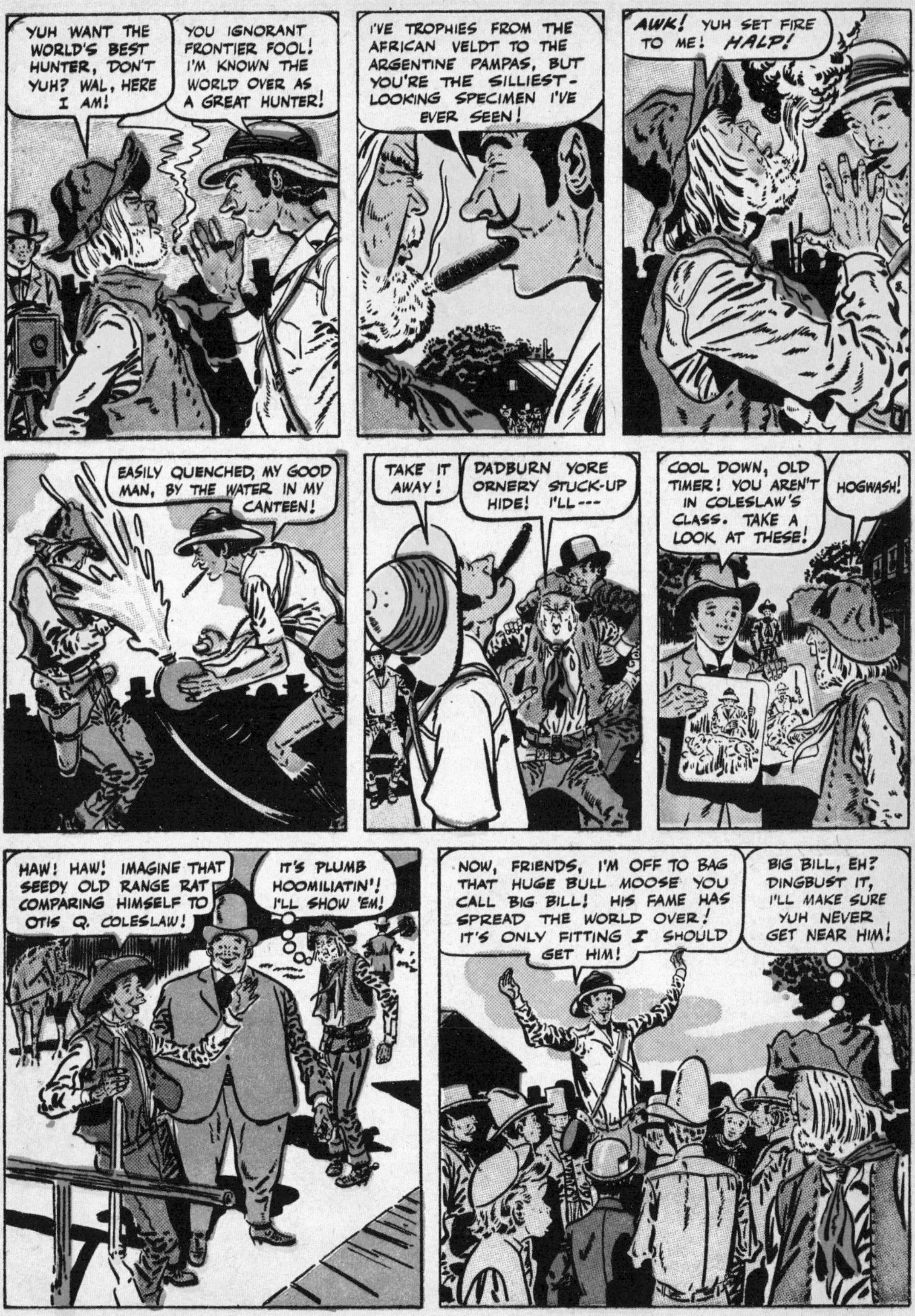
YUH WANT THE WORLD'S BEST HUNTER, DON'T YUH? WAL, HERE I AM!
YOU IGNORANT FRONTIER FOOL! I'M KNOWN THE WORLD OVER AS A GREAT HUNTER!
I'VE TROPHIES FROM THE AFRICAN VELDT TO THE ARGENTINE PAMPAS, BUT YOU'RE THE SILLIEST-LOOKING SPECIMEN I'VE EVER SEEN!
AWK! YUH SET FIRE TO ME! HALP!
EASILY QUENCHED, MY GOOD MAN, BY THE WATER IN MY CANTEEN!
TAKE IT AWAY!
DADBURN YORE ORNERY STUCK-UP HIDE! I'LL---
COOL DOWN, OLD TIMER! YOU AREN'T IN COLESLAW'S CLASS. TAKE A LOOK AT THESE!
HOGWASH!
HAW! HAW! IMAGINE THAT SEEDY OLD RANGE RAT COMPARING HIMSELF TO OTIS Q. COLESLAW!
IT'S PLUMB HOOMILIATIN'! I'LL SHOW 'EM!
NOW, FRIENDS, I'M OFF TO BAG THAT HUGE BULL MOOSE YOU CALL BIG BILL! HIS FAME HAS SPREAD THE WORLD OVER! IT'S ONLY FITTING I SHOULD GET HIM!
BIG BILL, EH? DINGBUST IT, I'LL MAKE SURE YUH NEVER GET NEAR HIM!

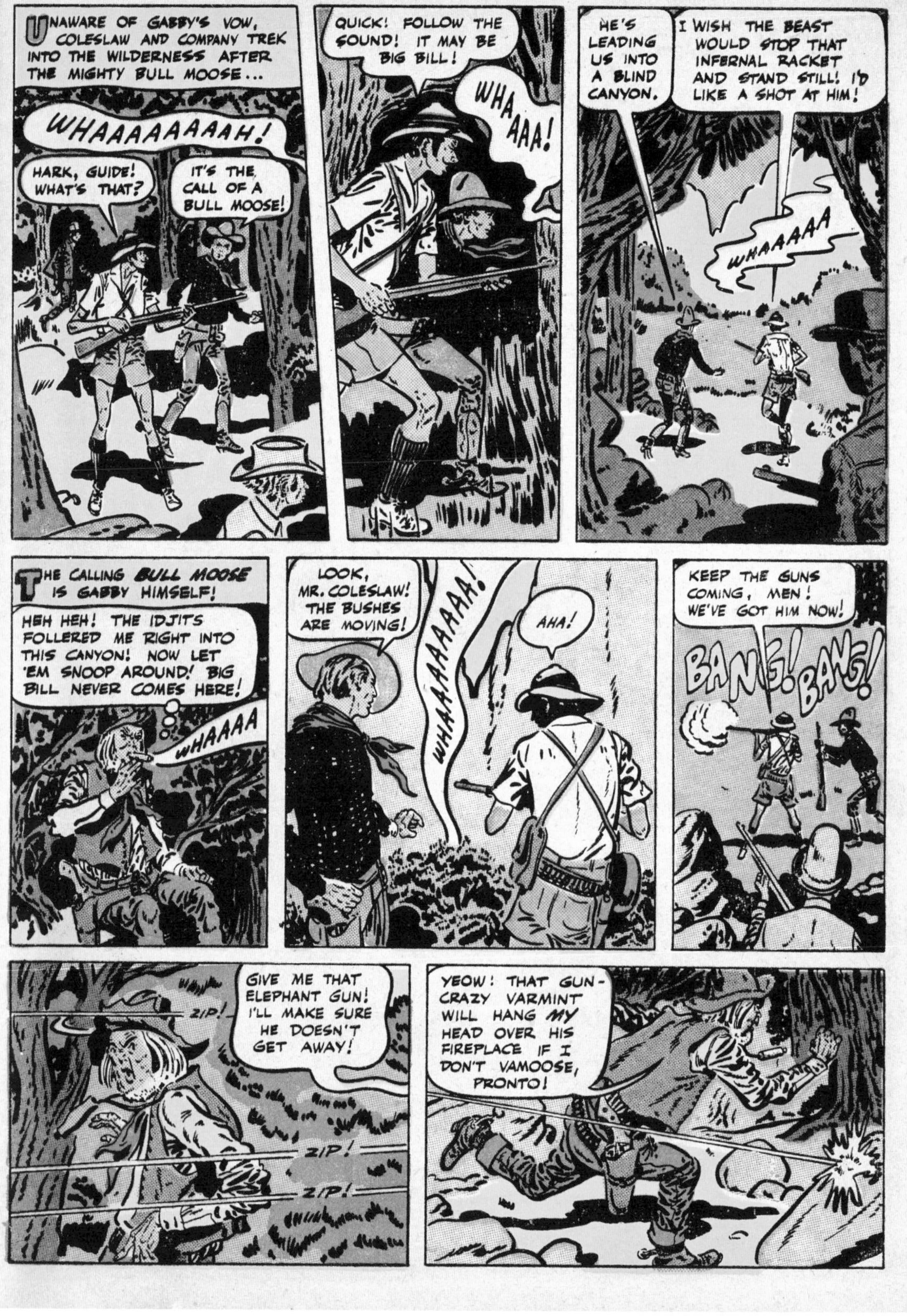
UNAWARE OF GABBY'S VOW, COLESLAW AND COMPANY TREK INTO THE WILDERNESS AFTER THE MIGHTY BULL MOOSE...
WHAAAAAAAAH!
HARK, GUIDE! WHAT'S THAT?
IT'S THE CALL OF A BULL MOOSE!
QUICK! FOLLOW THE SOUND! IT MAY BE BIG BILL!
WHAAAA!
HE'S LEADING US INTO A BLIND CANYON.
I WISH THE BEAST WOULD STOP THAT INFERNAL RACKET AND STAND STILL! I'D LIKE A SHOT AT HIM!
WHAAAAAA
THE CALLING BULL MOOSE IS GABBY HIMSELF!
HEH HEH! THE IDJITS FOLLERED ME RIGHT INTO THIS CANYON! NOW LET 'EM SNOOP AROUND! BIG BILL NEVER COMES HERE!
WHAAAA
LOOK, MR. COLESLAW! THE BUSHES ARE MOVING!
WHAAAAAAAAAA!
AHA!
KEEP THE GUNS COMING, MEN! WE'VE GOT HIM NOW!
BANG! BANG!
ZIP!
GIVE ME THAT ELEPHANT GUN! I'LL MAKE SURE HE DOESN'T GET AWAY!
ZIP!
ZIP!
YEOW! THAT GUN-CRAZY VARMINT WILL HANG MY HEAD OVER HIS FIREPLACE IF I DON'T VAMOOSE, PRONTO!

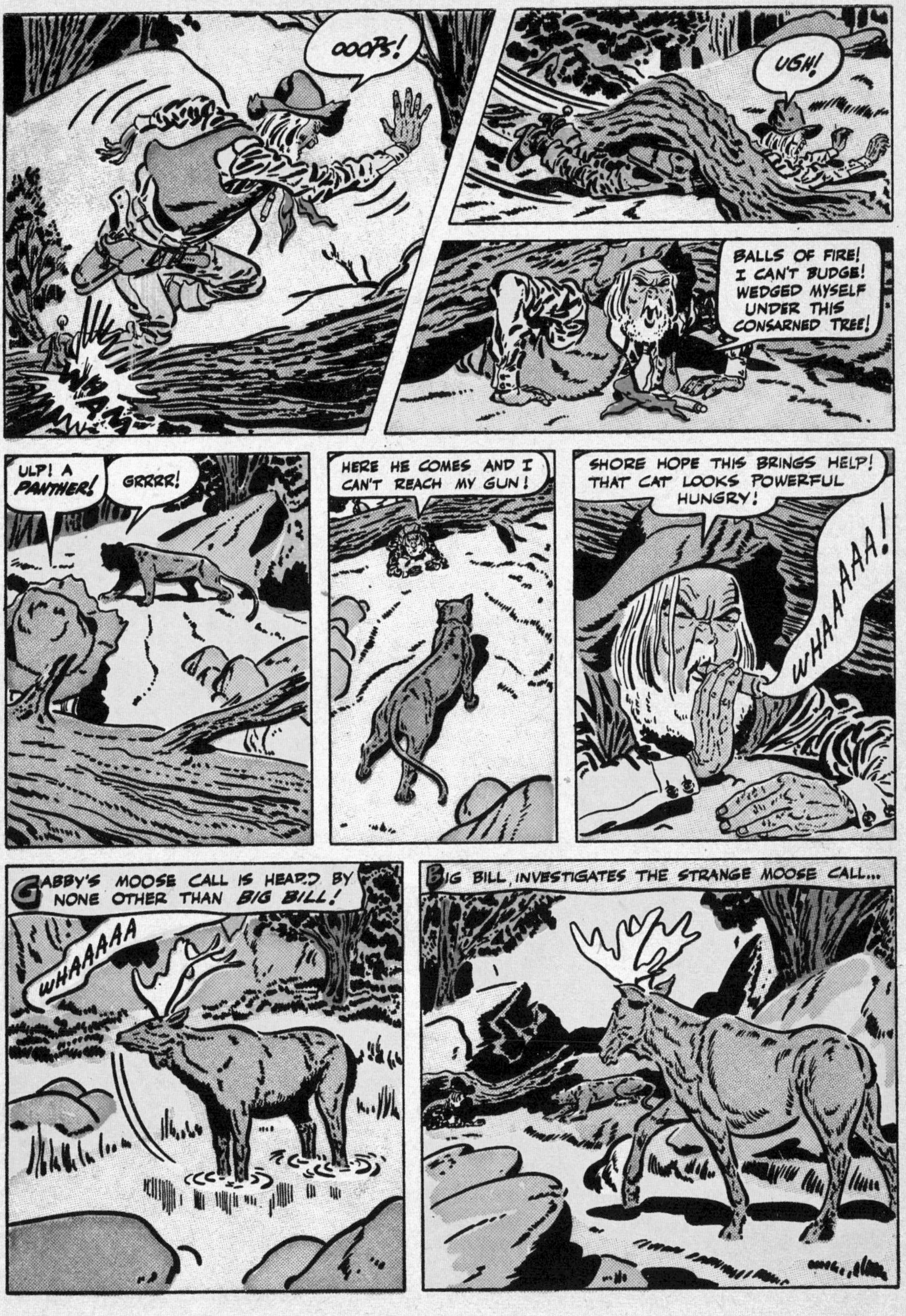
OOOPS!
WHAM
UGH!
BALLS OF FIRE! I CAN'T BUDGE! WEDGED MYSELF UNDER THIS CONSARNED TREE!
ULP! A PANTHER!
GRRRR!
HERE HE COMES AND I CAN'T REACH MY GUN!
SHORE HOPE THIS BRINGS HELP! THAT CAT LOOKS POWERFUL HUNGRY!
WHAAAAAA!
GABBY'S MOOSE CALL IS HEARD BY NONE OTHER THAN BIG BILL!
WHAAAAAA
BIG BILL INVESTIGATES THE STRANGE MOOSE CALL...

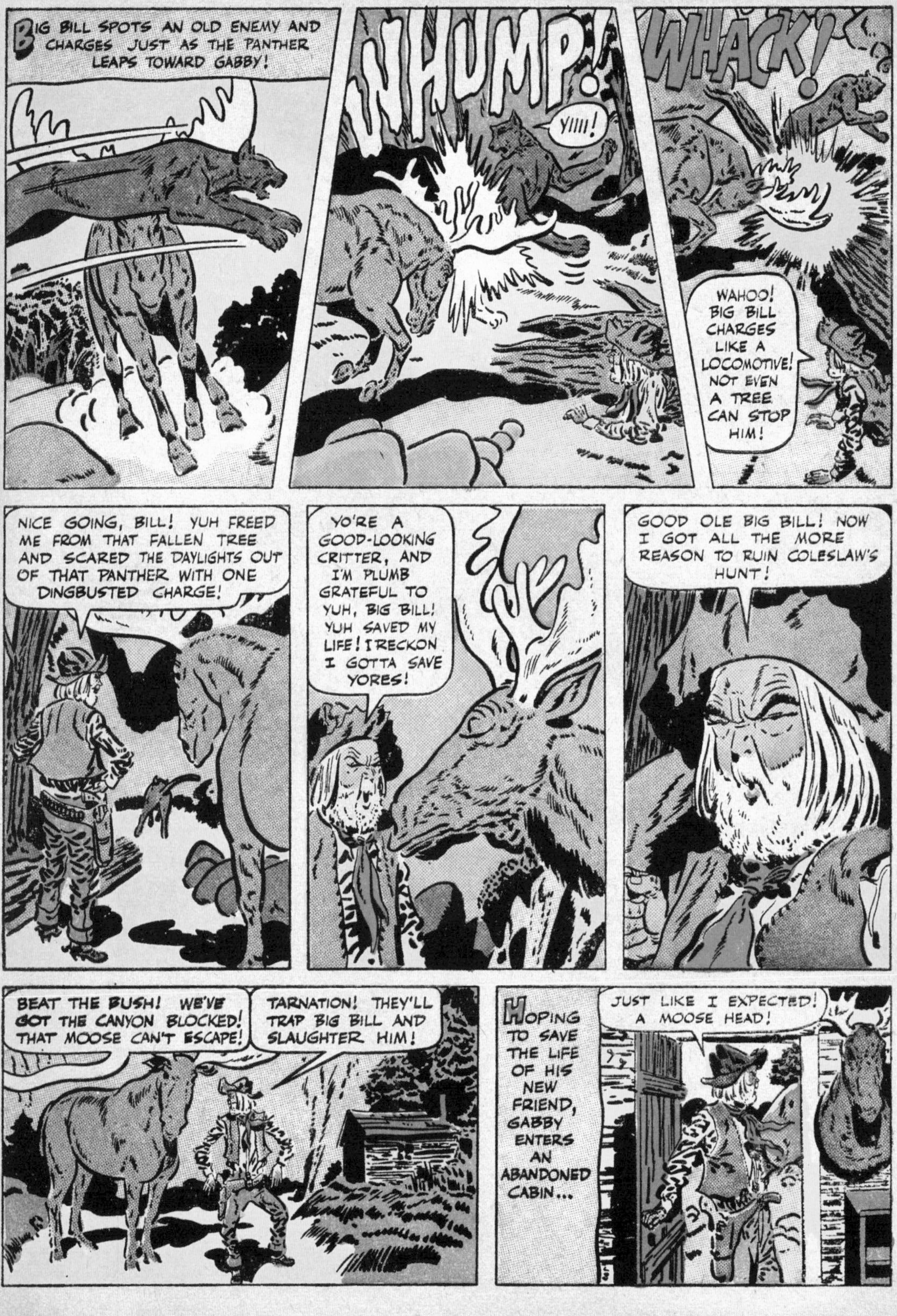
BIG BILL SPOTS AN OLD ENEMY AND CHARGES JUST AS THE PANTHER LEAPS TOWARD GABBY!
WHUMP!
YIII!
WHACK!
WAHOO! BIG BILL CHARGES LIKE A LOCOMOTIVE! NOT EVEN A TREE CAN STOP HIM!
NICE GOING, BILL! YUH FREED ME FROM THAT FALLEN TREE AND SCARED THE DAYLIGHTS OUT OF THAT PANTHER WITH ONE DINGBUSTED CHARGE!
YO'RE A GOOD-LOOKING CRITTER, AND I'M PLUMB GRATEFUL TO YUH, BIG BILL! YUH SAVED MY LIFE! I RECKON I GOTTA SAVE YORES!
GOOD OLE BIG BILL! NOW I GOT ALL THE MORE REASON TO RUIN COLESLAW'S HUNT!
BEAT THE BUSH! WE'VE GOT THE CANYON BLOCKED! THAT MOOSE CAN'T ESCAPE!
TARNATION! THEY'LL TRAP BIG BILL AND SLAUGHTER HIM!
HOPING TO SAVE THE LIFE OF HIS NEW FRIEND, GABBY ENTERS AN ABANDONED CABIN...
JUST LIKE I EXPECTED! A MOOSE HEAD!

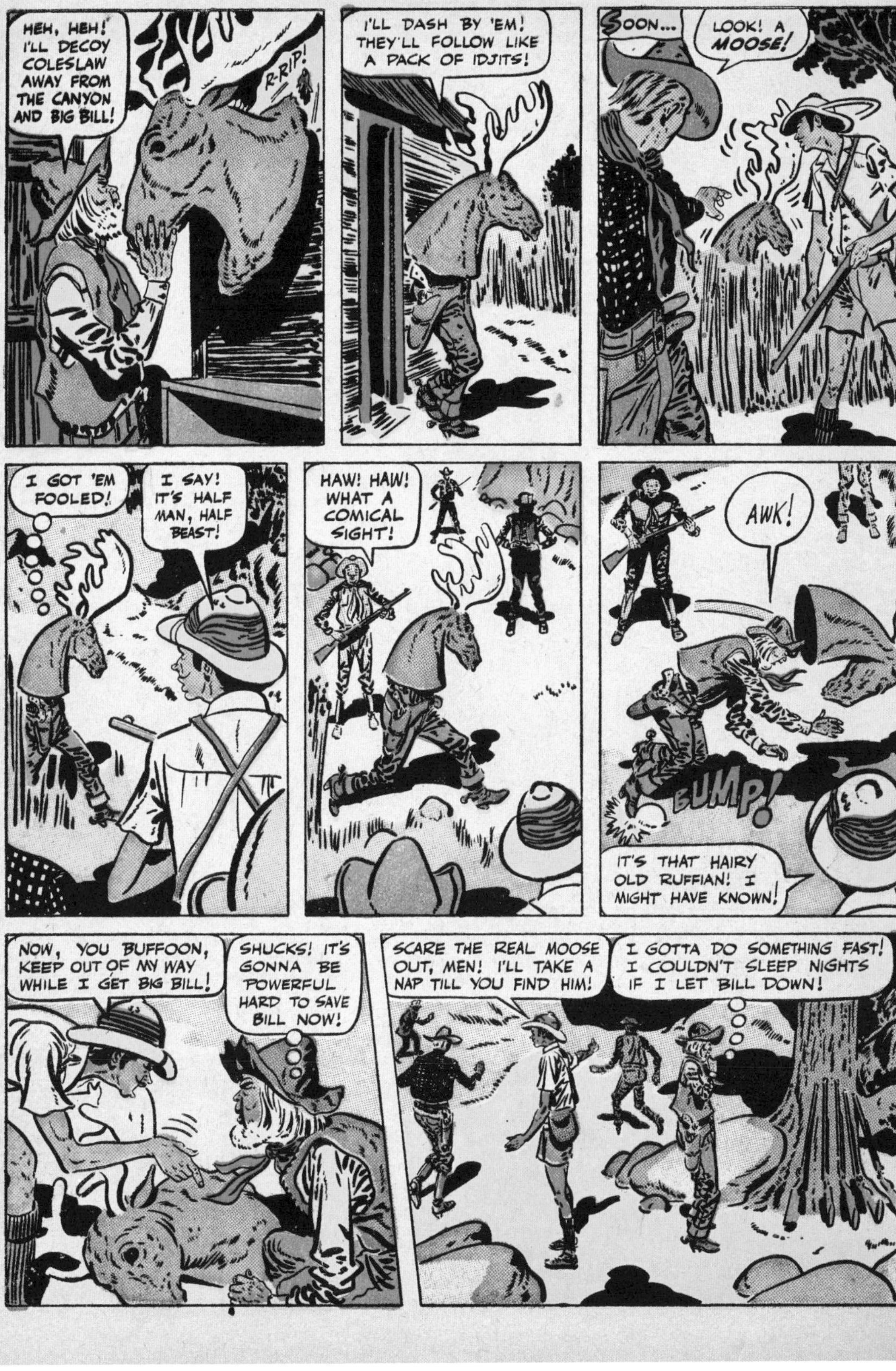
HEH, HEH! I'LL DECOY COLESLAW AWAY FROM THE CANYON AND BIG BILL!
R-RIP!
I'LL DASH BY 'EM! THEY'LL FOLLOW LIKE A PACK OF IDJITS!
SOON...
LOOK! A MOOSE!
I GOT 'EM FOOLED!
I SAY! IT'S HALF MAN, HALF BEAST!
HAW! HAW! WHAT A COMICAL SIGHT!
AWK!
BUMP!
IT'S THAT HAIRY OLD RUFFIAN! I MIGHT HAVE KNOWN!
NOW, YOU BUFFOON, KEEP OUT OF MY WAY WHILE I GET BIG BILL!
SHUCKS! IT'S GONNA BE POWERFUL HARD TO SAVE BILL NOW!
SCARE THE REAL MOOSE OUT, MEN! I'LL TAKE A NAP TILL YOU FIND HIM!
I GOTTA DO SOMETHING FAST! I COULDN'T SLEEP NIGHTS IF I LET BILL DOWN!

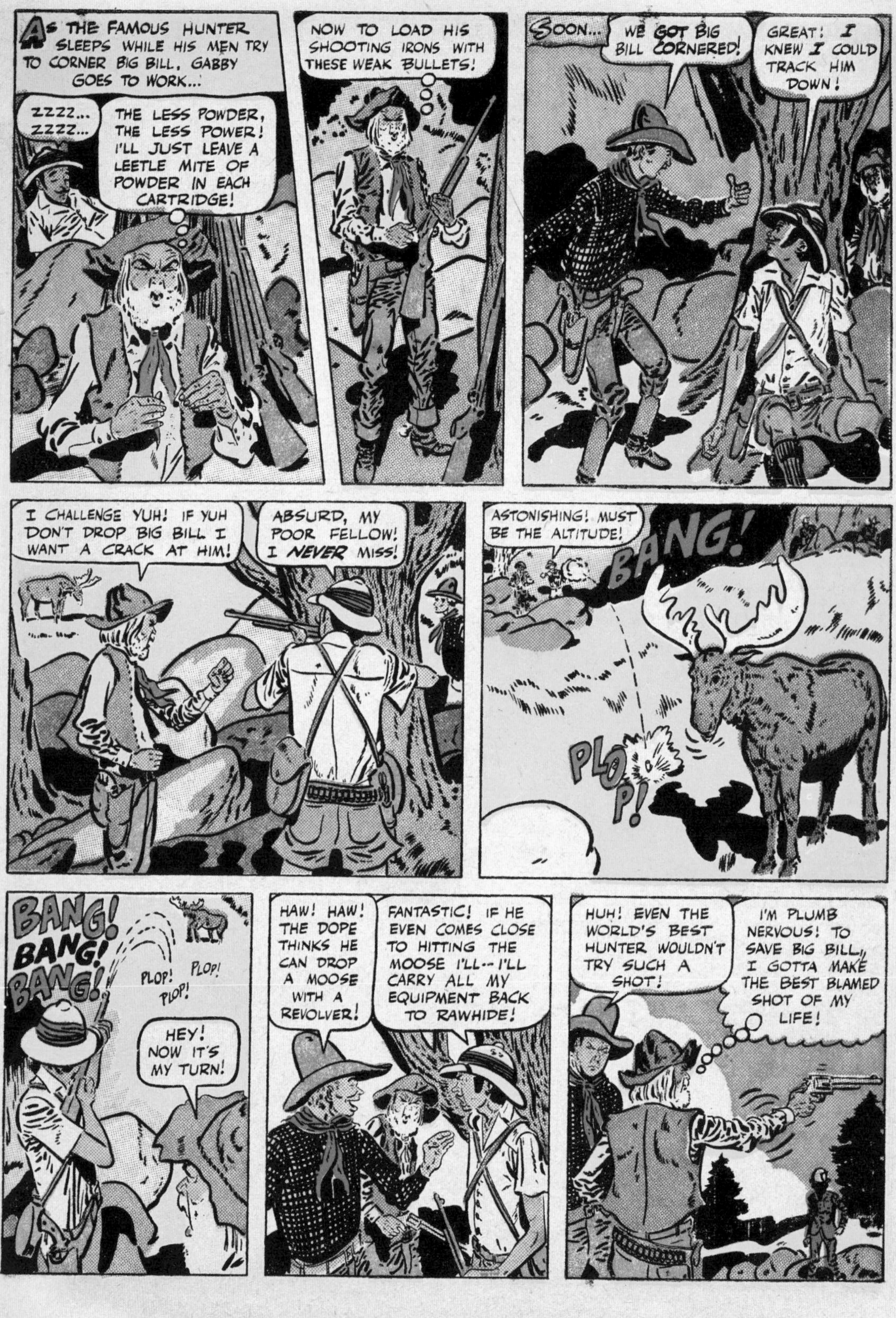
AS THE FAMOUS HUNTER SLEEPS WHILE HIS MEN TRY TO CORNER BIG BILL, GABBY GOES TO WORK...
ZZZZ... ZZZZ...
THE LESS POWDER, THE LESS POWER! I'LL JUST LEAVE A LEETLE MITE OF POWDER IN EACH CARTRIDGE!
NOW TO LOAD HIS SHOOTING IRONS WITH THESE WEAK BULLETS!
SOON...
WE GOT BIG BILL CORNERED!
GREAT! I KNEW I COULD TRACK HIM DOWN!
I CHALLENGE YUH! IF YUH DON'T DROP BIG BILL I WANT A CRACK AT HIM!
ABSURD, MY POOR FELLOW! I NEVER MISS!
ASTONISHING! MUST BE THE ALTITUDE!
BANG!
PLOP!
BANG! BANG! BANG!
PLOP! PLOP! PLOP!
HEY! NOW IT'S MY TURN!
HAW! HAW! THE DOPE THINKS HE CAN DROP A MOOSE WITH A REVOLVER!
FANTASTIC! IF HE EVEN COMES CLOSE TO HITTING THE MOOSE I'LL--I'LL CARRY ALL MY EQUIPMENT BACK TO RAWHIDE!
HUH! EVEN THE WORLD'S BEST HUNTER WOULDN'T TRY SUCH A SHOT!
I'M PLUMB NERVOUS! TO SAVE BIG BILL, I GOTTA MAKE THE BEST BLAMED SHOT OF MY LIFE!

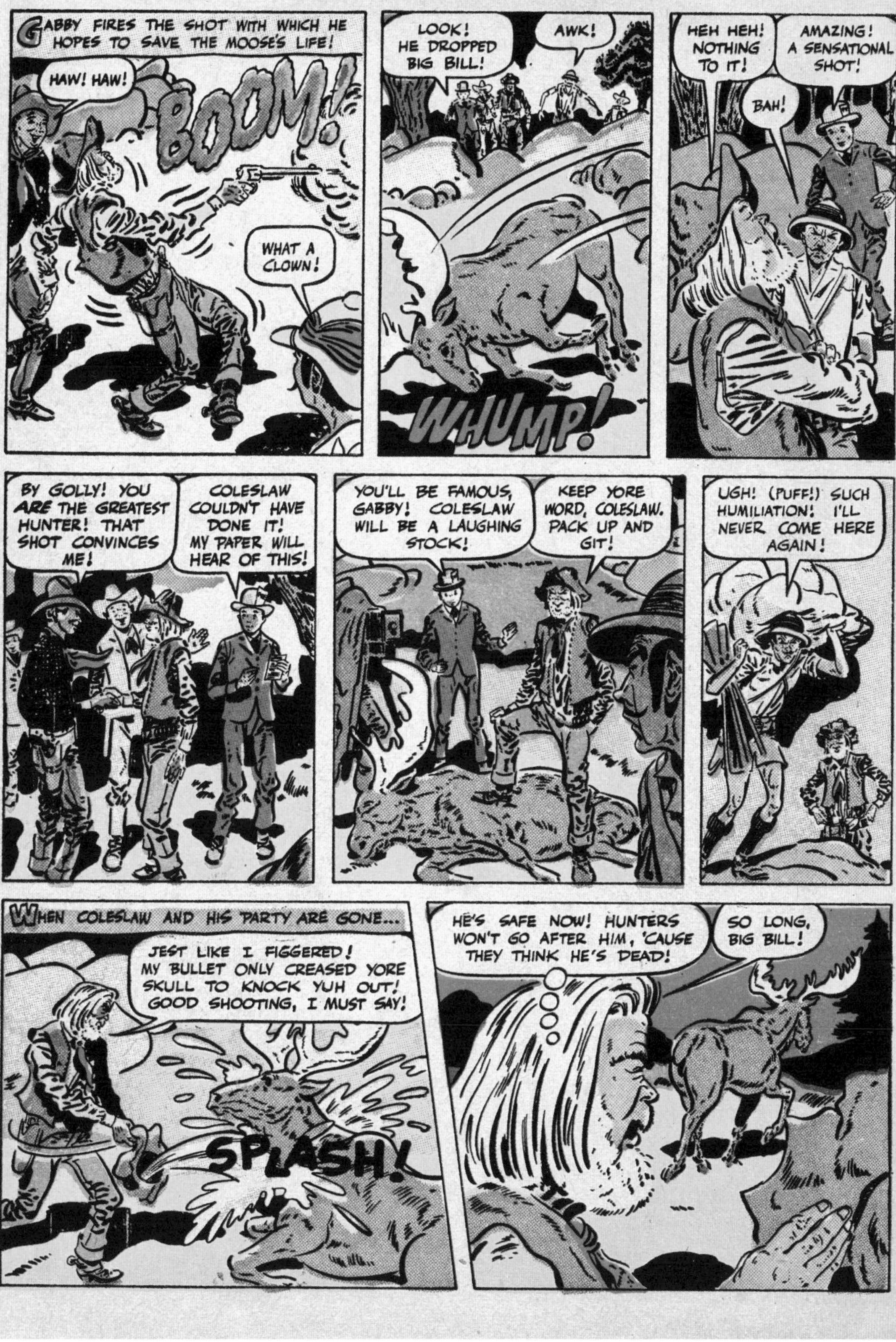
GABBY FIRES THE SHOT WITH WHICH HE HOPES TO SAVE THE MOOSE'S LIFE!
HAW! HAW!
BOOM!
WHAT A CLOWN!
LOOK! HE DROPPED BIG BILL!
AWK!
WHUMP!
HEH HEH! NOTHING TO IT!
AMAZING! A SENSATIONAL SHOT!
BAH!
BY GOLLY! YOU ARE THE GREATEST HUNTER! THAT SHOT CONVINCES ME!
COLESLAW COULDN'T HAVE DONE IT! MY PAPER WILL HEAR OF THIS!
YOU'LL BE FAMOUS, GABBY! COLESLAW WILL BE A LAUGHING STOCK!
KEEP YORE WORD, COLESLAW. PACK UP AND GIT!
UGH! (PUFF!) SUCH HUMILIATION! I'LL NEVER COME HERE AGAIN!
WHEN COLESLAW AND HIS PARTY ARE GONE...
JEST LIKE I FIGGERED! MY BULLET ONLY CREASED YORE SKULL TO KNOCK YUH OUT! GOOD SHOOTING, I MUST SAY!
SPLASH!
HE'S SAFE NOW! HUNTERS WON'T GO AFTER HIM, 'CAUSE THEY THINK HE'S DEAD!
SO LONG, BIG BILL!

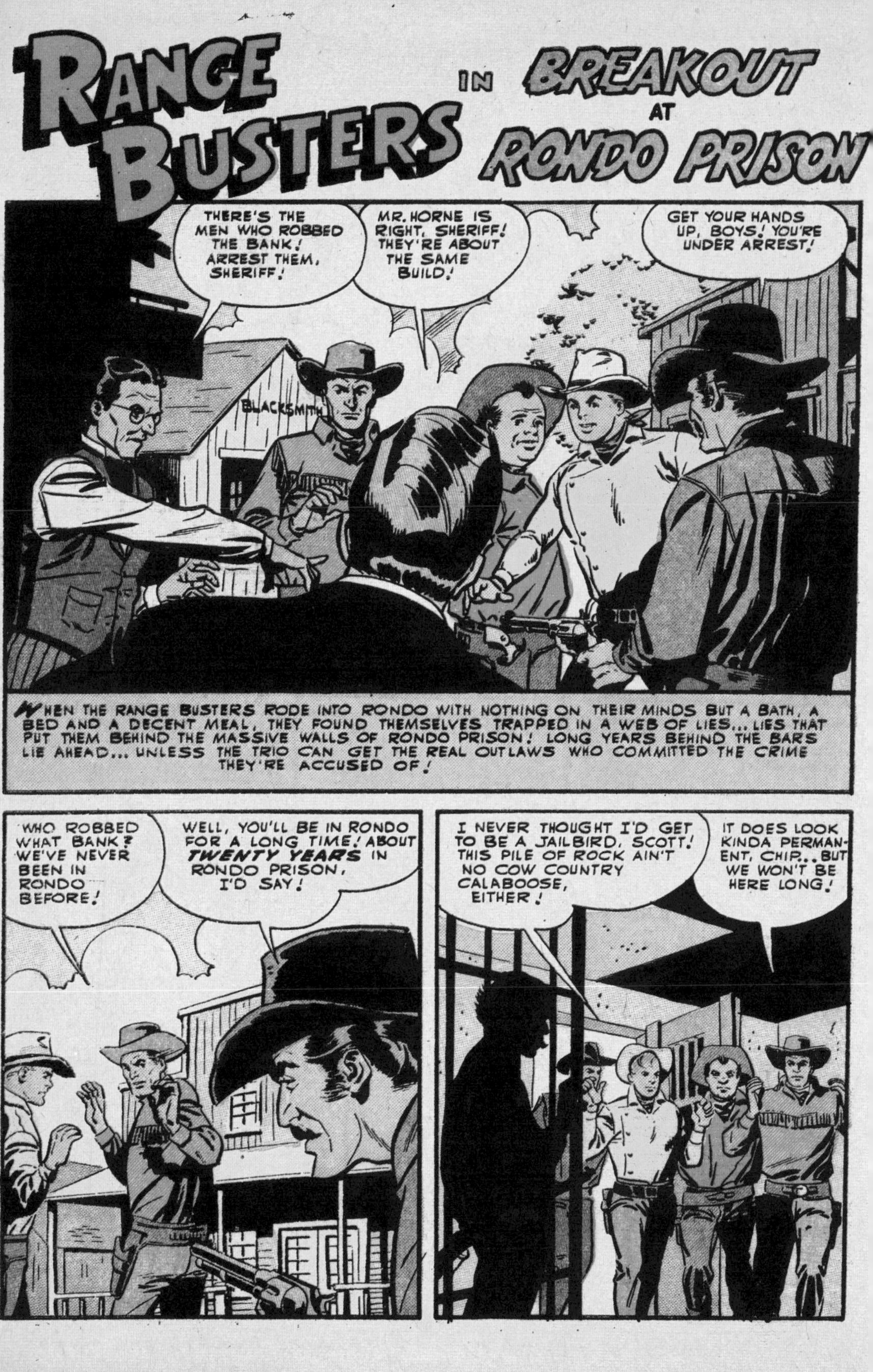
RANGE BUSTERS IN BREAKOUT AT RONDO PRISON
THERE'S THE MEN WHO ROBBED THE BANK! ARREST THEM, SHERIFF!
MR. HORNE IS RIGHT, SHERIFF! THEY'RE ABOUT THE SAME BUILD!
GET YOUR HANDS UP, BOYS! YOU'RE UNDER ARREST!
BLACKSMITH
WHEN THE RANGE BUSTERS RODE INTO RONDO WITH NOTHING ON THEIR MINDS BUT A BATH, A BED AND A DECENT MEAL, THEY FOUND THEMSELVES TRAPPED IN A WEB OF LIES... LIES THAT PUT THEM BEHIND THE MASSIVE WALLS OF RONDO PRISON! LONG YEARS BEHIND THE BARS LIE AHEAD... UNLESS THE TRIO CAN GET THE REAL OUTLAWS WHO COMMITTED THE CRIME THEY'RE ACCUSED OF!
WHO ROBBED WHAT BANK? WE'VE NEVER BEEN IN RONDO BEFORE!
WELL, YOU'LL BE IN RONDO FOR A LONG TIME! ABOUT TWENTY YEARS IN RONDO PRISON, I'D SAY!
I NEVER THOUGHT I'D GET TO BE A JAILBIRD, SCOTT! THIS PILE OF ROCK AIN'T NO COW COUNTRY CALABOOSE, EITHER!
IT DOES LOOK KINDA PERMANENT, CHIP... BUT WE WON'T BE HERE LONG!

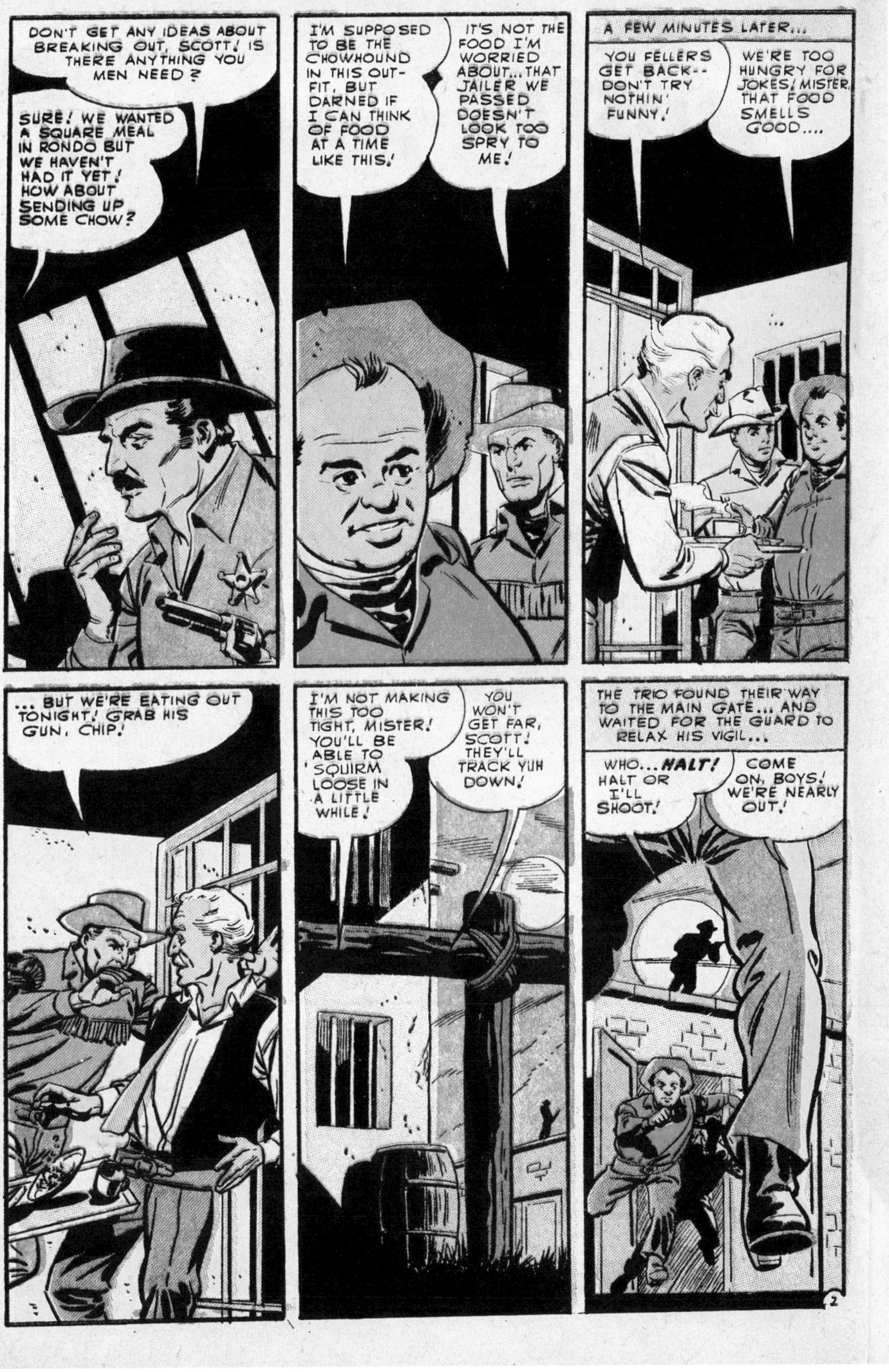
DON'T GET ANY IDEAS ABOUT BREAKING OUT, SCOTT! IS THERE ANYTHING YOU MEN NEED?
SURE! WE WANTED A SQUARE MEAL IN RONDO BUT WE HAVEN'T HAD IT YET! HOW ABOUT SENDING UP SOME CHOW?
I'M SUPPOSED TO BE THE CHOWHOUND IN THIS OUTFIT, BUT DARNED IF I CAN THINK OF FOOD AT A TIME LIKE THIS!
IT'S NOT THE FOOD I'M WORRIED ABOUT... THAT JAILER WE PASSED DOESN'T LOOK TOO SPRY TO ME!
A FEW MINUTES LATER...
YOU FELLERS GET BACK-- DON'T TRY NOTHIN' FUNNY!
WE'RE TOO HUNGRY FOR JOKES, MISTER. THAT FOOD SMELLS GOOD....
... BUT WE'RE EATING OUT TONIGHT! GRAB HIS GUN, CHIP!
I'M NOT MAKING THIS TOO TIGHT, MISTER! YOU'LL BE ABLE TO SQUIRM LOOSE IN A LITTLE WHILE!
YOU WON'T GET FAR, SCOTT! THEY'LL TRACK YUH DOWN!
THE TRIO FOUND THEIR WAY TO THE MAIN GATE... AND WAITED FOR THE GUARD TO RELAX HIS VIGIL...
WHO... HALT! HALT OR I'LL SHOOT!
COME ON, BOYS! WE'RE NEARLY OUT!
2

RANGE BUSTERS

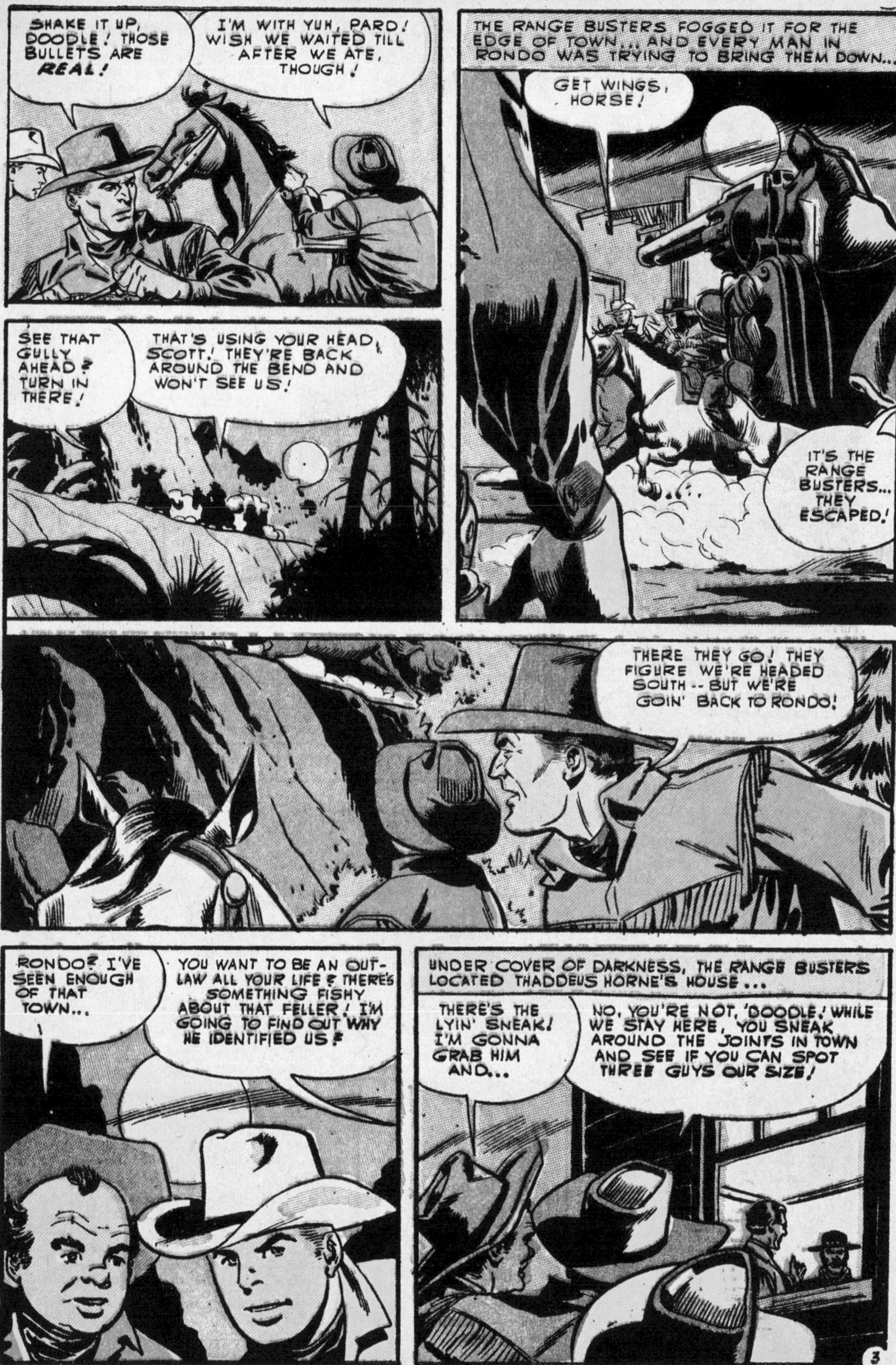
SHAKE IT UP, DOODLE! THOSE BULLETS ARE REAL!
I'M WITH YUH, PARD! WISH WE WAITED TILL AFTER WE ATE, THOUGH!
THE RANGE BUSTERS FOGGED IT FOR THE EDGE OF TOWN... AND EVERY MAN IN RONDO WAS TRYING TO BRING THEM DOWN...
GET WINGS, HORSE!
IT'S THE RANGE BUSTERS... THEY ESCAPED!
SEE THAT GULLY AHEAD? TURN IN THERE!
THAT'S USING YOUR HEAD, SCOTT! THEY'RE BACK AROUND THE BEND AND WON'T SEE US!
THERE THEY GO! THEY FIGURE WE'RE HEADED SOUTH -- BUT WE'RE GOIN' BACK TO RONDO!
RONDO? I'VE SEEN ENOUGH OF THAT TOWN...
YOU WANT TO BE AN OUTLAW ALL YOUR LIFE? THERE'S SOMETHING FISHY ABOUT THAT FELLER! I'M GOING TO FIND OUT WHY HE IDENTIFIED US?
UNDER COVER OF DARKNESS, THE RANGE BUSTERS LOCATED THADDEUS HORNE'S HOUSE...
THERE'S THE LYIN' SNEAK! I'M GONNA GRAB HIM AND...
NO, YOU'RE NOT, 'DOODLE!' WHILE WE STAY HERE, YOU SNEAK AROUND THE JOINTS IN TOWN AND SEE IF YOU CAN SPOT THREE GUYS OUR SIZE!
3

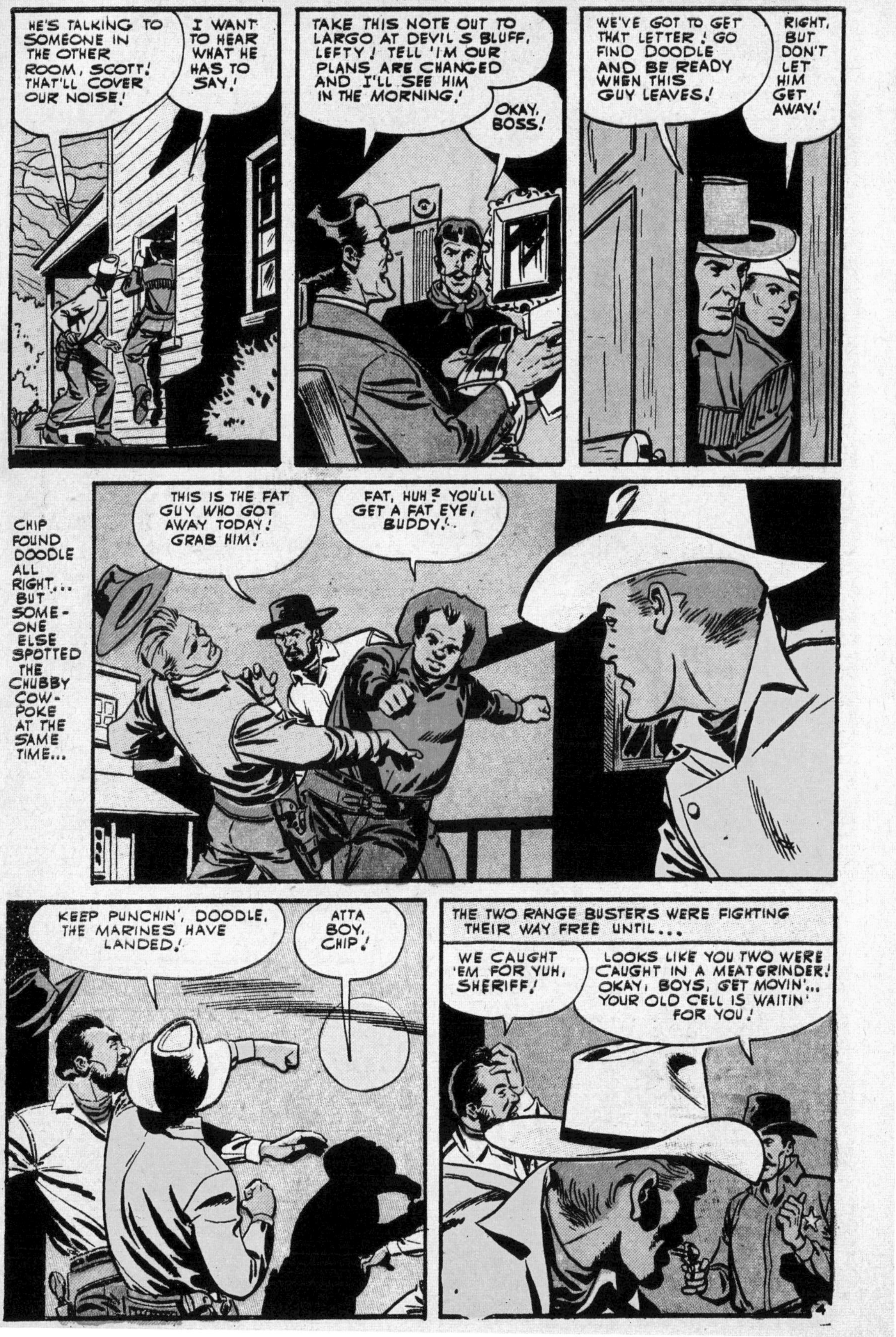
HE'S TALKING TO SOMEONE IN THE OTHER ROOM, SCOTT! THAT'LL COVER OUR NOISE!
I WANT TO HEAR WHAT HE HAS TO SAY!
TAKE THIS NOTE OUT TO LARGO AT DEVIL S BLUFF, LEFTY! TELL 'IM OUR PLANS ARE CHANGED AND I'LL SEE HIM IN THE MORNING!
OKAY, BOSS!
WE'VE GOT TO GET THAT LETTER! GO FIND DOODLE AND BE READY WHEN THIS GUY LEAVES!
RIGHT, BUT DON'T LET HIM GET AWAY!
CHIP FOUND DOODLE ALL RIGHT... BUT SOME-ONE ELSE SPOTTED THE CHUBBY COW-POKE AT THE SAME TIME...
THIS IS THE FAT GUY WHO GOT AWAY TODAY! GRAB HIM!
FAT, HUH? YOU'LL GET A FAT EYE, BUDDY!
KEEP PUNCHIN', DOODLE, THE MARINES HAVE LANDED!
ATTA BOY, CHIP!
THE TWO RANGE BUSTERS WERE FIGHTING THEIR WAY FREE UNTIL...
WE CAUGHT 'EM FOR YUH, SHERIFF!
LOOKS LIKE YOU TWO WERE CAUGHT IN A MEATGRINDER! OKAY, BOYS, GET MOVIN'... YOUR OLD CELL IS WAITIN' FOR YOU!
4

RANGE BUSTERS

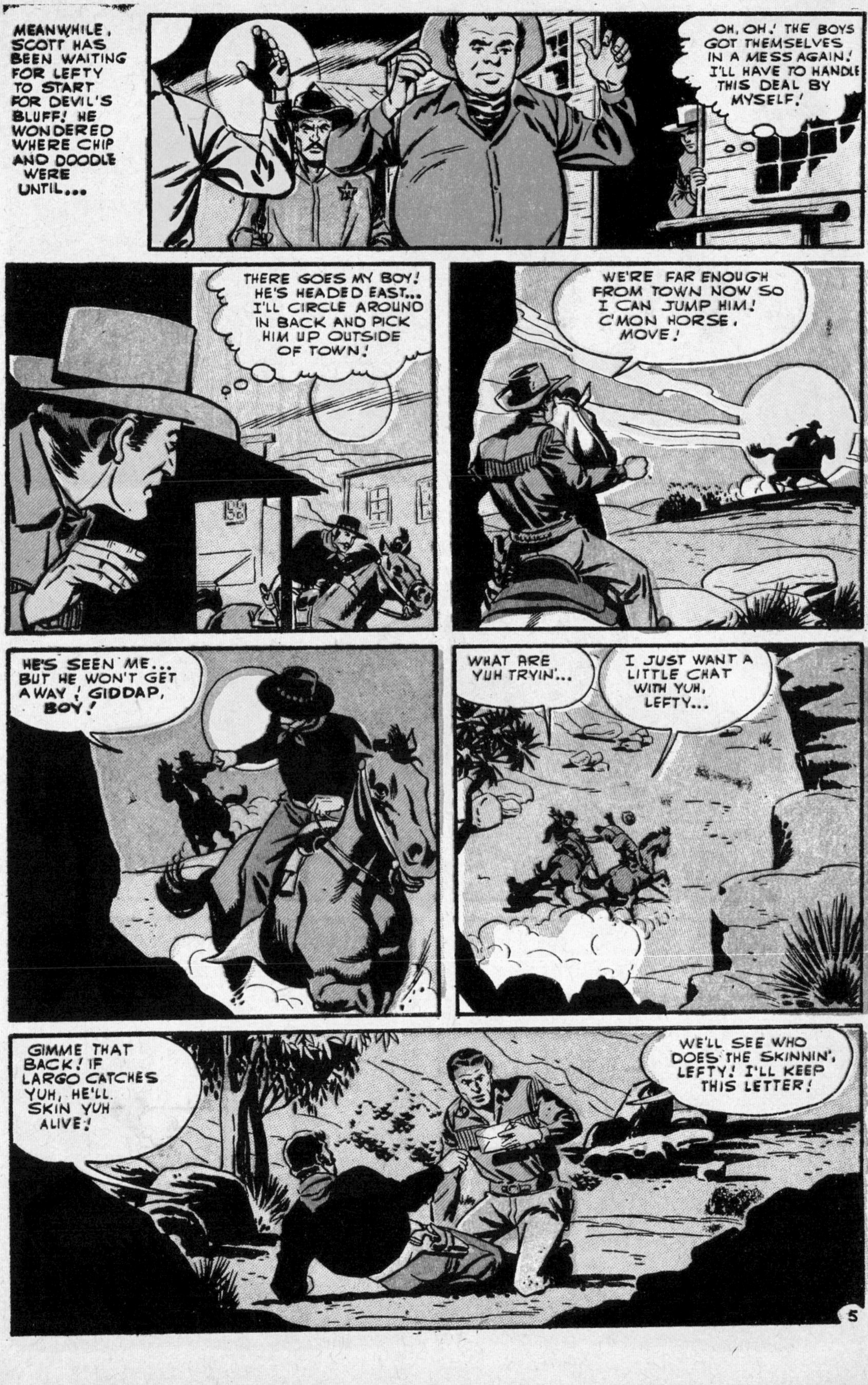

MEANWHILE, SCOTT HAS BEEN WAITING FOR LEFTY TO START FOR DEVIL'S BLUFF! HE WONDERED WHERE CHIP AND DOODLE WERE UNTIL...
OH, OH! THE BOYS GOT THEMSELVES IN A MESS AGAIN! I'LL HAVE TO HANDLE THIS DEAL BY MYSELF!
THERE GOES MY BOY! HE'S HEADED EAST... I'LL CIRCLE AROUND IN BACK AND PICK HIM UP OUTSIDE OF TOWN!
WE'RE FAR ENOUGH FROM TOWN NOW SO I CAN JUMP HIM! C'MON HORSE, MOVE!
HE'S SEEN ME... BUT HE WON'T GET AWAY! GIDDAP, BOY!
WHAT ARE YUH TRYIN'...
I JUST WANT A LITTLE CHAT WITH YUH, LEFTY...
GIMME THAT BACK! IF LARGO CATCHES YUH, HE'LL SKIN YUH ALIVE!
WE'LL SEE WHO DOES THE SKINNIN', LEFTY! I'LL KEEP THIS LETTER!
5

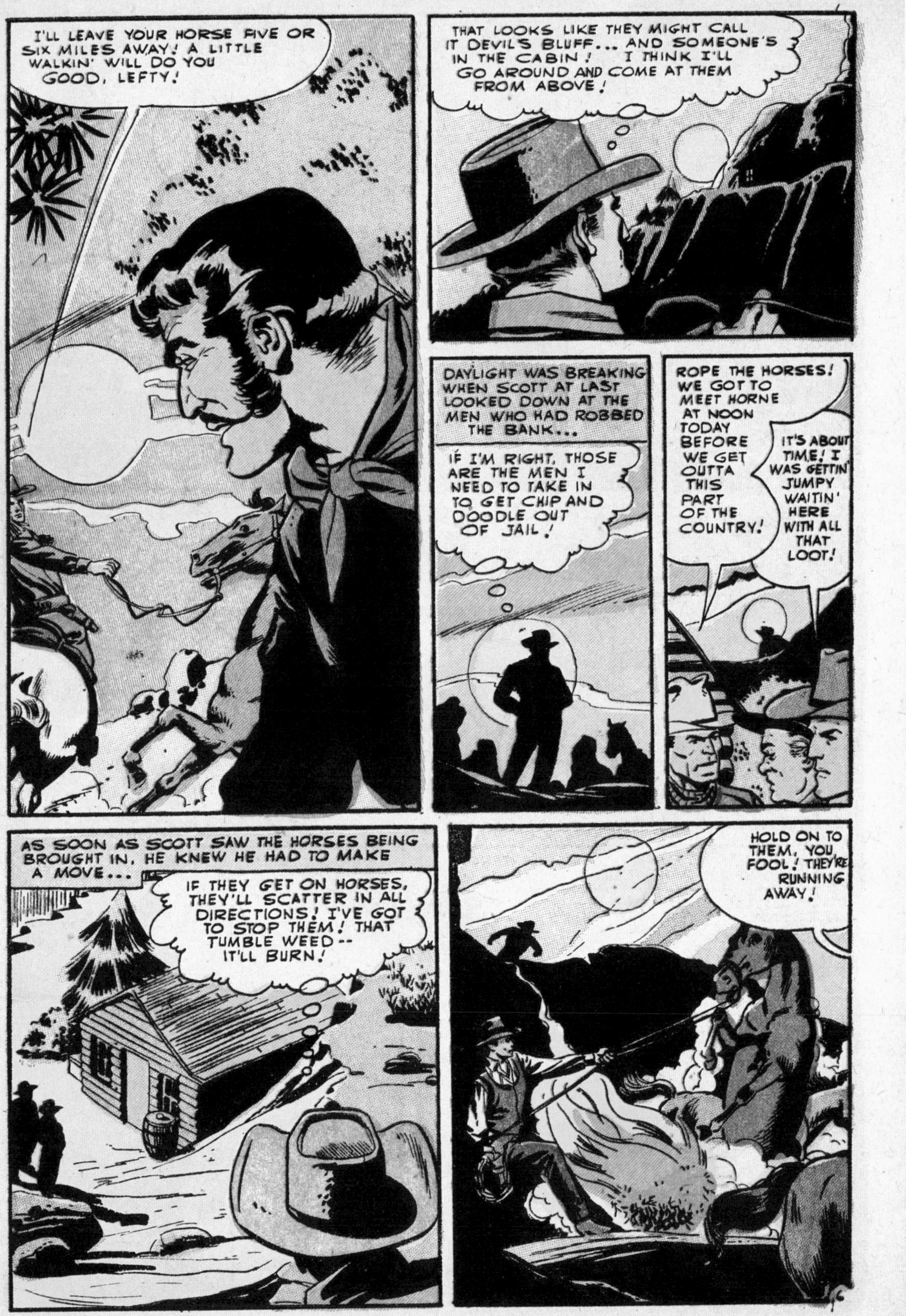
I'LL LEAVE YOUR HORSE FIVE OR SIX MILES AWAY! A LITTLE WALKIN' WILL DO YOU GOOD, LEFTY!
THAT LOOKS LIKE THEY MIGHT CALL IT DEVIL'S BLUFF... AND SOMEONE'S IN THE CABIN! I THINK I'LL GO AROUND AND COME AT THEM FROM ABOVE!
DAYLIGHT WAS BREAKING WHEN SCOTT AT LAST LOOKED DOWN AT THE MEN WHO HAD ROBBED THE BANK...
IF I'M RIGHT, THOSE ARE THE MEN I NEED TO TAKE IN TO GET CHIP AND DOODLE OUT OF JAIL!
ROPE THE HORSES! WE GOT TO MEET HORNE AT NOON TODAY BEFORE WE GET OUTTA THIS PART OF THE COUNTRY!
IT'S ABOUT TIME! I WAS GETTIN' JUMPY WAITIN' HERE WITH ALL THAT LOOT!
AS SOON AS SCOTT SAW THE HORSES BEING BROUGHT IN, HE KNEW HE HAD TO MAKE A MOVE...
IF THEY GET ON HORSES, THEY'LL SCATTER IN ALL DIRECTIONS! I'VE GOT TO STOP THEM! THAT TUMBLE WEED -- IT'LL BURN!
HOLD ON TO THEM, YOU FOOL! THEY'RE RUNNING AWAY!

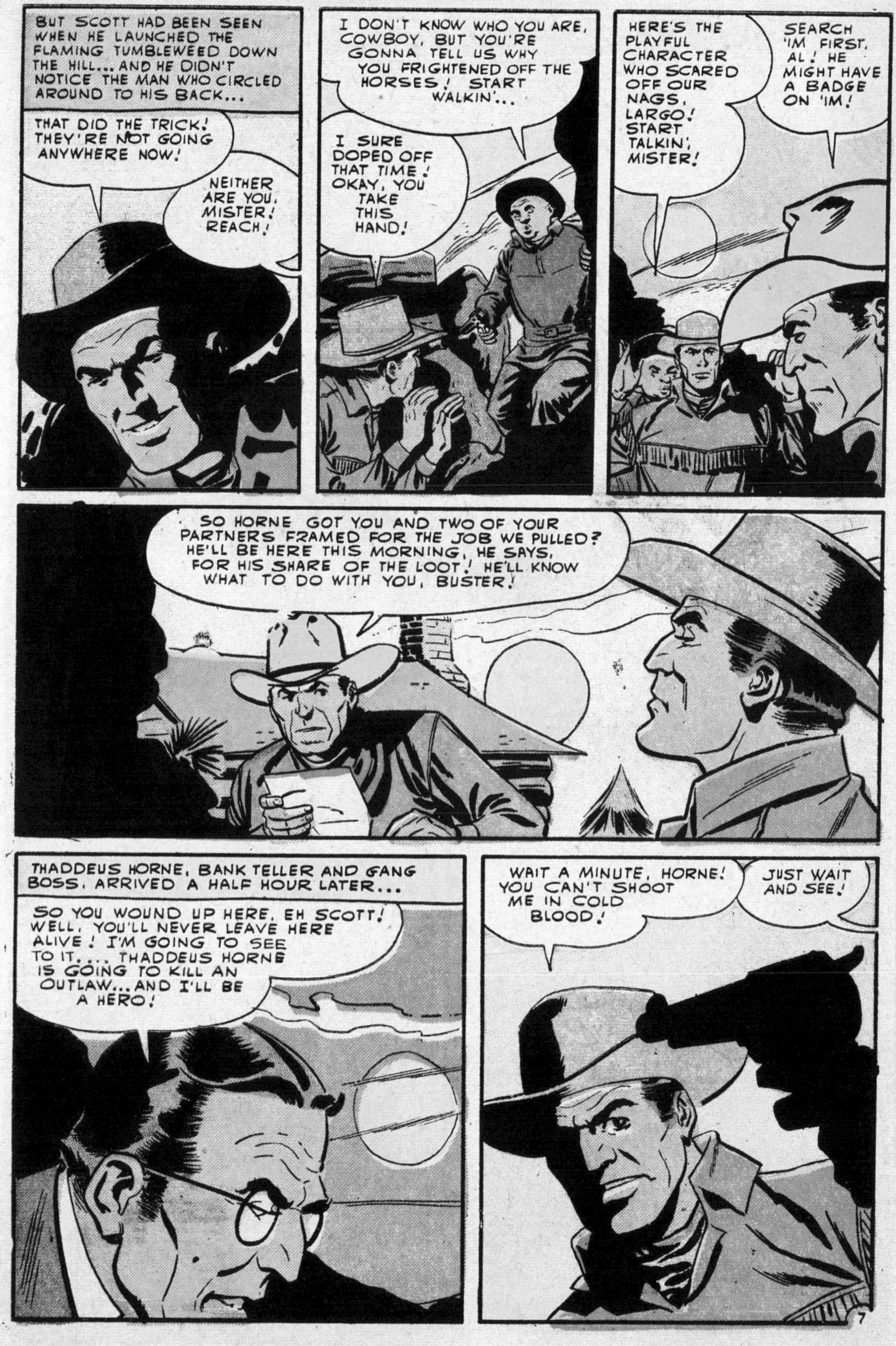
BUT SCOTT HAD BEEN SEEN WHEN HE LAUNCHED THE FLAMING TUMBLEWEED DOWN THE HILL... AND HE DIDN'T NOTICE THE MAN WHO CIRCLED AROUND TO HIS BACK...
THAT DID THE TRICK! THEY'RE NOT GOING ANYWHERE NOW!
NEITHER ARE YOU, MISTER! REACH!
I DON'T KNOW WHO YOU ARE, COWBOY, BUT YOU'RE GONNA TELL US WHY YOU FRIGHTENED OFF THE HORSES! START WALKIN'...
I SURE DOPED OFF THAT TIME! OKAY, YOU TAKE THIS HAND!
HERE'S THE PLAYFUL CHARACTER WHO SCARED OFF OUR NAGS, LARGO! START TALKIN', MISTER!
SEARCH 'IM FIRST, AL! HE MIGHT HAVE A BADGE ON 'IM!
SO HORNE GOT YOU AND TWO OF YOUR PARTNERS FRAMED FOR THE JOB WE PULLED? HE'LL BE HERE THIS MORNING, HE SAYS, FOR HIS SHARE OF THE LOOT! HE'LL KNOW WHAT TO DO WITH YOU, BUSTER!
THADDEUS HORNE, BANK TELLER AND GANG BOSS, ARRIVED A HALF HOUR LATER...
SO YOU WOUND UP HERE, EH SCOTT! WELL, YOU'LL NEVER LEAVE HERE ALIVE! I'M GOING TO SEE TO IT.... THADDEUS HORNE IS GOING TO KILL AN OUTLAW... AND I'LL BE A HERO!
WAIT A MINUTE, HORNE! YOU CAN'T SHOOT ME IN COLD BLOOD!
JUST WAIT AND SEE!
7

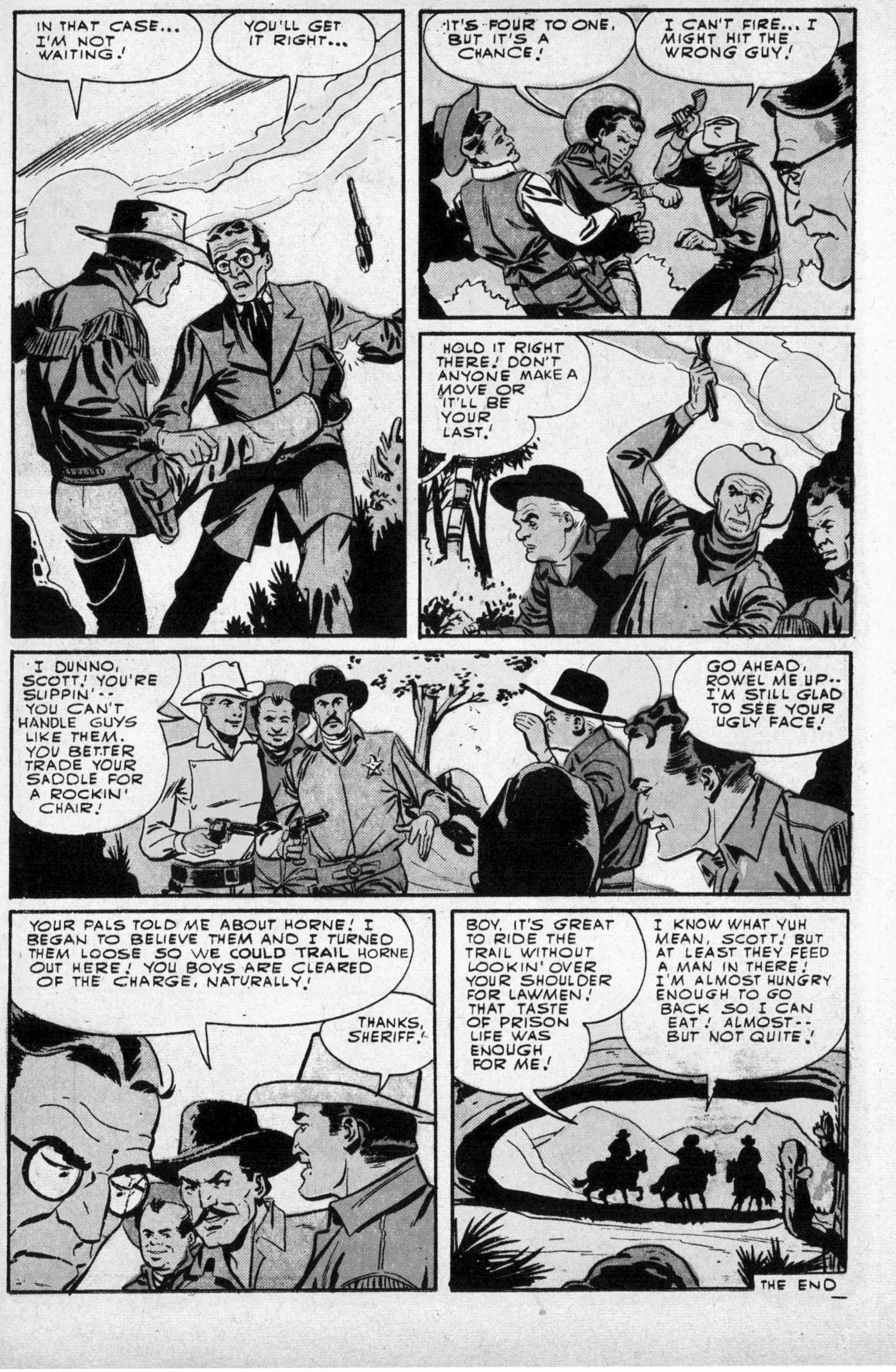
IN THAT CASE... I'M NOT WAITING!
YOU'LL GET IT RIGHT...
IT'S FOUR TO ONE, BUT IT'S A CHANCE!
I CAN'T FIRE... I MIGHT HIT THE WRONG GUY!
HOLD IT RIGHT THERE! DON'T ANYONE MAKE A MOVE OR IT'LL BE YOUR LAST!
I DUNNO, SCOTT! YOU'RE SLIPPIN'-- YOU CAN'T HANDLE GUYS LIKE THEM. YOU BETTER TRADE YOUR SADDLE FOR A ROCKIN' CHAIR!
GO AHEAD, ROWEL ME UP.. I'M STILL GLAD TO SEE YOUR UGLY FACE!
YOUR PALS TOLD ME ABOUT HORNE! I BEGAN TO BELIEVE THEM AND I TURNED THEM LOOSE SO WE COULD TRAIL HORNE OUT HERE! YOU BOYS ARE CLEARED OF THE CHARGE, NATURALLY!
THANKS, SHERIFF!
BOY, IT'S GREAT TO RIDE THE TRAIL WITHOUT LOOKIN' OVER YOUR SHOULDER FOR LAWMEN! THAT TASTE OF PRISON LIFE WAS ENOUGH FOR ME!
I KNOW WHAT YUH MEAN, SCOTT! BUT AT LEAST THEY FEED A MAN IN THERE! I'M ALMOST HUNGRY ENOUGH TO GO BACK SO I CAN EAT! ALMOST-- BUT NOT QUITE!
THE END

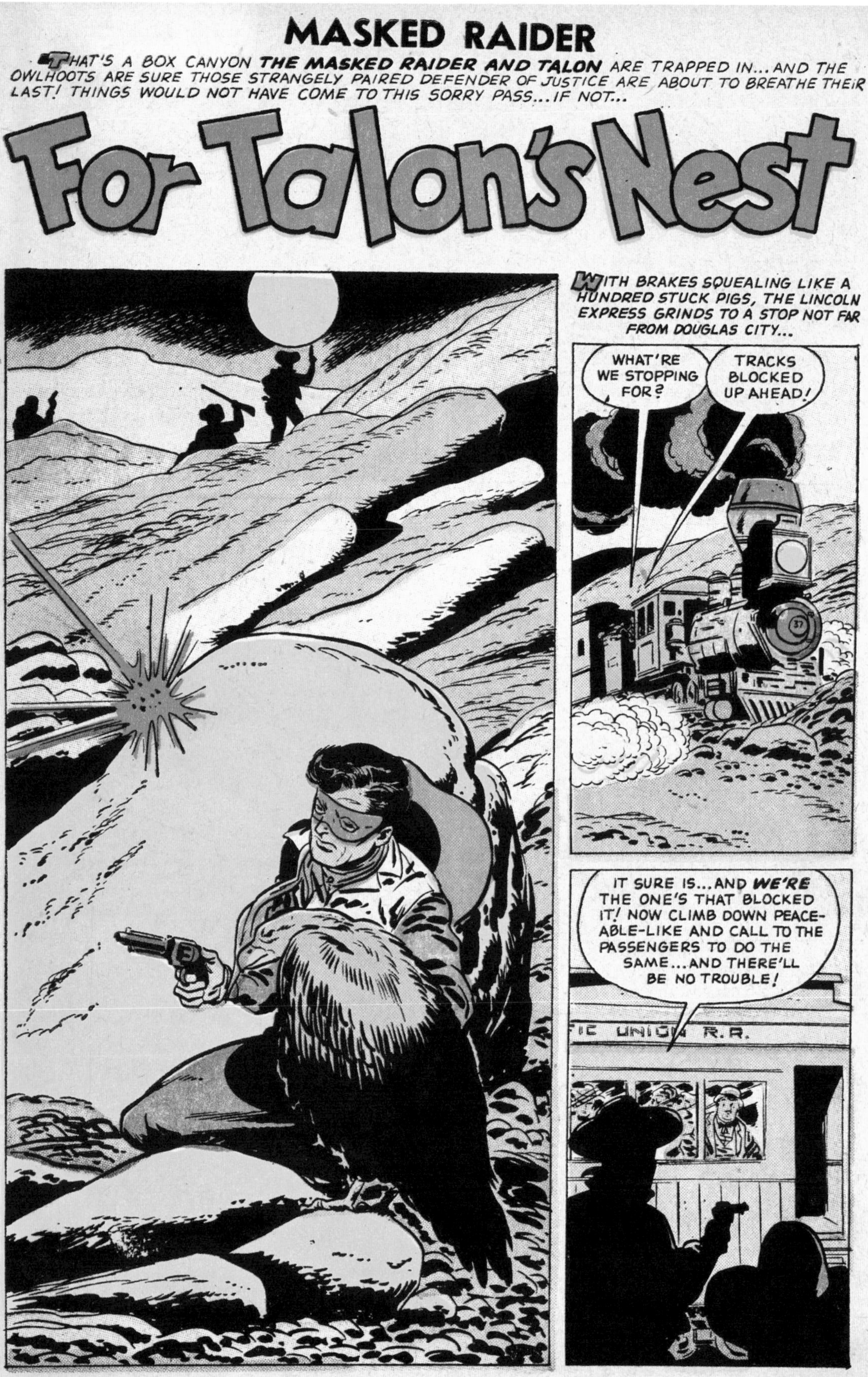

MASKED RAIDER
THAT'S A BOX CANYON THE MASKED RAIDER AND TALON ARE TRAPPED IN... AND THE OWLHOOTS ARE SURE THOSE STRANGELY PAIRED DEFENDER OF JUSTICE ARE ABOUT TO BREATHE THEIR LAST! THINGS WOULD NOT HAVE COME TO THIS SORRY PASS... IF NOT...
For Talon's Nest
WITH BRAKES SQUEALING LIKE A HUNDRED STUCK PIGS, THE LINCOLN EXPRESS GRINDS TO A STOP NOT FAR FROM DOUGLAS CITY...
WHAT'RE WE STOPPING FOR?
TRACKS BLOCKED UP AHEAD!
37
IT SURE IS... AND WE'RE THE ONE'S THAT BLOCKED IT! NOW CLIMB DOWN PEACE-ABLE-LIKE AND CALL TO THE PASSENGERS TO DO THE SAME... AND THERE'LL BE NO TROUBLE!
FIC UNION R.R.

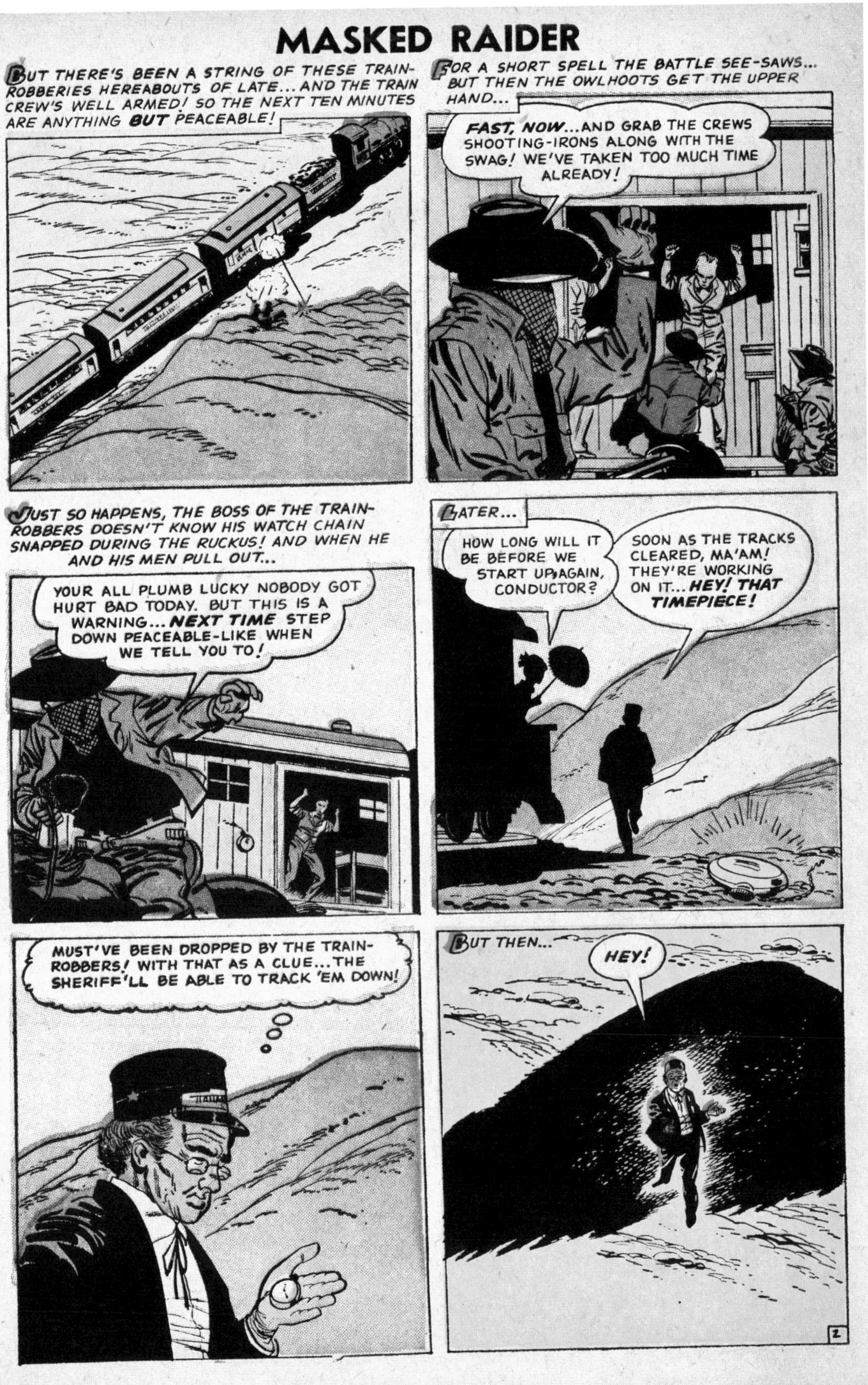
MASKED RAIDER
BUT THERE'S BEEN A STRING OF THESE TRAIN-ROBBERIES HEREABOUTS OF LATE... AND THE TRAIN CREW'S WELL ARMED! SO THE NEXT TEN MINUTES ARE ANYTHING BUT PEACEABLE!
FOR A SHORT SPELL THE BATTLE SEE-SAWS... BUT THEN THE OWLHOOTS GET THE UPPER HAND...
FAST, NOW...AND GRAB THE CREWS SHOOTING-IRONS ALONG WITH THE SWAG! WE'VE TAKEN TOO MUCH TIME ALREADY!
JUST SO HAPPENS, THE BOSS OF THE TRAIN-ROBBERS DOESN'T KNOW HIS WATCH CHAIN SNAPPED DURING THE RUCKUS! AND WHEN HE AND HIS MEN PULL OUT...
YOUR ALL PLUMB LUCKY NOBODY GOT HURT BAD TODAY. BUT THIS IS A WARNING... NEXT TIME STEP DOWN PEACEABLE-LIKE WHEN WE TELL YOU TO!
LATER...
HOW LONG WILL IT BE BEFORE WE START UP AGAIN, CONDUCTOR?
SOON AS THE TRACKS CLEARED, MA'AM! THEY'RE WORKING ON IT... HEY! THAT TIMEPIECE!
MUST'VE BEEN DROPPED BY THE TRAIN-ROBBERS! WITH THAT AS A CLUE... THE SHERIFF'LL BE ABLE TO TRACK 'EM DOWN!
BUT THEN...
HEY!
2

MASKED RAIDER

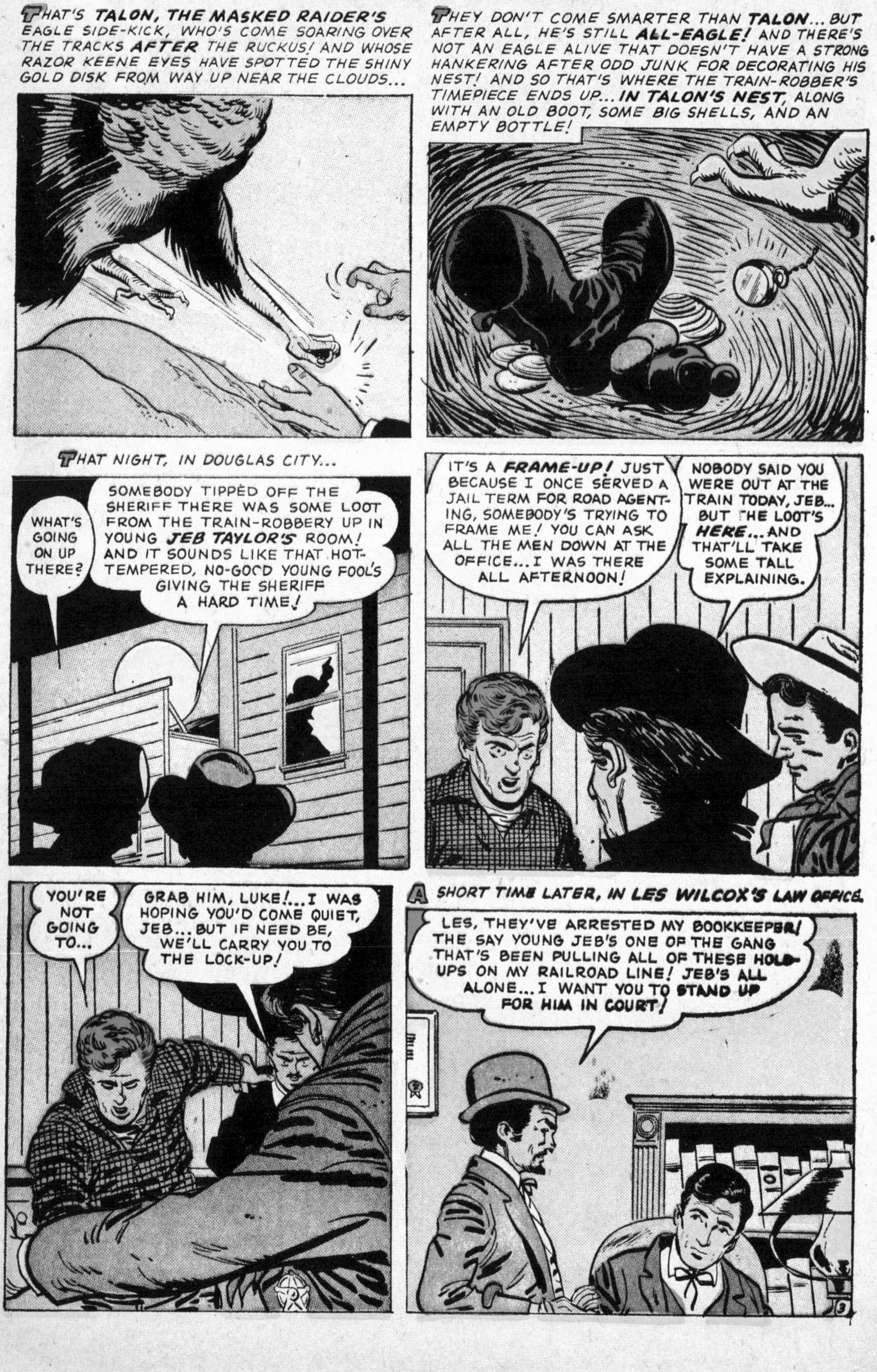
THAT'S TALON, THE MASKED RAIDER'S EAGLE SIDE-KICK, WHO'S COME SOARING OVER THE TRACKS AFTER THE RUCKUS! AND WHOSE RAZOR KEENE EYES HAVE SPOTTED THE SHINY GOLD DISK FROM WAY UP NEAR THE CLOUDS...
THEY DON'T COME SMARTER THAN TALON... BUT AFTER ALL, HE'S STILL ALL-EAGLE! AND THERE'S NOT AN EAGLE ALIVE THAT DOESN'T HAVE A STRONG HANKERING AFTER ODD JUNK FOR DECORATING HIS NEST! AND SO THAT'S WHERE THE TRAIN-ROBBER'S TIMEPIECE ENDS UP... IN TALON'S NEST, ALONG WITH AN OLD BOOT, SOME BIG SHELLS, AND AN EMPTY BOTTLE!
THAT NIGHT, IN DOUGLAS CITY...
WHAT'S GOING ON UP THERE?
SOMEBODY TIPPED OFF THE SHERIFF THERE WAS SOME LOOT FROM THE TRAIN-ROBBERY UP IN YOUNG JEB TAYLOR'S ROOM! AND IT SOUNDS LIKE THAT HOT-TEMPERED, NO-GOOD YOUNG FOOL'S GIVING THE SHERIFF A HARD TIME!
IT'S A FRAME-UP! JUST BECAUSE I ONCE SERVED A JAIL TERM FOR ROAD AGENTING, SOMEBODY'S TRYING TO FRAME ME! YOU CAN ASK ALL THE MEN DOWN AT THE OFFICE... I WAS THERE ALL AFTERNOON!
NOBODY SAID YOU WERE OUT AT THE TRAIN TODAY, JEB... BUT THE LOOT'S HERE... AND THAT'LL TAKE SOME TALL EXPLAINING.
YOU'RE NOT GOING TO...
GRAB HIM, LUKE!... I WAS HOPING YOU'D COME QUIET, JEB... BUT IF NEED BE, WE'LL CARRY YOU TO THE LOCK-UP!
A SHORT TIME LATER, IN LES WILCOX'S LAW OFFICE.
LES, THEY'VE ARRESTED MY BOOKKEEPER! THE SAY YOUNG JEB'S ONE OF THE GANG THAT'S BEEN PULLING ALL OF THESE HOLD-UPS ON MY RAILROAD LINE! JEB'S ALL ALONE... I WANT YOU TO STAND UP FOR HIM IN COURT!

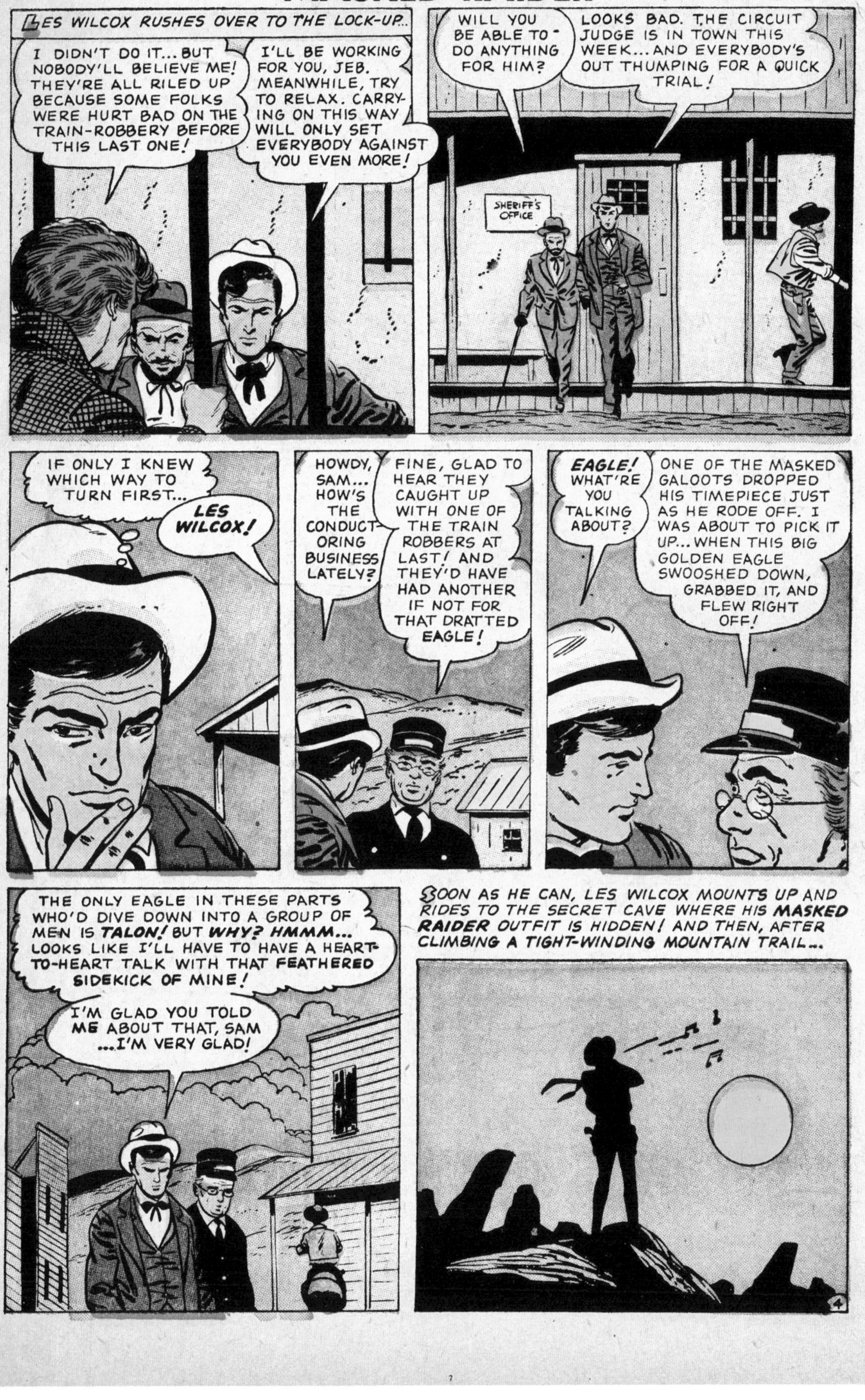
LES WILCOX RUSHES OVER TO THE LOCK-UP...
I DIDN'T DO IT... BUT NOBODY'LL BELIEVE ME! THEY'RE ALL RILED UP BECAUSE SOME FOLKS WERE HURT BAD ON THE TRAIN-ROBBERY BEFORE THIS LAST ONE!
I'LL BE WORKING FOR YOU, JEB. MEANWHILE, TRY TO RELAX. CARRYING ON THIS WAY WILL ONLY SET EVERYBODY AGAINST YOU EVEN MORE!
WILL YOU BE ABLE TO DO ANYTHING FOR HIM?
LOOKS BAD. THE CIRCUIT JUDGE IS IN TOWN THIS WEEK... AND EVERYBODY'S OUT THUMPING FOR A QUICK TRIAL!
SHERIFF'S OFFICE
IF ONLY I KNEW WHICH WAY TO TURN FIRST...
LES WILCOX!
HOWDY, SAM... HOW'S THE CONDUCTORING BUSINESS LATELY?
FINE, GLAD TO HEAR THEY CAUGHT UP WITH ONE OF THE TRAIN ROBBERS AT LAST! AND THEY'D HAVE HAD ANOTHER IF NOT FOR THAT DRATTED EAGLE!
EAGLE! WHAT'RE YOU TALKING ABOUT?
ONE OF THE MASKED GALOOTS DROPPED HIS TIMEPIECE JUST AS HE RODE OFF. I WAS ABOUT TO PICK IT UP... WHEN THIS BIG GOLDEN EAGLE SWOOSHED DOWN, GRABBED IT, AND FLEW RIGHT OFF!
THE ONLY EAGLE IN THESE PARTS WHO'D DIVE DOWN INTO A GROUP OF MEN IS TALON! BUT WHY? HMMM... LOOKS LIKE I'LL HAVE TO HAVE A HEART-TO-HEART TALK WITH THAT FEATHERED SIDEKICK OF MINE!
I'M GLAD YOU TOLD ME ABOUT THAT, SAM ...I'M VERY GLAD!
SOON AS HE CAN, LES WILCOX MOUNTS UP AND RIDES TO THE SECRET CAVE WHERE HIS MASKED RAIDER OUTFIT IS HIDDEN! AND THEN, AFTER CLIMBING A TIGHT-WINDING MOUNTAIN TRAIL...
4

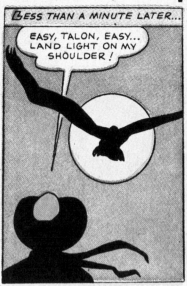

LESS THAN A MINUTE LATER...

EASY, TALON, EASY... LAND LIGHT ON MY SHOULDER!

YOUR NEST, TALON... SEE? BRING DOWN WHAT YOU HAVE IN YOUR NEST, ALL THE JUNK YOU LIKE TO COLLECT... *EVERYTHING* THAT'S IN YOUR NEST.

THE EAGLE TAKES AIR WITH A CLAP OF HIS GIANT WINGS! AND HE MAKES TRIP AFTER TRIP BETWEEN HIS EYRIE AND WHERE THE **MASKED RAIDER** *STANDS...*

THAT'S NOT IT... TRY AGAIN...

THAT'S IT! GOOD BOY, TALON! EASY NOW... WE DON'T WANT IT SMASHED! *I WANT TO BE ABLE TO READ IT'S OWNER'S NAME!*

IT'S THE NEXT DAY NOW, AND THE CIRCUIT JUDGE IS HOLDING COURT...

HOW CAN I TELL YOU WHO THE OTHER GANG MEMBERS ARE WHEN I'M NOT A MEMBER OF THE GANG?!

DON'T SHOUT, YOUNG MAN! MY HEARING'S JUST AS GOOD AS YOURS!

JUST THEN...

GOT A NOTE FOR YOU, SHERIFF. SOMEBODY MUST'VE SLIPPED IT UNDER YOUR OFFICE DOOR THIS MORNING.

AFTER READING THE NOTE, THE SHERIFF POW-WOWS WITH THE JUDGE, AND THEN...

COURT ADJOURNED FOR THE DAY.

WHAT'RE THEY DOING *THAT* FOR? JEB TAYLOR'S GUILTY ... IT'S WRITTEN PLAIN ALL OVER HIS FACE!

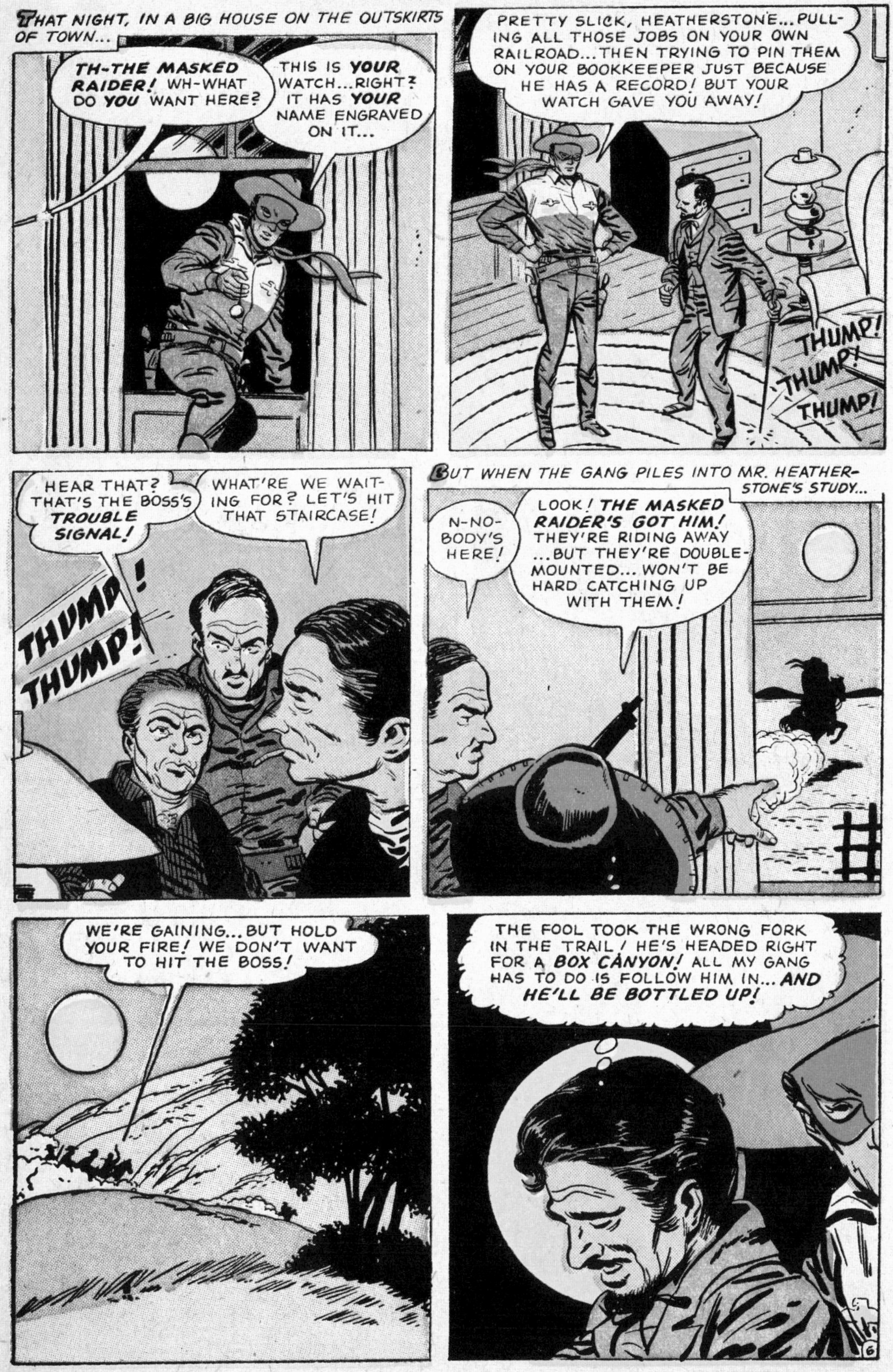
THAT NIGHT, IN A BIG HOUSE ON THE OUTSKIRTS OF TOWN...
TH-THE MASKED RAIDER! WH-WHAT DO YOU WANT HERE?
THIS IS YOUR WATCH...RIGHT? IT HAS YOUR NAME ENGRAVED ON IT...
PRETTY SLICK, HEATHERSTONE... PULLING ALL THOSE JOBS ON YOUR OWN RAILROAD...THEN TRYING TO PIN THEM ON YOUR BOOKKEEPER JUST BECAUSE HE HAS A RECORD! BUT YOUR WATCH GAVE YOU AWAY!
THUMP! THUMP! THUMP!
HEAR THAT? THAT'S THE BOSS'S TROUBLE SIGNAL!
WHAT'RE WE WAITING FOR? LET'S HIT THAT STAIRCASE!
THUMP! THUMP!
BUT WHEN THE GANG PILES INTO MR. HEATHERSTONE'S STUDY...
N-NOBODY'S HERE!
LOOK! THE MASKED RAIDER'S GOT HIM! THEY'RE RIDING AWAY ...BUT THEY'RE DOUBLE-MOUNTED... WON'T BE HARD CATCHING UP WITH THEM!
WE'RE GAINING...BUT HOLD YOUR FIRE! WE DON'T WANT TO HIT THE BOSS!
THE FOOL TOOK THE WRONG FORK IN THE TRAIL! HE'S HEADED RIGHT FOR A BOX CANYON! ALL MY GANG HAS TO DO IS FOLLOW HIM IN... AND HE'LL BE BOTTLED UP!
6

MASKED RAIDER

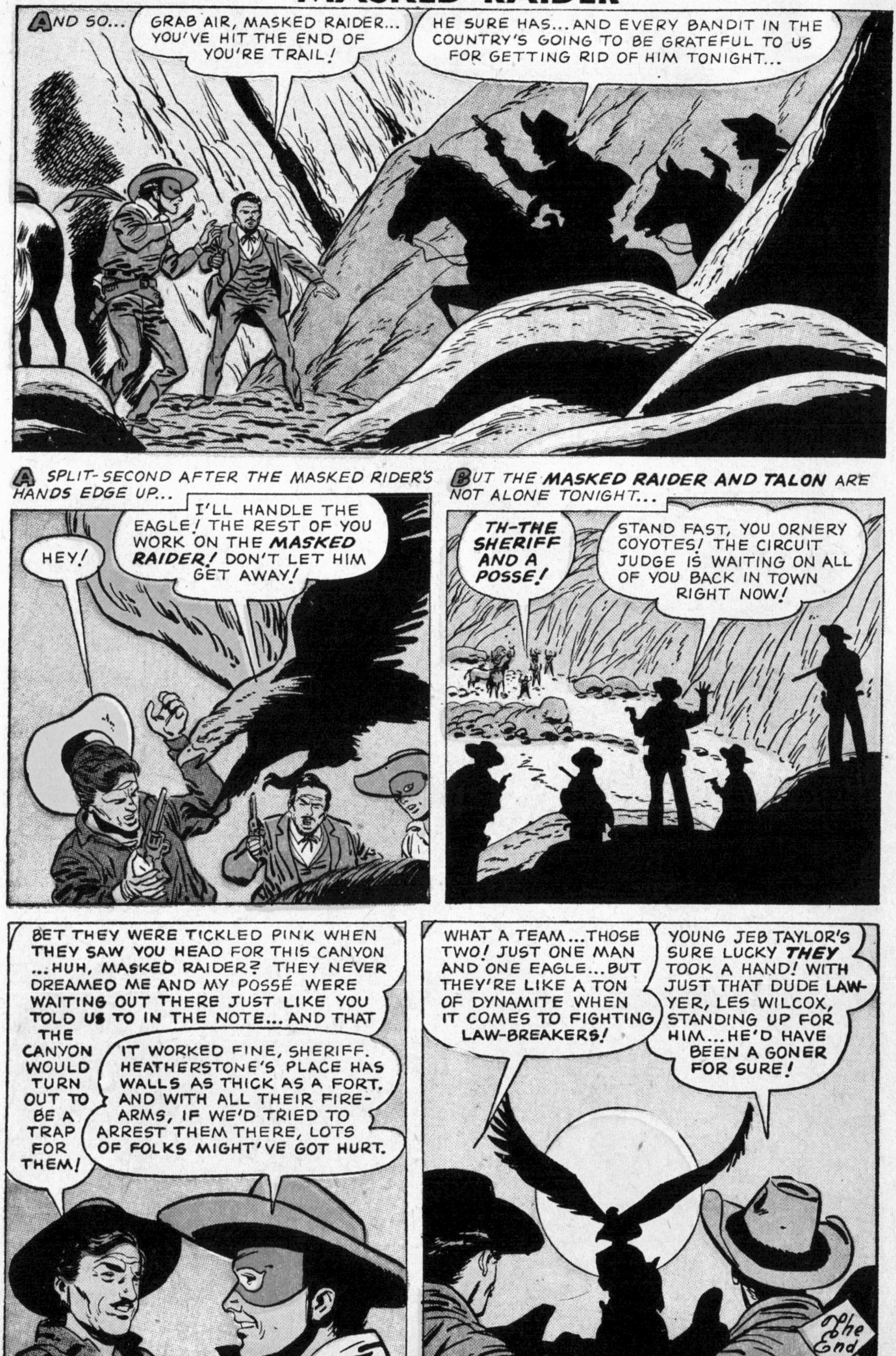
AND SO...
GRAB AIR, MASKED RAIDER... YOU'VE HIT THE END OF YOU'RE TRAIL!
HE SURE HAS... AND EVERY BANDIT IN THE COUNTRY'S GOING TO BE GRATEFUL TO US FOR GETTING RID OF HIM TONIGHT...
A SPLIT-SECOND AFTER THE MASKED RIDER'S HANDS EDGE UP...
HEY!
I'LL HANDLE THE EAGLE! THE REST OF YOU WORK ON THE MASKED RAIDER! DON'T LET HIM GET AWAY!
BUT THE MASKED RAIDER AND TALON ARE NOT ALONE TONIGHT...
TH-THE SHERIFF AND A POSSE!
STAND FAST, YOU ORNERY COYOTES! THE CIRCUIT JUDGE IS WAITING ON ALL OF YOU BACK IN TOWN RIGHT NOW!
BET THEY WERE TICKLED PINK WHEN THEY SAW YOU HEAD FOR THIS CANYON ...HUH, MASKED RAIDER? THEY NEVER DREAMED ME AND MY POSSÉ WERE WAITING OUT THERE JUST LIKE YOU TOLD US TO IN THE NOTE... AND THAT THE CANYON WOULD TURN OUT TO BE A TRAP FOR THEM!
IT WORKED FINE, SHERIFF. HEATHERSTONE'S PLACE HAS WALLS AS THICK AS A FORT. AND WITH ALL THEIR FIRE-ARMS, IF WE'D TRIED TO ARREST THEM THERE, LOTS OF FOLKS MIGHT'VE GOT HURT.
WHAT A TEAM... THOSE TWO! JUST ONE MAN AND ONE EAGLE... BUT THEY'RE LIKE A TON OF DYNAMITE WHEN IT COMES TO FIGHTING LAW-BREAKERS!
YOUNG JEB TAYLOR'S SURE LUCKY THEY TOOK A HAND! WITH JUST THAT DUDE LAW-YER, LES WILCOX, STANDING UP FOR HIM... HE'D HAVE BEEN A GONER FOR SURE!
The End

LD
UR
AND

---BECAUSE JOHN DAVY **ALWAYS** GETS WHAT HE WANTS!

LOCUSTS! THAT

OUR

HOLD IT, EVER

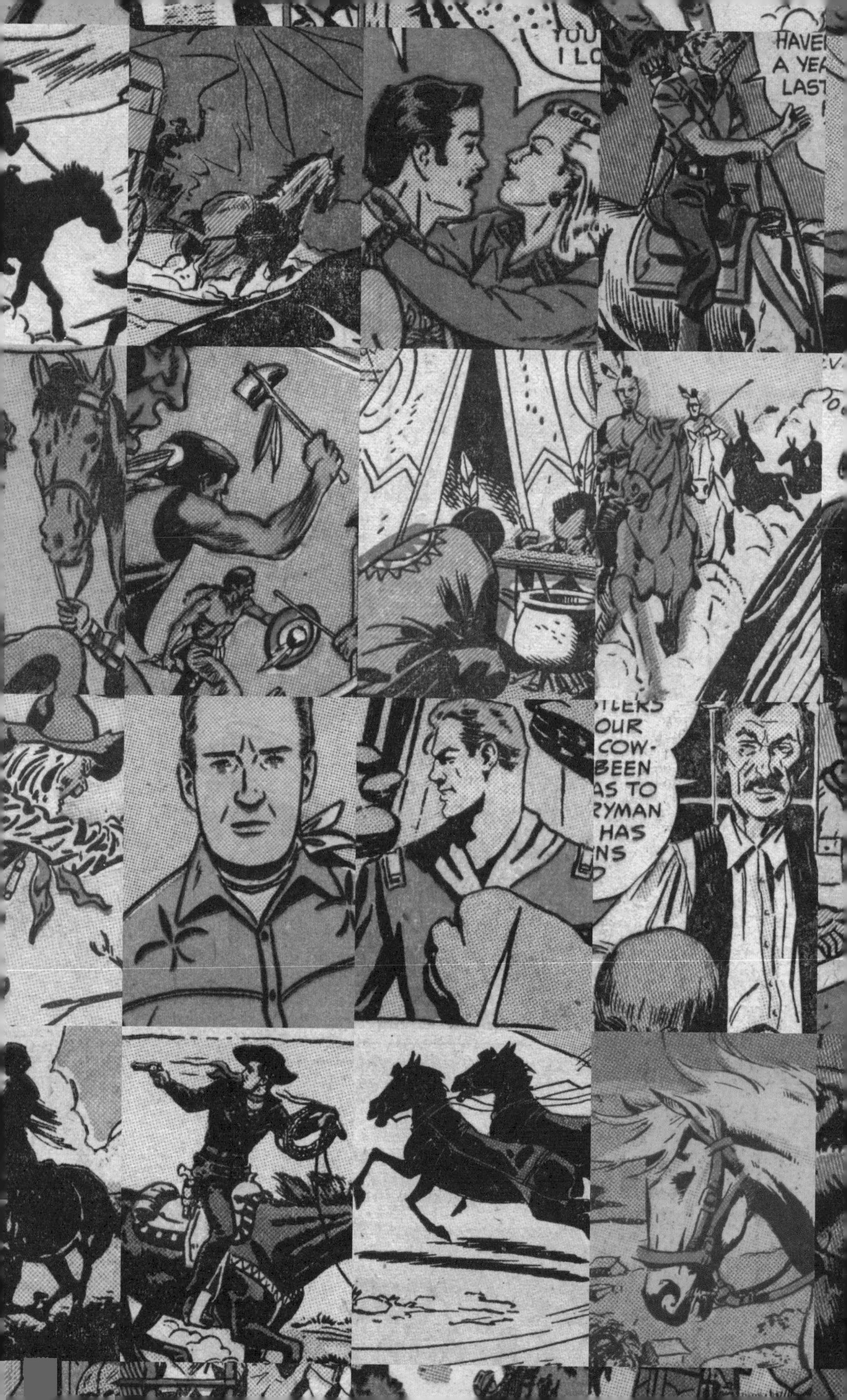
YOU
I LO
HAVE
A YEA
LAST
STLERS
OUR
COW-
BEEN
AS TO
RYMAN
HAS
NS